SHAKES

Renaissance humanists believed that if you want to build a just society you must begin with the facts of human nature. This book argues that the idea of a universal human nature was as important to Shakespeare as it was to every other Renaissance writer. In doing so it questio
Postmo
was ali
essentia
their ti
that fo
period,
and ou

ROBIN
Directc
Roehai
(Camb
2000).

THE UNIVERSITY OF
WINCHESTER

Martial Rose Library
Tel: 01962 827306

To be returned on or before the day marked above, subject to recall.

SHAKESPEARE'S HUMANISM

ROBIN HEADLAM WELLS

CAMBRIDGE
UNIVERSITY PRESS

CAMBRIDGE UNIVERSITY PRESS
Cambridge, New York, Melbourne, Madrid, Cape Town, Singapore, São Paulo, Delhi

Cambridge University Press
The Edinburgh Building, Cambridge CB2 8RU, UK

Published in the United States of America by Cambridge University Press, New York

www.cambridge.org
Information on this title: www.cambridge.org/9780521107235

First published 2005
This digitally printed version 2009

A catalogue record for this publication is available from the British Library

ISBN 978-0-521-82438-5 hardback
ISBN 978-0-521-10723-5 paperback

to Aurora
Lo! ever thus thou growest beautiful
Tennyson, Tithonus

Contents

vii

Preface

Renaissance humanists believed that if you want to build a just society you must begin with the facts of human nature. This book argues that the idea of a universal human nature was as important to Shakespeare as it was to every other Renaissance writer. In doing so it questions the central, defining principle of postmodern Shakespeare criticism. By 'postmodern' I mean criticism that's informed by what is generally termed 'Theory' (either spelt with a capital letter, or enclosed by inverted commas, or both, to distinguish it from the literary theory that existed before Barthes, Derrida and other French thinkers began to dominate Anglo-American criticism in the late 1960s). There are of course significant differences between Cultural Materialism and New Historicism, and between different kinds of feminism; where necessary I'll try to make these differences clear. But since anti-essentialism – the belief that there is no such thing as a universal essence of human nature – is a core principle shared by most versions of 'Theoretically'-informed criticism (but not by liberal feminism), I thought it best to avoid repetition of awkward lists of titles of critical schools by using the general term 'postmodern' when writing about critics who claim that Shakespeare was an anti-essentialist. However, with the exception of chapter 9, where I consider Althusser and Foucault and the strange history of anti-essentialism, I've tried to keep discussion of 'Theory' to a minimum. Readers who are interested to know where the notion of a Renaissance anti-essentialism comes from may want to go to chapters 1 and 9 first.

One other point of usage: some scholars use the word 'contemporary' in the sense of 'modern'. I've used it to mean 'living or occurring at the same time'; so for example, when I say that *King Lear* may possibly have set some contemporary playgoers thinking about social injustice, I'm talking about Shakespeare's original audiences. When I mean 'contemporary or nearly contemporary with ourselves' I use the word 'modern'.

All quotations from Shakespeare are from the modern-spelling *Complete Works*, edited by Stanley Wells and Gary Taylor (Oxford: Clarendon Press, 1986). Because I wanted to avoid making other Renaissance writers look old fashioned by comparison with Shakespeare, I've modernised all quotations from early modern printed books and modern original-spelling editions. However, I've left quotations from Chaucer and 'ancient' Gower in their original spelling. As Spenser wanted his poetry to look archaic I've also left him in the original spelling.

I am grateful to the Arts and Humanities Research Board for the award of a Research Leave Fellowship, and to the School of English and Modern Languages at Roehampton University for granting me a semester's study leave. I'm also grateful to Andrew Gurr, Emrys Jones and the late Inga-Stina Ewbank for their kind support.

A number of people have corrected errors and made helpful suggestions – advice which I'm afraid I didn't always take. But you can put that down to the folly of 'those that are in the vaward of our youth' (as Falstaff tells the Chief Justice). I owe thanks to Graham Bradshaw, Joseph Carroll, Trevor Dean, Michael Dobson, Peter Edwards, Ros King, Owen Knowles, John Lee, Fritz Levy, Kevin McCarron, Mike Pincombe, John Roe, Jerry Sokol, Stanley Stewart, Neil Taylor and Rowland Wymer. I owe a particular debt to Tom McAlindon, who first set me thinking about anti-essentialism. And I'm especially grateful to Cambridge's anonymous readers for invaluable advice.

Editors of the following journals have kindly given permission to reprint articles in a revised form: *The Ben Jonson Journal* (chapter 8), *Modern Language Review* (chapter 6), *The Shakespearean International Yearbook* (chapters 2 and 3), *Shakespeare Survey* (chapter 7). An earlier version of chapter 4 first appeared in *Renaissance Refractions: Essays in Honour of Alexander Shurbanov*, ed. Boika Sokolova and Evgenia Pancheva (Sofia: St Kliment Ohridski University Press, 2001).

Introduction

> A vision of a future social order [must] be based on a concept of
> human nature. If, in fact, man is an indefinitely malleable,
> completely plastic being, with no innate structures of mind and
> no intrinsic needs of a cultural or social character, then he is a fit
> subject for the 'shaping of behavior' by the State authority, the
> corporate manager, the technocrat, or the central committee. Those
> with some confidence in the human species will hope that this is not
> so and will try to determine the intrinsic human characteristics that
> provide the framework for intellectual development, the growth of
> moral consciousness, cultural achievement, and participation in a
> free community . . . We must break away, sharply and radically,
> from much of modern social and behavioral science if we are to
> move towards a deeper understanding of these matters.
>
> Noam Chomsky, 'Language and Freedom' (1972)[1]

Postmodernists do not share Noam Chomsky's views on human nature.
Cultural Materialists and New Historicists believe that talk of innate
structures of mind or intrinsic human needs is no more than ideological
mystification; in reality there are as many forms of human nature as there
are human societies. 'Constructionism', writes one leading American
Shakespeare scholar, 'is one of the basic propositions by which new
historicism as a way of reading has distinguished itself from humanism.
Where humanism assumes a core essence that unites people otherwise
separated in time and social circumstances new historicism insists on
cultural differences.'[2]

The belief that our minds are shaped largely by sensory experience is
not a new one. John Locke famously declared that at birth the mind was 'a
white sheet, void of all characters, without any ideas'.[3] But in denying the
existence of innate ideas Locke did not reject the principle of a universal
human nature. He argued that, although we may not come into the world
with ready-made notions of, let's say, truth or justice, we are nevertheless
equipped with faculties that enable us to learn what we need to know

as human beings, and it's those inborn faculties that define our humanity.[4] What concerned Chomsky was not the notion of the mind as a *tabula rasa* passively absorbing experience – though psychologists now dispute that idea – but the claim that we inherit no species-specific mental characteristics of any description. It was in the early decades of the last century that it became fashionable to argue that human nature was inherently unstable. 'On or about December 1910 human character changed', wrote Virginia Woolf in 1924.[5] 'There is nothing that can be changed more completely than human nature when the job is taken in hand early enough', declared Bernard Shaw ten years later.[6] Woolf and Shaw were being deliberately provocative. But the new denial of human nature wasn't just a matter of novelists and playwrights rhetorically asserting a modernist sense of cultural crisis. Anthropologists from Margaret Mead to Clifford Geertz agreed that human nature was infinitely malleable; even the central nervous system was thought to be a cultural artefact.[7] Sometimes referred to as the Standard Social Science Model, this constructionist view of humanity was the orthodox theory of mind in university social science departments for much of the twentieth century.[8]

For Chomsky there was something profoundly disturbing in the prospect of an Orwellian world in which human nature is fabricated by the state and truth merely an effect of power. It was also bad science. But since the 1970s there has been a revolution in the psychological and biological sciences. Where 'humanity' was once seen as a purely cultural construct, a consensus is now emerging among psychologists and neuroscientists that our minds are the product of a complex interaction between genetically determined predispositions and an environment that has itself been shaped by generations of human culture. The zoologist and polymath Edward O. Wilson has a phrase that sums it up well: we are, he says, the products of 'gene-culture coevolution'.[9] I will discuss the modern debate on human nature in more detail in chapter 9.

But literary postmodernists are suspicious of the truth claims of science and remain ideologically committed to the principle that the mind, and even gender, is shaped exclusively by social forces and owes nothing to our biological nature. It's true that some of anti-humanism's most passionate former champions have now modified their constructionist theories. But in doing so they have effectively abandoned the core principle of postmodern literary theory.[10] As the neo-Marxist critic Jean Howard explains, central to the New Historicist project is 'the attack on the notion that man possesses a transhistorical core of being. Rather, everything from "maternal instinct" to conceptions of the self are now seen to be the products of specific discourses and social processes'.[11] Postmodernists insist that we bring into the world no inherited predispositions that are typical of our species. It's not just a question of the infant mind being a blank sheet devoid of innate mental content; for the postmodernist there are none of the built-in rules that Locke thought were essential for processing experience. If there is nothing in our mental constitution that can be said to be intrinsically human, any Lockean notions of universal human rights[12] evaporate and we are left with a cipher waiting to be given shape and form by society. As Howard puts it, '*nothing exists* before the human subject is created by history'.[13] Stephen Greenblatt spells out this key principle of New Historicist criticism in one of his most influential essays: 'The very idea of a "defining human essence" is precisely what new historicists find vacuous and untenable.'[14]

Anti-essentialism is as fundamental to Cultural Materialism as it is to New Historicism. Alan Sinfield speaks for a whole generation of post-structuralist Marxist critics when he writes: 'as a cultural materialist I don't believe in common humanity'.[15] Reviewing the critical developments of the past twenty years, Jonathan Dollimore has recently reminded us that Cultural Materialism has always been 'resolute' in its rejection of 'universal humanism' and 'essentialist individualism'.[16]

Postmodernists believe that the notion of a transhistorical essence of human nature is an invention of the modern world. Citing Foucault – 'before the end of the eighteenth century, *man* did not exist'[17] – Cultural Materialists and New Historicists argue that to attribute essentialist ideas of human nature to Shakespeare and his contemporaries is an historical anachronism (though as I shall explain in my final chapter, Foucault meant something very different from what his followers took him to mean). In one of the truly seminal critical books of the late twentieth century – *Radical Tragedy* (1984) – Jonathan Dollimore declared that it wasn't until the Enlightenment that 'essentialist humanism' first made its appearance.[18] So influential was *Radical Tragedy*, and so great the continuing demand for it on university English courses, that a third edition has recently been published. In a foreword to the new edition Terry Eagleton tells us that the book is essential reading for the modern student: it's one of the '*necessary*' critical works of our time.[19] By the end of the twentieth century the consensus view in what had by then become mainstream Shakespeare criticism[20] was that to read this period through 'the grid of an essentialist humanism', as Dollimore put it, is to give a false picture of the age.[21] Shakespeare was in effect a postmodernist '*avant la lettre*.[22] Students were warned against the folly of supposing that Shakespeare's plays might have anything to do with human nature.[23] They were taught that in this period the human 'subject' was thought to be inherently unstable and fragmented;[24] that it wouldn't have occurred to people that they might have an inner self;[25] that the idea of creative originality was an entirely alien concept;[26] and that 'in the Renaissance our modern concept of the genius simply did not exist'.[27] As for gender, that was so indeterminate and had so little connection with biological nature that Elizabethans thought the mere act of putting on an actor's costume could literally turn a man into a woman.[28] Homosexuality hadn't yet been invented.[29]

The belief that Shakespeare and his contemporaries were radical anti-essentialists is not supported by historical evidence. On the contrary, wherever you look in Elizabethan England you find the same insistence on the importance of understanding human nature. As the political historian Janet Coleman reminds us, 'for all medieval and Renaissance thinkers, man's nature does not change over time . . . In all societies throughout history men can be observed to have demonstrated through their actions the same kind of nature, a nature that is specific to humans'.[30] For Elizabethan humanists – the word 'humanist' comes via Italian from the Latin '*humanitas*', whose primary meaning was 'human nature' – the proper study of mankind was man.[31] Humanist historiographers believed that the study of history was useful because, human nature being much the same in all ages, it could give the politician a valuable key to human action. Literary theorists defended poetry on the grounds that it gives you a much better insight into the way human beings behave than any scholastic treatise could do: one of the main justifications for reading literature was the belief that dramatic poetry could, as Hamlet puts it, hold the mirror up to nature and show us our characteristic human vices and virtues. People naturally argued about what human nature was like, but no one doubted that it existed. That it was important to understand human nature is something that seems to have been accepted by even the most unconventional thinkers. Montaigne's friend Pierre Charron summed up a commonplace of this period when he said that 'The first lesson and instruction unto wisdom . . . is the knowledge of our selves and our human condition.'[32]

Humanist philosophers from Cicero to A. C. Grayling have argued that any attempt to realise the ideal of a just society must begin with the facts of human nature.[33] Renaissance thinkers shared that belief. However, their intellectual world probably had more in common with Chaucer's than it does with our own. To emphasise the paramount importance that Renaissance thinkers accorded the study of human nature is not to suggest that their educational principles are relevant to the problems of the modern world (Elizabethan humanists showed no interest in the inductive approach to knowledge that was so soon to transform science). Nor is it to endorse Renaissance theories of civilisation (though there was a strong republican element in Elizabethan humanism, much humanist thought was unashamedly elitist). Rather it's an attempt to reconstruct unfamiliar ways of looking at things in the hope that this may correct certain misconceptions about Shakespeare's intellectual world that have become commonplaces in modern criticism. Dr Johnson said that the task of criticism was to improve opinion into knowledge.[34] As playgoers and readers we all have opinions about Shakespeare. But it's not until you have established the mental framework within which intellectual debate was conducted and meanings generated in the past that you can begin to judge a writer's response to 'the very age and body of the time his form and pressure' (*Hamlet*, 111.ii.23–4), or evaluate critically the worth of that response from a modern perspective.

Shakespeare's Humanism is about the centrality of human nature in Shakespeare's mental universe. Although in reasserting the importance of *humanitas* in the plays, it runs counter to the general tenor of mainstream, establishment Shakespeare criticism, it's not an argument for returning to the critical past. In my final chapter I'll suggest that, by listening to what other disciplines have to say about human nature, criticism can move on from an outdated anti-humanism that has its intellectual roots in the early decades of the last century to a more informed modern understanding of the human universals that literature has, in Ian McEwan's words, 'always, knowingly and helplessly, given voice to'.[35]

Shakespeare and English humanism

'And what are you reading, Miss – ?' 'Oh! it is only a novel!', replies the young lady, trying to hide her embarrassment. The narrator supplies the rejoinder that the imaginary young reader lacks the wit or the experience to come up with herself: 'in short, only some work in which the most thorough knowledge of human nature, the happiest delineation of its varieties, the liveliest effusions of wit and humour are conveyed to the world in the best chosen language'.[1]

Shakespeare would have had no idea what Jane Austen was talking about; her ironic defence of the novelist's art would have completely passed him by. It's not just that novels as we know them didn't exist in Elizabethan England; human nature didn't exist either. At least, that's what postmodernism tells us. In postmodern Shakespeare criticism it's taken for granted that Shakespeare and his contemporaries were anti-essentialists. That is to say, Elizabethans are thought to have had no general theory of humankind as a species: human beings had no existential 'centre'; they lacked any kind of unifying essence; they were 'frail, precarious, dispersed across a range of discourses'.[2] The idea of a humankind with universal characteristics and a more or less coherent inner self is something that didn't appear in Europe for another fifty years or so. This anti-essentialist view of humanity affected the way people wrote, their theories of authorship and originality, the way they thought about self-hood and gender, their view of history, and their attitude to authority. It informed their whole world view.

When these claims were first made in the 1980s they seemed perverse and counter-intuitive. After all, wasn't it Shakespeare who said that people the world over 'feel want, / Taste grief, need friends' (*Richard II*, III.ii.171–2)? Didn't Shakespeare tell us that 'One touch of nature makes the whole world kin' (*Troilus and Cressida*, III.iii.169)? But of course we can't assume that these were Shakespeare's own views. Perhaps we are meant to read statements like these ironically. At any rate, two decades later postmodernism's anti-essentialist reading of Renaissance intellectual culture no longer seems so shocking. But though these ideas have been thoroughly assimilated into mainstream Shakespeare criticism, it's not easy to find evidence for them in European intellectual history. In Elizabethan England, as in Continental Europe, intellectual and artistic life was permeated through and through by humanist thought, and Renaissance humanists believed that all social and intellectual inquiry must be grounded in an understanding of human nature. What Pope said about philosophy in 1734 was as true of the Renaissance as it was of the Enlightenment: humanists believed that the proper study of mankind was man.

Humanism was a highly self-conscious intellectual movement that devoted much thought to promotion of its own methods and ideals. Though humanists argued about the nature of 'man', they agreed both that there was an irreducible essence of human nature, and that it was important to understand what that essence consisted of. Human beings might have unique powers of rationality, but their nature was flawed: that's why civilisation is such a fragile thing. But knowledge of the generic limitations of human nature could help to guard against the consequences of human folly. If self-knowledge, meaning both awareness of your individual strengths and weaknesses and an understanding of humanity in general, was 'the chief part of wisdom', as Erasmus put it,[3] literature could help you to acquire that wisdom. By holding 'as 'twere the mirror up to nature' (*Hamlet*, iii.ii.22),[4] the arts of poetry and drama could help you to understand your 'human-kindness'. In its broadest sense, Renaissance humanism was a literary culture that concerned itself with the question of how to promote civilised values and at the same time guard against the barbarism to which the baser side of human nature always threatened to lead us.[5] Shakespeare's plays are a product of that humanist culture.[6]

THE PROPER STUDY OF MANKIND

The word 'humanist', first used in England in 1589,[7] is a translation of the Italian '*umanista*',[8] which meant someone who taught the *humanae litterae*, or 'liberal arts' as Prospero calls them (*The Tempest*, i.ii.74). The ruling ambition of the humanists was to recover the values of classical civilisation. Because civilisation was thought to have had its origins in oratory,[9] the study of classical eloquence formed the basis of humanist plans for a new system of education. Some humanists, like Petrarch, were

fiercely nationalistic; others, like Erasmus, deplored international rivalries
and cherished the ecumenical ideal of a world, or at least a Europe, united
by reason and learning.[10] But nationalists and internationalists alike
shared the belief that any programme of social reform must be based on
a true understanding of human nature. 'The first lesson and instruction
unto wisdom . . . is the knowledge of our selves and our human condition',
wrote Montaigne's friend Pierre Charron.[11]

'*Umanista*' in turn comes from the Latin '*studia humanitatis*'. In
classical Latin *humanitas* had three principal meanings: human nature;
civilisation, or culture; and benevolence, and this is how the word was
understood by sixteenth- and seventeenth-century English humanists. In
his Latin dictionary of 1565 the Elizabethan humanist Thomas Cooper
gave examples to illustrate these related meanings of *humanitas*, explaining that they could be summed up under three general headings: 'the
state of human nature common to us all'; 'liberal knowledge, learning,
humanity'; and 'courtesy, gentleness, humanity'.[12] When the seventeenth-
century poet Robert Aylett explained the meaning of 'humanity' he gave
the same priority to human nature: 'Humanity may have a threefold
sense, / man's nature, virtue, and his education / In humane arts'.[13]

Modern scholars describe Renaissance humanism as primarily an educational movement[14] and contrast it with the more generalised nineteenth
and twentieth-century use of the word to mean a concern with secular
values.[15] It's true that the pioneering figures in Renaissance humanism
were, in the main, editors, translators, and teachers who believed that a
systematic study of classical eloquence would help to bring about a more
civilised society. In Northern Europe in particular, humanists argued
that education meant that you had a duty to the state. In More's *Utopia*
the character of Peter Giles advises Hythlodaeus to act as counsellor to
some illustrious prince; in *The Governour* Sir Thomas Elyot claimed that
'the end of all doctrine and study' was 'good counsel';[16] in *Gorboduc*,
England's first Senecan tragedy, Sackville and Norton remind the young
Queen Elizabeth of the importance of listening to wise counsellors;
Shakespeare's Duke Vincentio remarks: 'if our virtues / Did not go forth
of us, 'twere all alike / As if we had them not' (*Measure for Measure*, 1.
i.33–5). Ben Jonson summed up the humanists' belief in the importance of
civic duty when he justified the study of poetry by saying that 'it offers to
mankind a certain rule, and pattern of living well, and happily; disposing
us to all civil offices of society'.[17] The ideal that inspired Renaissance
humanists was a just society, ruled, like Plato's imaginary republic, by a
wise and responsible oligarchy.

These generalisations about the emphasis in Northern Renaissance humanism on the practical application of learning are not in dispute. But at the same time it's important to keep in mind the origins of the term '*umanista*' and the significance that humanists attached to the study of human nature. This is something that hasn't been given much attention in modern Renaissance scholarship. As the word suggests, a humanist was someone who made it his business to understand humankind. Indeed how could you begin to plan the just society until you knew what kind of human problems you were dealing with? As the humanists' favourite Latin author, Cicero, had said, if you want to explain the meaning of justice, you must look for it in the nature of man.[18] So while modern scholars are right to distinguish between sixteenth-century and modern humanism – the one concerned with the recovery of classical culture, the other with the promotion of secular values – we need to be sure that we don't lose sight of the original concern of Renaissance humanists with the study of human nature.[19]

When More had Peter Giles advise Hythlodaeus on his civic responsibilities he was almost certainly thinking of Cicero. For Renaissance humanists Cicero was the supreme example of the philosopher who devoted his life to service of the state. Petrarch said of him, 'of all the writers of all ages and races the one whom I most admire and love is Cicero'.[20] In the *De officiis* Cicero wrote: 'Those whom Nature has endowed with the capacity for administering public affairs should put aside all hesitation, enter the race for public office, and take a hand in directing the government.'[21] His words were echoed in countless Renaissance treatises, plays and poems. The first classical text to be printed in Europe, *De officiis* was the most important of all Cicero's works for Renaissance humanists. It encapsulated, in a way that no other classical work did, the humanist ideal of the civilised life. Cicero's book is a treatise on the moral duties of a statesman. Writing in exile and in fear of his life, Cicero was concerned with the preservation of the republican values that he believed were the very foundation of civilisation and that were now in danger of extinction. But because he believed that ethical systems are derived from our essential characteristics as human beings rather than from some supernatural source, he devoted the first book of his treatise to an anatomy of human nature. Cicero begins by listing those universals that are the defining features of our humanity: the power of speech and reason, the ability to distinguish between cause and effect, sociability, a concern with family ties, a need for security, a desire for truth, hatred of unjust authority, an aesthetic sense, and so forth. Cicero argues that it's from these basic human characteristics that our moral sense is derived.

Having described the universals that define humanity as a species, Cicero then distinguishes between our generic nature and our particular characteristics as individuals:

> We are invested by Nature with two characters, as it were: one of these is universal, arising from the fact of our being all alike endowed with reason and with that superiority which lifts us above the brute. From this all morality and propriety are derived, and upon it depends the rational method of ascertaining our duty. The other character is the one that is assigned to individuals in particular.[22]

For Cicero the founding principle of all responsible action was an understanding both of humanity in general and of one's own particular strengths and weaknesses as an individual: 'we must so act as not to oppose the universal laws of human nature, but while safeguarding those, to follow the bent of our particular nature'.[23] That's why self-knowledge, in the sense in which Charron defined it – 'the knowledge of our selves and our human condition' – is of such paramount importance for Cicero and his humanist followers: only through an understanding of our human limitations can we hope to control the baser part of our nature and live virtuous lives that contribute to the public good. As Juan Luis Vives, the Spanish humanist and friend of Erasmus and More, put it: 'what greater practical wisdom is there than to know how and what the human passions are: how they are roused, how quelled?'[24]

That the ancient adage *nosce teipsum* – know thyself – is a key principle in humanist thought in general, and in Shakespeare in particular, is so well known that it hardly needs repeating.[25] Social identity may be a fluid and unpredictable phenomenon, oft got without merit, and lost without deserving, and dependent, like reputation, on circumstances; as Jaques says, 'one man in his time plays many parts' (*As You Like It*, II.vii.142). But we shouldn't confuse an individual's social role with his or her essential inner being. Renaissance writers go out of their way to insist on the distinction. In *Radical Tragedy* Dollimore cites Francis Bacon's essay 'Of Custom and Education' as evidence of an explicit anti-essentialism. 'Nature', wrote Bacon, 'nor the engagement of words, are not so forcible as custom.'[26] What Dollimore omitted to mention was that this essay is one of a pair.[27] In the companion piece Bacon character-istically put the other side of the argument, asserting the inviolability of that essential self which exists at a deeper level and is not affected by the vagaries of social behaviour: 'Nature is often hidden, sometimes over-come, seldom extinguished.'[28] Bacon's distinction between social role and inner self is one of the core principles of neo-Stoic thought. Just as modern clinical psychologists believe that, essential to emotional maturity is a stable self that travels with you from one social role to another, so humanists asserted the paramount importance of self-knowledge.

But as Renaissance humanists repeatedly insist, self-knowledge means more than just being familiar with your own personal strengths and weaknesses. Echoing Cicero, the Elizabethan psychologist Thomas Wright wrote: '[self-knowledge] consisteth of a perfect experience every man hath of himself in particular, *and an universal knowledge of men's inclinations in common*'.[29] We know that for humanists self-knowledge is 'the chief part of wisdom'. What needs to be emphasised, in view of the postmodernist assertion that Renaissance thinkers and writers either rejected, or were unfamiliar with, the idea of human universals, is the importance that humanists placed on an understanding of our generic human nature: that too was part of self-knowledge. Wherever you choose to look in this period – whether it's poetry, drama, sermons, historiography or psychology – you find the same endlessly repeated insistence on an essential core of universal humanity. As John Donne put it, 'all mankind is of one author, and is one volume'.[30] That doesn't mean that humanists believed that our lives are rigidly determined by biological necessity; what it does mean is that they recognised that the choices we make as individuals are constrained by the nature of our species.[31] Some people are more adaptable than others; but no one can change their fundamental nature. The importance of an understanding of that nature is something that all the major humanist writers insist on. In the famous essay 'On his Own Ignorance' Petrarch objected that, for all their pseudo-scientific learning, scholastic theologians ignored the essential question of 'man's nature, the purpose for which we are born, and whence and whereto we travel'.[32] Erasmus also attacked his contemporaries, protesting that scholastics derived their moral norms from abstract principles rather than human realities.[33] 'The first point of wisdom', he wrote in the *Enchiridion militis christiani*, 'is to know thy self',[34] by which he meant that anyone who aims to think seriously about how to live wisely and virtuously must begin with an understanding of what it means to be human. Erasmus' friend More, too, declared that knowledge of human nature must come first: people may go to university to study theology, but 'they do not start with that discipline. They must first study the laws of human nature.'[35]

THE LAWS OF HUMAN NATURE

At the core of Renaissance humanism is the belief that training in the liberal arts could inspire what Henry Peacham the Elder called a 'love of humanity and politic government'.[36] Like so much humanist thinking, it's an idea that has its origins in Cicero. In the dialogue *De oratore* Cicero has one of his characters rehearse the familiar story of humanity's progression from nomadic barbarity to a civilised state. Defending the power of eloquence, Crassus asks:

what other power could have been strong enough either to gather scattered humanity into one place, or lead it out of its brutish existence in the wilderness up to our present condition of civilization as men and as citizens, or, after the establishment of social communities, to give shape to laws, tribunals, and civic rights?[37]

Cicero refers to the same story in his oration in defence of his contemporary, the poet Archias (*Pro Archia poeta*), this time adding the details that allow us to identify the myth he's alluding to. Defending the dignity of the poet's calling, he wrote: 'the very rocks of the wilderness give back a sympathetic echo to the voice [of the poet]; savage beasts have sometimes been charmed into stillness by song'.[38] It was a well-known story: the poet who could tame wild beasts, and to whose words even rocks and stones were sympathetic, was Orpheus. Classical and Renaissance mythographers interpreted the Orpheus story as an allegory of the origins of civilisation. In the *Ars poetica* Horace wrote: 'While men still roamed the woods, Orpheus, the holy prophet of the gods, made them shrink from bloodshed and brutal living; hence the fable that he tamed tigers and ravening lions.'[39] Expanding Horace's brief reference to the Orpheus story, Renaissance humanists explained how it was the Thracian hero's eloquence that first persuaded humanity to abandon its barbaric way of life and form civil communities. In the *Arte of English Poesie* George Puttenham wrote:

It is feigned that Orpheus assembled the wild beasts to come in herds to hearken to his music, and by that means made them tame, implying thereby, how by his discreet and wholesome lessons uttered in harmony and with melodious instruments, he brought the rude and savage people to a more civil and orderly life.[40]

For Renaissance humanists the Orpheus story was a fable about the origins of civilisation and for that reason a justification for the study of eloquence. But it was also a fable about human nature. According to pagan myth, man degenerated to the state of barbarism described by Cicero and Puttenham after the deposition of Saturn. In the *Metamorphoses* Ovid told the story of how, as the golden age gave way to the ages of silver, bronze, and finally iron, men lost their primal innocence and began to behave in barbaric ways; war broke out; and Astraea, goddess of justice, fled from the earth.[41] Appalled by man's impiety, Jupiter resolved to exterminate the entire human race in a universal flood, relenting only when two solitary individuals, Deucalion and Pyrrha, were left alive. The Bible told a similar story of a loss of primal innocence, and divine displeasure in the form of a flood.

As a consequence of these ancestral calamities humanity has a divided nature: though our reason has been corrupted, we are susceptible of improvement. In his *Oration on the Dignity of Man* Pico della Mirandola imagined God telling man: 'Thou shalt have the power to degenerate into the lower forms of life, which are brutish. Thou shalt have the power, out of thy soul's judgement, to be reborn into the higher forms, which are divine.'[42] It's been argued that Pico's account of man's dual nature is evidence of an anti-essentialist view of humankind.[43] But this is to confuse an inherent capacity for change with lack of a defining essence. It's a fallacy that the Middle Ages was well aware of. St Augustine warned of those 'vain babblers' who 'because they have observed that there are two wills in the act of deliberating, affirm thereupon, that there are two kinds of nature'. The truth is, said Augustine, 'that in the acts of one man's deliberating there is one soul distracted between two contrary wills'.[44] Giordano Bruno made the same point in a book he published in London in 1585. Discussing the conflicting elements in the soul, he wrote: 'there are not two contrary essences, but only one essence subject to two extremes of contrariety'.[45] In his *Oration* Pico described man as 'our chameleon' ('*nostrum chameleonta*').[46] The fact that human beings have within them the potential for either amelioration or degeneration no more means that they lack an essence than the chameleon's ability to change its colour means that *it* lacks an essence. It means rather that the capacity for change is an essential feature of our fallen nature.

Pico's *Oration* happens to be the most celebrated statement of the humanist belief in man's divided nature. But the same principle was articulated everywhere in humanist writing. Edmund Spenser gave a classic Elizabethan statement of it in one of the key stanzas of *The Faerie Queene*, Book II:

> Of all Gods workes, which do this world adorne,
> There is no one more faire and excellent,
> Then is mans body both for powre and forme,
> Whiles it is kept in sober gouernment;
> But none then it, more fowle and indecent,
> Distempred through misrule and passions bace:
> It growes a Monster, and incontinent
> Doth loose his dignitie and natiue grace.[47]

Sidney also had this dualistic view of human nature in mind when he claimed that the final end of poetry was to 'lead and draw us to as high a perfection as our degenerate souls, made worse by their clayey lodgings, can be capable of'.[48] The same formulaic view of man's essentially divided nature continued to be rehearsed well into the eighteenth century.[49]

Though as we shall see in the next section, primitivists rejected the idea of a primal corruption of human nature, classic humanists were sceptical of the claim that man's natural state was one of harmonious tranquillity. As Robert Aylett wrote, 'every rude and savage nation, / Where gentle arts abide not, are inclined / To rustic force, and savage cruelty of mind'.[50] Central to the humanist philosophy of man is the belief that, although our reason and will may have been damaged by the follies of our ancestors, the arts of civilisation could, as John Dennis put it, 'restore the decays that happened to human nature by the Fall, by restoring order'.[51] The Elizabethan writer William Scott made the same point in a recently discovered manuscript treatise entitled *The Model of Poesy* (c. 1599): 'the farthest scope [of poesy is] to assist and direct nature to work as being ordained to reduce man to his former state of moral and civil happiness, whence he is declined in that unhappy fall from his original understanding and righteousness'.[52]

CHALLENGES TO THE HUMANIST VIEW OF MAN

Renaissance writers disagreed, as people have always done, in their estimate of human nature: optimists, like Erasmus, tended to stress man's innate love of truth; pessimists, like Machiavelli, emphasised his wickedness. But classic humanists shared a view of man's fallen nature, his vulnerability to temptation, and his capacity for improvement through the arts of civilisation. There were two main challenges to this meliorist view of humanity and the power of the arts to repair our fallen nature: primitivism and Protestant fundamentalism.

Two of the most important political treatises written in Tudor England – More's *Utopia* and Thomas Starkey's *Dialogue Between Pole and Lupset* – are dialogues that engage with primitivist and materialist views of human nature (since poststructuralist materialists believe that it's only prevailing economic arrangements that prevent us realising our true potential and living harmonious lives, primitivism and materialism tend in practice to amount to much the same thing). In *Utopia* Hythlodaeus is a materialist who believes in the malleability of human nature, while 'More' is a realist. Get rid of private property and you will abolish vice, says Hythlodaeus. But 'More' is sceptical: though social reform is urgently needed, changing the material circumstances of people's lives doesn't necessarily mean that they will revert to a life of harmonious sociability. Hythlodaeus agrees that this does indeed seem unlikely, but tells 'More' that his doubts would be dispelled if he had actually experienced the Utopian way of life for himself,[53] which seems, for some commentators, to clinch the argument. It's sometimes suggested that *Utopia* is More's blueprint for a communist society and that More himself was a radical anti-essentialist.[54] But this is to ignore the book's central irony. 'Utopia' means not only 'a good place', but also 'nowhere';[55] only in never-land do people automatically become wise and virtuous when you do away with private property. Because 'More' is made to look foolish by appearing to believe that a show of wealth is the true glory and ornament of the state, it may seem as if the author's sympathies are with the materialist. But in the final pages of the book Hythlodaeus, the anti-essentialist 'dispenser of nonsense', in effect demolishes his own argument when he says that the whole world would have converted to communism long ago were it not for the fact that pride is so deeply rooted in the human heart.[56] Materialist social theories are falsified by the unwelcome truth, at least as More seems to have seen it, about human nature.

Utopia is a humanist work, not just in its satire on the condition of England, its treatment of the question of civic duty, and its imaginative transformation of classical sources, but also because it suggests that a true understanding of human nature must be the starting point for any programme of social reform: ignore the facts of human nature and you will merely end up telling yourself fairy stories.

Human nature is also a key issue in Starkey's *Dialogue Between Pole and Lupset*, written some sixteen years after More published *Utopia*.[57] Starkey had studied civil law in Padua and for a time acted as adviser to Henry VIII's chief minister, Thomas Cromwell. He was one of the most active humanists of his generation in importing Italian ideas into England.[58] In the *Dialogue* he set out proposals for a far-reaching reform of the polity with all its 'faults and misorders and universal decays'. Like Cicero, he begins by establishing certain basic facts about human nature. Before Pole and Lupset get down to constitutional matters, they discuss the meaning of civilisation. What divides them is their radically opposed views of human nature: Pole is cast in the role of a primitivist who believes that humanity's natural dignity has been corrupted by city life. Appealing to the myth of the golden age, he argues that city life is alien to our true nature and that our best hope of living harmonious lives is to abandon civil institutions and return to a more natural existence. But Lupset is allowed to win the argument. Like Cicero (*De officiis*, 1.xvi.50–1), he believes that we have an innate desire for civil order. However, there's another, less congenial, side to our nature. Though Lupset agrees that corruption is rife in our cities, he counters Pole's primitivist case by arguing that the life of ancestral man was 'rude' and 'bestial', not the idyll imagined by poets and mythographers. Defining civil life as 'living together in good and politic order, one ever ready to do good to another, and as it were conspiring together in all virtue and honesty', he argues that society's problems stem from 'the malice of man' rather than from the corrupting influence of civil institutions. For Lupset the solution lies in reform of those institutions, not in an escape to nature.[59]

It's clear from the trouble that More and Starkey took to rebut idealistic views of human nature that primitivist arguments enjoyed some popularity in Tudor England – at least, popularity enough to make them seem worth countering. In 1511 the Florentine humanist Pietro Vermigli, known in England as Peter Martyr, published the first of his series of accounts of the voyages of Columbus, Cortes and other New-World explorers. Describing the lives of the native inhabitants of the Caribbean island of Hispaniola (now Haiti and the Dominican Republic), Peter Martyr reported that they lived 'without tillage or culturing of the ground, as we recall of them which in old time lived in the golden age'. Of the Cubans he wrote: 'these natives enjoy a golden age, for they know neither *meum* nor *tuum*'.[60] As Peter Martyr's English translator Richard Eden noted in the marginal commentary of his edition of *De novo Orbe*, these reports sometimes 'read much like Ovid his transformations'.[61] As reports of voyages of discovery flooded the press in the sixteenth century, phrases from the *Metamorphoses* continually recurred.[62] It's as if these early discoverers were not experiencing the New World directly, but seeing it mediated through Ovid's eyes and imagining that the primitive tribespeople they encountered were living proof of the reality of a primal golden age that had survived unscathed by civilisation. And when Montaigne wrote his celebrated essay 'Of the Caniballes' (English translation by John Florio in 1603), praising what he took to be the dignity and nobility of the native South Americans his servant had told him about, he too used Ovid's phrases to describe their communistic society. Florio's translation of 'The Caniballes' stuck in Shakespeare's mind, and when he had Gonzalo imagine his ideal communistic society in *The Tempest* it was Florio's words that he put into his mouth. But as we shall see in chapter 5, Shakespeare's own views on the question are probably closer to More's and Starkey's than to Montaigne's.

More and Starkey belonged to that brilliant circle of humanists that flourished in England in the late fifteenth and early sixteenth centuries.[63] In 1418 the Florentine scholar Poggio Bracciolini went to England to meet humanists and search English libraries for classical texts.[64] He was deeply disillusioned by the experience. He found no new classical texts, and no one seemed interested in discussing the new learning. To an Italian humanist England seemed like an intellectual wasteland. By the end of the century it was a different story. Commending More's *Utopia* to his friend Peter Giles, the Flemish scholar Jean Desmarais claimed that England could now boast 'men of such talent as to be able to contend with antiquity itself'.[65] And when Erasmus described his impressions of Henry VIII's court after meeting Linacre, Grocyn, Colet and More on his first visit to England in 1499, he made it sound like Castiglione's Urbino in its sophistication, its charm, and its learning:

I have never found . . . such a quantity of refinement and scholarship . . .When I listen to Colet it seems to me I am listening to Plato himself. Who could fail to be astonished at the universal scope of Grocyn's accomplishments? Could anything be more clever or profound or sophisticated than Linacre's mind? Did nature ever create anything kinder, sweeter, or more harmonious than the character of Thomas More? . . . It is marvellous to see what an extensive and rich crop of ancient learning is springing up here in England.[66]

But radical Protestantism wasn't interested in such social graces or such intellectual sophistication. Nor did it have any time for humanism's meliorist view of humankind. Like Erasmus and his Italian forebears, the great Tudor humanists had aimed to unite Christian piety with classical culture: faith, combined with the wisdom of the ancients, was the surest guide to virtuous living. But Calvinism, which became the official theology of the Church of England after the secession from Rome,[67] distrusted reliance on secular learning, or indeed self-improvement of any kind, as a means of influencing one's spiritual destiny. Because man's nature was irreparably damaged by the Fall, divine grace alone could ensure salvation. It was this Calvinist view of human nature that was enshrined in the Thirty-nine Articles approved by Convocation in 1562 and ratified by parliament in 1571.[68] In its most radical form it was a view of humanity that was deeply suspicious of poetry, music and drama. At best these things were a distraction from the serious business of living soberly in accordance with God's law and were likely to lead to licentious behaviour; at worst they encouraged the heresy that human nature was not so depraved that a sympathetic reading of the classics couldn't ameliorate our fallen condition. At the Reformation religious zealots destroyed what they could of England's great heritage of ecclesiastical art; in Elizabethan England their counterparts would have torn down the theatres if they'd been able to.

Though we don't know how strongly Shakespeare felt the ties of what many now believe was a Catholic upbringing, it's clear from plays like *Twelfth Night* and *Measure for Measure* that, as you'd expect of someone who made his living in the theatre, he had little sympathy for religious fundamentalism. But it's in a play that has nothing, ostensibly, to do with puritanism that the contrast between humanism and religious fundamentalism is most striking. Shylock may be a Jew, but he has all the characteristics of the stereotypical Elizabethan puritan: he runs a 'sober' house; he is self-righteous and thrifty; and he hates music, masquing and revelry. In symbolic contrast to Shylock's puritanical hatred of music is Lorenzo's poetic portrait of Orpheus in the final scene of *The Merchant of Venice*. As so often in the plays, Shakespeare seems to be giving us a symbolic contrast between two antithetical cultures: one takes a grimly negative view of human nature and is obsessively concerned with the question of salvation (there is much equivocation on the question of Jessica's salvation in *The Merchant of Venice*); the other believes that, flawed though our nature undoubtedly is, the arts of civilisation, and especially drama, can help us to become more enlightened citizens. In effect, Shakespeare is offering us a symbolic defence of his own art.

Though primitivists and religious fundamentalists challenged the humanist view of 'man', no one in this period denied that there was such a thing as human nature. Despite the general assumption in postmodern Shakespeare criticism that leading intellectuals rejected the idea of a universal human nature, all the evidence points in the opposite direction. Major and minor writers alike agreed with Charron that 'the first lesson and instruction unto wisdom is the knowledge of our selves and our human condition'. Even Machiavelli, most sceptical of political theorists, insisted that, if the past contained a lesson for the present, it was because human nature is fundamentally the same in all ages. And what are Montaigne's *Essays* but the most subtle of all disquisitions on the quirks and oddities of human nature?[69]

THE BARBARIAN AT THE GATE

Renaissance humanists were skilful propagandists for their own cause. In his *Life of Petrarch* the humanist historiographer Leonardo Bruni (1370–1444) recorded how it was Petrarch who first revived classical learning in Italy after the barbarians who overran Rome in the Dark Ages had almost completely extinguished literary culture: 'he had such grace of intellect that he was the first to bring back into the light of understanding the sublime studies, so long fallen and ignored . . .[he] was the first with a talent sufficient to recognize and call back to light the antique elegance of the lost and extinguished style . . . he rediscovered the works of Cicero'.[70] That Petrarch was an indefatigable promoter of the classics is certainly true; but he didn't exactly rediscover Cicero. Ancient learning hadn't been lost in the Middle Ages: classical culture was appropriated and reinterpreted,[71] and classical texts, including Cicero's *De inventione* and *De officiis*, were known and translated.[72] What Petrarch *was* responsible for was the idea of a Dark Age when barbarian forces extinguished classical learning. Although he sometimes used the traditional metaphor of Christ's life and teaching bringing light to a pagan world,[73] the image for which Petrarch is chiefly remembered reverses the medieval Christian idea of a time of pagan darkness giving way to Christian enlightenment, in favour of the Virgilian idea of renewal.[74] According to this alternative scheme of history, the light of classical culture was extinguished by a dark age of barbarity, which in turn was about to give way to a new age of culture and learning in the modern world. Petrarch's most fully developed expression of this idea is in the epic poem that he worked on for much of his writing life. Petrarch's *Africa* attempted to do for modern Italy what Virgil's *Aeneid* did for Rome. The poem creates an historical myth. As Virgil had used the device of the hero's encounter with the spirit of his father in the underworld as a way of prophesying the founding of Rome, so Petrarch imagines a dream in which his hero, Scipio Africanus, learns from his father of Italy's destiny. It's a pessimistic vision. Scipio the elder concludes his story with an account of the collapse of the Roman empire into barbarity. 'Ah, who can bear / to think that mankind's dregs, the base and vile / survivors of our sword, shall come to reign', cries the sorrowing Scipio.[75] But in the final lines of the poem Petrarch prophesies a new age of enlightenment. Ignoring the achievements of the later empire and the Middle Ages, he predicts a return to the glories of the past:

> a more propitious age will come again:
> this Lethean stupor surely can't endure
> forever. Our posterity, perchance,
> when the dark clouds are lifted, may enjoy
> once more the radiance the ancients knew.
>
> (IX.637–41)

In these concluding pages of *Africa* Petrarch created a mythical version of history, partly as a glorification of Italy, but also partly as a way of celebrating his own achievements. It was a highly successful piece of propaganda. When Bartolommeo della Fonte, professor of poetry and oratory at the University of Florence, delivered an oration on the great humanist poet thirteen years after Petrarch's death, all the ingredients of the Petrarchan myth were there. Della Fonte spoke of 'the devastation of Italy, the frequent barbarian invasions and overturn of the Roman cities'; he reminded his audience of how 'eloquence was so hostilely abused that it lay hidden for many centuries in squalor and darkness'; and he related how 'at length [eloquence] was brought forth into the light again by the works of the most noble poet, Francesco Petrarca'.[76] The canonisation of Petrarch as a voice crying in a cultural wilderness and preparing a way for others to follow was complete. It was not so much the veneration of classical culture in itself, as the sense of a heroic defeat of barbarism leading to a new age of enlightenment, that was the most characteristic feature of Renaissance humanism.

Petrarch's *Africa* deals with 'savage deeds' and 'dark events' (IX.574). Though Scipio ends his catalogue of Rome's victories in Book II with the story of the empire's decline, he reassures his son, as Virgil's Anchises had reassured *his* son, that in the course of time Rome would once again subjugate the world: 'You will yet wage great wars / on far flung fields and by your prowess win / a glory worthy to endure' (II.568–70). By introducing himself in the final book of the poem as narrator of the violent events he is commemorating, and by prophesying Rome's future military victories, Petrarch seems to arrogate to himself something of the heroic qualities of his characters. It's almost as if he himself is an epic warrior in the cause of civilisation. In reality his wars were purely literary ones. The barbarians to whose overthrow he had dedicated his whole professional life were not literal Goths and Vandals, but scholastics opposed to the new learning.

Erasmus also portrayed himself as an heroic opponent of barbarian forces. He called his first book *Antibarbarorum liber – Against the Barbarians –* and depicted himself in the book's title-page woodcut as Hercules defeating those traditional symbols of barbarity, the centaurs (Achilles' tutor Chiron was an exception to the centaurs' general reputation for wildness). But Erasmus' barbarians were actually contemporary theologians.[77] Like Bruni and della Fonte, Erasmus rehearsed the Petrarchan cliché about classical learning being extinguished during the Dark Ages. In a letter of 1489 he complained with wild Petrarchan exaggeration that, owing to 'the obstinate growth of barbarism', literature had 'so completely disappeared that not a trace of it remained to be seen'.[78] However, the subject of the *Antibarbari* was not the European Middle Ages, but those in the modern world who opposed the introduction of classical studies into the university curriculum. If Petrarch had a habit of overstating his case, so did Erasmus. Like some irritable sceptic attacking post-modern sophistry, he complained that 'there are those who want the Republic of Letters to be destroyed root and branch'; these opponents of the classics were 'uncouth people who detest the whole of literature . . . on some vague religious pretext'; they were like a 'savage horde' who hate 'the humanities . . . worse than a snake'.[79]

Civilisation and the threat to its survival is one of the defining themes of Renaissance humanism. As Roman civilisation had been destroyed by barbarian hordes, so too, according to Elizabethan humanists, learning in ancient Britain had suffered from the depredations of plundering tribes from the North. The Elizabethan political theorist Sir Thomas Smith claimed that it was barbarous Norsemen who destroyed 'our Christian faith and all good letters, which by means of these troubles and vexations, by little and little, began to perish away amongst us also'.[80] But in the last two decades of Elizabeth's reign there was a new spirit of confidence as poets celebrated England's literary renaissance, and political propagandists revived the old story of Britain's Trojan origins. Like Petrarch, they shamelessly used historical myth for nationalistic purposes. According to the twelfth-century chronicler Geoffrey of Monmouth, the British were heirs in a direct line of succession that went back to the ancient world.[81] When Elizabethan writers took up the British myth and traced their own queen's ancestry back to the legendary Brutus, great-grandson of Aeneas, they conflated the Troy story with the prophecies in Virgil's fourth *Eclogue*: Astraea, virgin goddess of justice, had returned to the earth – more precisely to England – and a new Troy (Troynovaunt) was even now witnessing a restoration of learning and culture on the banks of the

Thames. In *The Faerie Queene*, Spenser used fictional prophecy to suggest that Elizabeth, like Virgil's Augustus, was the direct descendant of Aeneas and her reign the fulfilment of a divine historical plan.[82] Three years after Spenser published the first three books of *The Faerie Queene* (1590) Gabriel Harvey wrote of the 'transplantation' of the arts of civilisation from Greece and Rome to England.[83] The same idea is the underlying theme of John Davies' narrative poem *Orchestra* (1596). Combining elements of the mythical British History with the idea of a continuous historical and geographical progress of the arts westwards, Davies suggested that it was the Elizabethans who were the true cultural heirs of the ancient world.[84]

THE ENEMY WITHIN

An essential ingredient in humanist propaganda was the idea of barbarian forces threatening the existence of civilised values. In the sixteenth century, European propagandists made the most of the very real threat to Christian civilisation posed by the Ottoman empire. Stories abounded of unspeakable Muslim cruelty.[85] Turks were a byword for barbarity: 'Let a Christian man . . . despise the committer of sacrilege, not the man; let him kill the Turk, not the man', wrote Erasmus in a formula that Shakespeare seems to have had in mind when he wrote *Othello*.[86] Under Suleiman the Great, Turkey had become an international power and presented a threat to the entire Christian world. In dedicating his *General History of the Turks* to James I, Richard Knolles warned that Ottoman ambitions would only be satisfied when the whole world was under Muslim rule, 'from the rising of the sun unto the going down of the same'.[87] Some years earlier in his heroic poem on the battle of Lepanto James himself had portrayed the Christian victory over the Ottoman navy in 1571 as an apocalyptic defeat of the whole barbarous 'Antichristian sect'.[88]

Portraying your enemy as Antichrist engaged in a war against the forces of truth and justice is a sure way of uniting the country in a common cause. But less partial commentators knew that Christians were just as capable of barbaric behaviour as Turks. 'Surely no Turkish power can overthrow us, if Turkish life [ie, our own barbarity] do not cast us down before', wrote Roger Ascham.[89] In an account of the Ottoman campaign in eastern Europe, he described the atrocities that followed a treacherous Christian truce:

This Turkish cruelty was revenged this last year in Hungary, when like promise of life was made, and yet all put to the sword, the Christians bidding the Turks remember Tripoli. To such beastly cruelty the noble feats of arms be come unto betwixt the Christian men and the Turks.

Mike Pincombe, who quotes this passage in a brilliant analysis of mid-century humanism, comments: 'What particularly appals [Ascham] is the ease with which supposedly enlightened Christians can degenerate to brutal inhumanity.'[90]

The ease with which apparently reasonable men can degenerate to brutal inhumanity is a recurring topic in Shakespeare's mature work. Cassio's words – 'To be now a / sensible man, by and by a fool, and presently a beast! / O, strange!' (*Othello*, II.iii.298–300) – sum up a theme that's central, not just to *Othello* and *The Winter's Tale*, where civilised men metamorphose into barbarians with symbolic speed, but to the entire humanist view of man and his divided nature. An ancient and familiar symbol of reason threatened by the treacherous passions is the city besieged by enemy forces.[91] Little wonder, then, that the Troy story haunted the imaginations of Renaissance writers, not just as a means of giving spurious authority to their own ruling houses by linking them dynastically with the ancient world, but as a symbol of our fallen human condition.[92] Here was an archetypal tale about a city that fell, not as a result of the military superiority of the enemy, but because of an act of treachery within. Humanists were fond of comparing themselves to Greeks, and their opponents to barbarous Trojans.[93] Though plays like *Hamlet* and *Othello* portray states under threat from an external aggressor, it's the psychology of the enemy within and the risk he poses to national security that's the real centre of dramatic interest in both plays.

If you are comfortable with the Romantic view of Hamlet as a tender and delicate prince caught up in a world of violence that's alien to his true nature, it may seem perverse to compare Shakespeare's hero with Antenor, the man who was responsible, so the story goes, for the fall of Troy.[94] It's true that Hamlet is interested in poetry and philosophy; but he's also fascinated by violence. His favourite piece of dramatic poetry is a particularly brutal episode from a play about the Trojan war; he secretly admires the irredentist who has been laying siege to his own city; and before he dies he actually nominates that avenger as Denmark's next ruler. Othello, too, seems to have the Troy story somewhere at the back of his mind. What could possibly justify the murder of a woman, guilty or not? Though, like Cassio, Othello is devastated by the thought of his injured reputation, the only reason he will admit to himself for killing his wife is the possibility that she may undermine national security. As he's about to murder her, Othello murmurs to himself: 'Yet she must die, else she'll betray more men' (v.ii.6). Like Troy, Cyprus is a community under siege. The Greek island is the last outpost of the civilised world, a garrison beleaguered by barbarian forces. In circumstances such as these, 'in a town of war / Yet wild, the people's hearts brimful of fear' (II.iii.206–7), you cannot have another Helen corrupting your troops. Though Othello doesn't appear at any point to be conscious of the parallel between Cassio's fortunes and his own, the latter's thoughts on his descent into brutality apply with equal force to Venice's heroic commander. In the play's last scene, as Othello finally identifies himself with the barbarian he has been appointed to defeat ('And say besides that in Aleppo once / Where a malignant and a turbaned Turk . . .'), we see the full irony of Iago's words about the two sides of our human nature:

> If the beam of our lives had not
> one scale of reason to poise another of sensuality, the
> blood and baseness of our natures would conduct us
> to most preposterous conclusions.
>   (I.iii.326–9)

Humanists tell us that self-knowledge is 'the chief part of wisdom'. One of the characteristic ironies of Shakespeare's mature work is his heroes' failure to recognise in their own conduct the very barbarism they claim to see in others. It's when Othello begins to behave like 'an erring barbarian' (I.iii.354) himself that he suspects Desdemona of reverting to feral ways like a half-trained hawk (III.iii.264). It's when Lear abrogates the responsibilities of a civilised parent that he compares his own daughter to a savage:

> The barbarous Scythian,
> Or he that makes his generation messes
> To gorge his appetite, shall to my bosom
> Be as well neighboured, pitied, and relieved
> As thou, my sometime daughter.
>   (Folio, I.i.117–120)

And it's when Leontes abandons all semblance of *humanitas* that he refuses to use his wife's royal title on the grounds that to honour one so devoid of decency would be to reduce social distinctions to barbarous uniformity. 'Thou thing', he tells the innocent Hermione,

Which I'll not call a creature of thy place
Lest barbarism, making me the precedent,
Should a like language use to all degrees,
And mannerly distinguishment leave out
Betwixt the prince and beggar.

(II.i.84–9)

The idea that the fragility of civilisation is due, not to economic conditions, or false ideology, but to some latent barbarism lurking in our ancestral psyche may have little to say to postmodern anti-essentialists; but it's a theme that's at the heart of Renaissance humanism.

SHAKESPEARE'S HUMANISM

Like Erasmus, Shakespeare could be satirical when he wanted to at the expense of humanism's enemies. In *2 Henry VI* the buffoonish Jack Cade attacks Lord Saye for corrupting the country's youth by the introduction of grammar schools:

Thou hast most traitorously corrupted
the youth of the realm in erecting a grammar school;
and, whereas before, our forefathers had no other books
but the score and the tally, thou hast caused printing
to be used and, contrary to the King his crown and
dignity, thou hast built a paper-mill. It will be proved
to thy face that thou hast men about thee that usually
talk of a noun and a verb and such abominable words
as no Christian ear can endure to hear.

(*2 Henry VI*, IV.vii.30–8)

Henry VI is an early play, and the anachronistic tirade against learning that Shakespeare puts into Cade's mouth (the real Cade died in 1450) makes a fool of the political agitator in a way that none of the later plays does even when the common people are portrayed as politically irresponsible, as they are in *Julius Caesar* and *Coriolanus*. Cade is almost like the butt of one of Erasmus' invectives against the opponents of humane learning. But of course the speech is actually a tribute to the educational reforms of the Tudor humanists and their vision of a new polity based on study of the classics. Compromised though that vision was by a series of rulers determined to use education as an instrument of national policy,[95] the reformed grammar-school curriculum[96] was responsible for the birth of classical studies in England. The old medieval educational system had emphasised training for warfare and knowledge of the classics of chivalric literature. In replacing this with a curriculum that involved translation of the greatest Latin poets as well as a systematic grounding in rhetoric, logic, and composition based on creative imitation, Tudor grammar schools ensured that every schoolboy knew the classics by heart. This in turn led to a new generation of translators. Among the Latin authors that were 'englished' in the sixteenth century were Cicero, Florus,[97] Horace, Livy, Lucan, Ovid, Plautus, Seneca, Tacitus, Terence and Virgil. To those can be added such modern classics as Castiglione, Contarini, Guicciardini, Machiavelli and Petrarch.

Though their aim had been to create an educated governing class, the early Tudor humanists had in effect laid the foundation for a new national literary culture based on adaptation and reinterpretation of the classics. Puttenham tells us how Wyatt's and Surrey's imitations of Petrarch (a modern classic) transformed English poetry;[98] Sackville and Norton's imitation of Seneca started a fashion that was to become one of the richest seams in English Renaissance tragedy; Arthur Golding's translation of Ovid's *Metamorphoses* provided Shakespeare with phrases for some of his most celebrated virtuoso set-pieces. It was not just that literature was now a proper subject for study and imitation; in the last two decades of the sixteenth century there was a new sense of confidence in the power of English as a literary language. Poets knew they were writing for posterity and that their work would be read in centuries to come; dramatists (and their censors) knew that they now had at their command a linguistic instrument capable of powerfully influencing public opinion (Marlowe's *Tamburlaine* is like a virtual realisation of Thomas Wilson's claims for the power of rhetoric: 'If the worthiness of eloquence may move us, what worthier thing can there be, than with a word to win cities and whole countries?'[99]). A new confidence in the power of literature can be seen too in the assurance with which Puttenham and Sidney justify the art of poetry in their treatises on poetics. Literary genius (see chapter 8) is a mysterious phenomenon, and it would be pure speculation to claim that Shakespeare's plays couldn't have been written without the background of a strong humanist literary culture. But it's difficult to imagine anyone devising such sophisticated metadramatic defences of the dramatist's art as Shakespeare does in the late tragicomedies (see chapter 5) except as part of a culture of humanist apologetics in response to the attacks of religious fundamentalists.

Shakespeare's immersion in Latin poetry has been exhaustively documented: the plays show his knowledge of the classics on almost every page.[100] They also show their humanist origins in the themes they dramatise. Repeatedly they come back to those matters that concern Duke

Vincentio in *Measure for Measure*: 'the properties of government', 'our city's institutions', 'the terms for common justice', 'the nature of our people' (1.i.1–9). In play after play Shakespeare deals with the past and the lessons it has for the modern world; with the problem of tyranny; with the responsibilities of rulers and subjects; with war and the question of whether and under what circumstances it can be justified. Shakespeare wasn't of course the only late Elizabethan playwright to dramatise humanist themes.[101] Lyly's *Campaspe* makes comedy out of the politics of war; Heywood's *Edward IV* considers the problem of what to do about a tyrannical ruler, and invites us to draw parallels between contemporary events and fifteenth-century history; the anonymous *Thomas of Woodstock* deals with the question of the rights of subjects to resist unjust authority. What seems to be unique to Shakespeare is the emergence for the first time in English drama of psychologically plausible characters who give the illusion of having interior lives, but who are at the same time representative figures in the drama of humanism's great symbolic battle between *humanitas* and *feritas*.

Shakespeare's debt to Tudor humanism and its educational reforms is apparent also in the form of his plays. In a formula that sounds strikingly similar to E. M. W. Tillyard's order/disorder model of Elizabethan intellectual life, Cultural Materialism proposes that we ask whether Shakespeare's plays endorsed or subverted 'the dominant order'.[102] Quite apart from the fact that the 'dominant order' in Elizabethan and Jacobean England wasn't a single homogeneous entity, but a volatile mixture of rival aristocratic groups who disagreed violently on key policy issues, this Manichaean approach to English Renaissance drama inevitably reduces complex works of art to a formula that would have seemed crude to Shakespeare and his contemporaries. More and Starkey were the products of a humanist culture that taught its pupils how to argue from both sides of a question.[103] So was Shakespeare. The result was a dramatic art that resists the kind of question that Cultural Materialism wants us to ask. In the 1940s, 1950s and 1960s, historicists began to re-read Shakespeare and his contemporaries in the light of Renaissance rhetorical theory. Rosalie Colie commented on the Renaissance interest in the rhetorical figure of paradox: 'one element common to all these kinds of [rhetorical] paradox is their exploitation of the fact of relative, or competing value systems. The paradox is always involved in dialectic: challenging some orthodoxy, the paradox is an oblique criticism of absolute judgment or absolute convention.'[104] At about the same time Norman Rabkin argued that it was this dialectical habit of thinking that put Shakespeare's plays 'out of the reach of the narrow moralist, the special pleader for a particular ideology, the intellectual historian looking for a Shakespearean version of a Renaissance orthodoxy'.[105] W. R. Elton recognised the same humanist commitment to debate as a method of dealing with ethical problems when he described the structure of the typical Shakespeare play as 'a dialectic of ironies and ambivalences, avoiding in its complex movement and multi-voiced dialogue the simplifications of direct statement and reductive resolution'.[106] Shakespeare's plays reflect their humanist origins, not just in their themes and their adaptation of the classics, but in their dialectical form.

Does the fact that the plays typically seem to hold conflicting arguments in unresolved equilibrium mean that Shakespeare had no opinions of his own? That seems unlikely when you consider the controversial nature of the issues he dealt with, particularly in his middle and later work.[107] *Hamlet*, for example, reflects contemporary concern over the succession question and seems to make oblique allusion to Essex's recent attempt to open negotiations with James VI about a possible military takeover; *Macbeth* deals with the paradox of violent action in defence of civilised values in a way that makes James' own views on political obedience look simplistic; *Coriolanus* portrays a disunited military society at a time when foreign policy was the subject of heated argument between militarists and moderates at court; *The Tempest* alludes to James' controversial plans for resolving European political conflict through dynastic marriage. These were all matters that divided public opinion. Yet none of the plays can be read as unequivocal endorsements of, or satires on, the government. Indeed it would be surprising if they could. Shakespeare was plainly interested in politics; but he was above all an artist writing both for the stage and for publication,[108] and one of the characteristics of great literature has always been a sense of the irreducible complexity of the moral and political issues it deals with. Despite his royal patronage, Shakespeare seems to have been less interested in acting as a spokesman for, or critic of, the government, or even in attacking or defending particular constitutional models, than in analysing the human causes of failure in different types of polity. And that, a Renaissance humanist would say, all comes down to a matter of what Charron called a 'knowledge of our selves and our human condition'. Renaissance historiographers defended the study of history on the grounds that, since human nature is the same in all ages, we can learn important lessons from the past, and so predict how people might behave in the future (see chapter 7, p. 136). Literary theorists defended poetry on the grounds that it gives you a much better insight into the way human beings behave than any scholastic treatise could do.[109] Rather than asking whether Shakespeare was for or against 'the state', it would probably make more sense to take Hamlet's account of 'the purpose of playing' and ask what the plays tell us about the form and pressure of their time as they hold the mirror up to our human-kindness.

THE DECLINE OF NATURAL LAW THEORY

One of the fundamental principles of Renaissance humanist anthropology was the belief that humankind was, as James I's physician Helkiah Crooke put it, 'an Epitome or compend of the whole creation'.[110] The idea was that, in a world framed according to Pythagorean principles, the same rules could be observed throughout the created universe. Minds, bodies, states, families: all were thought to be based on certain timeless, universal laws.[111] The same principles of order, degree, balance and equilibrium were repeated on every plane of existence. Just as the proportions of the ideal human body reflected the mathematical structure of the universe, so too the balance of humours in a well tempered mind reflected the balance of elements in nature,[112] though in a fallen world that precarious balance was all too vulnerable to sudden and violent change.[113] 'Hence it is that man is called a *Microcosm*, or little world', wrote Crooke in his *Micro-cosmographia*.[114] It's this analogy between microcosm (man) and macro-cosm (the universe) that a minor character in *King Lear* is referring to when he talks about Lear outstorming nature's fury in 'his little world of man' (Quarto, viii.9).

Belief in the old theory of correspondence between microcosm and macrocosm lingered on long after the medieval cosmos had been super-seded by a Copernican universe. Francis Bacon endorsed the general principle that man was 'an abstract or model of the world' even as he attacked the absurd lengths that alchemists went to in elaborating the idea.[115] Walter Ralegh repeated the idea in his *History of the World*, saying that man was 'an abstract or model, or brief story of the universal'.[116] On the very eve of civil war Sir Thomas Browne wrote: 'To call ourselves a microcosm, or little world, I thought it only a pleasant trope of rhetoric, till my near judgement and second thoughts told me there was a real truth therein.'[117] But by the 1640s, when Browne wrote *Religio Medici*, the microcosmic analogy had been gradually losing its power as an explana-tory model of human nature for at least a century. With it was disinte-grating too the old Ciceronian theory of a universal law of nature that was common to all nations and that, in Starkey's words, 'inclined and stirred [humankind] to civil order and loving company'.[118] With complete indifference to the philosophical premises of medieval and Renaissance political theory, Machiavelli wrote of a harshly competitive world where man's aggressive instincts knew no natural bounds. Montaigne too was sceptical of traditional theories of natural law, claiming that the humanists' celebration of the dignity and rationality of man was testimony to little more than the vanity of our imagination.[119] But if sceptics like Machiavelli and Montaigne helped to demolish the whole metaphysical edifice of natural law and analogical thinking, that doesn't mean that they rejected the idea of a universal human nature. Quite the reverse. It was Machiavelli's belief that, though times may change human nature doesn't, that was the basis of his pragmatic theory of history: knowledge of the past is valuable to the politician because it's not providence, but human beings with their predictable foibles, jealousies and lust for power who determine the course of history. And if Montaigne came to the conclusion that man's grand theories of natural law are nothing but self-delusion, it's because he recognised that an unfounded belief in our own powers of rationality is something that seems to be indelibly written into human nature: 'presumption is our natural and original infirmity'.[120]

As the medieval universe grew more and more dilapidated, it seemed to many writers that, not just the fabric, but the very foundations of moral and civic life had been demolished. ''Tis all in pieces, all coherence gone', wrote John Donne in his *Anatomy of the World*.[121] But no one claimed that human nature was also in pieces; that was the one indisputable thing that had survived. Now that the old religious, philosophical and pseudo-scientific certainties were no more, it seemed to many that all that was left was 'the thing itself' (*King Lear*, III.iv.100), unaccommodated man stripped of all his mythological and metaphysical trimmings. In the nineteenth century Jules Michelet and Jacob Burckhardt came close to suggesting that in the Middle Ages man lacked any real sense of an interior self (see below, chapter 9, p. 187); that idea has long since been rejected by modern Renaissance scholarship. But the claim that the idea of a universal human nature was alien to the Renaissance mind is something that seems to be unique to postmodern literary criticism and is unsupported by any documentary evidence. How did it come about that professional scholars were so easily persuaded by an idea that was so patently without foundation? As I'll argue in my final chapter, it probably all comes down to a misreading of a single book – Michel Foucault's *The Order of Things*.[122]

CHAPTER 2

Gender

During the Long Parliament England's puritan revolutionaries conducted an experiment: they tried to change human nature. In June 1647 Parliament decreed that Christmas, along with Easter, Whitsun and all the other traditional festivals of the Church year, was to be abolished. Wakes, feasting, dancing, church ales, Christmas holly bushes and unseemly merry-making had no place in the new godly society, so they were made illegal. The experiment failed. The puritan revolution could no more stamp out people's natural love of feasting, merry-making and dancing than the nineteenth-century English public school system could obliterate adolescent boys' obsession with sex. So unpopular were the government's attempts to suppress Christmas celebrations that in 1646 protestors took over the streets of Canterbury, set up holly bushes outside their houses, gave out free drinks, and broke open the city gaol. The militia had to be brought in to quell the riots.[1]

Though Christmas festivities weren't legally abolished until 1647, the puritan campaign against the old Church rituals goes back to the Reformation. Evangelical clergy attacked anything that had a taint of the old religion. Because the seasonal festivals were so closely linked with Catholicism, they had to go. Despite the revival of pre-Reformation customs under Mary, seasonal celebration declined over the second half of the century. Between 1584 and 1586 there was a parliamentary campaign to reform the Church. A bill prohibiting sports and games on Sundays would have become law if Elizabeth, who did not share the views of the more militant members of her Privy Council, had not vetoed it. But old customs die hard. Lords of misrule continued to be a feature of Christmas festivities in great houses, colleges and Inns of Court long after Elizabeth's accession. Archbishop Grindal gave orders for their suppression in 1576;[2] Phillip Stubbes was still complaining about them in 1583.[3] But in the last two decades of Elizabeth's reign there was a sentimental reaction against the humourless piety of the godly reformers, and writers began to look

31

back nostalgically to an age of popular merry-making. At about the time Shakespeare was writing *Twelfth Night*, William Warner evoked a sentimental picture of merry England enjoying traditional Christmas fare: 'At Yule we wonten gambol, dance, to carol, and to sing. / To have good spiced stew, and roast, and plum-pies for a King.'[4] It was not a scene that would have pleased Elizabeth's more pious clergy. With growing hostility between moderates and evangelical militants in Parliament and the Privy Council, Christmas had become a political issue.

THE POLITICS OF 'TWELFTH NIGHT'

All this makes *Twelfth Night* a much more topical play than it's usually thought to be. Had Elizabeth herself not had a certain amount of sympathy with the old rituals, a play whose title made overt reference to the traditional twelve-day Christmas festival, and that pointedly mocked puritan asceticism, might well have been censored. Sir Toby Belch would no doubt have been delighted with Warner's picture of merry Englanders with their 'ale and cakes';[5] but evangelical reformers would have been less pleased. It's not just that the play contains a lot of buffoonish merry-making. With its farting and belching aristocrats who take delight in humiliating their puritan victim, it looks like a riposte to those reformers who wanted to abolish Christmas. Indeed, since Twelfth-Night celebrations had long been associated with papism, it ran a serious risk of being charged with Catholic propaganda.

To make matters worse, the play seemed to be making light of the military question. An important element in radical Protestantism was the belief that the government should act decisively to restore military values to a society that had, in the Earl of Essex's words, grown generally 'unwarlike, in love with the name, and bewitched with the delight of peace'.[6] In his *Schoole of Abuse* (1579) the anti-theatrical pamphleteer Stephen Gosson complained about the decline of England's military culture: 'Our wrestling at arms, is turned to wallowing in ladies' laps, our courage to cowardice, our running to riot, our bows into bowls, and our darts to dishes.'[7] What more alarming example of the decadence that concerned Gosson than *Twelfth Night*? With its epicurean appetites, heady perfumes, lubricious music and sexual dalliance, Orsino's court is a veritable temple of paganism. But not content with portraying a sybaritic world dedicated to the pleasures of love, the play seems to be making incompetence in the martial arts a joking matter. (The farcical build up of Viola's and Sir Andrew's reputation for ferocity in III.iv is one of the funniest scenes in the play.)

What would have been even more inflammatory to puritan sensibilities was the sexual ambiguity of the whole play. It was bad enough having unattached, unchaperoned young women roaming the country forming unconventional liaisons with powerful landowners. But that wasn't all. One of the things that worried puritan reformers about the theatre was the way it seemed to make men effeminate. To evangelical Protestants disguise of any kind was anathema. Having a boy actor playing a mature woman impersonating a man – and so obviously enjoying the whole experience – was enough to fuddle the mind of any godly citizen. To the puritan sensibility the result of this kind of behaviour was inevitable: it's obvious that Shakespeare's duke has been corrupted by the ambiguities of the situation and has allowed himself to fall half in love with the winsome 'boy' who acts as his go-between. Though Orsino has no hesitation in marrying 'Cesario' when it turns out that 'he' is really a woman in disguise, he prolongs the fiction as long as possible. Clearly there's something about his pretty young assistant that he finds himself drawn to. For aficionados of mistaken-identity farce all this is a distinct improvement on *A Comedy of Errors*. Instead of the mechanical confusions of Shakespeare's only truly Plautine comedy, you now have a nicely ambiguous love interest, together with a bit of affectionate mockery of the self-indulgent lover who thinks he's suffering from the malady that the Middle Ages called *amor heroycus*.[8] Orsino's court is a high-camp world that defines its own elaborate artifice by alluding to the mock-serious conventions of the great medieval love treatises.[9] It's like an adult version of Lyly's innocent schoolboy comedies, with the erotic potential of cross-dressing now intimated in knowing innuendo and hints of forbidden pleasures. But puritans weren't interested in such dramatic subtleties: indeed you could hardly ask for better proof of the theatre's tendency to encourage sexual deviancy. And of course the greatest scandal of all is the fact that Shakespeare doesn't seem to regard this sexual ambivalence as a scandal, merely as a charmingly foolish affectation that must sooner or later come to an end.

This deplorably liberal attitude towards sexual matters is exacerbated by the way Shakespeare treats the one obviously same-sex relationship in the play. The first time we see Antonio he is pleading with Sebastian, like a Petrarchan lover supplicating an indifferent mistress, not to leave him (II.i.1–2). We know that in Shakespeare it's quite normal for men to use the language of love when they are in fact talking about nothing more than friendship. For example, when Cassius complains to Brutus, 'I have not from your eyes that gentleness / And show of love as I was wont to have' (*Julius Caesar*, 1.ii.34–6) it's obvious that he is thinking about political rather than amorous alliances. But when Antonio urges Sebastian not to 'murder' him (in the way that disdainful Petrarchan mistresses have a habit of doing) for his love (31) he's not talking politics. At the end of the scene he has a short soliloquy in which he reveals his true feelings for his beautiful young friend: 'come what may, I do adore thee so / That danger shall seem sport, and I will go' (39–43). This may be one more variation on the familiar literary theme of unrequited love; but it's not the kind of love that any self-respecting puritan could tolerate.

What does Shakespeare do to censure such decadent behaviour? Nothing. Though Antonio admits that it was infatuation that made him risk the full severity of the law by defying his sentence of banishment from Illyria, no penalty is enforced. In fact he seems to have been completely forgotten about at the end of the play when the central characters are paired off. Written at a time when the militant-Protestant campaign for a toughening of the nation's moral fibre had just come to a spectacular and disastrous climax,[10] *Twelfth Night* is a provocative challenge to reformist ideas about seasonal merrymaking, festive cross-dressing and the theatre. But above all it's the play's insouciance regarding sexual matters that must have outraged godly reformers.

However, this is not the way the play has been seen in recent mainstream Shakespeare criticism. For postmodern critics *Twelfth Night* is a play about class and gender struggle. Far from suggesting an easy-going, anti-puritan attitude towards sexuality, the disguise that's such an important part of the play's comic design is a sign of deep social anxiety about gender identity. People – and that includes Shakespeare – apparently believed that gender was so unstable, and so vulnerable to cultural influences, that the mere act of putting on female clothing could physically turn a man into a woman.[11]

GENDER INSTABILITY

How do we know that Renaissance writers believed that gender was purely a matter of social construction with no basis in nature? What evidence is there that this caused deep cultural anxiety? The answer is not a straightforward one. Postmodern interest in Renaissance theories of gender begins, as do so many topics of modern Shakespearean debate, with Stephen Greenblatt. In *Shakespearean Negotiations* Greenblatt proposed the notion of 'social energy'. He wanted to argue that *Twelfth Night* shares certain assumptions about the instability of gender with those he has found in a seventeenth-century French treatise on hermaphrodites (or intersex, as such people prefer to be known), so he developed a theory that would allow him to establish a connection between the two. But the connection is not a simple matter of source and influence.

Because they exhibit characteristics of both sexes, intersex cannot be categorised unequivocally as male or female; they may even appear to metamorphose from one sex to another at different stages of their physical development. Generalising from one medical example, Greenblatt tells us that Renaissance writers regarded sexual difference as a fluid and uncertain phenomenon: 'in Renaissance stories . . . sexual difference . . . turns out to be unstable and artificial at its origin'.[12] Since intersex do not by definition conform to the single-sex norm, it might be supposed that you could hardly draw conclusions about the thought of a whole age on the question of gender from one exceptional example. But the Renaissance mentality was different from ours, Greenblatt tells us. This is a period when the normal was habitually defined with reference to the abnormal, or 'prodigious': 'where the modern structuralist understanding of the world tends to sharpen its sense of individuation by meditating upon the normative, the Renaissance tended to sharpen its sense of the normative by meditating upon the prodigious'.[13] So in other words, if you want to find out what ordinary people thought about gender difference, the place to go to is treatises on intersex and other sexual oddities. Had Shakespeare been reading these treatises? We don't know. But Greenblatt argues that the question isn't really important; his theory of 'social energy' means that Shakespeare didn't have to have read a particular text to share its discursive assumptions:

The relation I wish to establish between medical and theatrical practice is not one of cause and effect or source and literary realization. We are dealing rather with a shared code, a set of interlocking tropes and similitudes that function not only as the objects but as the conditions of representation.[14]

What this means in practice is that, because in *Twelfth Night* you have a woman played by a boy actor disguising herself as a man and actually being mistaken for one, the play is obviously illustrating those theories of sexual indeterminacy that you find in treatises on intersex. It is, in effect, 'a reified form of medical discourse'.[15]

Or is it? Depending, as it does, not on proven sources or 'literary realisation', but on 'interlocking tropes and similitudes', Greenblatt's notion of 'social energy' is difficult either to prove or disprove. The most you can say is that certain ideas about sexual indeterminacy may have been in the air at the time, and that if they were, Shakespeare could possibly have absorbed them and turned them into art. But even then it seems to be stretching the point a bit far to compare mistaken-identity farce – still a staple part of the modern amateur-dramatic repertory – with an obscure medical treatise on sexual abnormalities. But leaving aside these methodological problems, let's consider the claim that the Renaissance had a special interest in prodigies, and that the normal was habitually defined by reference to the abnormal. There's no doubt at all that in Renaissance Europe people were interested in human stories that were in any way out of the ordinary. But that's probably true of most societies. In Victorian England it was fairground freaks that fed the public appetite for the grotesque. Now it's the tabloid press. Nor is our modern taste for the bizarre confined to lower socio-economic groups. In 2000 two top university presses published books with titles like *The Two-Headed Boy and Other Medical Marvels* (Cornell University Press) and *Half a Brain is Enough*, the latter being the story of a boy who had the complete right hemisphere of his brain surgically removed and lived to tell the tale (Cambridge University Press). Three years later Harper Collins published a best-selling academic study of some of the more sensational human mutations titled *Mutant: On the Form, Varieties and Errors of the Human Body*. There doesn't appear to be anything remarkable in the Renaissance fascination with prodigies: the grotesque seems to be a perennial subject of human interest.

But what about the assertion that in the Renaissance people habitually defined the normal with reference to the abnormal? In the absence of any supporting argument it has to be said that this is not a convincing claim. As you would expect, Renaissance physicians were concerned with departures from the norm. But they didn't define that norm by reference to the abnormal. In his book of anatomy James I's physician explained that in order to recognise a pathological condition you had to start with the healthy organism: 'he that knows what should be the natural disposition of every part will be best able to judge when Nature declineth from that integrity, and how far the declination is from the true and genuine constitution'.[16] Anthropologists, too, appealed to an ideal norm. In the standard works of metaphysical anthropology that we know Shakespeare either read or had access to – books like Pierre de La Primaudaye's *The*

French Academie (1586), Pierre Charron's *Of Wisdome* (1601), Thomas Wright's *The Passions of the Mind in General* (1601) or John Davies' *Microcosmos* (1603) – one theme is paramount, namely, that if we want to comprehend ourselves as human beings we have to understand those universal laws of which the human body is one manifestation. Far from defining the normal by reference to the abnormal, anthropologists did the opposite: they defined the proportions of the human body by reference to an abstract metaphysical ideal. It was not just that, as one writer put it, 'the body of man is no other but a little model of the sensible world, and his soul an image of the world intelligible';[17] the physical proportions of the human body were thought to be based on the same mathematical principles on which the universe itself was built. Leonardo da Vinci's Vitruvian Man, showing a human figure inscribed in a circle within a square, is the best known example of this Pythagorean tradition of describing the ideal proportions of the body in terms of universal mathematical principles, though there are plenty of others.[18]

The same analogy between the cosmos and 'the little world of man' (*King Lear*, Quarto, viii.9) formed the basis of Renaissance humoural psychology. Pierre de La Primaudaye summed up a psychological commonplace when he wrote: 'as there are four elements of which our bodies are compounded, so there are four sorts of humours answerable to their natures',[19] which is why it was said that 'our lives consist of the four elements', as Sir Toby puts it (II.iii.9). Like physicians and anthropologists, psychologists defined the normal by reference to an ideal. They argued that temperamental oddities resulted from an imbalance in the four humours, which in an ideal state would be evenly balanced so that they cancelled out each other's excesses in the same way that the four elements had been designed by God to co-exist in dynamic equilibrium.[20] In *Cynthia's Revels* Jonson described his idealised scholar-poet Crites as 'One, in whom the humours and elements are peaceably met, without emulation of precedency.'[21] Shakespeare's Mark Antony praises Brutus in similar terms (*Julius Caesar*, v.v.73–4). Renaissance thinkers knew that fallen man was a contrarious creature who was never short of ingenious ways of betraying his Maker's plans. But they had a very clear idea of what he *should* be like: in essence he was a 'little world made cunningly / Of elements and an angelic sprite', as John Donne put it.[22] When James's physician published his book of anatomy he gave it a title – *Microcosmographia* – that reflected what everyone knew about the fundamental principles on which the human body was framed.[23]

These ideas were not some provincial eccentricity. Nor is there any
difficulty proving their currency: evidence that people thought of man as a
'little world made cunningly' can be found everywhere in the literature of
the period.[24] The microcosmic analogy embodied generally accepted
thinking about human physiology and psychology in medieval and Renaissance Europe. As for gender, that was an all-too-familiar story: in a
hierarchical universe men were supposed to embody the higher principle
of rational intelligence, while women represented the capricious emotions
which, since the Fall, have threatened to usurp the rightful jurisdiction of
reason. When the Dutch physician and theologian Levinus Lemnius
wrote, 'a woman is not so strong as a man, not so wise and prudent,
nor hath so much reason, nor is so ingenious in contriving her affairs as a
man is',[25] he was articulating a commonplace so indubitable that only
exceptional writers (like Shakespeare) had the wit to challenge it, though
not even Shakespeare imagined that there weren't certain essential differences between men and women. Education could change people's behaviour; indeed for humanists the whole point of studying the liberal arts was
to inspire virtuous action.[26] But as the example of Caliban seems designed
to illustrate, however hard you tried, you couldn't change a person's
fundamental nature. 'Such as we are made of, such we be', says Viola
(II.ii.32).

Despite the flaws in Greenblatt's argument – flaws that some might
regard as disabling – his claim that Renaissance writers believed that
gender was inherently unstable quickly became accepted as a given in
postmodern Shakespeare criticism. However, the fact remained that
Greenblatt's theory of something called 'social energy' silently and invis-
ibly pulsing through the body politic was all a bit vague. Phrases like
'historically contingent' and 'categorical understanding'[27] gave the notion
an air of methodological rigour, but they didn't satisfy the scholar's desire
for historical accuracy. In an essay called 'Transvestism and the "body
beneath"' Peter Stallybrass undertook to give the argument about Renaissance theories of gender instability a more secure factual basis by
looking at what English anti-theatrical writers said on the subject.[28] It's
well known that religious opponents of the theatre didn't care for transvestites.[29] Citing Deuteronomy 22:5 – people who dress in the clothes of
the opposite sex are an 'abomination unto the Lord' – anti-theatrical
pamphleteers made it clear that cross-dressing was a crime against God
and nature. But what did they say about gender identity?

Stallybrass considers William Prynne, self-appointed scourge of the
theatre in Caroline England. Prynne was a pamphleteer *extraordinaire*

and an inveterate quarreller. One contemporary said of him that if 'the Apostle come from Heaven, sent thence to constitute a Government [Prynne] would dissent from, and wrangle with him'.[30] His most famous book – really a grotesquely inflated pamphlet – is *Histriomastix*, the 'scourge of players'. It represents the culmination of the anti-theatrical tradition. Published in 1633, it consists of over a thousand pages of invective against the theatre citing every conceivable classical and Christian writer who ever had anything to say against plays and play-acting. What interests Stallybrass is Prynne's thoughts on the effects of cross-dressing in the theatre. Apparently Prynne believed that dressing boy actors up as women didn't just effeminate them; it could actually bring about a physical transformation and turn them into women. Indeed he talks of male actors being 'metamorphosed into women on the stage'.[31] Stallybrass believes that Prynne's materialism enables us to see the truth that Shakespeare's comedies exemplify, namely, that gender is, as Greenblatt puts it, 'unstable and artificial at its origin'. It's only later generations that have deluded themselves with 'a fantasized biology of the "real"'.[32]

It's true that there is something undeniably odd about Prynne with his paranoid fear of Jesuit plots and his obsessive preoccupation with the evils of the theatre. As William Lamont writes in his biography, he 'wanted England to be a community where men were abstemious, serious-minded, short-haired and shunned plays'.[33] But not even Prynne was foolish enough to believe that cross-dressing could literally turn you into a woman. The sentence from which Stallybrass has taken the phrase about boys metamorphosing into women reads as follows: '*May we not daily see our players metamorphosed into women on the stage, not only by putting on the female robes, but likewise the effeminate gestures, speeches, pace, behaviour, attire, delicacy, passions, manners, arts and wiles of the female sex*' (Prynne likes italics and uses them fairly indiscriminately).[34] What Prynne obviously means is that, by wearing women's clothes and affecting female manners it's almost *as if* these actors had actually become women. Only someone who didn't understand how figurative language works would assume that Prynne meant that you could see boy actors literally changing into women every day of the week.

That Prynne is speaking metaphorically when he talks about boys metamorphosing into women is clear from a passage that Stallybrass omits to mention. To illustrate Prynne's materialist view of gender he quotes this phrase: 'a man's attiring himself in woman's array . . . perverts one principal use of garments, *to difference men from women*'.[35] Stallybrass takes this to mean that, since there's no innate difference between the two sexes, clothes could determine a person's gender; they could quite literally 'metamorphose boy into woman'.[36] Does Prynne really mean that it's clothes that decide our gender? We need to see the phrase in context to understand what he is actually talking about. On the next page Prynne explains why he finds transvestism so abhorrent:

> *men's . . . wearing of women's garments* . . . [is] an unlawful thing . . . because it transforms the *male in outward appearance into the more ignoble female sex, and nullifies that external difference between them, which it ought to do.*[37]

This passage makes it clear what Prynne really means. Far from claiming that there are no innate differences between the two sexes and that it's clothing that determines our gender, Prynne is saying the opposite. At the creation God decreed that men and women should be different in kind: men are the superior sex and women are 'ignoble'. It's these essential differences that clothes should emphasise. In a diatribe against assertive women, the anonymous author of the misogynist pamphlet *Hic Mulier* (1620) wrote: 'Remember how your Maker made for our first parents coats, not one coat, but a coat for the man, and a coat for the woman . . . and the man's coat fit for his labour, the woman's fit for her modesty.'[38] For Prynne, as for the author of *Hic Mulier*, clothes are an outward sign of an inner reality. To ignore Deuteronomy's prohibition is to violate that sacred principle. But Prynne makes it clear that even then the male transvestite can only mimic a woman '*in outward appearance*'; he doesn't literally become one.

So much for Prynne's materialist view of gender. But perhaps the oddest thing about Stallybrass' argument is the assumption that a paranoid religious zealot writing thirty years after Elizabeth's death, who was opposed to everything that the theatre stood for, should somehow provide us with an accurate diagnosis of what Stallybrass calls 'the transvestite theatre of the Renaissance'.[39] To claim that, despite its mockery of fundamentalist bigotry, *Twelfth Night* nevertheless shared the very obsessions of those it was satirising is to stretch credibility to breaking point.[40] I will return later to the question of whether it's appropriate to use the term transvestite when writing about festive disguise comedy.

By the time Prynne published *Histriomastix* there was already a long tradition of anti-theatrical pamphleteering. In *Men in Women's Clothing: Anti-theatricality and Effeminization* Laura Levine deals with the Elizabethan pamphleteers Gosson and Stubbes. Her book is about how Shakespeare gave imaginative embodiment to the anti-theatricalists' fear that 'men really could be turned into women'.[41] Echoing Stallybrass' argument, she explains that, 'at the root of pamphlet attacks lay the fear that costume could actually alter the gender of the male body beneath the costume'.[42] This fear is first articulated in a pamphlet that 'was to establish the terms of attack and defense for another sixty years'.[43] Stephen Gosson's *School of Abuse* hints at what later writers make explicit, namely, that wearing women's clothes could turn 'boy actors' into women. Levine writes: 'in the years of mounting pamphlet war this [concern with gender instability] evolves into a full-fledged fear of dissolution, expressed in virtually biological terms, that costume can structurally transform men into women'.[44] To make no mistake about Gosson's seminal role in initiating the debate on gender instability, she repeats the point in the next chapter, explaining that 'Phillip Stubbes clarified [Gosson's] claim even as he heightened it by insisting that male actors who wore women's clothing could literally "adulterate" male gender.'[45]

All this sounds clear enough. However, when you go back to *The School of Abuse* it's difficult to find substantiating evidence for any of Levine's assertions. The passage to which her footnote refers us has got nothing to do with either clothing or boy actors. It's about music. Levine says that Gosson talks 'curious[ly]' and 'cryptically'[46] about theatre effeminating the mind. It's true that he complains about the degenerate state of the theatre in Elizabethan England, but he's no more cryptic than any other Euphuistic writer of the period. In this section of his pamphlet Gosson rehearses the familiar argument in which good government ('the politic laws in a well governed commonwealth') is compared to musical harmony (Exeter uses the same analogy in *Henry V*, 1.ii.180–3); but when music is corrupt, that's usually a sign of a decadent society. To support his point he cites Plutarch on the misuse of music: 'Plutarch complaineth, that ignorant men, not knowing the majesty of ancient music, abuse both the ears of the people, and the art itself: with bringing sweet comforts into the theatres, which rather *effeminate the mind,* as pricks unto vice, than procure amendment of manners, as spurs to virtue.'[47] Much of what Gosson says about the theatre concerns the ancient world. His theme is how the arts have degenerated in modern times. Nowhere does he so much as mention boy actors, cross-dressing or gender.

There is a similar problem with Levine's other main source. In the *Anatomy of Abuses* (1583) Phillip Stubbes complains that men or women who wear the other sex's clothes 'adulterate the verity' of their own nature.[48] Levine says that Stubbes is talking explicitly about 'boy actors who wear women's clothing'.[49] But he isn't. Like Prynne, Stubbes is a religious zealot who attacks anything that gives people enjoyment: lords of misrule, games, fairs, football, ale, wakes, festivals, dancing, music, cards, tennis, bowls, and of course plays. The phrase that Levine cites is from a misogynist chapter entitled 'A particular description of the abuses of women's apparel.' Stubbes uses it as an opportunity to attack perfume, makeup, dyed hair, hats, earrings, big ruffs, small ruffs, scarves, capes, petticoats and practically every other item of women's clothing that you could think of. But he says nothing about the theatre. In the section Levine is referring to, Stubbes is talking about female transvestites ('women wearing doublets'), not boy actors wearing women's clothing. He finds them repellent. So shameless are they in the way they flaunt their 'doublets and jerkins' that he imagines that they would even change their sex if they could: 'if they could as well change their sex, and put on the kind of man, as they can wear apparel assigned only to man, I think they would'.[50] But not even a transvestite can do that, at least not without the help of a surgeon. Stubbes does have a chapter on the theatre in which he says that plays encourage bawdry, foolery and heathen idolatry.[51] But like Gosson, he says nothing about boy actors or theatrical cross-dressing.

Although it's true that some anti-theatricalists were concerned with transvestism, they don't confuse it with boy actors in drag. Nor should we. In the modern world, entertainers like Barry Humphries (Edna Everage) and Paul O'Grady (Lily Savage) make a career out of female impersonation. But they aren't transvestites. There's no reason to assume that boy actors who played female parts on the stage were transvestites either.

The claim that fear of biological transformation is at the root of the pamphlet attacks on the theatre is based on a misconception. What the anti-theatricalists were objecting to when they discussed clothing was the discrepancy between outward appearance and inner reality. Because 'our corrupt nature is more prone and ready to embrace the error of man than the truth of God', the godly must be continually on their guard against mistaking 'an outward, false and corrupt profession' for an 'inward spirit and faith', or so said the self-righteous puritan separatist Robert Browne (he's the one Sir Andrew can't abide – III.ii.30).[52] For Protestant reformers any form of disguise was morally dangerous;[53] at worst it could lead you into the arms of that grand illusionist, Pope-Antichrist. Antichrist 'misleadeth everyone to his mischievous business', wrote Robert Browne;[54] 'an illusion is the work of Satan', wrote the virulently anti-Catholic William Perkins.[55] It was this belief in the spiritual and moral consequences of distorting the inner truth that explains the anti-theatricalists' concern with cross-dressing. Stubbes protested that transvestites falsify their own true nature; Prynne complained that acting requires men 'to seem that in outward appearance which they are not in truth'.[56] Such pronouncements reflect a belief, not in the fluidity of gender, but in essential, God-given differences.

Despite the fact that there is nothing in the anti-theatrical pamphlets to suggest that their authors were so credulous as to believe that theatrical disguise, or even transvestism, could physically transform men into women, the myth that people were anxious at this time about gender instability has been thoroughly assimilated into mainstream Shakespeare criticism.[57] Stephen Orgel tells us that in Renaissance England people feared 'the fragility, the radical instability of our [sexual] essence'.[58] Dympna Callaghan says that anti-theatricalists believed that 'the soul resides in the clothes'.[59] Stephen Cohen writes: 'The ontological anxiety rooted in the inessentiality and malleability of the self is . . . the fear of a monstrous, self-mutating subject'.[60] Valerie Traub explains that, in contrast to our own time, 'erotic desires and practices' were not 'generally linked to a sense of personal identity' in Renaissance England.[61] David Scott Kastan believes that our understanding of 'the Renaissance sex-gender system' has been 'powerfully' illuminated by Levine and others.[62] Underpinning these claims is a postmodern belief in the constructed nature of gender, a belief that anti-theatricalists and, bizarrely, the very playwrights they were attacking, are said to have shared. But that belief is also based on a misconception.

CONSTRUCTING GENDER

In postmodern Shakespeare criticism it's taken as a given that gender differences are the result of social programming and owe nothing to biology. There can after all, as Catherine Belsey explains, 'be no specifically [gendered] identity if identity itself does not exist'.[63] And since in postmodernist thinking the notion of essential selfhood is 'epistemologically insupportable',[64] it follows that gender can have no basis in nature. Jean Howard writes: 'Materialist . . . feminism . . . assumes that gender differences are culturally constructed and historically specific, rather than innate.'[65] Karen Newman also takes it for granted that 'identity, sexual difference, and even sexuality itself are constructed rather than "natural"'.[66] So does Stephen Orgel: 'gender [is] obviously not a fixed category'.[67] Though token acknowledgement is sometimes made of an authority (usually a French thinker like Lacan or Kristeva),[68] no clinical evidence is offered in support of these claims; they are presented as self-evident truths. The postmodern belief that gender is the exclusive product of environmental influences with, as Judith Butler puts it, 'no ontological status apart from the various acts which constitute its reality',[69] is an extreme version of what is sometimes called the Standard Social Science Model of human nature.[70] Proponents of this model argue that inherited predispositions count for little; environment and social conditioning are the overriding determinants of our identity. This is true not just of social identity in general, but even of gender. Orgel reflects this behaviourist belief in the constructed nature of gender when he claims that in Elizabethan England gender was only determined after about the age of seven when male and female children started being dressed differently; until that age their gender was 'interchangeable' and could presumably go either way.[71] So powerful was the influence of behaviourist thinking in the last century that as recently as 1992 a standard A-Level psychology textbook stated that 'gender is primarily a social phenomenon, and . . . [gender] identity is learned'.[72] Clinching evidence cited in support of this claim was the remarkable story of David Reimer, a tale as tragic and bizarre as anything you could find in a Renaissance book of prodigies.[73]

Reimer was born a normal male child in 1965. But when he and his twin brother were being circumcised by cauterisation, David's penis was accidentally destroyed. His parents were counselled by the celebrated Johns Hopkins behaviourist John Money, who explained to them that at birth gender is indeterminate. Since we are born with no innate sense of gender identity, a child could be constructed as either male or female provided that the appropriate socialisation took place within the first two years of life. He recommended that the baby should be surgically re-assigned as a female. Impressed by Money's theory of gender neutrality, the parents accepted his advice. Now called Brenda, the child was brought up as a girl: 'she' was dressed as a girl, given girl's toys and generally encouraged to behave in the way Western society expects girls to behave. In 1972 Money described the Reimer case in a book on gender identity.[74] Although he acknowledged that it was too soon to give a final judgement, he claimed that all the indications were that the experiment had been a complete success: now seven years old, Brenda was to all intents and purposes a perfectly normal girl. It looked like the strongest possible confirmation of the behaviourist belief in the malleability of gender.

The real story was very different. In 1995 the BBC interviewed Reimer for a 'Horizon' programme on gender identity. Instead of a well-adjusted young woman, Reimer was now a married man. So deeply traumatised had he been by his unalterable sense of false identity, that he had chosen to undergo multiple surgery to confirm what he knew intuitively was his true gender.[75] He said he felt that throughout his childhood he had been living a lie. Money had assured Reimer's parents that, since we are all born with an unformed sense of gender, children could be constructed as either sex. Yet despite castration, hormone treatment and years of the most conscientious and supportive social conditioning, Reimer said that for as long as he could remember he knew that he was in the wrong gender. He was horrified when he learnt that his case was being cited by behaviourists as proof of gender neutrality. It was that discovery which made him decide to go public. 'You know who you are', he told an interviewer, 'it's in you; in your genes; in your brain; nobody has to tell you who you are.'[76]

Transsexuals also report a sense of being in the wrong gender. It might be thought that transsexuals were proof of behaviourist claims for gender indeterminacy. Here are people who seem to enact Ovid's tales of trans-formation, voluntarily metamorphosing, with the surgeon's help, from one sex to another. 'Transsexualism . . . is one . . . manifestation of the constructedness of gender', writes Marjorie Garber.[77] In reality the op-posite is true. Transsexualism is proof of the power of prenatally deter-mined gender identity. Neurobiologists now believe that gender is not just a matter of social conditioning or even of chromosomal difference, but also of the hormones to which the foetus is exposed in the uterus. Flood a female foetus with testosterone and its brain will develop male characteristics; deprive a male foetus of testosterone and its hypothalamus will be more like that of a female.[78] Those differences remain an irrevers-ible part of the brain's neuronal architecture and may be the reason why transsexuals feel that they are imprisoned in the wrong body. At all events, their innate sense of gender identity is so resistant to years of social conditioning that they are prepared to undergo expensive and painful surgery to restore them to what they believe is their true gender. 'Trans-sexualism', writes Jan Morris in her autobiography, 'is a passionate, lifelong, ineradicable conviction, and no true transsexual has ever been disabused of it.'[79] Recent research on how babies acquire a sense of gender identity suggests that it's the hormones to which the prenatal brain is exposed that determine our gender, with cultural influences powerfully reinforcing innate dispositions. Only when they are sure about the stabil-ity of their own identity do children begin to relax their conservative view of gender roles and accept that girls can do boys' things and vice versa.[80]

There are, of course, good reasons for challenging conventional notions of femininity and masculinity. Throughout history men have denied women full legal rights on the grounds that they are inferior to men and unfitted by 'nature' to take a full part in civic or commercial life or to receive equal wages. Such assumptions need to be continuously challenged. But it's one thing to acknowledge the obvious fact that our behaviour and our sense of our personal identity are influenced by our social environment, and quite another to claim that gender is, as Orgel puts it, 'mutable, constructed, a matter of choice'.[81] Garber argues that the whole subject of gender construction is 'undertheorized'.[82] In view of the discrepancy between postmodern theory and empirical reality, it's difficult to avoid the conclusion that the problem is not so much a lack of theory, as a lack of evidence to support the radical constructionist case. With the Standard Social Science Model looking increasingly untenable, there is now an emerging consensus among neurobiologists and psychologists that gender identity is not exclusively a matter of biological or of environmental influences, but of an interaction between the two.[83] Psychologist Diane Ruble writes: 'our need is to understand better the delicate and complex balance of biological and cultural influences in gender role development'.[84]

SOME LIKE IT HOT

Anti-theatricalists were concerned about the effect of the theatre on people's morals. There's nothing particularly surprising in that: apologists for the theatre also thought that plays could change people's outlook and behaviour.[85] But there's no evidence that either pro- or anti-theatricalists thought that theatrical costume could turn men into women or vice versa. There's even less evidence that Shakespeare thought it could; as Linda Woodbridge rightly says, 'transvestite disguise in Shakespeare does not blur the distinction between the sexes but heightens it'.[86] There is one Elizabethan play in which a cross-dressed girl is physically transformed into a boy. But the metamorphosis is a joke. Because the two central characters in *Gallathea* have fallen in love with each other while disguised as boys, Lyly has to find a device that will allow everything to be tied up neatly at the end of the play. His solution is a *dea ex machina*. Venus proposes that one of the girls be turned into a boy. To prevent arguments about who it's going to be, she decrees that neither will know until they get to church. Gallathea and Phillida happily agree, and the play ends with a witty little Epilogue from Gallathea about the irresistible power of love.

Lyly was one of Shakespeare's major sources of comic inspiration. What Shakespeare got from *Gallathea* was not a superstitious belief in gender transformation, but a sophisticated form of mistaken-identity farce that allowed for some wonderfully ironic dialogue in which characters test each other's responses while taking care not to put themselves at risk by giving too much away. Echoes of Lyly's amorous nonsense can be plainly heard in *Twelfth Night* in scenes like ii.iv. Though Viola can see that Orsino finds her attractive, and drops strong hints of where her own feelings lie, she has to be careful not to break the spell before she's sure of him.

Neither Lyly nor Shakespeare seems particularly anxious about gender. Certainly they have none of Stubbes' hangups about transvestism. What can't be denied, though, is the fashion for theatrical double cross-dressing in this period. All-male acting companies meant that female characters had to be played by cross-dressed males. But this doesn't explain the appeal of the boy-playing-a-girl-playing-a-boy motif. If *Twelfth Night* is not about gender anxiety, what is the cultural significance of this particular kind of disguise?

Transvestism exists in most cultures and takes many different forms. Transvestites may be heterosexual, homosexual, or transsexual. Modern researchers seem to be agreed on two things: first, that transvestism is closely associated with sexual arousal (one transvestite told Peter Ackroyd, 'when I dress it feels as if I have a continual orgasm'),[87] and second, that its psychological causes are unknown.[88] But postmodern Shakespeareans write as if there were no difference between the psychological compulsion to wear the clothes of the opposite sex, and cross-dressing as entertainment. It's true that there is some overlap between the two: transvestites may perform in clubs and bars, while theatre actors working in plays involving cross-dressing may privately be transvestites. But it would be just as mistaken to suppose that every male who ever acted in a single-sex performance of a Shakespeare play is a closet transvestite as it would to assume that the accountant or the lorry driver who gets a kick out of secretly putting on his wife's underwear is no different from the professional Noh or Kabuki actor. Admittedly, Orsino finds the whole idea of falling in love with a 'boy' amusing and relishes the thought of seeing 'him' in women's clothes (v.i.271). But the erotic potential of the situation is treated as a joke: the facile banter that the play's misunderstandings give rise to in the final scene doesn't suggest that Shakespeare is dealing with a serious case of fetishistic transvestism. It's more a matter of being sufficiently comfortable with unconventional sexual relationships to be able to make them the subject of comedy.

In the introduction to *Erotic Politics: Desire on the Renaissance Stage* Susan Zimmerman writes: 'Cross-dressing, or transvestism, is a convention alien to the mainstream of modern theatrical practice . . . but central to the erotic dynamic of Renaissance drama.'[89] This is a puzzling claim. Though boys' acting companies, with the institutionalised tradition of female impersonation that they entailed, have long gone, cross-dressing is as popular in the entertainment world now as it always was. Pantomime, with its preposterous dames, shows no signs of disappearing; films like *Tootsie* and *Mrs Doubtfire* were box-office winners; in August 2001 members of the American Film Institute voted *Some Like it Hot* the funniest film of the last century. It often seems to be forgotten in postmodern Shakespeare criticism that *Twelfth Night* is also a comedy. In a recent article on the social changes that feminism has brought about Jeanette Winterson argued that there is now 'a [sexual] playfulness on the streets that gender politics misses'.[90] *Twelfth Night*'s best critics have always recognised that playfulness. In mistaken-identity farce part of the fun for an audience comes from something that seems to be as universal as comedy itself: the pleasure we all seem to take – in fiction at least – in seeing people deceived by appearance. *Twelfth Night* plays on that universal interest in deception; its sense of fun comes from an easy tolerance of unconventional sexual relations.[91] Goethe was right when he argued that 'The twofold charm [of female impersonation] comes from the fact that this person is not a woman, but rather portrays a woman.'[92] He could have been writing about either *Twelfth Night* or *Some Like it Hot*. The joke of Wilder's film lies not in the audience's sense that Tony Curtis and Jack Lemmon have been physically transformed into a couple of broads, but the fact that ditzy Marilyn can't see that beneath the drag are two libidinous males who are not likely to be doing much sex changing. *Twelfth Night* also emphasises the differences between the sexes rather than their interchangeability (though unlike *Some Like it Hot*, the play gets its laughs mainly at the expense of men, not women).[93] The dramatic irony of Viola's remark to Olivia about not being what she seems (III. i.139) would lose its spice if she were actually turning into a man. The knowledge that Shakespeare's cross-dressed heroine is really a boy in drag turns Goethe's 'two-fold charm' into a three-fold joke.

While we obviously need to be clear about the difference between transvestism as a psycho-sexual phenomenon and the pleasures of theatrical disguise, it would be wrong to suggest that all cross-dressed entertainment is politically innocent. Classical Japanese theatre may be a completely institutionalised part of an establishment culture, but camp performances by rock musicians like David Bowie or Alice Cooper are intentionally provocative. They deliberately set out to violate bourgeois notions of respectability and decency. There is also an anarchic element in the medieval mumming tradition. Though mumming was sometimes part of court entertainment in the Middle Ages (a contemporary account survives of an elaborate mumming at Richard II's court in 1377),[94] informal revellers in cross-dressed disguise were recognised as a threat to law and order; in 1414 Lollard heretics actually plotted a coup against 'the King and Holy Church' under the guise of mummers.[95] When England's revolutionary puritans made Christmas illegal in 1647 they weren't being kill-joys just for the sake of it; they understood the subversive potential of festive merrymaking. Garber claims that 'the appeal of cross-dressing is clearly related to its status as a sign of the constructedness of gender categories'.[96] What seems more likely is that its appeal comes from the *frisson* of pleasure we get from the breaking of taboos. Puritans could see that perfectly well; so could the Taliban (both, incidentally, were responsible for the most atrocious acts of cultural vandalism).[97] If you want political obedience it doesn't do to let people get too festive. Not for nothing did the anti-theatricalists cite Deuteronomy: for fundamentalists like Stubbes and Prynne here was a kindred spirit. Its author was a patriarch whose angry God (6:15–16) encouraged his chosen people to destroy the religious culture of their tribal neighbours and desecrate their sacred places (12:2–3). *Twelfth Night* is genially subversive of that fundamentalist mentality. The world it portrays is an easy-going aristocratic world of romantic love, sexual tolerance and childish pranks. Its main characters are certainly 'idle shallow things' (III.iv.121–2), and they all come in for a certain amount of satire. But the play invites us to see them as less obnoxious than the puritans who wanted to do away with the theatre along with football, wakes, and festive cross-dressing. Above all, *Twelfth Night* celebrates what Olivia calls a 'generous . . . free disposition' (I.v.87–8).

CHAPTER 3

Value pluralism

'Hath not a Jew hands, organs, dimensions, senses, affections, passions?'
(*The Merchant of Venice*, III.i.55–6). Shylock's most famous speech has
been read by many critics as a defence of the persecuted outsider. With its
powerful rhetoric and its sense of the dignity of the human spirit, this is
one of Shakespeare's great set pieces, comparable with Henry V's medita-
tion on the cares of kingship, or even Hamlet's soliloquy on suicide.
Appealing, as he does, to a universal humanity that transcends ethnic and
cultural differences, Shylock comes across, not just as the victim of
Christian prejudice, but as a tragic figure of almost heroic proportions.
Yet within half a dozen lines he has metamorphosed into a pantomime
buffoon. As Tubal's 'bad' news of Jessica's betrayal alternates in symmet-
rical sequence with the 'good' news of Antonio's misfortunes, Shylock's
ludicrously exaggerated reactions make him an obvious target for the
mockery of the street boys who follow 'crying "His stones, his daughter,
and his ducats!"' (II.viii.24). What are we to make of such contradictory
images? Was Shakespeare sympathetic to the Jewish outsider? Or did
he share the anti-Semitism that was the norm in late medieval and
Renaissance Europe?

It's understandable that, after the greatest crime against humanity in
recorded history, twentieth-century criticism should have been preoccupied with Shakespeare's treatment of the Jewish question (even to the extent of claiming that Shakespeare himself was a Jew).[1] But with so few
Jews in England and no Holocaust to prick their consciences, Elizabethans
didn't see themselves as having a Jewish problem. It's true that Jews were
routinely vilified, as they had been since their expulsion from England in
1290.[2] But their tiny numbers meant that they weren't perceived as a
national issue. Though conflict between Jews and Christians is undeniably at the centre of *The Merchant of Venice*, the play is not about whether
you should be supporting one side or the other. Indeed it goes out of its
way to challenge such a reductive approach to ethical and political

questions. Renaissance thinkers believed that the key to an informed understanding of history, politics and morality lay in self-knowledge: to know yourself was to understand the peculiarities of humankind as a species. As Ben Jonson put it, before he can advise others, 'a man must be furnished with a universal store in himself, to the knowledge of all nature: that is the matter, and seed-plot; there are the seats of all argument, and invention. But especially, you must be cunning in [that is, knowledge-able about] the nature of man.'[3] Being 'cunning in the nature of man', is what *The Merchant of Venice* is all about. The play hints at the problem of self-knowledge in its opening scene. In the very first line of the play Antonio confesses that he is a puzzle to himself, and goes on to admit that he has much ado to know himself (1.i.6). Shakespeare's play is artfully designed to set us thinking about our contrarious humanity and the complex ethical choices it generates.

SHYLOCK THE PURITAN

The Merchant of Venice is in every sense an artful play. It's full of self-conscious parallels and contrasts: there are two main plots linked by the motif of a bond (Antonio and Portia both talk about the conse-quences of defaulting on their bond – 1.iii.134–5; III.ii.172–4); there are also two trials, two contrasting locations, two merchants, two fathers (though Portia's father is dead, his influence lives on), and two daugh-ters. Informing these stylised parallels and contrasts is the antagonism between Christians and Jews and their respective values. Portia's appeal to the 'quality of mercy' (IV.i.181) and Shylock's insistence on the letter of the law suggest an obvious opposition between Christian charity and pagan vindictiveness, or perhaps between Old and New Testament views of justice. This conflict of values is part of a broader series of structural oppositions. On one side there is Belmont, Portia, love, music, poetry, moonlight, and 'human gentleness and love' (IV.i.24); on the other there is Venice, Shylock, the world of financial com-petition, puritanical asceticism, and ancient hatreds. But as is usually the case in Shakespeare, simple-looking binary opposites turn out to be anything but straightforward. The Christians can be just as un-pleasant as Shylock.[4] Think of Antonio's public humiliation of Shylock, or the vindictive things that Gratiano says in the trial scene, taunting his enemy when the tables are turned, and demanding summary execution. Not even Portia is above telling 'quaint lies' (III.iv.69) to achieve her ends.

However, plays change their meaning over time. The elements that modern audiences find most disturbing in *The Merchant of Venice* would probably not have bothered the average Elizabethan theatregoer, while conversely, Elizabethans would have been aware of social and religious nuances that may be lost on us. Particularly troubling to modern critics is Shylock's enforced conversion: to the modern sensibility it's difficult to reconcile Portia's fine words about charity with the court's subsequent denial of the Jew's right to the religion that is the very core of his ethnic identity. This is unlikely to have bothered Elizabethan theatregoers. Compared with the fate that was meted out to Catholic heretics like Edmund Campion, Shylock's sentence is lenient. Moreover, conversion of the Jews to Christianity was such a central, and proverbial, part of sixteenth-century apocalyptic that it's unlikely that an Elizabethan audience would have regarded Shylock's sentence as unreasonable. After all, hadn't St Paul himself said that 'all Israel shall be saved' (Rom. 11:26), which the Geneva Bible glossed as meaning that Christians have a duty to work for the conversion of the Jews by spreading the gospel and 'the good tidings of salvation which they preached'?[5] Elizabethan exegetes believed that conversion of the Jews was the last stage in the grand historical plan outlined in Daniel's interpretation of Nebuchadnezzar's dream (Daniel 2:31–44).[6] The surprising thing about *The Merchant of Venice* is not that Shakespeare could have written a play that seems to give such free expression to anti-Semitic prejudice,[7] but that in an age when dramatists and their audiences had few inhibitions about such matters, it asks us to question that prejudice. Despite Portia's flagrant deception of a court of law, most Elizabethan theatregoers would probably have agreed that by the end of Act IV mercy had been shown and justice done; Shylock's conversion was clearly a matter of being cruel only to be kind.

However, that's not to say that Shylock would have been an uncontroversial figure for a contemporary audience. Though he is portrayed as a Jew, his values seem almost indistinguishable from those of a puritan: he is thrifty and self-righteous ('What judgement shall I dread, doing no wrong?' – IV.i.88); he hates music, masquing and revelry; his house is 'sober' (II.v.36); he places great importance on his family (unlike his wifeless, 'prodigal' adversary); and his idea of justice is based on the old *lex talionis*. Jews may not have been a pressing social issue in Elizabethan England, but puritans certainly were. They weren't just killjoys who disapproved of feasting and merrymaking. They wanted to close the theatres; they sought to control government policy; they wanted to criminalise adultery; and, most dangerous of all for Catholics, they were anxious to see the sternest possible measures taken against heretics.[8] And for convicted proselytisers that meant public execution with the usual live disembowelling, and sometimes removal of the still-beating heart. For a playwright with Catholic connections they were a very unwelcome presence indeed. In *Twelfth Night* and *Measure for Measure* Shakespeare satirised puritans quite openly. But in Elizabethan England you had to be careful when dealing with religious matters. In *The Merchant of Venice* Shakespeare was more circumspect than he was in the two later plays, and used a politically uncontroversial hate-figure to stand for the puritan sensibility. The link was not entirely arbitrary. As a way of confirming their status as God's chosen people, some fundamentalist puritans actually referred to themselves as Israelites. 'We are the same Israelites . . . [who] shall be sent unto the land promised us . . . [in] this Queen's day that now reigneth', wrote the puritan Ralph Durden.[9] In the seventeenth century some Levellers actually called themselves 'Jews' and advocated the adoption of the Torah as the basis for English legislation.[10] The parallel between puritans and Jews was sufficiently familiar to be made a topic of anti-puritan satire. In 1608 one pamphleteer published a spoof apology supposedly written by a Jew who becomes a puritan: 'if I am to say on my honour why I am become a Calvinist, I shall have to confess that the one and only reason which persuaded me was that among all the religions I could find none which agreed so much with Judaism, and its view of life and faith . . .the Jews everywhere are at pains to cheat people. So are we.'[11]

In the twenty-first century no dramatist with any sensitivity to racial issues would think of using a Jew as an easy symbol for what he or she regarded as undesirable religio-political tendencies. But Elizabethans had no qualms about racial stereotyping; Elizabeth actually gave orders for the city of London to be ethnically cleansed of 'Negars and Blackamoors'.[12] Though Portia avoids being openly rude to her African suitor, she makes it clear that she doesn't care for those of 'his complexion' either (II.vii.79). In much the same way that *Othello* draws on the popular Elizabethan association of Moors with the darker side of human nature, so *The Merchant of Venice* adapts an earlier play about a scheming Jew (Marlowe's *Jew of Malta*) and casts him in the role of ascetic, self-righteous avenger.

In symbolic contrast to Shylock's religious fundamentalism is the humanist world of Belmont. In the final act of the play we almost forget Shylock's 'ancient grudge' (I.iii.45) and his puritanical hatred of festivity as we enter a magical world of music and enchantment. As with the forests in *A Midsummer Night's Dream* and *As You Like It*, the sense that this is a purer, more innocent world free from the discords of daily life turns out to be an illusion. The stories that Lorenzo and Jessica playfully exchange at the beginning of Act v are all tales of death or betrayal and give the lie to any idea that marriage can be relied on to set your life permanently in order. But if there is an obliquity in human nature that somehow makes a mockery of our best intentions, the remedy, humanists believed, lies not in puritan self-mortification, but in cultivating the better side of our nature through the arts of civilisation. That's the point of the Orpheus story which Lorenzo tells Jessica. Surprisingly few critics even mention Lorenzo's long speech. Yet, like the framing biblical symbols of storm and rainbow in *The Tempest*, it's a crucial part of the play's design. In part it's imaginative mood painting in preparation for the reunions that follow. But it also has a symbolic function. So familiar was Orpheus as a humanist symbol of the civilising power of the arts and their ability to reform the more barbarous elements in our nature that a contemporary audience would have little trouble in seeing that, as so often in the plays, Shakespeare is making a coded defence of his own dramatic art in response to puritan attacks on the theatre. It's the opposition between puritan and humanist sensibilities, rather than the conflict between Christian and Jewish values, that's the significant structural contrast in the play.

THRIFT

Whether we describe them as Christians or humanists, it seems as if Shylock's enemies are just as given to underhand ways of dealing with their opponents as he is. Trickery is a central motif in *The Merchant of Venice*. During their negotiations in I.iii Shylock reminds Antonio of the story of Jacob and Laban. It's not a particularly edifying tale. Antonio assumes that it must be about justifying the taking of interest (74). But it's really about what Shylock euphemistically calls 'thrift' (89). When Jacob decides to leave Laban's service and set up on his own, Laban asks his nephew what payment he would like. Jacob proposes that, when the time comes for him to leave, he should take all the pied animals in Laban's flock. Laban agrees to this arrangement. But then, using some genetically implausible methods, Jacob craftily ensures that Laban's ewes produce an exceptional number of pied lambs, with the result that his leaving present is a lot larger than Laban had bargained for. For Shylock the moral of the story is about looking after your own interests: 'This was a way to thrive; and he was blest;' he tells Antonio, 'And thrift is blessing, if men steal it not' (88–9). Laban's sons are naturally not pleased and accuse Jacob of trickery (Genesis 31:1). Though Jacob is the grandson of 'our holy Abram' (71), and himself the progenitor of the twelve tribes of Israel, neither he nor Laban comes out of the story particularly well. Both are guilty of deception. While Laban disingenuously offers Jacob his elder daughter rather than the one his nephew had actually been courting, Jacob deceives not only his uncle, but also his father and his brother (Shakespeare parodies Jacob's deception of his father in II.ii). Even when Shylock has finished his story, Antonio seems oddly blind to the meaning of this cautionary tale of 'thrift' and repeats his point that Shylock must in some way be trying to justify the taking of interest (93). But there's also a lesson in the story for Shylock: while Antonio ignores the theme of trickery, Shylock forgets that it was Rachel who stole her father's images when she eloped with Jacob (Genesis 31:19). Had he thought of this he might have put a closer guard on his own daughter and prevented her from 'stealing' away (v.i.15) with the treasured ring that his wife had given him before they were married.

But the real dramatic relevance of the Jacob and Laban story to their own situation is something that neither Shylock nor Antonio is in a position to see. Like Laban, Shylock is a deceiver who meets his match in someone who is an even more adept schemer than he is.

Portia's own willingness to use 'thrift' is not confined to the 'quaint lies' she tells in the trial. There are two references in the play to the story of Jason and the Argonauts. In I.i Bassanio compares Portia's hair to the golden fleece and tells Antonio that 'many Jasons come in quest of her' (172). Later, when Gratiano is telling Salerio of his and Bassanio's success in their quest for a wife, he says 'We are the Jasons; we have won the fleece' (III.ii.239). There is also a reference to Medea (v.i.13), the enchantress who deceives her father by using secret arts to help the foreigner whom she hopes to marry and thus ensure Jason's success in the tasks that Aeëtes has set him (Ovid, *Metamorphoses*, VII.7–99). As many commentators have noted, there's a strong suggestion that Portia is giving her own Jason a helping hand when she arranges for a song, whose first three lines just happen to rhyme with 'lead', to be played while he's choosing the right casket. But puritans apart, no one would claim that this is a particularly egregious piece of deception; it's merely another example of the play's theme of bending the rules. A more serious kind of fraud is Portia's impersonation of a lawyer.

It's often argued that in the trial scene Shakespeare was alluding to the two rival legal systems that existed in Elizabethan England: common law and equity.[13] Common law relied on precedent and custom; equity, an alternative system administered by the Lord Chancellor through the Court of Chancery, was based on abstract principles of natural justice. Portia is said to appeal to equity when it looks as if common law is going to result in an inhuman verdict. But decisions based on equity were a matter for judges, not plaintiffs. Portia's speech about mercy is an appeal, not to the legal principle of equity, but to Shylock's humanity.[14] When that fails, she concedes Shylock's point that the law of contract must take its course, and proceeds to build her case on a sophistical quibble. Her response to Bassanio's suggestion that she 'do a little wrong' and manipulate the law to Antonio's advantage is emphatic rejection: 'It must not be. There is no power in Venice / Can alter a decree establishèd' (IV.i.212–16). Yet this is exactly what she does. It's true that Shylock's bond says nothing about blood, but it's obvious that Shylock couldn't take his pound of flesh without spilling blood. That's the whole point of it. It may not be very nice, but if Antonio didn't like it he shouldn't have agreed to it. Of course, in strictly legal terms the whole trial is a nonsense. What responsible court of law would sanction the outcome of a trial in which the advocate, who also plays judge, is an imposter with no legal qualifications? What responsible court of law would even consider such a preposterous contract in the first place? This is the world of fairytale, not the Elizabethan Court of Chancery. Dramatically, though, it makes perfectly good sense. Shylock seeks vengeance against his persecutor; Portia appeals to his better nature; he knows he has a strong case and rejects her appeal, so she resorts to trickery. In the fairytale world of the play the agreement that Antonio signed was a legally binding document, and Portia's argument is a violation of the spirit of that bond. She's using Machiavellian trickery to defeat cunning, or as the duke puts it in *Measure for Measure*, applying 'craft against vice' (III.i.533).

Whether or not it was legitimate to use 'craft against vice' was a disputed question in the sixteenth century. It was usually debated in the context of rulers and their responsibilities (I'll deal with this in the next chapter). In the *Education of a Christian Prince* Erasmus said that rulers should be wise, just and honourable in their dealings with their subjects.[15] But in his own book on the subject of princes, Machiavelli said that for a ruler to deal openly, decently and honourably with his subjects would be disastrous. We live in what Portia calls 'naughty times' (III.ii.18). To stay ahead of the game an astute prince has got to be cunning: 'A ruler who wishes to maintain his power must be prepared to act immorally when this becomes necessary.'[16] Erasmus said that the wise rulers must suppress the baser part of their nature; Machiavelli said they must suppress the better part of their nature.

Political theorists knew that there was more to 'the great *Doctor of State, Macchiavell*'[17] than the caricature portrayed in books like Innocent Gentillet's *Discourse Against Machiavell.*[18] But to puritans deception of any kind was anathema, even deception in a just cause. In a pamphlet called *Th' overthrow of Stage-Plays* the puritan writer John Rainoldes warned that deception can never be allowed, even if the results seem to justify it: 'the spirit of truth teacheth us that it is not lawful for us to doe evil, that good may come thereof'. Stage plays are a double form of lying. Not only do they often involve characters deceiving each other, but the very act of putting on theatrical costume is in itself a form of deception. Worst of all is when male actors impersonate women. 'If a man might save his life, or benefit many, by putting on a woman's raiment, yet ought he not to do it, because it is evil', wrote Rainoldes.[19] That Shakespeare doesn't seem to share this concern with the evils of theatrical impersonation is hardly surprising; he did, after all, make his living in the theatre. As if to show his distaste for puritan anti-theatricalism, he takes the deception one stage further by having his cross-dressed boy actor impersonate a male lawyer.[20] Indeed he actually has Portia boast of the lies she will tell the world. From a Christian point of view her deceit is a triumphant success: the vindictive Jew is caught in his own trap and an innocent life is saved.

CONUNDRUMS

But however you rationalise the use of an 'honest and laudable deceit'[21] in what contemporary audiences would probably have considered a worthy cause, the fact remains that Christian conduct in this play often seems to contradict the New Testament values the characters themselves claim to stand by. Though Salerio claims, for example, that Venice's merchant is the kindest gentleman that ever trod upon the earth (II.viii.35), Antonio himself admits that he has no qualms whatever about abusing Jews in public. When Shylock reminds him how he spat at him and called him insulting names, Antonio frankly admits 'I am as like to call thee so again, / To spit on thee again, to spurn thee too' (I.iii.124–9). Is this the act of a Christian gentleman? If this were a realistic play you could explain the anomaly by saying that Antonio is a complex character whose psychological makeup involves a mixture of conflicting elements. But this isn't realism. It's more a question of Shakespeare giving us such contradictory information about his characters that any attempt to make psychological sense of them is bound to fail. It's almost as if he is going out of his way to confuse our responses. Nor is this a device that's confined to the play's major characters.

Jessica is a good example of a kind of stylised characterisation that works by self-cancelling opposites. When she arrives in Belmont after eloping with her Christian lover, she has one of those quibbling conversations that Shakespeare's clowns obviously enjoy, but which are apt to seem tedious to modern audiences. Launcelot is worried about Jessica betraying her father's trust and says he's concerned about the state of her soul. 'Be o' good cheer,' he tells her, 'for truly I think you are damned' (III.v.4–5). The only thing that might save her, he tells Jessica, would be if she were a bastard and not the Jew's daughter. In other words, only if the sins of the mother were visited upon the child might her own sin be mitigated (5–10). But Jessica is a feisty young woman and isn't going to be put down by such self-contradictory nonsense. 'I shall be saved by my husband', she retorts, 'He hath made me a Christian' (17–18), to which Launcelot replies: 'the more to blame he!' (19). Are we supposed to condemn her because she has betrayed her father's trust and married his enemy, or are we supposed to approve of her because she has become a Christian? Is she saved or is she damned? Is Lorenzo to be applauded or blamed for converting her? It's impossible to say. Nor is the confusion due simply to careless writing. The play's stylised structural patterns are far too contrived to put all these anomalies down to muddled thinking.

In II.vi Lorenzo tells Gratiano how much he loves Jessica:

> Beshrew me but I love her heartily,
> For she is wise, if I can judge of her;
> And fair she is, if that mine eyes be true;
> And true she is, as she hath proved herself;
> And therefore like herself, wise, fair, and true,
> Shall she be placèd in my constant soul.
>
> (52–7)

In a less artful play these lines could be read simply as a conventionally stylised declaration of romantic love. But the rhetorically patterned language draws attention to the problem they contain. Only a few lines earlier Jessica had reminded Lorenzo that 'love is blind, and lovers cannot see / The pretty follies that themselves commit' (36–7). Yet now her doting lover assures Gratiano that his eyes are true and his judgement sound. What seemed like a simple declaration of love begins to look rather complicated: *is* Jessica fair? *has* she proved herself true? *can* Lorenzo's judgement be trusted? It's not a question of Jessica being a complex character who can't be pigeon-holed like a cipher in a Jonsonian comedy of humours. On the contrary, she's a minor figure with no real psychological depth who happens to get caught up in the conflict between her father and his Christian enemies. Nor is it a matter simply of needing to know a bit more about her. As with Antonio, it's more a question of Shakespeare presenting us with contradictory information: one bit of information is cancelled out by another that is diametrically opposed to the first. She is *both* apostate *and* convert, damned *and* saved. These contradictions are summed up in Launcelot's farewell to Jessica at the end of II.iii:

> Adieu. Tears exhibit my tongue, most beautiful
> pagan; most sweet Jew; if a Christian do not play the
> knave and get thee, I am much deceived.
>
> (II.iii.10–12)

In the real world there's no reason why Jews shouldn't be sweet and pagans beautiful. But this isn't the real world; it's a dramatic world of stylised conundrums and irresolvable paradoxes. If Jessica is an enigma, so too is her lover. Launcelot says he suspects that Lorenzo will play the knave and marry Jessica. Yet in Christian eschatology conversion of the Jews is part of God's endgame plan for the world. How can Lorenzo be a knave if he is cooperating with divine will in converting a Jew to Christianity?

Launcelot's teasing oxymorons illustrate one of the play's most characteristic devices: the portrayal of characters, not as the embodiment of one humour or another, or as largely good or bad, or even as realistic mixtures of both, but as combinations of incompatible elements. Is Antonio the kindest gentleman that ever trod upon the earth as Salerio claims he is, or is he a rather unpleasant anti-Semite? Is Bassanio an honest lover who, alone among the suitors, shows himself worthy of Portia's hand, or is he an opportunistic fortune hunter who risks his friend's life in the hope of winning the Belmont lottery? Is Shylock the heroic, persecuted alien, or is he, like Marlowe's Barabas, little more than a pantomime Jew? While everyone has a mixture of strengths and weaknesses in their psychological makeup, you cannot be at one and the same time the kindest of mortals *and* a persecutor of minorities, or a paragon of integrity *and* a deceiver.

This motif of self-cancelling information isn't only a matter of characterisation. Shakespeare also uses it in the verbal quibbles and conundrums that are such a distinctive feature of the play. Here's an example:

at the beginning of Act II Launcelot Gobbo gets himself into a state about whether or not he should leave Shylock and go to Belmont with Jessica:

> Certainly my conscience will serve me to run
> from this Jew my master. The fiend is at mine elbow
> and tempts me, saying to me 'Gobbo, Lancelot Gobbo,
> good Lancelot,' or 'good Gobbo,' or 'good Lancelot
> Gobbo—use your legs, take the start, run away.'
>
> . . . well, my conscience says, 'Lancelot, budge not';
> 'Budge!' says the fiend; 'Budge not', says my
> conscience. 'Conscience,' say I, 'you counsel well';
> 'Fiend,' say I, 'you counsel well.' To be ruled by my
> conscience I should stay with the Jew my master who,
> God bless the mark, is a kind of devil; and to run away
> from the Jew I should be ruled by the fiend who, saving
> your reverence, is the devil himself. Certainly the Jew
> is the very devil incarnation; and in my conscience,
> my conscience is but a kind of hard conscience to offer
> to counsel me to stay with the Jew. The fiend gives the
> more friendly counsel. I will run, fiend. My heels are
> at your commandment. I will run.
>
> (II.ii.1–29)

On one level this is just a piece of comic nonsense, probably designed to show off Will Kempe's talents as a comic actor. But at a more serious level it's telling us something about the nature of moral choice. The way Launcelot defines his dilemma means that it's impossible to resolve. It's true that he does finally decide to leave Shylock; but the moral problem hasn't been resolved. On the one hand Launcelot has got the devil at his side tempting him to leave his master. But on the other hand his master *is* the devil, at least he seems like one to Launcelot. In effect, Launcelot has got the devil on both sides of his moral equation. The way he phrases his problem means that the question simply can't be answered. A bit later in the same scene he says 'I am a Jew if I serve the Jew any longer' (113) – another perfect conundrum.

The most significant use of this stylised motif comes immediately after the very climax of the play where we have another ethical conundrum. In the trial scene Portia cleverly finds a loophole that will allow her to save Antonio's life. The legal argument she uses certainly smacks of trickery; indeed her whole performance is a piece of deliberate deception. Nevertheless the end seems to justify the means, and the Christians are overjoyed. In fact there's a pretty unpleasant display of triumphalism on the

Christian side of the courtroom. Very soon, though, the Christians find that the shoe is on the other foot. The business with the doctor and his clerk and Bassanio's and Gratiano's betrothal rings may look like another piece of comic foolery. Structurally, though, it's significant. In effect it's a kind of mock trial after the main trial is over. Like the courtroom trial, it involves more 'quaint lies'.

The motto on the lead casket – 'Who chooseth me must give and hazard all he hath' (II.vii.16) – might almost stand as an epigraph to *The Merchant of Venice*. Hazard, and in particular the reversal of fortune, is one of the play's characteristic motifs. You find it in III.i when Tubal's good news alternates with the bad. You find it too in the very next scene: no sooner does Bassanio discover that he has chosen the right casket than he learns of Antonio's misfortunes (III.ii.241–2). Now, after their success in the trial, the triumphant lovers once again discover that their fortunes have apparently sunk, like Antonio's ships. Unlike the caskets, where the chooser simply gets it right or wrong, there's no correct answer to their problem. Whatever they do is going to look bad. If they give the doctor and his clerk their rings they'll be guilty of betraying their betrothal vows; if they deny them, they'll be guilty of gross ingratitude. Like Launcelot Gobbo, they're in a no-win situation. If this were a realistic play you could speculate about Portia's motives: did she engineer the situation simply for the fun of playing 'a thousand raw tricks' (III.iv.77)? Did she want to force Bassanio into making a choice between herself and her male rival? Was she trying to teach these 'bragging Jacks' a lesson in humility after Gratiano's unpleasant performance in the courtroom? Or perhaps she wanted to remind them of Christ's words about casting out the beam in your own eye before judging others (Matt 7:1–5)? No doubt there's some truth in all of these suggestions. But psychological realism isn't this play's mode. The real point of Bassanio's and Gratiano's dilemma is its insolubility; it's another conundrum.

VALUE PLURALISM

In his elegy on Shakespeare Ben Jonson referred to his subject as 'My gentle Shakespeare',[22] and wrote in his notebook: 'He was (indeed) honest, and of an open, and free nature . . . and gentle expressions.'[23] Was Shakespeare the man really open, free and gentle by temperament, or did his professional persona conceal a 'tiger's heart', as his enemies suggested?[24] As far as our understanding of the plays is concerned, the answer is immaterial. Whether or not Shakespeare lived according to his own precepts, the plays repeatedly suggest that reason is 'nobler' than fury, and that 'the rarer action is / In virtue than in vengeance' (*The Tempest*, v.i.26–7). But if he did mean us to believe that 'human gentleness and love'[25] are better than 'ancient grudges', what's the point of all those conundrums in *The Merchant of Venice*? If the play really is arguing for the superiority of New Testament values over retaliatory notions of justice, and a humanist acceptance of the social and moral value of the arts, why the seemingly deliberate confusions?

In *The Merchant of Venice* everyone judges everyone else.[26] Lorenzo and Launcelot both judge Jessica, while Shylock says the devil will judge her. Shylock invites Launcelot to judge the difference between himself and Bassanio. The suitors have to judge the caskets – more riddles and conundrums there – while at the same time they themselves are being judged by Portia. The Christians judge Shylock; then the judges are themselves put on trial, so to speak. Finally, the audience itself is all the time judging Shakespeare's characters and trying to make sense of them. And while it shows these judgements going on, the play reminds us, not just that complex moral choices may be involved in any act of judgement, but that choice of one good often seems to entail rejection of another good that has an equal claim on our conscience.

Many critics have written on Shakespeare's studied ambivalence.[27] Diomedes' cynical response to Paris' question, 'Who in your thoughts merits fair Helen most, / Myself or Menelaus?' (*Troilus and Cressida*, iv.i.55–6) epitomises a kind of ethical conundrum that's typically Shakespearean. 'Both alike . . .,' replies Diomedes, 'Both merits poised, each weighs nor less nor more, / But he as he: which heavier for a whore?' (56; 67–8). Stylised conundrums, and the dramaturgical technique of presenting both sides of an argument, owe much, no doubt, to the training that every Elizabethan grammar-school boy received in the art of arguing *in utramque partem*.[28] They may also owe something to the humanist interest in Pyrrhonian scepticism (Sextus Empiricus' *Pyrrhoniae hypotyposes*, or *Outlines of Pyrrhonism*, was translated into English in 1590/ 1.)[29] Writing towards the end of the first century AD, Sextus set out at tedious length the Pyrrhonist belief that, since truth is unknowable, judgement on ethical questions must always be suspended. Thomas Nashe told his readers that Sextus gave 'the name of good or ill to everything', explaining that 'out of [his] works (lately translated into English for the benefit of unlearned writers) a man might collect a whole book of this argument'.[30] But the paradoxes in *The Merchant of Venice* suggest a position that's quite different from the classical sceptic's habit of 'opposing to every proposition an equal proposition', as Sextus put it.[31] Shakespeare's paradoxes suggest, not that truth is unattainable, or that judgement must always be suspended, but that when a choice has to be made between rivalrous positions, that choice will often involve loss of an alternative good. This view of ethics is sometimes called 'value pluralism'. The person who is most closely associated with it is Isaiah Berlin.[32]

Berlin reminds us that, in a tradition that goes back to Plato's *Republic*, idealist philosophers have argued that all positive values are in the end compatible with one another. They must be, because they emanate from the ultimate Platonic Form of the Good. That's what the Elizabethan Great Chain of Being was all about with its related doctrines of analogy and correspondence. It was a model of the universe designed to show that all phenomena and all values are generated by the same universal blueprint. In one of his Holy Sonnets John Donne described himself in a famous phrase as 'a little world made cunningly / Of elements, and an angelic sprite'.[33] If humanity was in a real sense a microcosm of the larger order of things, then it followed logically that human values should conform to those universal laws. They are part of a harmonious interlocking system in which the human and the cosmic are aspects of one another. Renaissance writers called this system of universal ethical imperatives 'natural law'.[34] In a classic statement of this principle Richard Hooker explained that natural law 'comprehendeth all those things which men by the light of their natural understanding evidently know . . . to be beseeming or unbeseeming, virtuous or vicious, good or evil, for them to do'.[35] English Renaissance exponents of natural law were aware of sceptical challenges to this idealist view of ethics long before Sextus Empiricus was translated into English. Sixty years earlier, Thomas Starkey warned of the 'pestilent persuasion of them, which say and affirm betwixt vice and virtue no difference be but only strong opinion, and fancy'.[36] Starkey didn't deny that positive law varies from one country to another. He wrote: 'this law [civil law] taketh effect of the opinion of man, it resteth wholly in his consent, and varieth according to the place and time, in so much that in diverse time and place, contrary laws are both good, and both convenient to the politic life'. But he claimed that civil law is rooted in natural law: 'this law [natural law] is the ground and end of the other, to the which it must ever be referred . . . for civil ordinance is but as a mean to bring man to observe this law of nature, in so much that if there be any civil law ordained which cannot be resolved thereto, it is of no value, for al good civil laws spring and issue out of the law of nature'.[37] Natural law theorists believed that, although opinion as to what constitutes justice may vary from one state to another, or even from one city to another, all positive law has its basis in those universal principles that, in Hooker's words, 'men by the light of their natural understanding evidently know to be good or evil'.

Berlin's rejection of the idealist view of ethics is based on the belief, not that the truth is unknowable, but that any value system inevitably involves choices between incommensurables. In the widely cited essay 'Two Concepts of Liberty' he wrote:

> The world that we encounter in ordinary experience is one in which we are faced with choices between ends equally absolute, the realization of some of which must inevitably involve the sacrifice of others . . . If, as I believe, the ends of men are many, and not all of them compatible with each other, then the possibility of conflict – and of tragedy – can never wholly be eliminated from human life, either personal or social. The necessity of choosing between absolute claims is then an inescapable characteristic of the human condition.[38]

A few years after Berlin wrote 'Two Concepts of Liberty' Norman Rabkin put forward a similar argument in a book on Shakespeare. Adapting the quantum theories developed by the physicist Niels Bohr in the 1920s, Rabkin suggested that the principle of complementarity 'provides a writer with the basis of a mimesis which appeals to the common understanding because it recalls the unresolvable tensions that are the fundamental conditions of human life'.[39]

Berlin's value pluralism and Rabkin's complementarity shouldn't be confused with either Pyrrhonian scepticism or postmodern relativism. While Pyrrhonists believe that all propositions can be answered with equally valid counter-propositions, relativists argue that values can only be judged from the perspective of the culture that produces them. If, as postmodernists believe, there's no such thing as a universal essence of human nature, you cannot claim that some value systems are superior to others. This means that, if all cultures are morally equivalent, it would be illogical to condemn regimes that, let's say, forbid the education of women, or whose judicial systems prescribe such legal penalties as amputation for petty theft, or stoning to death for rape (that is, for being the victim of rape). If those things are sanctioned by some cultures, it's not for others to condemn them. But as many philosophers have pointed out, radical relativism is not just politically irresponsible; it's also pragmatically self-refuting. If you claim that, under no imaginable circumstances can moral truths be absolute or objective, you are asserting precisely what relativism denies, namely, a universal truth.[40]

At the core of postmodern relativism is a rejection of the notion of supernaturally sanctioned universal values. But you don't have to appeal to a transcendent being to recognise that there are such things as universal values. It's an historical fact that, as Shakespeare's Hector points out,

> There is a law in each well-ordered nation
> To curb those raging appetites that are
> Most disobedient and refractory.
> (*Troilus and Cressida*, II.ii.179–81)

The fact that Hector follows this with a *volte-face* in which he denies everything he's just been saying about the folly of keeping Helen doesn't invalidate his defence of universals; it's more a testimony to the emotive power of Troilus' ideal of 'manhood and honour' (45). Nor is he appealing in these lines to a supernatural principle; with little of the verbosity that is characteristic of his more bombastic speeches, he's simply making an empirical observation: in contrast to ancient heroic societies, where disputes were typically resolved by appeal to the kind of archaic honour code embraced by both sides in *Troilus and Cressida*, 'well-ordered nations' have legal systems designed to restrain barbaric behaviour. That desire for order and justice appears to be just as much a part of our universal human nature as the raging appetites which our laws are designed to curb.

Throughout history both civilised and pre-civilised societies have framed laws or codes of conduct that seek to control the more barbarous side of our nature. But however carefully they are framed, such laws can never provide an infallible guide to moral conduct. It's in the nature of human value systems that we can never entirely avoid conflict between rivalrous goods or evils. Bassanio's and Gratiano's dilemma over their betrothal rings is a tragicomic illustration of this truth: through no fault of their own they face an impossible choice between two equally compelling demands on their consciences. Isaiah Berlin believed that, although there may be no answer to the conundrums that life regularly confronts us with, an understanding of the conflictual nature of human values is the first step towards a tolerant society. If we acknowledge that value judgements are rarely simple, and that a decision in favour of one good may involve loss of another good that we hold equally dear, then we may be less hasty in our judgement of others.

The Merchant of Venice portrays a world of ethnic hatred and racial intolerance. But to ask, as so much twentieth-century criticism did, whether the play is anti-Jewish or pro-Jewish is to miss the point of

Shakespeare's stylised, self-consciously patterned conundrums. It would be equally mistaken to assume that it's endorsing some kind of moral relativism. It's true that Portia tells Nerissa that 'Nothing is good, I see, without respect' (v.i.99). But from the context of her remark it's clear that she isn't making a case for moral relativism. Illustrating her point about the way our perception of things can be distorted by circumstances, she gives an example from public life:

> A substitute shines brightly as a king
> Until a king be by, and then his state
> Empties itself as doth an inland brook
> Into the main of waters.
>
> (94–7)

The fact that we may mistake a deputy for the real thing doesn't mean that they are of equal status. On the contrary, it's failure to allow for the fact that 'things by season seasoned are' (107) that leads to such simple errors of judgement. In reality, Portia is saying, all things have their 'right praise and true perfection' (108). Repeatedly the play shows us that, while some codes of value are inherently preferable to others, our social transactions may require us to make moral choices, not between good and evil, but rather between rivalrous and incompatible goods. This pluralist view of ethics isn't unique to Shakespeare. Indeed it might be said to be the basis of much of the world's greatest literature; certainly it's the basis of most tragedy. What is exceptional about this play is the fact that a sense of the plural nature of human values is not just a vision that informs the action, but, in part at least, the play's subject. *The Merchant of Venice* is about understanding our selves as moral and political beings, and the irresolvable paradoxes that result from the peculiarities of our humanity. It suggests that being 'cunning in the nature of man' (in Jonson's phrase) can make us more tolerant in our dealings with others.

CHAPTER 4

Social justice

Michel Foucault's *Discipline and Punish* is a work of extraordinary imaginative power. Its influence on postmodern Shakespeare criticism can hardly be exaggerated. For a time in the 1980s and 1990s it was impossible to open a collection of Cultural Materialist or New Historicist essays without finding an analysis of this Elizabethan play as a epitome of the carceral society, or that Jacobean play as covert legitimation of state violence through the production and containment of subversion. Through his gifted populariser Stephen Greenblatt, Foucault spoke to a generation of Shakespeareans in a way that no other analyst of bourgeois society had done before. In this chapter I'll discuss a classic Foucauldian reading of *Measure for Measure* that sees the play as a dramatic picture of a police state in-the-making where citizens are subjected to new forms of surveillance, and delinquent sexuality is produced as a way of justifying more punitive forms of social control. Does a presentist reading of this kind need to justify its claims by reference to the text itself with its structural parallels and contrasts, verbal patterning, biblical motifs, and other artistic devices by which meanings are generated? Probably not. If your ultimate purpose is not to recover unfamiliar ways of thinking, but to enlist Shakespeare as a spokesman for postmodern theories of culture, then there's no reason to be bound by the text. 'Creative' reading against the grain is a perfectly acceptable procedure in postmodern literary criticism. What *is* important, I shall argue, is to be clear about the difference between a presentist and an historicist approach.

ANATOMISING THE 'POLICE-UNIVERSE'

Foucault wasn't the first to denounce the oppressive nature of modern bourgeois society. A long tradition going back at least as far as Wordsworth's Preface to *The Lyrical Ballads* had deplored the dehumanising influence of industrial society, and contrasted life in the modern world with the

imagined harmony of a pre-industrial age. But it was the *kulturkritiker* of
the Frankfurt School who seem to have been Foucault's main source of
visionary inspiration for *Discipline and Punish*. In developing Marx's
principle of man's alienation under capitalism, Theodor Adorno and Max
Horkheimer argued that it was 'the power of the system' rather than a
conscious strategy on the part of 'the rulers' that was responsible for the
spiritual impoverishment of modern man.[1] A central theme in *Dialectic of
Enlightenment* was the power-that-is-knowledge. Writing during the
Second World War, Adorno and Horkheimer argued that the horrors
of the modern world were traceable directly to the baleful influence of the
Enlightenment. 'The power of progress is the progress of power', they wrote
in a chiasmic formula that became almost *de rigueur* in New Historicist
criticism. Though the Enlightenment liberated humanity from supersti-
tion, the scientific rationalism that it unleashed has since been used to inflict
a far more insidious kind of enslavement of our minds. When science
destroyed the gods of the old animistic world, it replaced them with the
technology that now controls our lives. The result was 'the total schematiza-
tion of men'.[2]

Herbert Marcuse also saw instrumental reason as the bane of modern
life. In his influential *One Dimensional Man* he argued that the 'technological rationality' that was the Enlightenment's legacy to the modern
world had become a means of endorsing and consolidating the interests of
'the powers that be'.[3] The modern state might have abandoned terror in
favour of technology as a way of controlling our minds, but its power had
not diminished. On the contrary, 'the scope of society's domination over
the individual is immeasurably greater than ever before'.[4] Like Adorno
and Horkheimer, Marcuse believed that blame for the ills of a society that
specialised in the control of people's minds lay, not with individuals, but
with 'the power of the system'. The phrase that summed up his despairing
view of the modern world was a remark by Roland Barthes that he chose
as one of his chapter epigraphs: 'In the present state of history, all political
writing can only confirm a police-universe.'[5] In their analyses of the effects
of the Enlightenment and the 'technological rationality' it gave rise to,
neither Adorno and Horkheimer nor Marcuse made any attempt to weigh
the evils of, say, industrial disease and workplace injury against the
advantages of mass immunisation and the discovery of penicillin, or the
growth of bureaucracy against more progressive labour laws and universal
franchise. For them the legacy that the Enlightenment bequeathed to the
modern world has been an unmitigated disaster: 'the fully enlightened
earth radiates disaster triumphant'.[6] Such is the power of 'the system' that

the 'police-universe' is able now to control, not just our bodies, but our innermost thoughts.

To readers of *Discipline and Punish* all this is familiar. Uncompromising hostility to the Enlightenment; the state's abandonment of torture in favour of new technologies for controlling the mind; the identification of knowledge with power; a tendency to disregard documented abuses of human rights in favour of a critique of more abstract crimes against the soul[7] – though all these were important themes in *Discipline and Punish*, none was exactly new. It was Foucault's repository of arcane facts, his eye for compelling anecdote, and above all his rhetorical gifts, that captured the imaginations of postmodern academics.

Foucault's analysis of what he called the 'carceral society' owes much to the work of the Frankfurt School. However, for his own critique of the Enlightenment Foucault adopted an historical approach, tracing the development of systems of state punishment in France from the middle of the eighteenth century to the third decade of the nineteenth. But his real subject was much larger than this timescale implies. Foucault tells us that he is writing 'the history of the present'.[8] He is concerned, in other words, to uncover the historical processes that led, not just to our present penal system, but to those 'mechanisms of normalization' that reach their tentacles into every mind and turn us into obedient servants of the state. In his opening chapter Foucault reproduces a contemporary account of the judicial torture of a would-be regicide in 1757. The report describes in lingering detail the almost unimaginably brutal public torments to which criminals were routinely subjected under the old order. Such spectacular displays of mutilation and dismemberment were designed detail by detail as a symbolic re-enactment of the crime that had been, or in this case might have been, committed. But as Enlightenment ideas of humanity and social utility began to permeate society, the old judicial atrocities gave way to a more rational approach to the whole subject of punishment. By the 1830s criminals were no longer being tortured in public. The emphasis was now on correction rather than retribution; in place of punishment as a spectator sport, you had a highly regulated system of correction designed to avoid gratuitous pain and ensure that punishment was commensurate with humane principles. Penal reformers were concerned above all that punishment should be a rational process that would not only protect society but reform the offender. If re-education is your aim, it's obviously no good simply packing offenders off to rot in obscure dungeons. They need to be held in well-lit establishments where their behaviour can be observed and their progress monitored. The modern prison system was born.

It might be thought that a more humanitarian approach to the problem of punishment and correction was cause for at least qualified approval; that a bureaucratised penal system, degrading to the spirit though it might be, was at least preferable to live disembowelment. But not for Foucault. In his opening chapters he makes it clear that the supposed humanitarian reforms of the eighteenth century disguised a darker purpose. The monstrous brutalities of the *ancien régime* might have gone; but they had been replaced by something far more sinister: 'what was emerging was . . . not so much a new respect for the humanity of the condemned . . . as a tendency towards a . . . closer penal mapping of the social body'.[9] This is the core of Foucault's argument. What might look to the uncritical eye like humanitarian reform was actually a whole new 'technique of power', a new 'mode of subjection' whose purpose was the production of compliant subjects.[10] Technology had replaced spectacle. When the public executioner and vivisectionist was pensioned off, he was replaced by 'a whole army of technicians . . .: warders, doctors, chaplains, psychiatrists, psychologists, educationalists'.[11] Though ostensibly they were there to superintend the process of correction, their real function was to control the mind. They were agents of the new technology of surveillance. And what was true of the prison system was true, for Foucault, of society as a whole. Jeremy Bentham's notorious panopticon – his plan for a circular prison building containing at its centre the watchtower from which each prisoner's activities could be observed at every hour of the day or night – served for Foucault as a symbol of the new surveillance society. Just as Coleridge's description of Piranesi's prison etchings burnt themselves into De Quincey's memory as a graphic image of his own torments, so Bentham's panopticon summed up for Foucault the techniques by which the new 'carceral society' observed, controlled, and acquired knowledge of its subjects.

For Foucault, as for Adorno and Horkheimer, knowledge is power. And power is not just about restraint and control; it's about who decides what counts as real. 'Power produces;' Foucault explains, 'it produces reality'.[12] That's why the newly bureaucratised penal system was such an important element in the post-Enlightenment state: incarceration was the 'omnipresent armature' of the 'panoptic society'.[13] It might look as if the 'carceral network' was there to protect society from the criminal. Not so. Its purpose was to *produce* delinquency in order to justify the exercise of authority: 'In effect, the great continuity of the carceral system throughout the law and its sentences gives a sort of legal sanction to the disciplinary mechanisms'; its object is to 'legitimate [a] disciplinary power' whose ultimate purpose is 'the fabrication of the disciplinary individual'.[14] This is what Foucault meant when he said in his opening chapter that the carceral society 'gives[s] birth to man as an object of knowledge'.[15] Extending itself into every corner of the carceral society, power is an impersonal self-replicating system whose job is the construction of subjects. As Foucault develops his theme it becomes clear in what sense *Discipline and Punish* is a history of the present: it's we who now inhabit the carceral society:

> The judges of normality are present everywhere. We are in the society of the teacher-judge, the doctor-judge, the educator judge, the 'social worker'-judge; it is on them that the universal reign of the normative is based; and each individual, wherever he may find himself, subjects to it his body, his gestures, his behaviour, his aptitudes, his achievements. The carceral network . . . with its systems of insertion, distribution, surveillance, observation, has been the greatest support, in modern society, of the normalizing power.[16]

Foucault's interest in cruelty and physical punishment has often been noted.[17] But passages like this suggest something different – a genuine paranoia. The world he's describing might sound like that of the East German Stasi or Pinochet's Chile. But it's not. Foucault isn't writing about the great police states of the twentieth century where neighbours were encouraged to inform against each other and dissidents would disappear in the night. Nor is he warning us, as Huxley and Orwell did, of the future dystopia to which present social policies are in danger of leading us. His aim is not to extrapolate from existing social tendencies and imagine what terrors we might stumble into in the future; his subject is the here and now, the horror of the *normal*, everyday world of laudable intentions, political compromise, and betrayed ideals that we in the Western democracies thought we knew so well. The task he had set himself was to defamiliarise that world and expose the surveillance systems that control our lives so successfully that we are largely unaware of them. Like the Wachowskis' *Matrix* films, Foucault's carceral society is a nightmare world of purely indifferent, impersonal malevolence. In such a world 'it is useless to believe in the good or bad consciences of judges, or even their unconscious . . . [because] it is the economy of power that they exercise, and not that of their scruples or their humanism'.[18] Morality has no part in Foucault's thinking. The object of his apocalyptic jeremiad is not criminal politicians, corrupt governments, misguided social policies, or even the global capitalist economy (Joseph Conrad had warned of the consequences of that as early as 1904 in *Nostromo*), but rather the blind technologies of power that have taken control of our minds since the

Enlightenment and whose sole purpose is the construction of 'disciplinary individuals' that will serve 'the system'.

SHAKESPEARE'S CARCERAL SOCIETY

Foucault once compared one of his earlier books – *The Order of Things* – to a novel.[19] *Discipline and Punish* also has something of the appeal of good fiction. It has a strong storyline; it has plenty of arresting incidents; and it's brilliantly told. The fact that an author may have got most of his key historical facts wrong[20] isn't a matter of overriding concern to the reader of fiction. What does matter is the power of the writer's vision. And that's something that *Discipline and Punish* has in abundance. We all like a good dystopia. So compelling was Foucault's nightmare vision of the carceral society with its panoptic technologies of surveillance that the book's obvious faults – notably its neglect of real social problems in favour of the metaphysics of power, and its refusal to consider genuine humanitarian reform as anything but an extension of 'the reign of the normative' – could be overlooked, and its anti-humanist vision applied to the analysis of literary texts. Renaissance plays were particularly good material to work on. With their dark Senecan themes of tyranny and corruption, and their self-declared interest in political power, they were ripe for reinterpretation. *Measure for Measure* would seem to fit the Foucauldian bill perfectly. 'Hence shall we see / If power change purpose, what our seemers be' (I.iii.53–4), says Shakespeare's 'duke of dark corners' (IV.iii.153) as he prepares to spy on his deputy. Here's a play, much of whose action takes place in a prison, where citizens are placed under covert surveillance by the state, and subversion is produced in order to divert attention from more systemic problems and justify the exercise of authoritarian power. At least, that's what Jonathan Dollimore argues in a seminal Cultural Materialist reading of *Measure for Measure*.[21]

Dollimore begins his essay with a statement of the play's central theme: 'In the Vienna of *Measure for Measure* unrestrained sexuality is ostensibly subverting social order; anarchy threatens to engulf the State unless sexuality is subjected to renewed and severe regulation. Such . . . is the claim of those in power.'[22] To say that 'those in power' believe that sexuality must be subjected to more severe regulation sounds like a contradiction of the play's manifest concern – hinted at in its punning title – with the idea of 'measure' in the sense of the Italian '*misura*', meaning moderation, proportion, an avoidance of extremes. But Dollimore does warn us that his reading is going to be a paradoxical one. He explains that, taking it for granted that sexuality is 'intrinsic to human nature', traditional interpretations of the play generally assume that *Measure for Measure* has got something to do with the question (controversial for Shakespeare's contemporaries) of how it should be restrained. Dollimore rejects this essentialist approach, arguing that the play shows sexuality to be not so much part of our biological makeup as an effect of power. In *The History of Sexuality* Foucault explained that what we take to be a biological phenomenon is in reality a discourse through which the state ensures that we internalise social norms. Common sense might suggest that the state would want to suppress, or at least moderate, sexuality. But according to Foucault the reverse is true: in the post-industrial world 'power delineated [sexuality], aroused it, and employed it as the proliferating meaning that it had always taken control of lest it escape; it was *an effect with a meaning value*'.[23] In other words, just as the carceral society creates delinquency in order to construct its subjects as 'disciplinary individuals', so the modern state fabricates sexuality as an excuse for tighter social control. Dollimore believes that the same is true of Shakespeare's world: 'What Foucault has said of sexuality in the nineteenth and twentieth centuries seems appropriate also to sexuality . . . in earlier periods: it appears to be that which power is afraid of but in actuality is that which power works through . . . [it] has produced the subjects of authority as surely as any ideology.'[24] Dollimore believes that we can see this process at work in *Measure for Measure*. Although 'those in power' make a show of cracking down on sexual offenders, the truth is that it's the state that has chosen to identify and encourage certain kinds of sexual behaviour as a threat to social order. By 'constructing' those who offend against sexual norms as dissidents and allowing them to flourish, the state is able to justify new forms of surveillance and new punitive measures:

Whatever subversive identity the sexual offenders in this play possess is a construction put upon them by the authority which wants to control them; moreover control is exercised through that construction. Diverse and only loosely associated sexual offenders are brought into renewed surveillance by the State; identified in law as a category of offender (the lecherous, the iniquitous) they are thereby demonised as a threat to law. Like many apparent threats to authority this one in fact legitimates it: control of the threats becomes the rationale of authoritarian reaction in a time of apparent crisis . . . Arguably then the play discloses corruption to be an effect less of desire than authority itself.[25]

What is the ultimate purpose of this production and containment of sexual subversion? In *Discipline and Punish* Foucault explained that, by producing delinquency and submitting offenders to new methods of surveillance, the carceral society fabricates disciplinary subjects. It's for essentially the same reason that Shakespeare's duke submits his people to what Dollimore describes as 'a much more sophisticated and effective mode of surveillance'; his sole object is 'subjection',[26] that is to say, the construction of subjects who have so completely internalised the ideology of 'those in power' that they believe themselves to be free, rational agents.

Readers who know *Measure for Measure* might be forgiven for thinking that this doesn't sound much like the play they are familiar with. Far from seeking more repressive measures against sexual offenders, Duke Vincentio is concerned to temper the excessive zeal of his puritan deputy.[27] And though it's true that he does keep a close eye on both Angelo and Isabella, it might be thought that it's stretching things a bit far to suggest that this amounts to a 'sophisticated and effective mode of surveillance', with all that that implies in the world of Foucauldian discourse. As for the farcical prison scene in which Pompey invites Barnadine with mock politeness to rise and be hanged, only to be told by Barnadine that, with a hangover like his, he has no intention of being executed at that time in the morning (IV.iii.20–57) – anything further from the spirit of Foucault's carceral technologies would be difficult to imagine. But there's no rule in literary criticism to say that presentists shouldn't read texts against the grain if this helps to overthrow the existing social order. An historicist would strongly disagree with such an approach, but would no doubt acknowledge that there will probably never be a consensus on the function of literary scholarship.[28] Presentism only becomes a problem when its counter-textual readings are confused with an attempt at authentic reconstruction of a past intellectual world.

For someone committed to the advancement of Theory, Dollimore is surprisingly reticent about his own theoretical position. He tells us that his aim is to consider the historical conditions that prevailed at the time the play was written, and that he wants to address the problem of what the play doesn't say about the victims of an oppressive system of government. What's not clear is whether, in representing the play as a dramatic picture of a surveillance society, Dollimore is writing as an historicist, a deconstructionist, or a presentist. Is he attempting to reconstruct a fragment of Jacobean intellectual life with its cultural divisions and impassioned arguments (an historicist reading), showing how the text undermines itself in such a way as to expose meanings that may be the opposite of what Shakespeare intended (a deconstructive reading), or simply recruiting Shakespeare as a Foucauldian anti-essentialist in the cause of social struggle in the modern world (reading against the grain)? On the one hand he talks about 'political strategy in this period', which suggests that he's speaking as an historicist and giving us new insight into the kinds of discourses that informed political thought in Jacobean England; on the other hand, he not only ignores the play's overt themes of self-knowledge and social justice, but makes statements about the characters and their actions that don't tally with what's in the text. An against-the-grain reader can of course make up the facts and use them as the basis of a presentist version of the play that no one can quarrel with: as Sidney said of poets, he who affirms nothing, never lies.[29] But a deconstructive reading involves responding to what's actually in the play and showing how the text contradicts itself, in this way revealing meanings to a modern reader that were unavailable to the author or his contemporaries. On the assumption that historical deconstruction has more to recommend it than arbitrary reading against the grain (or in other words making it up), it may be useful to rehearse some of the more obvious themes that a deconstructive reading would need to engage with.

DEBATE IN MEASURE FOR MEASURE

In the early decades of the last century – long before Roland Barthes announced the death of the author – it was fashionable to argue that, because a writer can never be in possession of all the possible interpretations his or her text might be open to, consideration of authorial intention should play no part in literary criticism (see chapter 8, pp. 157–8). But since it's unlikely that the stylised artistic patterns that are such a typical feature of Shakespeare's dramaturgy somehow assembled themselves without conscious thought on Shakespeare's part, it would seem to tie the critic's hands unnecessarily to rule out authorial intention.[30] That's not to suggest that works of literature have 'a single "theological" meaning', as Barthes put it;[31] indeed with a humanist debate play where rival arguments are played off against each other, it would make little sense to talk about a single, definitive meaning. Rather it's to suggest that, when a writer repeats certain key words and devises complex verbal and structural patterns, it's because he or she wants us to think about the matters that are being drawn to our attention in this way. Let's begin with the play's key words.

In Act II Scene ii Angelo and Isabella meet for the first time. They immediately start arguing. She tries to persuade him to show pity and remit her brother's death sentence. He refuses, telling her that the law must take its course. At first she's inclined to accept his decision: 'O just but severe law!' (II.ii.41). But when Lucio urges her not to give up so easily, she again appeals to Angelo's pity, telling him that mercy is more important in a judge than the trappings of office (63–5). As their argument develops over the next fifty or so lines, the words 'law', 'judge', 'judgement', and 'mercy' echo through the scene and beyond it, establishing one of the play's central topics of debate. He tells her that the law must be impartial, and that to show mercy to one offender would be unjust to others. She urges him to recall that we are all subject to a higher judge (77–81), reminding him, in effect, of the Sermon on the Mount (Matt, 7:1–3). When Angelo continues to resist her appeals to his mercy, she reminds him of another verse from the Sermon on the Mount – 'first cast out the beam of thine own eye' (Matt, 7:5) – and asks him if he can be sure that he has no sin in himself: 'Go to your bosom; / Knock there, and ask your heart what it doth know / That's like my brother's fault' (140–2). Her point has struck home, though Angelo doesn't admit it to her. In a punning aside he confesses salaciously, 'She speaks, and 'tis such sense / That my sense breeds with it' (145–6).

Two scenes later they meet again, and Angelo makes his infamous sexual proposal. As they renew their argument about justice, mercy, and the law, they are like two stubborn critics, each with his own inflexible interpretation of the same play. But this time the roles are reversed (a repeated motif in the play), and it's Isabella who is now put on the spot by an appeal to charity (II.iv.63–4). She's in an impossible position. Should she risk damnation in saving another's life? Or should she preserve her own virtue and cause another's death? Whatever she decides to do will involve violation of a principle that's as important to her as life itself. Shakespeare is fond of such artificial conundrums, as we saw in chapter 3. But *Measure for Measure* isn't about the pseudo-scholastic question of whether it's a greater act of virtue to save a brother's life or your own soul; Isabella's dilemma is a stylised reminder of the irreducible complexity of the issues that human value systems tend to throw up. As the plot unfolds, it becomes clear that the real question that the play's key words are inviting us to think about is those two opposed views of justice that are summed up in Matthew 5:38–9 – the Old Law and the New.

In her argument with Angelo, Isabella was obviously thinking about the Sermon on the Mount: don't be too hasty in judging others until you've examined your own soul, she tells him, or as St Matthew puts it in the words that the play's title alludes to, 'Judge not, that ye be not judged. For with what . . . measure ye mete, it shall be measured to you again'

(7:1–2). But as Portia says in *The Merchant of Venice*, it's a good divine who follows his own instructions (1.ii.14–15). When Isabella realises later in the play that Angelo has double crossed her, she forgets Christ's advice a bit earlier in the Sermon about turning the other cheek (Matt, 5: 38–9) and demands vengeance: 'O, I will to him and pluck out his eyes!' (IV. iii.116). Warning her that he may appear to side with Angelo (IV.vi.5–7), the duke decides to test her charity by seeing if she is prepared show mercy to the man she thinks has killed her brother. Once Angelo has confessed to his crime, Vincentio pretends to subscribe to a retaliatory view of the law. Though his words echo the phrases of the Sermon on the Mount, the sentiments he's expressing are those of the Old Testament prophets (Exodus, 21: 24, Leviticus, 24: 20, Deuteronomy, 19: 21):

> The very mercy* of the law cries out
> Most audible, even from his proper tongue,
> 'An Angelo for Claudio, death for death'.
> Haste still pays haste, and leisure answers leisure;
> Like doth quit like, and measure still for measure.
>
> (v.i.404–8)

But the duke is playing devil's advocate. Having undergone one of those miraculous changes of heart that are so familiar in romance literature, Isabella joins Mariana in pleading for the life of the man who has deceived them both. She has passed her test. As the play ends with forgiveness all round, it's clear that the duke's apparent vindictiveness was merely a show of severity. In reality his is a penitential conception of justice whose ultimate purpose is not the avenging of wickedness but the spiritual good of the sinner.[32]

Contemporary theatregoers would most likely have responded in different ways to Shakespeare's polemic. Fundamentalist Protestants (if there were any in the audience) would not have taken kindly to Shakespeare's satirical portrait of the hypocritical puritan with his harsh interpretation of the law; those of a more tolerant disposition would probably have welcomed Vincentio's penitential view of justice. Their response would no doubt have been complicated by the ambiguous figure of the duke himself.

Measure for Measure was first performed shortly after James I's accession. The duke's admission that he doesn't like staging himself to the public gaze (1.i.68), together with the lines in which Angelo talks

---

*That is, payment (Latin *merces* – wages).

about crowds causing unintended offence to their 'well-wished king'
(ii.iv.26–30) sounds like an obvious allusion to James and his dislike of
the 'foolish throngs' (24). The play also seems to echo James' interest in
justice and equity, his dislike of puritans, and his belief in the importance
of 'measure' or moderation.[33] With hostilities between fundamentalists
and moderates in the Privy Council ready to break out again as soon
as James' political honeymoon was over, it was a topical theme that
Shakespeare was addressing. But *Measure for Measure* is by no means a
straightforward compliment to Shakespeare's new patron. Though
Vincentio insists in response to Lucio's slander that there's no question
of the duke's wisdom (iii.i.400), in reality there is. In a long speech in
Act i he confesses to Friar Thomas that it was his failure to punish those
who had broken the law that has resulted in the present state of disorder:
'We have strict statutes and most biting laws, / The needful bits and curbs
to headstrong weeds, / Which for this fourteen years we have let slip'
(1.iii.19–21). When the friar points out that he could perfectly well have
dealt with the problem himself without bringing Angelo in to do the job
for him, he admits his past error, but claims, with rather doubtful logic,
that it would be unfair if he himself were now to reimpose the law: 'Sith
'twas my fault to give the people scope, / 'Twould be my tyranny to strike
and gall them / For what I bid them do' (35–7).

What are we meant to make of all this? In some scenes the duke looks
like a Machiavellian schemer; in others he looks like a conscientious and
well-meaning ruler who is determined to govern wisely and humanely. To
talk of wisdom or humanity is of course to lay yourself open to the charge
of political naivety. In postmodern criticism the virtues that Isabella and
Angelo argue about – mercy, pity, humility – are no more than ideological mystification designed to produce compliant subjects who will
passively accept their rulers' edicts. There's some truth in this. Ever since
Christianity became an imperial religion in the fourth century, rulers have
found it useful to commend the New Testament virtues of passivity and
obedience. But that doesn't mean that all rulers are ruthless opportunists
concerned with nothing more than self-aggrandisement. One of the
criticisms that's frequently made of Foucault's *Discipline and Punish* is
that it treats all forms of humanitarian action merely as an extension of
the technologies of power. As we've seen, there's no room in Foucault's
mental universe for any distinction between genocidal tyranny and
humane political leadership. He himself said that there's no point in
appealing to humanitarian principles, because those in authority are
merely agents of some metaphysical principle called power. Cultural

Materialists echo Foucault's emphasis on the power of 'the system'. Alan Sinfield writes: 'It is not individuals but power structures that produce the system within which we live and think',[34] and Richard Waswo comments approvingly: 'I don't think this can be improved on as a summary of what we have to learn . . . from . . . postmodern . . . materialism.'[35] However, it's difficult to avoid the conclusion that a model that's unable to distinguish between a Stalin and a Gandhi is of limited value to either the historian or the literary critic.

As a Foucauldian, Dollimore is sceptical of the notion of integrity, claiming that when Duke Vincentio talks of princely virtue this is merely 'a strategy of authority'.[36] It's true that the duke admits with Machiavellian candour that a ruler may sometimes have to use 'craft against vice' (III.additional lines 57). But for Shakespeare's contemporaries the epithet 'Machiavellian' didn't simply mean unprincipled pursuit of power; there were many versions of Machiavelli in this period. Conservatives like the popularist Innocent Gentillet condemned Machiavelli as peddler of a pernicious doctrine that had destroyed 'not this or that virtue, but even all virtues at once'.[37] But more thoughtful writers recognised his importance as a political thinker. In his *Six Bookes of Politickes* (1589) the influential Flemish neo-Stoic philosopher Justus Lipsius defended the principle of 'honest and laudable deceit' when political circumstances required it.[38] Jean Bodin also justified the use of calculated deception if it meant that you could win political advantage in a just cause. In a discussion that would have interested James I, Bodin argued that it's naïve to suppose that 'goodness, bounty and courtesy' are necessarily the mark of an effective ruler:

to the contrary it happeneth often that the state of a city or commonweal [is] ruinated by the too much lenity and facility of [a simple ruler] . . . For by the too much sufferance and simplicity of too good a king, it cometh to pass that flatterers, extortioners, and men of most wicked disposition . . . enjoy the principal honours, offices, charges, benefits, and preferments of the commonwealth . . . whereby the common people are gnawn unto the very bones, and cruelly made slaves unto the great.[39]

Though Bodin and Lipsius defended the principle of Machiavellian *realpolitik*, they made it clear that deceit can only be justified if it's ultimately for the good of the state.

Machiavelli's *Prince* created a storm of controversy in sixteenth-century Europe. Much of the debate turned on the question of the difference between a tyrant and a just ruler. Though it was generally agreed that the former was someone who abused his authority, and the latter a ruler who used 'honest and laudable deceit' for the good of the state, opinion about whether someone was a tyrant or a just ruler was bound to depend to some extent on your perspective. As Bodin explained, 'Things oft times fall out that, for the variety of times, places, persons, and other occasions presenting themselves, princes are constrained to do such things as may seem unto them tyrannical, and unto others commendable.'[40] Shakespeare's history plays are centrally concerned with *realpolitik* and the question of what makes an effective ruler. So is *Measure for Measure*. Isabella accuses Angelo of tyranny (II.ii.110; II.iv.115), while the duke discusses with the provost the question of whether his deputy is behaving in a tyrannical way (IV.ii.85). But the key question, which the play inevitably leaves open, is whether the duke himself is a tyrant or a benign Machiavel. The problem with using Foucault as a theoretical model for analysing Renaissance drama (or any other body of literature) is that fine distinctions of the kind that Bodin and Lipsius were making get lost, and everything is reduced to the same transhistorical formula: because of the impersonal self-replicating nature of power, it means that wherever you look, at whatever point in history, you find authority legitimating itself by the production and containment of subversion.

If the debates that were going on in contemporary political treatises are anything to go by, it's not at all clear that Shakespeare's original audiences would have seen *Measure for Measure* as a text-book case of the construction of sexuality as a way of creating and containing disciplinary subjects. What's more likely is that they would have seen the play as part of a debate on the nature of effective rule. Machiavelli argued that the best way to give advice to a new ruler was to cite the example of his own actions.[41] In creating a dramatic portrait of a ruler who is strikingly reminiscent of James I, not just in his merits but also in his faults, Shakespeare seems to be following the familiar epideictic convention of advising princes by means of a balance of praise and blame. The result is an open-ended play that has more to do with airing questions of governance and holding the mirror up to nature than providing definitive answers.

Though *Measure for Measure* leaves key questions in suspension, one thing is clear: whatever your own opinion of James I, and regardless of your views on religious fundamentalism and its attitude to sexuality, it's certainly not true to say that *Measure for Measure* is about 'the state' reacting in an authoritarian way at a time of crisis. Dollimore claims that the play's transgressors 'are exploited to legitimate an exercise in authoritarian oppression'.[42] Authoritarian oppression is exactly what Duke Vincentio tries to avoid. As head of state, he admits that it's his own negligence that has resulted in the present crisis. But far from trying to 'demonise' those who break the city's sexual laws, or seeking to submit them to a more punitive system of control, he's concerned to temper the excesses of his puritan deputy. Vincentio wants his court to understand the need for moderation: the law must be upheld, but it must be tempered with mercy. Whatever the duke's faults may be – and political cowardice seems to be among them – his is above all a tolerant, sympathetic view of humanity that is the reverse of Foucault's repressive, impersonal carceral society. Instead of using his power to construct 'disciplinary individuals' who can be deceived into internalising a false ideology, he tries to do the opposite. Just as Vincentio had, according to Escalus, 'contended / especially to know himself' (iii.i.490–1), so his aim is to help his subjects to better understand themselves and their human-kindness. A postmodernist would no doubt say that any attempt to persuade people that sexuality is part of our biological nature is itself false ideology. But it's one thing to accept Foucault's assertion that sexuality has nothing to do with nature (though it's unlikely that this would get much support from modern biologists and psychologists), and quite another to argue, against all the evidence, that Renaissance intellectuals shared that insight.

SELF-KNOWLEDGE

In postmodern Shakespeare criticism it's generally accepted that, far from being a universal feature of human nature, the sense of selfhood that most of us take for granted is an historically specific phenomenon. 1660 is the favourite date for the emergence of this new version of humanity, though some critics put it a few decades earlier. Before the appearance of the modern self people didn't have much sense of interiority. They were, so to speak, surface beings. In the nineteenth century Jules Michelet and Jacob Burckhardt made similar claims about the emergence of a modern sense of self, though they located it in the fourteenth century. But these claims were rejected by modern Renaissance scholarship many decades ago (see chapter 9, p. 187). As we saw in the previous chapter, there's no evidence that people lacked a sense of self in Elizabethan England. Wherever you look in the literature of this period you find people talking about the inward being and distinguishing it from the outer self. It's true that Renaissance writers echo the familiar Stoic advice about the pressure to dissemble in public life. But this doesn't mean they believed that human beings lacked an essential inner self or that human nature itself was a figment of the new bourgeois imagination. Indeed it was argued that, the more a politician or a statesman might be driven for professional reasons to assume a public mask, the greater the need to remain faithful to his true nature. Like so much humanist thinking, this idea probably originates in Cicero.

In the *De officiis* Cicero cites many cases of politicians who had to conceal their true feelings and act a part in public life.[43] But though he acknowledged that the pressures of political life may mean that you have to conceal your real feelings, he emphasised that you should never suppress your true nature: 'For we must so act as not to oppose the universal laws of human nature, but, while safeguarding those, to follow the bent of our own particular nature.'[44] Seneca, who knew better than most people the dangers of public life, also discussed the art of self concealment, arguing that, while it's best to live a life of candid simplicity, you lay yourself open to danger if you are always open with everyone you have to deal with. However, if circumstances mean that you are forced to conceal your true self, it's important to keep sane by maintaining contact with the inner man. 'Above all,' he wrote, 'it is necessary for a man to estimate himself truly.'[45] Cicero and Seneca were among the most widely read Roman authors in sixteenth-century England. So deeply rooted in neo-Stoic thought is the distinction between what Claudius calls the 'exterior' and the 'inward man' (*Hamlet*, ii.ii.6) that it becomes an almost formulaic way of praising integrity. For example, when Sidney cites Aeneas as a model of virtue, he commends Virgil's hero for the control he shows both 'in his inward self, and . . . in his outward government'.[46] In *Measure for Measure* the difference between outward show and inner reality is as important as it is in *Hamlet*. 'O, what may man within him hide, / Though angel on the outward side!' thinks the duke to himself as he meditates on the contradictions of human behaviour (iii.additional lines 51–2).

For Renaissance humanists knowledge of your inner self is a key to wise action. As Vives put it, 'what greater practical wisdom is there than to know how and what the human passions are: how they are roused, how quelled?'[47] But as we've seen (Chapter 1, pp. 10–11), when humanists talked about self-knowledge they meant an understanding, not just of your own personality, but of human-kind in general. '[Self-knowledge] consisteth of a perfect experience every man hath of himself in particular, and an universal knowledge of men's inclinations in common', wrote Thomas Wright.[48] Because it was thought that any just legal system should be based on the laws of human nature, it was essential for an effective ruler to have a knowledge of what Pierre Charron called 'our human condition'. Again, it's an idea that goes back to Cicero. In the *De officiis* he argued that, although legal systems vary from one country to another, the laws of any particular society should be based on the universal nature of humanity.[49] Cicero elaborated the distinction between what he called civil law (*ius civile*) and universal law (*ius gentium*) in another treatise. *De legibus* was one of the most influential of all Roman philosophical works. Cicero's principle of right reason (*recta ratio*) was the source for Renaissance theories of natural law;[50] it was the basis of Milton's Christian-humanist ethic in *Paradise Lost*. The core of Cicero's theory of law is the idea that justice must be based on the facts of human nature. Our task, he wrote, is to 'explain the nature of Justice, and this must be sought for in the nature of man'.[51] It's an ancient maxim that Escalus is echoing when he says that Duke Vincentio 'contended especially to know himself'.

With the decline of civic humanism in the seventeenth century, Cicero's emphasis on the importance of integrity in rulers came to be viewed more critically. It was Machiavelli who taught people to be sceptical about the humanist assumption that virtue and utility must always go together. When he argued in *The Prince* that an effective ruler might have to oppose a virtuous course of action in favour of one that might seem ethically dubious, he was implicitly acknowledging that human value systems inevitably involve choices between incommensurables. One good – a strong independent state for example – may mean negation of another good: openness and honesty on the part of its ruler. But though he saw that the good and the useful are not always compatible, Machiavelli shared Cicero's belief that an effective ruler must have a thorough knowledge of humankind. Informing his whole view of history, was the belief that human nature was the same in all ages. By analysing the reasons for people's behaviour in the past you could predict how they might behave in the future. A ruler who had, to paraphrase Charron, a knowledge both of himself and the human condition in general, held a key that was essential to good government. *Measure for Measure* is about both kinds of self-knowledge.

MEASURE

We know from earlier plays – especially *The Merchant of Venice* and *Twelfth Night* – that Shakespeare distrusted puritan extremists. In *The Merchant of Venice* Shylock's joyless asceticism is contrasted with the

Christians' love of music and merriment. If both sides have their faults, the chief lesson that vindictive Christians like Gratiano, as well as Jews, have to learn is the importance of compassion. In *Measure for Measure* the satire on puritanism is made more pointed by the pairing of two of the central characters. Angelo and Isabella may look superficially like sinner and saint, but they have much in common. Both are high minded ascetics who deny their sexuality and appear to have completely mastered their feelings. At first sight they seem like the antithesis of the low-life characters with their frank and open attitude to sex. But under pressure they go from one extreme to another. Though word has it that Angelo is not susceptible to 'the wanton stings and motions of the sense' (I.iv.58), the truth is that he's as vulnerable to his emotions as the next man. Even he is perplexed by the violence of the feelings that Isabella's chastity arouses in him (II.ii.167–92). Her passion is equally violent: in the very act of rejecting the thought of sex with Angelo, her passionate nature reveals itself in sado-masochistic images of naked, lacerated bodies (II.iv.100–4). Claudio too goes from one extreme to another, first accepting the duke's Stoic counsel about being prepared for death (III.i.42–3), then pleading with his sister to let him live (134). As the duke says, his emotions are as changeable as the moon (24–5).

Reversal of roles and fluctuation from one extreme to another is an important motif in *Measure for Measure*. Just as the play's characters swing from one emotional pole to another, so under Angelo's influence the city itself goes from an extreme of licence to one of excessive restraint. 'Why, here's a change indeed in the commonwealth', says Mistress Overdone when she hears that the city's brothels are to be demolished (1.ii.96–7). What Claudio tells Lucio about his death sentence is as true of Vienna as it is of his own fortunes. 'Whence comes this restraint?' asks Lucio. 'From too much liberty', answers Claudio (1.ii.116–17). He then moralises the point in one of the play's many *sententiae* on human nature:

> As surfeit is the father of much fast,
> So every scope, by the immoderate use,
> Turns to restraint.
>
> (118–20)

Duke Vincentio knows that it's his own preference for 'the life removed' (1.iii.8) and his neglect of his princely duties that has provoked the present civic crisis. Though he has no sympathy for debauchery and tells Lucio irritably that 'severity must cure it' (III.i.365), he also knows that the remedy doesn't lie in Angelo's kind of repressive rule. Angelo's attempt to stamp out illicit sex altogether suggests a disastrous ignorance, not just of his own nature, but of humankind in general. As so often in the plays, Shakespeare puts the shrewdest words into the mouths of his knaves and villains. Exasperated by Elbow's stupidity as they go about the business of rounding up the pimps and brothel keepers, Escalus asks, 'Which is the wiser here, justice or iniquity?' (II.i.165). Ironically, the answer is in one sense iniquity. Unlike Angelo, Pompey knows that you'll never succeed entirely in suppressing illicit sex. When Escalus tells him that prostitution is to be outlawed in Vienna, he replies, 'Does your worship mean to geld and spay all the / youth of the city?' (220–1). The provost also knows that fornication is a universal feature of human society: 'All sects [ie, classes], all ages, smack of this vice' (II.ii.5). Lucio knows it too: 'it is impossible to extirp it quite . . . till eating and drinking be put down' (III.i.367–8). The point is not that brothels are a desirable feature of any city; rather that, given the realities of human nature, they are probably inevitable. At least, they seem to be a fairly constant element in city life in the ancient as well as the modern world.

Dollimore argues that the function of the low-life characters in *Measure for Measure* is to illustrate the coercive power of ideology as it first constructs people as sexual subjects and then contains the subversion it has knowingly created.[52] The play itself would seem to suggest something more familiar. The low-life characters in *Measure for Measure* serve as a reminder, not of the socially constructed nature of sexuality, but of what Iago calls the 'blood and baseness of our natures' (*Othello*, I.iii.328). If the best men are 'moulded out of faults', as Mariana claims in another of the play's *sententiae*, and 'become much more the better / For being a little bad' (V.i.436–8), that's probably because, understanding their own weaknesses, they have a more tolerant view of humanity than puritan zealots like Angelo, and don't expect to find perfection in others. The difficulties that Angelo and Isabella get themselves into suggest that it makes no more sense to deny human sexuality than it does to give it free reign: both are likely to lead to 'preposterous conclusions' (*Othello*, I.iii.329).

Renaissance humanists were inspired by the aim of realising a classical ideal of the just society. But they were sufficiently practical to know that any programme of social reform has got to begin by acknowledging the facts of human nature. As Cicero had said, if you want to define justice you've got to look for it in the nature of man. And that's what Duke Vincentio's machinations in the last two acts of the play are ultimately all about. The elaborate pretence of the bed-trick may not convince a modern audience that it's got anything serious to say, especially following, as it does, the semi-realistic, tragic mode of the first three acts. But this is the world of Renaissance tragicomedy where riddles, conundrums, and folk-tale motifs are used to figure ethical and political problems. For Angelo and Isabella the metadramatic contrivances of the fourth and fifth acts are like a romance, directed by the duke, in which they themselves are actors, one of them unwitting, the other half aware of the real part she's playing. Its purpose is to hold the mirror up to nature and show virtue her own feature and scorn her own image. Angelo learns that Isabella was right about knocking at your heart and asking what it knows before judging other people; Isabella learns to practise the mercy she once preached. Both learn that Mariana's tolerant view of humanity is preferable to their own neurotic perfectionism. It's not just St Matthew's phrases, but also a classical ideal of *misura*, or measure, that the play's title alludes to.

A POSTMODERN SHAKESPEARE?

Is there any truth in Dollimore's Foucauldian analysis of *Measure for Measure* as a dramatic picture of a surveillance society? His essay has certainly been influential. For a postmodernist like Richard Wilson, Dollimore's reading of the play is indisputable. In a chapter titled 'Discipline and punish in Shakespearean comedy' he writes:

> *Measure for Measure* . . . provides a conspectus of the Damoclean methods of the disciplinary state, as Jonathan Dollimore has shown . . . The play presents a power that has learned the lesson of modernity, that subjection is obtained not by oppression, but by self-repression. The state over which Vincentio presides has long ago begun the experiment of abandoning its public violence in return for private discipline of its citizens, and it knows its legitimacy depends upon its incitement of transgression.[53]

It's true that in some ways early Jacobean England must have been very like the world that Foucault evoked in the opening chapter of *Discipline and Punish* (though quite unlike the surveillance society he described in the latter part of the book). Catholics were kept under close scrutiny; the government operated an active spy network aimed at the detection of Catholic plots against the crown; and Catholic proselytisers were hunted down and dismembered in ways that were every bit as macabre as the torture of Robert-François Damiens in 1757. But *Measure for Measure* doesn't deal with those matters. To justify a claim that Elizabethan or Jacobean writers shared Foucault's vision of the way power works in 'surveillance' societies, or even that they analysed that system without realising they were doing so, you would really need to choose a different play. With its ever-watchful agents representing some higher power, and its hints of the gruesome fate that heretics could expect in Elizabethan England, Marlowe's *Doctor Faustus* suggests itself as a possibility. *Measure for Measure* also deals with religious and judicial issues; but it's not about religious persecution or the hunting down of heretics. And it's certainly not about the construction of sexuality as a way of creating disciplinary subjects.

Shakespeare was suspicious of any kind of extreme religious fundamentalism. Like Cicero, he appears to have believed that any humane system of justice must begin with an acknowledgment of the facts of our universal humanity; like Machiavelli, he seems to be saying that effective rulers, devious as they may sometimes have to be, need to have a thorough knowledge of human nature. This may not be a welcome conclusion for postmodernists, but it would probably make more sense to acknowledge Shakespeare's humanist themes for what they are and then deconstruct them, rather than claim that he was a postmodernist *avant la lettre*. It's not impossible to imagine a coherent deconstructive reading of *Measure for Measure*. But such a reading would need to address the play's overtly articulated themes of self-knowledge, justice, and human nature and show how they undermine themselves. It's also possible to imagine an historicist reading that challenged the play's essentialist concern with human nature. But that would have to show that its keywords were used in a consistently ironic way, and that the structural parallels and contrasts that point to a concern with universal truths about human sexuality were designed for ironic effect. It would need to show too that the proverbs and *sententiae* about human nature spoken by all the major characters were either said with tongue in cheek, or were intended to make those characters look foolish or misguided. Though such a reading is conceivable, it seems inherently unlikely. Shakespeare was certainly aware of relativist arguments of the kind that Thomas Starkey addressed in the introduction to his *Dialogue Between Pole and Lupset* (see chapter 5). But his treatment of those ideas in *Troilus and Cressida* seems designed to make them look absurd.[54] *Measure for Measure*'s *sententiae* on human nature; its emphasis on self-knowledge; its paralleling of two puritanical characters who are disastrously lacking in self-knowledge; its satiric reminder of the less pleasant side of human nature; its thoughts on the difference between a tyrant and a just ruler; and its central theme of justice, mercy and 'measure' – all these point, not to a fable about the legitimation of authority by the construction and containment of sexual subjects, but to an anatomy of government that takes as its premise the Ciceronian principle that 'justice . . . must be sought for in the nature of man'. It's true that its portrayal of a well-intentioned though devious and rather weak-minded ruler who is keenly interested in justice, but dislikes the 'obsequious fondness of the crowd' (II.iv.28–9), might be thought a rather risky way of complimenting a new patron. (Even more risky, one would have thought, is the suggestion that when it comes to women, the play's ruler-figure is 'not inclined that way' – III.i.386.) But double-edged though the compliment may be, it's difficult to avoid the conclusion that *Measure for Measure* is a Christian humanist play, not a postmodern text.

CHAPTER 5

Men, women and civilisation

One of the defining features of civilised states that distinguishes them from many primitive societies, and a few modern fundamentalist religious ones, is the existence of laws that deny individuals the right to take personal revenge for crimes against themselves or their families. In *Hamlet* a Viking code of heroic values (represented by Fortinbras and the ghost of Old Hamlet) is contrasted with Horatio's philosophic stoicism.[1] The former valorises retaliatory vengeance, the latter an indifference to misfortune. In *Othello* the Venetian republic – famed for its legendary political wisdom – is threatened by the forces of barbarism in the form of the Ottoman empire; the two are symbolically brought together when the soldier charged with defending Venice against the barbarian, resorts not to a court of law, but to an archaic honour code in satisfaction of a supposed wrong. While humanists saw their task as the defence of civilisation against barbarism, they believed that the greatest danger didn't always come from an external enemy. The archetypal example of a city that fell as a result of help from within was Troy. In both *Hamlet* and *Othello* the ultimate threat to state security comes, not from an invading power, but from within the city gates. Though both tragedies reflect humanist distrust of heroic values, it's only in *Hamlet* that there's any talk of the liberal arts, and even then Hamlet seems more interested in heroic poetry than in the civilising power of the arts. In his last two tragicomedies Shakespeare returns to the humanist theme of conflict between civilisation and barbarism. But now the liberal arts are given particular emphasis. In these plays barbarism is countered with a *humanitas* that's evoked in terms, not of judicial bodies and legislative assemblies, but of the imaginative arts of poetry, music, song, and by implication, drama.

ART AND NATURE

In all four of Shakespeare's late tragicomedies there's a pattern of estrangement, suffering and reconciliation. Some critics have argued that the form of these plays derives from medieval drama with its structural patterns based on the Passion and Resurrection.[2] It's been suggested that, with their emphasis on penance and redemption, the tragicomedies reflect a specifically Catholic view of the Passion narrative.[3] There's much in the plays to support such a Christian, and perhaps specifically Catholic, interpretation: Pericles 'puts on sack-cloth' (*Pericles*, s.d., xviii.22–3); Belarius observes 'morning's holy office' (*Cymbeline*, iii.iii.4); Leontes performs a 'saint-like sorrow' (*The Winter's Tale*, v.i.2); Prospero lives in a 'poor cell' (*The Tempest*, i.ii.20) and at the end of the play asks for prayers to relieve his despair (Epilogue, 15–16). And of course, central to *The Winter's Tale* is the archetypal Christian mythos of 'things dying' and 'things new-born' (iii.iii.111). In a play involving suffering, penance and renewal, the idea of springtime rejuvenation following a period of 'saint-like sorrow' is bound to suggest those fundamental events of the Christian calendar: the Crucifixion and Resurrection. So deeply embedded in the national consciousness was the story of the Passion, and so vital a part did it play in the rituals of daily life, that for a contemporary audience Christian associations would have been difficult to avoid. But to claim that the Passion narrative is the 'hermeneutical key'[4] to *The Winter's Tale* is to ignore the play's humanist meanings.

Pagan mythology also tells of an archetypal experience of suffering and resurrection that affects the whole future course of human existence. The Proserpina story that Perdita recalls in iv.iv is a myth-of-origin.[5] In Book v of the *Metamorphoses* Ovid tells how the seasonal cycle of death and renewal only came about after Pluto abducted Proserpina, and Ceres neglected her duties as she sought her missing daughter. Though Jupiter decrees that Pluto must allow his reluctant partner back to the upper world for six months every year, fate is against her. The consequence of eating the seven pomegranate seeds is an annual period of desolation as Proserpina returns to the underworld and nature mourns her absence (*Metamorphoses*, v.385–567). Nature's primal equilibrium had been lost forever, and the cause was an act of sexual violence.

It's been suggested that Shakespeare may have substituted pagan deities for Christ in the tragicomedies partly because the 1606 Act of Abuses prevented players from referring directly to the 'name of God or of Jesus Christ, or of the Holy Ghost', and partly because a blend of paganism and Christianity would have made his treatment of the Passion story seem less like subversive Catholicism.[6] It's true that Catholics were more receptive to classical learning than radical Protestants were. But we shouldn't assume that these pagan motifs in the plays were merely a way of camouflaging a Christian message. There are elements in the tragicomedies that can't be interpreted as a disguised Christianity.

One of the ruling ambitions of Renaissance humanists was to reconcile pagan learning and Christian piety. Though radical Protestants strongly disagreed with them, humanists believed that, in a world where no one could claim to be exempt from the penalties of the fall, the *humanae litterae* could assist in repairing that primal damage. 'The final end [of poetry] is to lead and draw us to as high a perfection as our degenerate souls, made worse by their clayey lodgings, can be capable of', wrote Sidney in the *Apology for Poetry*.[7] 'The farthest scope [of poesy is] to assist and direct nature [in restoring] man to his former state of moral and civil happiness', wrote William Scott in *The Model of Poesy* (c. 1599).[8] These claims for the rehabilitative power of poetry were a commonplace of Italian Renaissance criticism.[9] Filtered through the work of popularisers like Castiglione, they were also a commonplace of English humanism and continued to inform thinking about the arts long after Shakespeare's death. 'The end . . . of learning is to repair the ruins of our first parents', wrote Milton in his tractate on Education.[10] 'The great design of arts is to restore the decays that happened to human nature by the Fall, by restoring order', wrote John Dennis sixty years later.[11] The conversation between Polixenes and Perdita on art and nature in the fourth act of *The Winter's Tale* deals with the same *topos*. It's like a miniature humanist dialogue on the civilising power of what Prospero calls the 'liberal arts' (*The Tempest*, I.ii.73).

In what sounds like a paraphrase of George Puttenham's discussion of poetics, Polixenes tells Perdita that there is 'an art / Which does mend Nature – change it rather' (IV.iv.95–6).[12] If we substitute the liberal arts for gardening, and human nature for flowers, then it's clear that Polixenes is talking about what generations of humanists were agreed on, namely, that the arts can change human behaviour for the better. Lorenzo uses the same phrase about changing nature in *The Merchant of Venice* when he tells Jessica that there's no one 'so stockish, hard, and full of rage / But music for the time doth change his nature' (v.i.81–2). Polixenes' ostensible theme happens to be gardening rather than music, but his drift is the same as Lorenzo's: there is an art which does mend nature. This is a fundamental principle in humanist thought, and though many Protestants as well as Catholics endorsed it, it has nothing to do with Christian doctrine.

The relationship between art and nature is a familiar debating *topos* in this period.[13] Puttenham's discussion in the final chapter of the *Arte of English Poesie* is one example; Spenser's Bower of Bliss is another. The first is concerned primarily with poetics, the second with morality. While both make it clear that the arts are a powerful agent for change, Spenser versifies a commonplace of the period when he shows that they can be used either to improve or to corrupt.[14] As Shakespeare's Duke Vincentio puts it, 'music oft hath such a charm / To make bad good, and good provoke to harm' (*Measure for Measure*, IV.i.14–15). What's true of music goes for the arts in general. As many commentators have noted, Polixenes seems to take a classic humanist view of art and nature in his conversation with Perdita, suggesting that nature's deficiencies can be remedied by art, while she argues from a primitivist position, expressing distaste at the idea of adulterating 'great creating nature' with human artifice. It used to be thought that Shakespeare shows his sceptical view of primitivism by allowing Polixenes to win the argument.[15] However, this reading of *The Winter's Tale* has been challenged in two late twentieth-century studies of Shakespeare's theory of poetic drama.

In *Shakespeare's Poetics* Ekbert Faas argues that Shakespeare reverses 'mainstream' Renaissance ideas about the relationship between art and nature, rejecting the notion that art 'fills out the deficiencies of nature'.[16] In the introduction to his influential 1963 edition of the play Frank Kermode wrote: 'in the end the play seems to say (I borrow the language of Yeats) that "whatever is begotten, born and dies" is nobler than "monuments of unageing intellect"'.[17] Faas agrees: 'Shakespeare's art . . . avoids the idealization of Yeats' Byzantium poems and instead reenacts the dying generations of nature's rhythms . . . *And that . . . is the message conveyed by* The Winter's Tale *as a whole*'.[18] More recently, Pauline Kiernan has endorsed Faas' revisionist reading of the play in *Shakespeare's Theory of Drama*. She writes:

Perdita exposes the absurdity of art which arrogantly attempts to imitate, perfect and surpass nature . . . There she stands, the embodiment of budding springtime, of the fertile earth and its future fruits, full of life, warmth, movement and beauty, and asks us to imagine her being mended, or rather, changed, by art into a painted image which Florizel would only desire because she was painted . . . she has effectively silenced the traditional theorists and adherents of the concept of art as an idealising re-presentation of nature, by showing what a pointless exercise it all is. Adulteration, depravity and sterilisation are the price that must be paid for that improvement of nature whose purpose is to glimpse the perfection created by the First Maker.[19]

It's true that nature is a vital element in *The Winter's Tale*'s design. By alluding to the Proserpina story Shakespeare is self-consciously linking his own drama of human suffering and reunion with the Ovidian myth of nature's self-renewal. But nature isn't simply a matter of 'warm' maidens and 'budding springtime'. In retelling the Proserpina story as a seasonal myth-of-origin Ovid had linked winter's cruelty with the darker side of human nature. *The Winter's Tale* reminds us of that link. If we ourselves are part of nature, human passions can be as destructive as winter storms. And it's those passions that the play is all about. The trouble with Faas' and Kiernan's interpretation of the art/nature debate is their literalism. When Kiernan says 'we do not need artifice . . . to make things "better than nature bringeth forth"'[20] she makes the play sound like a scholastic treatise: 'Which is superior, art or nature? Discuss, making full use of rhetorical *copia*'. There's no question about the age's preoccupation with art and nature: mid-sixteenth-century Italian theorists like Castelvetro, Cinthio, Minturno, Ricci, Speroni and Varchi devoted acres of print to the problem of whether poets owe more to one or to the other.[21] Platonists tended to emphasise native genius; Aristotelians tended to stress art and discipline. Horace said that both were important (see chapter 9, p. 169). But as any theatregoer will tell you, *The Winter's Tale* is no dry technical discourse. That the play is in part a self-reflexive commentary on the nature of its own dramatic art is not in dispute; indeed, together with *The Tempest* it's probably Shakespeare's most serious *apologia* for the theatre. I'll return later to this aspect of the play. But that's not the first thing that strikes an audience. This is a tragicomedy that begins by overwhelming you with its cruelty, and then goes on to charm you with its magical story of repentance, love and miraculous transformation. Like the 'old tales' the play repeatedly refers to, it's obviously a fable of some kind. But what is it telling us about the meaning of such destructive passion?

A SHORT MADNESS

Countless critics have looked for a psychological explanation for Leontes' bizarre behaviour. In a variation on the traditional hunt for a plausible cause, Catherine Belsey has recently suggested that the king's jealous anger has its origins in the aggression that Jacques Lacan believed was inseparable from romantic love, and therefore endemic in the bourgeois nuclear family.[22] But for historicists speculation about the causes of Leontes' insane cruelty is probably beside the point, especially if it turns Shakespeare into a Lacanian analyst, *avant la lettre*, of the bourgeois love-which-is-really-hate (not for nothing has Lacan been called 'the shrink from hell').[23] We all know that jealousy can be an overwhelming emotion. But Renaissance critics tended to interest themselves more in the nature and consequences of violent passion than its causes. 'Anger', writes Sidney echoing Horace and Seneca, '[is] a short madness.' He goes on: 'let but Sophocles bring you Ajax on a stage, killing and whipping sheep and oxen, thinking them the army of Greeks, with their chieftains Agamemnon and Menelaus, and tell me if you have not a more familiar insight into anger than finding in the schoolmen his genus and difference'.[24] Like Sidney's literary examples, *The Winter's Tale* invites us to think about the meaning of a 'short madness'. But in doing so it also invites us to ponder those great commonplaces of humanist criticism: can the liberal arts really make us into better people? can they really repair the ruins of our first parents? For a critic like Sidney there's not much to be gained by speculating about the causes of violent emotion because the answer was obvious. John Gower, whom Shakespeare named as the Chorus of *Pericles*, summed up an axiomatic principle of medieval and Renaissance Christian-humanist thought when he said that the reason why 'love is falle into discord' in this 'world of Stiel' is because of the sins of our first parents.[25]

But for primitivists the answer was not so simple. They believed that if, as 'ancient' Gower put it, 'love is fro the world departed',[26] that's not because of some primal act of sin, but because city life, the court, or perhaps civilisation in general, has corrupted our natural virtue. Thomas More considered these arguments in *Utopia* (1518); Thomas Starkey gave them an airing a few years later in his *Dialogue Between Pole and Lupset* (*c.* 1529–32). Montaigne reopened the whole question with his celebrated essay 'Of the Caniballes' (English translation by John Florio in 1603).[27] Which view did Shakespeare incline to, the Christian-humanist, or the primitivist? I'll come back to this question in a later section. In the meantime we need to deal with an objection that's been made with some consistency over the past two decades to the very terms in which the primitivist debate was couched.

NEO-PLATONIC MAGIC

Postmodernists claim that Shakespeare and his contemporaries were our own intellectual precursors. Catherine Belsey, for example, tells us that Shakespeare was 'a Saussurean *avant la lettre*';[28] Jonathan Dollimore finds evidence in *Measure for Measure* of a Foucauldian view of sexuality;[29] Richard Wilson believes that *Julius Caesar* 'appears to anticipate so much of postmodernism'.[30] This isn't simply a matter of using postmodern Theory to read Shakespeare against the grain of Renaissance thought. Since the mid 1980s it's been generally accepted in mainstream criticism that Shakespeare and his contemporaries were themselves radical anti-humanists. One of the few critics to consider in any detail the historical evidence for Renaissance anti-essentialism is Dollimore. In *Radical Tragedy* he discusses a number of Renaissance thinkers, who, he claims, adumbrated a radical anti-humanism in their writing. But his evidence has been shown to be flawed.[31] Let's take one example – his citation of the great Italian humanist Giovanni Pico della Mirandola – and this will lead us back to *The Winter's Tale* and its debt to Italian neo-Platonism.

Dollimore's thesis is that Jacobean tragedy is a good deal more politically subversive than we realised. These plays 'de-centre' humanity, showing us that we are the product, not of some timeless metaphysical blue-print, but of social forces that shape our entire being. In doing so they draw on a body of radical thought that challenged traditional ideas about human nature. One of these supposedly radical thinkers is Pico. In a well known passage in the *Oration on the Dignity of Man* Pico imagines God telling humankind that he has given them the choice of either ameliorating their fallen condition, or of ascending to higher realms of being (see Introduction). Dollimore takes this to be evidence of a modern decentred view of humanity: like the postmodernists he seems to anticipate, Pico apparently recognised that our nature is not fixed, but infinitely malleable; we have, in truth, no universal essence.[32]

However, you don't have to read very far in the *Oration* to discover that this interpretation stands Pico's Pythagorean humanism on its head. Far from de-centring mankind Pico does the exact opposite: 'We have placed thee at the world's centre' ('*medium mundi*'), God tells man.[33] The reason for this is that man is a kind of world in miniature ('a little world made cunningly', as Donne put it). Like the twelfth-century Chartrian neo-Platonists before him, and like countless Renaissance writers after him,

Pico believed that man was in a literal sense a microcosm of the universe. That's not to say that the human body is in some poetical sense *like* the universe; it means rather that the same universal laws apply to bodies, families, states, buildings and the universe itself.[34] If you believe, as many people still did in the seventeenth century, that the microcosm / macrocosm analogy expressed a scientific truth, it meant that, by understanding your own essence, you could acquire knowledge of nature's laws. That's why the old adage 'know thyself' was so important for Pico and practically every other Renaissance writer:[35] by knowing yourself you could begin to understand nature. These ideas aren't the eccentric product of some provincial backwater of Renaissance philosophy; they represent the core of a metaphysical anthropology that goes back to the Pythagoreans and that survived at least until the eighteenth century.

Far from being anti-essentialists, the great Renaissance humanists had a clearly worked-out sense of humankind's essentially divided nature: as a species we are capable either of realising our human *telos* and aspiring to heaven, or of descending to the level of the brutes. But how could humanity improve its fallen condition? For the civic humanist the answer was a practical one: education in the liberal arts in preparation for a life of public service. But fifteenth-century Italian neo-Platonists took a more philosophical approach. Basing their theories on the ancient doctrine of correspondence between microcosm and macrocosm, they developed an ambitious programme of spiritual renewal. In the *Timaeus* Plato suggested that there was a natural affinity between the cosmos and the human soul: because the same harmonic principles that controlled the revolutions of the heavenly bodies also governed the human soul, sympathetic use of music could restore harmony to a discordant soul.[36] It was this idea that the Florentine neo-Platonist Marsilio Ficino attempted to put into practice. Combining Plato's theory of correspondence between man and cosmos with Hermetic lore, Ficino tried to discover the secret of the magical power that legend attributed to the songs of Orpheus. He decided that the answer must be for the singer to imitate the music of the spheres. By supplicating the appropriate planetary influence, the Orphic singer could draw down the influence of the astral deities and absorb a 'certain celestial virtue'.[37]

Ficino claimed to have succeeded in realising this Orphic ideal of inspired communication. But although contemporary audiences were said to have been moved by his performances, there is, as often seems to be the case with charismatic teachers who claim divine inspiration, a strong suggestion of charlatanism in Ficino's writing. Whether or not

Shakespeare had read Ficino we don't know. In Italy and France his influence was enormous. His commentary on Plato's *Symposium* alone (*De amore*) inspired more than thirty Italian works in the century following its first circulation in manuscript.[38] In England his reception was more muted. The publication of Giordano Bruno's *De gli heroici furori* in England in 1585 gave currency to Ficino's ideas, but the book didn't meet with the reception Bruno hoped for (see chapter 6, pp. 123–5). He dedicated it to Sidney in the belief that he would be sympathetic to his neo-Platonic ideas. But Sidney was suspicious of Bruno's speculative theories, recognising that they were at best merely self-deceiving vanities (see for example, *Astrophil and Stella*, 5, 71, 72). Shakespeare also mocked Bruno's heroic pretensions in plays like *Romeo and Juliet* and *A Midsummer Night's Dream*.

But scepticism about some of the more extravagant claims of would-be hierophants like Ficino and Bruno doesn't mean that Shakespeare rejected entirely the world of Hermetic neo-Platonism, at least not as a way of thinking about art. As Wayne Shumaker has pointed out, no reader of *The Tempest* can fail to see that Prospero is a magician: he raises a storm, controls a sylph-like spirit, casts spells over those he wants to bring under his influence, wears a magic cloak, and is apparently aided by 'a most auspicious star' (I.ii.183).[39] Is all this, as Shumaker suggests it may be, simply a metaphor for the power of the artist to conjure up imaginary worlds and work his magic on our sensibilities?[40] Certainly this seems to be the case in *The Winter's Tale*, where apparently magical effects are revealed as carefully staged illusions produced by a woman who is in reality no magician but simply a member of Leontes' court who wants to impress on her king the importance of love, trust and forgiveness. There are no heroic frenzies here. Shakespeare is giving dramatic expression to neo-Platonic commonplaces about the affective power of the arts that, in a diluted form, were part of the common stock of humanist thought in Renaissance Europe.

The most famous and the most influential of the many imitations and popularisations of Ficino's ideas is Castiglione's *The Courtier*. In Book 1 Count Lodovico Canossa gives a defence of music against the charge of superficiality. As he explains how there is a natural sympathy between the heavenly spheres and the human soul, and how music can uplift the spirit and incline us towards virtue, he is summarising a body of thought that goes back through Ficino to Macrobius, Boethius and Plato and ultimately to the Pythagoreans in fifth-century Greece. Castiglione wrote:

It hath been the opinion of most wise philosophers that the world is made of
music, and the heavens in their moving make a melody, and our soul is framed
after the very same sort and therefore lifteth up it self, and (as it were) reviveth
the virtues and force of it self with music.[41]

Shakespeare versifies these same ideas when he has Lorenzo deliver a
lecture on the music of the spheres (*The Merchant of Venice*, v.i.55–88).[42]
For Lorenzo, as for Ficino, the figure who best exemplifies the affective power of music is Orpheus. But the Orpheus story isn't just about the
power of music. Renaissance mythographers treated it as an allegory of
the birth of civilisation. In the *Arte of English Poesie* Puttenham explained
that Orpheus' taming of the wild beasts was a fable illustrating the process
by which people were originally persuaded to abandon their barbaric life
and embrace 'a more civil and orderly life'.[43] Henry Peacham the Elder
made the same familiar point: it was through Orpheus' 'prudent art of
persuasion [that people] were converted from that most brutish condition
of life, to the love of humanity and politic government'.[44] Bacon said that
Orpheus symbolised the superiority of 'sweet and gentle measures' over
brute strength.[45]

CONJURING REMEMBRANCE

There are no musicians in *The Winter's Tale*, at least none that plays a
leading role. But it's not difficult to see that Paulina is like a female
version of Orpheus using the magical power of the arts to move her royal
audience. Shakespeare seldom used stories from classical mythology without altering them in some significant way. *Othello*, for example, seems to
invert the Pygmalion story. Like the Cypriots in Ovid's tale, Othello
grows horns on his head – or imagines he does – in reaction to the news of
his wife's supposed adultery. But instead of praying that a marble statue
might be brought to life to compensate him for his torture, he persuades
himself that a living woman can be turned into cold, alabaster perfection:

> Let me not name it to you, you chaste stars.
> It is the cause. Yet I'll not shed her blood,
> Nor scar that whiter skin of hers than snow,
> And smooth as monumental alabaster.
>
> (v.ii.1–5)

Shakespeare also draws on the Pygmalion story in the final scene of *The
Winter's Tale*.[46] In Ovid it's the grieving Orpheus who tells the story of
Pygmalion's misogyny and the miraculous creation of an idealised woman
who will never betray her husband. Paulina seems to combine the roles of

Pygmalion and Orpheus, using her 'magical' arts to persuade Leontes of
the power of love, and warning him not to cause his wife to die a second
time as Orpheus did. Though Paulina isn't a musician herself, music is an
important part of her performance. As she prepares for the statue to come
to life she calls for music to awaken it (v.iii.98).

Paulina's 'magical' art is of course a deception. Discussing the statue
scene, Faas argues that, in misleading his audience into thinking that a
miraculously life-like statue is a genuine piece of sculpture, Shakespeare is
showing the superiority of nature over art. Quoting another critic, he
writes: 'Art has not defeated nature; nature has defeated art.'[47] Kiernan
agrees. Dealing with the same scene she writes: ' "defective" nature is made
to triumph over painted image, when Shakespeare's "lawful" art exposes
the inadequacy of counterfeit art'.[48]

There are two problems with these readings of the play's finale. The
first concerns the categories that Faas and Kiernan appeal to; the second is
to do with the nature of dramatic illusion. Reading the statue scene in the
light of the debate between Polixenes and Perdita, both critics assume that
Shakespeare is dealing with some kind of competition between art and
nature. When Faas argues that Paulina's statue shows us nature defeating
art, he alludes again to Yeats' 'Sailing to Byzantium': 'the birds in the
trees, even though they are dying generations, are preferable to the birds
of hammered gold and gold enameling'.[49] But Yeats was talking in
metaphors. What tormented his sixty-year-old 'troubled heart' was not
whether metal birds are preferable to live ones, but the question of what to
do with his life: should he try to forget about the body with all its desires
and frustrations and devote himself to the life of the mind ('Choose Plato
and Plotinus for a friend'), or is the life of the senses (the 'horrible
splendour of desire') the only one worth living?[50] It's a theme that Yeats
returned to time and again in his later poetry.

Shakespeare too was writing metaphorically. But his subject was quite
different from Yeats'. When Renaissance humanists tell us that the
purpose of the arts is to repair the ruins of our first parents they aren't
asking us to choose between the life of the mind and the life of the body,
or at least only indirectly. They are suggesting that the liberal arts are
capable of inspiring in us what Peacham calls a 'love of humanity and
politic government'. Paulina's carefully stage-managed performance is
also about those things, not about whether 'the true voice of feeling' is
better than 'the false beauty proceeding from art', as Keats put it.[51] She
wants to make sure that Leontes' change of heart is permanent and that he
won't return to his old barbaric ways, so she puts him through the kind of

test that we've seen before in Shakespeare's romances: Duke Vincentio testing Isabella's charity when he pretends to disbelieve her story about Angelo's duplicity is one example; Rosalind asking Orlando, after she's tested his performance as a wooer and corrected some of his misconceptions about love, to believe that she can work miracles is another. Paulina's 'magic' is of a more serious kind than Rosalind's. She wants her statue to remind Leontes of his sins in the hope that the remorse aroused by such a moving experience will confirm his resolve to remain true to Hermione's memory. And the magical 'artistry' works. Reminded in such an extraordinary way of his long-dead wife, Leontes confesses:

> I am ashamed. Does not the stone rebuke me
> For being more stone than it? O royal piece!
> There's magic in thy majesty, which has
> My evils conjured to remembrance.
> (v.iii.37–40)

Orpheus was said to have tamed not just wild beasts, but even rocks and stones, with the magic of his song. Paulina is working with a heart whose stony cruelty has already been softened by penance. But her humanist magic completes the civilising of a barbarian. As an Orphic 'magician' she's concerned with conjuring remembrance, not with whether sculptures are better or worse than the things they imitate.

The second problem with Faas' and Kiernan's reading of the statue scene is to do with the question of dramatic illusion. Of course Paulina's statue is a deception. But then in one sense so is all art. It's not just a matter of illusionist painting deceiving the eye, or even of story writers asking us to believe in the existence of fictitious worlds. As Puttenham explains, figures of rhetoric themselves are

in a sort abuses or rather trespasses in speech, because they pass the ordinary limits of common utterance, and be occupied of purpose to deceive the ear and also the mind, drawing it from plainness and simplicity to a certain doubleness, whereby our talk is the more guileful and abusing, for what else is your *metaphor* but an inversion of sense by transport; your *allegory* by a duplicity of meaning or dissimulation under covert and dark intendments . . . and many other ways seeking to inveigle and appassionate the mind.[52]

The more skilful the rhetorician's 'trespasses', the more effective the persuasion. That's what Touchstone is talking about when he says, 'the truest poetry is the most / feigning' (*As You Like It*, iii.iii.16–17), meaning in one sense that the best poetry is that which imitates nature most skilfully, but in another sense that it's in the very nature of rhetoric to draw the mind 'from plainness and simplicity to a certain doubleness'. In a literal sense all drama is 'feigning'. What does the dramatist do but invite us to believe in actors pretending to be kings or knaves? But even as he asks us to suspend our disbelief and imagine that Richard Burbage is the Prince of Denmark, or Robert Armin a French court jester, Shakespeare reminds us that the insubstantial pageants of the stage are no more than illusions designed to 'inveigle and appassionate the mind'. This is what critics have agreed to call metadrama: Shakespeare is asking us to reflect on the power of theatrical illusion. The statue scene in *The Winter's Tale* may be unlike anything else in Shakespeare, but the fact that it involves illusion doesn't mean that art has in some way been 'defeated' by nature. Nor does it challenge those humanist ideas about the civilising power of the liberal arts that Shakespeare inherited from Renaissance Italy through critics like Puttenham and Sidney. If it challenges anything it's the primitivist belief in the essential goodness of humankind.

PRIMITIVISM

In *Shakespeare's Theory of Drama* Kiernan suggests that Perdita's innocent scepticism shows what a 'pointless exercise' it is to try to improve on nature.[53] Renaissance thinkers were divided on the question of whether or not nature was in need of improvement. But they didn't regard the matter as pointless. Indeed they believed that it was an issue of such fundamental importance that no attempt to plan a just society could begin until it had been resolved. One of the most important political documents to emerge from Tudor England was Starkey's *Dialogue Between Pole and Lupset*. Starkey's book was a radical proposal for a constitutional monarchy. Before setting out a solution to his country's problems Starkey, like Cicero before him, established certain basic truths about human nature (as Cicero said, if you want to explain the nature of justice, you must look for it 'in the nature of man' – see chapter 4, p. 83). For Starkey that involved disposing of the sentimental belief in natural virtue. The primitivist argument is put into the mouth of Pole. Pointing to the corruption in England's towns and cities, Pole argues that, since men lived more virtuously in the primitive world, it's clear that human beings are by nature unfitted for civic life:

if this be civil life and order to live in cities and towns with so much vice and misorder me seem man should not be born thereto, but rather to life in the wild forest, there more following the study of virtue, as it is said men did in the golden age wherein man lived according to his natural dignity.[54]

But Lupset replies that, if corruption is rife in the modern world, that's due not to the contaminating effect of civilisation, but to a flaw in human nature itself: 'the fault is neither in the cities nor towns neither in the laws ordained thereto, but it is in the malice of man, which abuseth and turneth that thing which might be to his wealth and felicity to his own destruction and misery'.[55] For Starkey the answer to England's social and political problems lies, not in a return to nature, but in effective government.

It's unlikely that Shakespeare would have read Starkey's *Dialogue*: fearing the king's reaction to his proposals for limiting the powers of the crown, Starkey sensibly decided not to publish his treatise. But Shakespeare would certainly have known More's *Utopia* with its similarly sceptical treatment of primitivist ideas (see chapter 1, p. 15). And like every other grammar-school educated Elizabethan, he would have been familiar with the myth that the rhetoric books told of the birth of civilisation from the liberal arts. How could people 'have been brought by any other means, to live together in fellowship of life, to maintain cities, to deal truly, and willingly obey one another, if men at the first had not by art and eloquence [been] persuaded [of] that which they full oft found out by reason?' asked Thomas Wilson in his *Arte of Rhetorique* (1560).[56] For Renaissance humanists the arts are not simply a decorative adjunct to courtly life; they are the basis of civilisation itself.

For the other side of the argument we know exactly what Shakespeare had been reading. Gonzalo's primitivist vision of an egalitarian utopia where men and women live virtuously in harmony with nature, with no laws and no governance (*The Tempest*, II.i.148–73), comes straight from Montaigne's essay 'the Caniballes'. For Montaigne the South American Indian is a living reproof of European civilisation. In our pride we call these people savages, says Montaigne; but in reality they are no more savage than the wild fruits that nature produces unaided. If anything, it's those plants that we have altered by selective propagation that should be called savage: 'in those [natural plants] are the true and most profitable virtues, and natural properties most lively and vigorous, which in these we have bastardised, applying them to the pleasure of our corrupted taste'.[57] Then, in the passage that Gonzalo echoes, Montaigne goes on to give an idealised picture, based partly on Ovid's account of the golden age, of a primitive community uncorrupted by the false values of civilisation.

Was Shakespeare signalling that he endorsed Montaigne's primitivism when he had Gonzalo quote from the 'Caniballes'? Jonathan Bate believes

that Gonzalo 'speaks conventional humanist wisdom'.[58] But a belief in
man's innate goodness has no part in conventional humanist thinking.[59]
Nor does the belief that 'Letters should not be known' (II.i.155). The
whole point of humanism's emphasis on the liberal arts was the belief that
they could help to reform our fallen nature. From the way this scene is
organised it seems unlikely that we are expected to endorse Gonzalo's
primitivist ideas. Like Jaques' speech on the seven ages of man, his
performance has the feel of a set piece; certainly it's something whose
phrases he has memorised. But he isn't allowed to deliver it uninter-
rupted. As he speaks, Antonio and Sebastian taunt him for his inconsist-
ency: though Gonzalo's commonwealth would have no rulers, 'Yet he
would be king on't', sneers Sebastian (II.i.162). You could argue that
Antonio and Sebastian represent the corruption of modern civilisation
that Montaigne was satirising. Dramatically, however, their interruptions
have the effect of puncturing an illusion, rather in the same way, though
less benignly, that Rosalind dispels Orlando's sentimental illusions about
love and marriage in *As You Like It*.

But it's Caliban who represents the strongest argument against a
primitivist reading of Shakespeare's tragicomedies. Since the mid 1970s
it's been generally accepted that Prospero is a coloniser who has appropriated Caliban's island and turned its owner into a slave in his own
territory.[60] (Caliban's rights of ownership of the island are by no means
clear: he himself is the second-generation son of an immigrant who
terrorised the native inhabitants of the island – 1.ii.258–94.) As I've argued
elsewhere, the colonialist reading of the play is an anachronism.[61] *The
Tempest* has a long and complex afterlife: in retrospect Prospero's treatment of Caliban might seem to suggest the mentality of a European
coloniser. But that's all. Whatever his views about savages – and for this
period they seem fairly enlightened – Prospero has no interest in colonis-
ing the island. In fact he can't wait to get away from it. To understand
Caliban's symbolic significance we need to ask how he fits into the play's
overall thematic design. *The Tempest* is not about commercial exploitation, or the founding of a new civilisation through subjugation of
indigenous peoples; it's about the patching up of an old one by peaceful
means. Like James I, Prospero has an ambitious scheme for uniting old
political enemies through diplomatic marriage. He is above all a peace-
maker. Offered by fate the opportunity to take revenge on his old
enemies, he chooses instead to forgive them.

But though political reconciliation is a central theme in *The Tempest*,
there's another lesson for Prospero in the events that led to his exile.

Prospero was ousted from his dukedom because, like Duke Vincentio in *Measure for Measure*, he was a negligent ruler. It was his naïve faith in humanity that 'awakened an evil nature' in his opportunistic brother (1.ii.93) and provided the chance for a coup. If, as *Julius Caesar* so vividly shows, politics is a dirty business, the successful ruler is one who has a healthy Machiavellian distrust of his fellow politicians. In *The Tempest* Shakespeare rebuts Montaigne's sentimental belief in natural virtue partly through parody (Gonzalo's vision of an ideal commonwealth) and partly by showing that in some men there seems to be a potential for evil that needs to be guarded against. But it's Caliban who represents his most emphatic rejection of Montaigne's primitivism.

Montaigne claimed that among his Brazilian Indians (whom he never actually met) there was 'ever perfect religion, perfect policy, perfect and complete use of all things'.[62] In other words they are noble savages. Caliban, by contrast, is spectacularly ignoble. He may have an ear for music (though so did Homer's sirens), but he's also smelly, treacherous, and as Miranda discovers to her cost, sexually rapacious. It's inevitable that later generations should compare this sort of representation of the pre-civilised world and its inhabitants with the attitudes of colonisers and slave owners; this is an inescapable part of the play's afterlife. But for Shakespeare Caliban is a symbol, not of exploitable commercial potential, but of the darker side of human nature. He is a reminder of why the modern world – that is, Shakespeare's world – needs effective government.

In *The Tempest* it's a benignly ineffectual courtier who puts the case for a primitivist view of human nature; in *The Winter's Tale* it's an innocent foundling. Perdita doesn't know that she's really a princess. Nor does she know that it was her own father's barbaric behaviour that has put her in such an anomalous position. It's that behaviour which gives the lie to her own belief in nature's goodness. If there had been some grounds for Leontes' storm of jealousy we might be inclined to sympathise with his injured feelings while deploring his actions. Though most of us no longer believe in the Old Testament principle of an eye for an eye, there is in most human societies a strong sense that the punishment should fit the crime: the greater the provocation, the more leniently we treat the criminal. It's the baselessness of Leontes' 'short madness' that's so unsettling. Just as Prospero's negligence seems to have 'awakened an evil nature' in his brother, it's as if spontaneously, in this civilised world of 'gifts, letters, loving embassies' (I.i.28), some dormant, atavistic evil has been stirred into life. Shakespeare invites us to read these opening scenes symbolically. In their infancy Leontes and Polixenes were so close that it's as if they belonged to a prelapsarian world of pastoral innocence:

> We were as twinned lambs that did frisk i' th' sun,
> And bleat the one at th' other. What we changed
> Was innocence for innocence. We knew not
> The doctrine of ill-doing, nor dreamed
> That any did.

But it would be self-deception to imagine that that pastoral idyll could continue; the golden age is no more than an ancestral memory. Polixenes goes on:

> Had we pursued that life,
> And our weak spirits ne'er been higher reared
> With stronger blood, we should have answered heaven
> Boldly, 'Not guilty', the imposition cleared
> Hereditary ours.
>
> (1.ii.69–77)

Hermione replies with courtly banter: 'By this we gather / You have tripped since' (77–8). But the implicit moral of Polixenes' story is more serious than she imagines. Within thirty-odd lines Leontes is beginning to show signs of a monstrous jealousy. It's perfectly understandable that, no longer believing in the reality of original sin, modern readers should want to look for a naturalistic cause for such cruelty in Leontes' psychological makeup. But Shakespeare belonged to a world where most people still believed in the literal truth of the Genesis story. Leontes' causeless jealousy is a symbolic reminder of the fact that, for all our civility, none of us is entirely exempt from the effects of that sin that is 'hereditary ours'.

When Perdita talks to Polixenes about art and nature she knows none of this. Like Montaigne, she feels that breeding exotic plants is like bastardising nature, and compares it with deceitful social behaviour. But though she hasn't consciously experienced nature's cruelty for herself, she unwittingly alludes to an archetypal example of that evil when she compares herself to the goddess whose rape was the cause and origin of nature's fall. Almost in the same breath that Perdita declares her maidenly trust in nature's goodness, she unconsciously reminds us of its darker side.

MENDING NATURE

Like *The Tempest*, *The Winter's Tale* deals with the theme of international relations and the reconciling of old differences through diplomatic

marriage. Some scholars think that the play was first performed as part of
the festivities that marked the investiture of James' elder son Henry as
Prince of Wales in 1610. Certainly the description of Mamillius as a
'gallant child' of 'greatest promise' (i.i.37–40) sounds like a pointed
allusion to Prince Henry. What Shakespeare couldn't have known when
he had Mamillius die in iii.ii was that Prince Henry, who was regarded by
his supporters as England's own 'greatest promise', was himself to die of a
mysterious fever two years later in 1612. In the following year his sister
Elizabeth married the Elector of the Palatinate. And we know that, as part
of the celebrations for this dynastic marriage, *The Winter's Tale* was
performed at court.

For all the topicality of its internationalist theme, *The Winter's Tale* is
not a *pièce à clef*. Shakespeare may be warning of the dangers of irresponsible rulers, but there's no reason to assume that this was a coded attack on
his own patron. The consequences of tyrannical rule is a familiar theme in
the comedies, histories and tragedies alike, and we have no evidence that
James took exception to any of the plays Shakespeare wrote after 1603.
Neither is *The Winter's Tale* a proto-romantic allegory about nature
triumphing over art. Still less is it a postmodern fable about a world of
de-centred creatures who are the product of social and ideological forces
that shape their entire beings. Like some behaviourist experiment from
the 1920s, it's almost as if Perdita's story is designed as a refutation of anti-
humanist theories about the infinite malleability of human nature. Growing up in a distant land among rural knaves and simpletons, Perdita
should, according to constructionist theory, have turned out to be indistinguishable from any other Bohemian Dorcas or Mopsa. In fact, she
retains, quite implausibly, all the natural graces of her royal birth. The
noble foundling who illustrates the overriding power of breeding by
'hiding royal blood in rural vein'[63] is a popular motif in this period.
Caliban's story also looks like a refutation of constructionist theory. John
Lee writes: 'It is hard to envision a situation of more crushing cultural
power, or a better dramatization of Foucault's sense that the birth of the
prison is a part of the history of the birth of the modern soul [than
Caliban's education under Prospero]. Yet Caliban grows up different,
unwilling to accept his culturally given identity.'[64]

The Winter's Tale is a tragicomedy about archetypal passions. Drawing
on a long tradition of Continental humanist writing, it suggests that,
although the potential for atavistic cruelty still seems to lurk in the
human psyche (though more in some people than others, and probably
more in men than in women), any propensity we may have for barbarous

behaviour can either be exacerbated or tamed by cultural influences. Humanists believed that, although you may not be able to change a person's fundamental nature (as Viola says, 'Such as we are made of, such we be' – *Twelfth Night*, II.ii.32), there are few who can't be improved by the arts of civilisation. Unique among the liberal arts is drama itself. Combining the 'magical' Orphic arts of music and story-telling, tragi-comedy holds the mirror up to our nature, showing us in stylised form both what we are, and what we are capable of becoming. At least that's what Shakespeare seems to be suggesting when he has Paulina tell Leontes 'it is required / You do awake your faith' (v.iii.94–5). There's no reason why Christian audiences shouldn't read an ulterior religious sense into these lines; but their primary meaning is an appeal to an 'erring barbarian' to believe that artists can do magical things. Metaphorically, it's a drama-tist's *apologia* for the benign power of theatrical illusion. These humanist ideas may have little to say to postmodern readers. But for the historicist part of the appeal of the past is its otherness: they do things differently there.

CHAPTER 6

Love and death

In no other Elizabethan play are love and death so closely intertwined. In his opening sonnet the Chorus of *Romeo and Juliet* tells us that the young couple's love has the mark of death on it (9). No sooner have the lovers met than they start thinking about death. That Romeo, as an aspiring Petrarchist, should have premonitions of 'untimely death' cutting short a 'despised life' (I.iv.110–11) is only to be expected: it goes with the role. As Mercutio puts it, 'Alas, poor Romeo, he is already dead: stabb'd with a white wench's black eye' (II.iv.13–14). But Juliet too is preoccupied with death. At first she wonders how she will cope if it should turn out that Romeo isn't free: 'If he be married, / My grave is like to be my wedding bed', she tells her Nurse (I.v.132–3). When she learns that Romeo is a Montague it seems as if the old Petrarchan conceit about the dear enemy has come horribly true:

> My only love sprung from my only hate!
> Too early seen unknown, and known too late!
> Prodigious birth of love it is to me,
> That I must love a loathed enemy.
>
> (I.v.136–9)

Surprised to hear Juliet talking in Petrarchan couplets, the Nurse asks her what's going on. Juliet admits that it's something she's picked up from Romeo: 'A rhyme,' she says, 'I learnt even now / Of one I danc'd withal' (140–1). Part of the ironic scheme of *Romeo and Juliet* is the way conceits seem to have a habit of coming true. When Juliet hears the news of Tybalt's death and Romeo's banishment, her double grief seems too much to bear: 'I'll to my wedding-bed; / And death, not Romeo, take my maidenhead' (III.iii.136–7). But when Romeo leaves her for Mantua it's his life that she worries about:

> O God, I have an ill-divining soul!
> Methinks I see thee, now thou art below,
> As one dead in the bottom of a tomb;
>
> (III.v.54–6)

108

As events draw towards their conclusion, the theme of untimely death is embroidered with increasingly fantastic imagery. 'Death lies upon her like an untimely frost, / Upon the sweetest flower of all the field', says Capulet over her apparently lifeless body. And then picking up Juliet's earlier image of the coffin-as-marriage-bed, he tells Paris, in a piece of grotesque metaphysical whimsy, that his place in the bridal bed has been usurped by a rival:

> O son, the night before thy wedding day
> Hath Death lain with thy wife. There she lies,
> Flower as she was, deflowered by him.
> Death is my son-in-law, Death is my heir;
> My daughter he hath wedded;
>
> (IV.v.35–9)

In the final scene Capulet's image of death as ravisher is in turn picked up and developed by Romeo. Finding Juliet as if asleep in a 'womb of death' (V.iii.45), he marvels at her life-like beauty, imagining that death, like an incubus, has sucked out her soul leaving her unmarked body for its own pleasures:

> Ah, dear Juliet,
> Why art thou so fair? Shall I believe
> That insubstantial Death is amorous,
> And that the lean abhorred monster keeps
> Thee here in dark to be his paramour?
>
> (101–5)

Death is a constant presence in *Romeo and Juliet* and the subject of its most inventive imagery. Traditionally the play has been seen as a story of youthful love tragically blighted either by fortune, or by irresponsible parents, or even by the lovers' own folly. But for postmodern readers the play's interlinking of love and death has an even darker meaning. Postmodernists question the very existence of romantic love, seeing it not as a universal human emotion that leaves people – young women in particular – vulnerable to exploitation, but as one of ideology's most successful confidence tricks.

AMOROUS DEATH

In *Tales of Love* Julia Kristeva argues that the intense feelings that Romeo and Juliet have for each other could never survive the bourgeois institution of marriage; the only way to preserve such passion is to immortalise it in death. But, she explains, it's not love that drives them towards the grave. Noting that Juliet herself frankly states that 'My only love [is] sprung from my only hate' (1.v.136), she argues that the real key to Romeo's and Juliet's passion is hatred. What they really desire is each other's death: 'hatred is the keynote of the couple's passionate melody'.[1] It's true that Juliet says 'I must love a loathed enemy.' But Kristeva omits to quote the immediately preceding lines, which make it clear that Juliet's exclamation is in response to the news that her Nurse has just given her about her lover's family: 'His name is Romeo, and a Montague; / The only son of your great enemy' (134–5). Unless you are looking for subconscious meanings – in which case you can make her words mean pretty much whatever you like – Juliet's intention couldn't be plainer: she's in love with Romeo, but their families are at loggerheads, thus making him a 'loathed enemy' in her *parents'* eyes (139). The whole point of her remark, or rather the way she makes it, is that it's a Petrarchan conceit that's somehow become a metaphoric reality; or to put it another way, it's a conceit that relies for its point on the transformation of another conceit. When literary lovers talk about the 'dear enemy' and complain about 'living deaths, dear wounds, fair storms and freezing fires',[2] they're referring to the combination of irresistible beauty and icy indifference that, according to the rules of the game, is supposed to characterise all true Petrarchan mistresses. But this isn't a Petrarchan relationship. Being in love with the son of your father's enemy is *like* being a Petrarchan lover who finds himself irresistibly drawn to a cruel mistress, which in turn is *like* being buffeted by 'fair storms' or tortured by 'freezing fires'. To assume that Juliet literally loathes her lover is to turn an elegantly stylised double conceit into a rather crude, and wildly inappropriate, statement of fact.

Amplifying her argument, Kristeva quotes the marvellous lines from III.ii in which Juliet anticipates the sensual joys of her marriage night (though for some reason Kristeva prints them as prose). As she thinks about the pleasures to come, Juliet weaves a series of conceits round the idea of 'love-performing night': she asks night to draw her curtain so that prying eyes won't see Romeo coming to her; she says lovers don't need light 'to do their amorous rites' since their own beauties are illumination enough; she sweetly asks 'civil night' to teach her how to lose the game of love she is about to play for her virginity; and she asks night to hide their blushes until, their embarrassment overcome, the act of true love will seem like 'simple modesty'. Then, in the lines quoted by Kristeva, she creates a charming conceit about how she imagines Romeo might one day be immortalised as a constellation:

Come, gentle night, come, loving black-brow'd night,
Give me my Romeo; and, when he shall die,
take him and cut him out in little stars,
and he will make the face of heaven so fine
That all the world will be in love with night,
And pay no worship to the garish sun.

(17–25)

The ironic allusion to Ovid's story of the stellification of Julius Caesar following the assassination (*Metamorphoses*, xv. 843–51) is no doubt unconscious on Juliet's part. For all its stylisation, the effect of her conceit, like the rest of the speech, is paradoxically one of artless candour. In *The Spanish Tragedy* Kyd created a brilliantly convincing (and equally stylised) portrait of sensuality combined with ruthlessness in the character of Bel-imperia. But no other writer in this period ever evoked such a delicate sense of 'true love acted [with] simple modesty'. But that's not the way Kristeva reads these lines. For her there's something 'infernal' in Juliet's supplication to night; her love has a 'sombre blindness' about it; her desire is 'closely umbilicated' with death. In imagining Romeo immortalised in the night sky for all lovers to marvel at, Juliet is in reality expressing 'her unconscious desire to break up Romeo's body'.[3] Under the misleadingly tender surface of this scene the real emotion is hatred, says Kristeva, 'a hatred that antedates the veil of amorous idealization'. The true pleasure that Juliet anticipates is the orgasmic prospect of Romeo's death.[4]

Kristeva's postmodern reading of *Romeo and Juliet* owes much to Denis de Rougemont's *Love in the Western World*, first published in 1939. De Rougemont's interpretation of medieval myth is compelling, and Kristeva is not the only postmodernist to have been inspired by it. It's a story that's worth retelling. Comparing Shakespeare's play with the Tristan and Iseult story, he argued that what *Romeo and Juliet* is really about is not tragic waste, but the desire for death. The Tristan story exists in many versions, but at the centre of them all is a passion that's hopeless because it's forbidden. De Rougemont describes the story as the 'one great myth of European adultery'.[5] Commanded by his uncle, King Mark of Cornwall, to bring Iseult back from Ireland to be his bride, Tristan inevitably falls in love with her himself, and she with him. But it's no ordinary love that binds them. Through an irony of fate Tristan and Iseult drink a love potion that Iseult's mother has prepared for her daughter and King Mark. Bound together by a magic that neither of them can undo, Tristan and Iseult are condemned to a life of torment. Even their death is

dogged by tragic irony. As he lies dying of a poisoned wound, Tristan –
now married to the daughter of the Duke of Brittany – sends a ship to
Cornwall pleading with Iseult to be with him at the end. He arranges, like
Theseus in the Minotaur story, that if she agrees to come, the sails of the
returning ship will be white; if she refuses, they will be black. In her
jealousy, Tristan's wife, ironically also called Iseult (he only marries her
for her name), tells him that the sails are black, and so with broken heart
he dies. Iseult arrives too late and finding her lover dead, also dies. As if to
mark such exceptional love, a miracle occurs: out of their graves spring
two intertwined trees as a symbol of their perpetual union.

In an argument that seems to have been inspired by Johann Huizinga's
Waning of the Middle Ages, de Rougemont says that the whole point of the
Tristan story is its exquisite anguish. In no ordinary story, and certainly in
no story of happy love, would it be possible to sustain such intensity of
passion. Imagine what would have happened if they had actually been
able to marry. Iseult would have become Mme Tristan, and their passion
would have subsided into mundane domesticity.[6] For passion to survive
you need insurmountable obstacles. If the external obstacles are insuffi-
cient, then you have to invent new ones. By marrying Iseult of the White
Hands, Tristan makes himself permanently unavailable to the other
Iseult. In so doing he ensures that the passion that would have died had
they somehow been able to marry is indefinitely prolonged. Linked in a
cruel covenant from which neither can escape, Tristan and Iseult suffer a
mutual torment that's almost indistinguishable from hatred. 'At times',
says de Rougemont, 'there pierces through their excessive passion a kind
of hatred of the beloved.'[7] Eventually the need for obstacles becomes an
end in itself, and the passion that had originally been their *raison d'être*
now serves the ultimate obstacle – death itself:

Unawares and in spite of themselves, the lovers have never had but one desire –
the desire for death! . . . In the innermost recesses of their hearts they have been
obeying the fatal dictates of a wish for death; they have been in the throes of the
active passion of Darkness.[8]

De Rougemont's analysis of the Tristan story is thrillingly transgressive
of all our tidy middle-class ideas about marriage and families. It's also
frankly élitist. Like Aldous Huxley's Savage (*Brave New World* was
published in 1932), Tristan and Iseult evince a 'noble purity' in their
suffering that's unattainable by the masses; unlike the bourgeoisie with
their 'picture-postcard idyll' of marriage, theirs is 'a privileged mode of
understanding' that sets them apart as superior beings. For de Rougemont

this is why medieval chivalric romance is so important: it embodies, as no other genre has done, the truth about the need – at least of those superior spirits who are capable of experiencing it – for a passion so intense that it transcends the need for happiness, or even life itself:

The outstanding find made by European poets, what distinguishes them first and foremost among the writers of the world, what most profoundly expressed the European obsession by suffering as a way to understanding, is the secret of the Tristan myth; passionate love at once shared and fought against, anxious for a happiness it rejects, and magnified in its own disaster – *unhappy mutual love.*[9]

And this, according to de Rougemont, is the great truth that Shakespeare expresses in *Romeo and Juliet.* His characters too are united in a hopeless passion; they too are kept apart by obstacles beyond their control; they too seem to be obsessed with death. In fact, says de Rougemont, Shakespeare's play is the last great resuscitation of the myth before Wagner's *Tristan und Isolde*:

Sprung out of the depths of a spirit avid of transfiguring torments, out of the abysmal night in which the lightning flash of love plays now and then on features motionless and fascinating . . . resurrected all of a sudden in its full stature, as though stunned by its provocative youth and drunk with rhetoric, on the threshold of the Mantuan tomb [Verona, actually] here once again the myth stands forth in the glow of a torch which is being held aloft by Romeo.[10]

De Rougemont's rhetoric is stirring, but there are a number of flaws in his argument. First, and most obvious, is the fact that, unlike Tristan and Iseult, Romeo and Juliet are not adulterers; by Act III they are married. If the Tristan story is the 'one great myth of European adultery' it's puzzling to hear it claimed that a tale of married love that goes tragically wrong is a revival of this myth. Second, although Romeo and Juliet do face obstacles to their love, there's a strong sense in the final scene that with patience and diplomacy their parents' opposition could have been overcome: the play concludes, not with a magical tree symbolising the irresolvable mystery of adulterous passion, but with an exchange of gifts: Capulet gives Montague the dowry that would have been Juliet's, and Montague reciprocates with a statue to a young woman who would have been a 'true and faithful' wife (v.iii.295–301). Third, Romeo and Juliet don't create obstacles; they do their best to overcome them, often against the advice of others. Fourth, while it's true that the couple are certainly preoccupied with death, they seek it only as a desperate alternative to the prospect of life without their marriage partner. De Rougemont claims that in the Tristan story 'the approach of death acts as a goad to sensuality'.[11] Romeo, by contrast, talks of death as a 'love-devouring' annihilator of all that matters to him (II. vi.7), while Juliet sees it as a hopeless last resort: 'If all else fail, myself have power to die' (III.v.243). Finally, de Rougemont takes no account of the huge difference in sensibility and technique that separates *Romeo and Juliet* from the world of Old French romance. The twelfth-century poem on which de Rougemont largely based his interpretation, is a magical story. But the success of the *Roman de Tristran* depends largely on Béroul's gift for narrative and his wonderful eye for detail (as for example, when King Mark, finding Tristan and Iseult sleeping in the forest with a naked sword between them, is able so easily to remove Iseult's ring while she sleeps because her finger has now grown thin with care and suffering).[12] Béroul's characters are, as de Rougemont rightly says, 'depicted physically and psychologically in an entirely conventional manner. He is "the strongest"; she, "the most beautiful", he, the knight; she, the princess; and so on. It is impossible to believe that any human feeling can grow between such rudimentary characters.'[13] In complete contrast, the remarkable thing about *Romeo and Juliet* is the illusion that Shakespeare creates of real people who have inner lives. Romeo's Petrarchisms are not simply the formal register of an early tragedy, comparable with the heroic couplets that everyone speaks in a Dryden tragedy. Petrarchism, as I'll explain below, is partly a way of characterising an adolescent egotism that causes Romeo's friends much amusement, and partly a device for satirising a particular kind of intellectual affectation that was popular in some circles in the 1580s and 1590s. In the absence of any analysis by de Rougemont of the text itself, it has to be concluded that his reading of the play doesn't stand up to critical scrutiny.

Just as E. M. W. Tillyard, once the standard authority on Shakespeare's Histories, was long ago superseded by more modern criticism, so de Rougemont is no longer cited by medievalists as an authority on Old French literature.[14] But neither the obvious flaws in his argument, nor his frank élitism, concerned Kristeva: her reading of the play was essentially a reworking of his argument. Jonathan Dollimore also cites de Rougemont in a discussion of *Romeo and Juliet*, agreeing with Kristeva that death is the lovers' true goal: 'death', he argues, 'does not so much defeat desire as emerge from within it, as the dynamic of desire itself; as love, or rather death, at first sight'.[15] But where Kristeva reads the play as an adolescent psychodrama, Dollimore believes that *Romeo and Juliet* is an adult's (presumably Shakespeare's) fantasy about what he calls the 'erotics of death'. This fantasy has two elements. The first is a 'desire' for the death of a child so that it will be exempted from the tyranny of time. So when

Capulet, weeping over the apparently lifeless body of his daughter, cries
'Death lies upon her like an untimely frost, / Upon the sweetest flower of
all the field', he is apparently experiencing a mixture of grief and attrac-
tion: 'hence that desiring gaze'. According to Dollimore, Capulet *desires*
his daughter's death almost as a kind of consummation because 'death
arrests beauty: transience, decay, decline . . . are averted in and through
death'.[16] It's true that people derive genuine consolation from the kitsch
that's an indispensable part of our own funeral culture, a taste that's
reflected in the long history of sentimental productions of *Romeo and
Juliet* from Garrick to Zeffirelli,[17] including most recently Luhrmann's
treatment of the death scene in *William Shakespeare's Romeo and Juliet*.
No doubt the bunches of flowers, often accompanied by cards inscribed
with mottos like 'Die young stay pretty', that appear at roadsides to mark
the deaths of teenage traffic-accident victims offer similar consolation. But
it's one thing to acknowledge that many people find relief in a sentimental
escape from reality, and quite another to suggest that the parents who
suffer such loss find a paradoxical pleasure in the death itself. That's an
argument that's unlikely to impress those who have actually watched a
child die, and belongs more to the kitsch-world of *Peter Pan* than to
Shakespeare.

The second element of the fantasy that Dollimore believes is enacted in
Romeo and Juliet is the excitement that adults are said to derive from
observing adolescent sexuality. This part of his argument has no element
of kitsch about it. Critics have often accused Romeo of immaturity in the
way he switches his attentions so easily from Rosaline to Juliet. But
Dollimore argues that, far from being a mark of his adolescence, Romeo's
'mobile', 'compulsive' sexuality, is a sign of maturity. Desire, for Romeo,
'is a serious business, a state of lack which, if not exactly indifferent as to
its objects, is prepared to substitute and replace them with that incon-
stancy which "true" love always disavows but never avoids. There is no
distinction here between true and false, mature and adolescent love.'[18]
The surprising thing about Dollimore's argument is not his frank approval of what the Fox TV network calls 'Adultman' values, but the fact
that he treats Shakespeare's characters as if they were sexual automata in
a pornographic novel. 'Mobile' sex is a familiar enough motif in both
pulp pornography and art novels. But while 'compulsive repetition', as
Dollimore calls it, may be fun to do, it's highly tedious to read about,
unless the writer's characters also exist in another dimension beyond the
sexual. The reason why a book like *My Secret Life* palls so quickly when
another, like *The Swimming Pool Library* (or more recently *The Line of*

Beauty) makes compelling reading is that 'Walter' is incapable of bringing his one-dimensional characters to life, while Alan Hollinghurst has a true novelist's ability to create the illusion of inner depth, and a life beyond the bedroom where people are capable of giving each other emotional pleasure and pain. In *An Anthropologist on Mars* Oliver Sacks recalls a conversation with the autistic writer Temple Grandin about her interest in science-fiction soap:

'I can really relate to Data', she said as we drove away from the farm. She is a *Star Trek* fan, as I am, and her favourite character is Data, an android who, for all his emotionlessness, has a great curiosity, a wistfulness, about being human. He observes human behaviour minutely, and sometimes impersonates it, but longs, above all to *be* human. A surprising number of people with autism identify with Data, or his predecessor, Mr Spock.[19]

Only in the strange world of literary postmodernism, with its de-centred human beings who lack inner selves and are incapable of communicating with each other, would anyone think of taking such complex, fully realised characters from a Renaissance play, reducing them to sexual androids, and then writing appreciatively about their very *absence* of humanising qualities.

NEW INVENTIONISM

Common to Kristeva's and Dollimore's readings of *Romeo and Juliet* is an indifference to the play's intellectual context. Their main concern is to reveal the power of ideology in constructing us as its subjects. If human beings are the product of historically specific discourses, that means that even our seemingly most instinctive drives and passions are in reality social artefacts. What, for example, could be more natural or more universal than maternal love? Or so we imagine. In the 1970s and 1980s it was fashionable to argue that, like all our other emotions, maternal love is a socially constructed phenomenon that's present in some societies and not in others. In *Centuries of Childhood*, first published in 1960 as *L'Enfant et la vie familiale sous l'Ancien régime*, Philippe Ariès (who wasn't a medievalist) claimed that in the Middle Ages the idea of childhood simply didn't exist; not until the seventeenth century did people start thinking of childhood as a distinct phase of human development.[20] Building on Ariès' speculative ideas about medieval childhood, Lawrence Stone argued in his enormously influential *The Family, Sex and Marriage* (1977) that, because children weren't really seen as individuals in Shakespeare's England, people didn't go in for parental affection: 'the family was an open-ended, low-keyed, unemotional, authoritarian institution which served certain essential political, economic, sexual, procreative and nurturant purposes'. At a time when infant death was an all-too-familiar experience, emotional investment in children was thought to be 'imprudent'; maternal 'love' only developed when social conditions made it viable.[21]

Similar claims were made about romantic love and homosexuality. The idea that romantic love was an historical invention goes back at least as far as the 1930s. Medievalists argued that, far from being a universal human experience, romantic love had a specific origin in the aristocratic courts of eleventh-century Provence.[22] But it was Michel Foucault who extended these arguments to sexuality in general, claiming that the way we think and behave as sexual beings has got nothing to do with our biological nature; rather it's an effect of power. Sexuality, for Foucault, is the product of those discourses through which the state constructs us as disciplinary subjects and ensures that we internalise social norms. By fabricating sexuality the state provides itself with justification for the exercise of ever tighter social control (see chapter 4, p. 73). Romantic love is one form of sexuality that has been fabricated by 'the state'; homosexuality is another (according to Foucault, the idea of homosexuality was invented in 1870).[23]

In recent years these new-inventionist arguments have been challenged by revisionist scholars working in a number of disciplines. Medievalists who have made specialist studies of the family now believe that maternal affection 'exists as far back in time and as widely in space as there are proper sources to document it';[24] anthropologists have concluded from studies of rich and poor, rural and metropolitan communities from Australia to Zambia that the anguish of young love – what Pope calls the 'craving void left aching in the breast' (*Eloisa to Abelard*, 94) – is not an invention of Western leisured classes, but a perennial human experience;[25] gay historians have shown that the new-inventionist belief that a sexual practice can only exist in a culture if that culture has a language for it is not borne out by historical evidence (and, moreover, gives support to the homophobic argument that society has no obligation to grant civil rights to those who choose to pursue a lifestyle that queer theorists themselves claim has no basis in nature).[26]

POOR PETRARCH'S LONG DECEASÈD WOES

Postmodern readings of *Romeo and Juliet* like Kristeva's and Dollimore's aim to expose the relentless grip that ideology has on our minds. What looks superficially like a young woman's vulnerability in a world of irresponsible parents and impulsive young men is really a story about her susceptibility to bourgeois discourse. She imagines that what she's experiencing is romantic love; in reality it's the aggression that, according to Lacan, is the ruling emotion in our psychic life.[27] What these presentist readings don't tell us is how Shakespeare's contemporaries might have responded to the play's satire. To recover some of the meanings that *Romeo and Juliet* may have had for an Elizabethan audience we need to reconstruct a literary discourse that was familiar enough to literate Elizabethans, but that's largely lost on the modern playgoer. The language of heroic love might seem arcane to most of us, but as historians know, the heroic ideal was a politically sensitive topic in the 1590s;[28] indeed it was one that filled Erasmian humanists with alarm. I'll return to this question at the end of the chapter.

For Elizabethan poets the dominant discourse for writing about love and death, and the link between them, was Petrarchism. That link was usually treated as an elaborate literary game. In *The Apparition* Donne's speaker tries to win round a cruel mistress by threatening to haunt her as a ghost after she has killed him with her disdain. Critics used to talk about Donne's grim realism as he evokes 'the cold rage of thwarted lust'.[29] But as Donald Guss showed so brilliantly many years ago, there's nothing particularly personal about *The Apparition*; the poem is a reworking of a long tradition of Petrarchan lyrics in which the scorned lover gets his revenge by returning to haunt the disdainful mistress.[30] Nor does Donne's poem ask us to ponder any profound truths. It's merely an elegant literary joke that depends for its effect on knowledge of the *topos* that it so wittily adapts. The poem is imitation at its most sophisticated. *Romeo and Juliet* also requires of its audience a good knowledge of Petrarchan commonplaces to appreciate the clever tricks that it plays with conventional formulae. But Petrarchism wasn't a single, unified phenomenon. By Shakespeare's time it already had a two-hundred-year history and meant different things – in some cases diametrically opposite things – to different people.[31]

There could hardly be a greater contrast of sensibilities than that between Petrarch himself and his most notorious imitator in Elizabethan England, Giordano Bruno (I'll discuss him later). Petrarch wrote the *Rime sparse* and the *Trionfi* over a number of years between the 1330s and the 1370s, continuing to revise the *Rime* until his death in 1374. This means that even the last of the poems were written half a century before a reliable text of Plato's *Symposium* was available in Florence.[32] The timing is significant. Despite the much-quoted lines from the envoy to his epic poem *Africa*, in which the great humanist looks forward to a new enlightened age of artistic accomplishment informed by the spirit of classical antiquity (see chapter 1, p. 20), there's no trace in Petrarch of that boundless belief in human perfectibility typical of Florentine neo-Platonism. The great theme of both the *Rime* and the *Trionfi* is the transience of earthly pleasures, and the need for philosophic resignation. 'O time,' he writes in the beautiful sonnet 355, 'O revolving heavens that fleeing deceive us blind and wretched mortals, O days more swift than wind or arrows! Now through experience I understand your frauds.'[33] Though Petrarch learns to reject his youthful infatuation, there's no sense that the changing course of his love can lead to an ennoblement of his own spirit. With greying hair and his passion gone, Petrarch longs for death because it will put an end to the long years of sadness and enable him to see his beloved Laura once more. In *The Triumph of Time* he paradoxically says how much better it is to die young:

> O therefore, I say, how blind are they thereto
> That think it much better for to die in age
> Than lying in the cradle to go that passage!
> To how many men had it been far passing better,
> Yea, and I affirm it a thousand times more sweeter,
> To have died being young than to have died old?[34]

But his preoccupation with mortality has nothing to do with de Rougemont's 'active passion of Darkness' or Dollimore's 'erotics of death'; if Petrarch longs for release from the torments of this life it's because he recognises that the spiritual world is the only true reality. When Laura appears to him in a dream on the night following her death, he asks whether she is alive or dead. Her reply is 'I am alive . . . And thou art dead (and so still shall be) / Till that the last hour that taketh thee / From the earth'.[35] Both in the *Rime* and the *Trionfi*, Petrarch learns as he grows older that, if Laura now returns his love, it's because he has at last understood that true love has no part in the world of the senses.

It's one of the ironies of literary history that such deeply serious meditative poems should have inspired so much literary frivolity. Poems like *The Apparition* owe their inspiration, however, not to Petrarch himself, but to fifteenth- and sixteenth-century imitators like Serafino and Guarino with their 'fantastic arguments, emotional extravagance, and peregrine comparisons'.[36] Romeo's conceits also belong to this tradition of what Guss calls 'extravagant Petrarchism'.

THE SIEGE OF LOVING TERMS

For Benvolio and Mercutio, Romeo's Petrarchisms are something of a standing joke. Romeo makes his first entrance a few moments after Prince Escalus has broken up the street fight between Benvolio and Tybalt in 1.i. 'What fray was here?' Romeo asks Benvolio, and then answering his own question, says, 'Yet tell me not, for I have heard it all.' The speech that follows, in which he compares love with fighting, is a compendium of Petrarchan clichés:

> Why then, O brawling love! O loving hate!
> O anything, of nothing first create!
> O heavy lightness! serious vanity!
> Mis-shapen chaos of well-seeming forms!
> Feather of lead, bright smoke, cold fire, sick health!
> Still-waking sleep, that is not what it is!
> This love feel I, that feel no love in this.
>
> (1.i.172–81)

After this barrage of hackneyed oxymorons it's not surprising that Benvolio's response to Romeo's question 'Dost thou not laugh?' is a weary 'No, coz, I rather weep . . . At thy good heart's oppression' (181–2). But Romeo is impervious to irony. Taking his cousin's words literally, he reads him another lecture on the nature of love:

> Love is a smoke rais'd with the fume of sighs;
> Being purg'd, a fire sparkling in lovers' eyes;
> Being vex'd, a sea nourish'd with loving tears.
> What is it else? A madness most discreet,
> A choking gall, and a preserving sweet.
>
> (188–92)

All this pseudo-literary anguish is occasioned by a young woman called Rosaline who clearly doesn't care for Romeo's style of wooing: 'She will not stay the siege of loving terms', he complains, 'Nor bide th' encounter of assailling eyes' (210–11). Happily for Rosaline the siege is soon at an end. After the Capulet ball Romeo transfers his undying affections – and his Petrarchan rhetoric – to Juliet. Wandering about in Capulet's orchard trying to catch a glimpse of his new beloved, he runs through some of the standard lines in the Petrarchist's repertoire, much as a musician might warm up with some arpeggios before an important performance. Thus, to the Petrarchan neophyte it's unthinkable that the light shining from

Juliet's window could be just an ordinary candle; it must be the first light of dawn and Juliet the rising sun. Her radiance naturally outshines the moon, so if the moon looks a bit off colour ('sick, and green') that's only to be expected: she's envious to see her own beauty eclipsed by Juliet's. Equally obvious is the reason why two stars in the night sky seem to look unusually bright: it's because they needed a break and asked Juliet's eyes to take their place until they got back. And of course no litany of Petrarchan conceits would be complete without the old one about being a glove on your lady's hand so that you can be pressed against her cheek without her noticing (II.ii.2–25).

Benvolio and Mercutio have heard all this kind of thing before and aren't impressed. 'Romeo! humours! passion! lover!' shouts Mercutio as he and Benvolio hunt their young innamorato in the darkness of the orchard, 'Appear thou in the likeness of a sigh; / Speak but one rhyme and I am satisfied; / Cry but "Ay me!" pronounce but "love" and "dove" ' (II.i.7–10). But there's no reply. 'The ape is dead,' says Mercutio (16). Benvolio and Mercutio are men of the world and are not unduly troubled when they can't find Romeo: 'Now will he sit under a medlar tree, / And wish his mistress were that kind of fruit / As maids call medlars when they laugh alone', says Mercutio in a conceit that's rather less genteel than those favoured by Romeo. Juliet, by contrast, is young and inexperienced. Unlike these men-about-town, she doesn't know that, according to the rules of the game that Romeo is playing, you are meant to be cold and aloof when your lover reveals his wounded heart, and that you're supposed to freeze the flames of his passion with your icy disdain. Instead she tells him she's in love and asks him if he loves her. At first Romeo doesn't realise that she's not playing his game. 'Lady, by yonder blessed moon I vow,/That tips with silver all these fruit trees tops . . . ', he begins. But she cuts him off, telling him that oaths aren't necessary, especially oaths about the inconstant moon. All that matters is that they love each other (107–15). Such simplicity is touching. But it's also very dangerous in a world where young men think nothing of killing for the sake of family honour; where parents are little better than quarreling children; where duennas are good for comic relief and little else; and where 'women, being the weaker vessels, are ever thrust to the wall' (I.i.15). Small wonder that the play is full of premonitions of disaster. Beginning as a playful burlesque on Petrarchan manners, the play modulates into a tragic satire on heroic love. Heroic love is a bizarre concept. Its chief exponent in Elizabethan England was Giordano Bruno.

AMOR HEROYCUS

Bruno is best known for two things: his theory of the infinite universe, and the fact that he was burnt alive in Rome in 1600 for his heretical views. Between 1583 and 1585 Bruno was in England where he wrote several philosophical treatises (including the *De l'infinito universo e mondi*), and made a number of enemies. He used to be thought of as an otherworldly intellectual, too preoccupied with the life of the mind to concern himself with anything as mundane as human relations.[37] From John Bossy's book on *The Embassy Affair*, however, he emerges as a skilful and ruthlessly professional secret agent (Bossy claims that, while Bruno was staying with Michel de Castelnau, the French ambassador in London, he helped to bring down the Earl of Throckmorton, who was executed in May 1584 on a charge of plotting a Catholic invasion).[38] While working to destroy Throckmorton's reputation, Bruno was busy building his own. His plan did not go quite the way he intended. Asked in the summer of 1583 to lecture in Oxford,[39] he invited his academic audience to abandon their blinkered pedantry and attend to the wisdom of a magus. Though no text survives of the lectures, the following passage from his *Cena de le Ceneri* (1584) gives some idea of the way Bruno attempted to win over his listeners:

Behold now, standing before you, the man who has pierced the air and penetrated the sky, wended his way amongst the stars and overpassed the margins of the world, who has broken down those imaginary divisions between spheres . . . which are described in the false mathematics of blind and popular philosophy. By the light of reason, with the key of most diligent enquiry, he has thrown wide those doors of truth which it is within our power to open and stripped the veils and coverings of nature. He has given eyes to blind moles, and illuminated those who could not see their own image in the innumerable mirrors of reality which surround them on every side . . . (and so on).[40]

The Oxford doctors weren't impressed. Their displeasure at the arrogance of their egotistical and opinionated visitor was not appeased when it turned out that a substantial part of his first lecture was plagiarised verbatim from Ficino.[41]

The hostility of the Oxford faculty towards Bruno wasn't simply a matter of style. Bruno represented everything that post-Erasmian classical humanism deplored. Rejecting medieval Aristotelian metaphysics, humanism was inspired by an ideal of *humanitas* based on scrupulous scholarship and the recovery of classical texts.[42] But for Hermetic neo-Platonists, a revived metaphysics based partly on the work of the pre-Socratic Hermes Trismegistus (actually written in the second and third centuries A D) was the key to a divine understanding of the universe. When Bruno spoke in the *Cena de le Ceneri* of penetrating the sky and breaking down the imaginary divisions between the spheres, he was echoing Ficino's belief in the power of sympathetic magic to liberate man from the material world and endow him with divine knowledge. As Frances Yates put it, a man like Bruno couldn't fail to arouse violent reactions in Oxford; his whole philosophy was 'madly impossible in a Protestant country that had been through the Erasmian reform'.[43]

Oxford may have regarded Bruno as an intellectual charlatan (as it has since done with other visiting European intellectual gurus), but the cool reception he received there didn't dampen his missionary zeal. Two years later he wrote a treatise on love in which he once again presented himself as an inspired hierophant, heroically striving to release the human spirit from its mental shackles. 'Those who can praise themselves by the laurel,' he wrote in the *De gli eroici furori*, 'are those who sing worthily of heroic things, who instruct heroic souls through speculative and moral philosophy.'[44] The *Eroici furori* belongs to a long tradition of Italian love treatises going back to Dante in which the writer provides commentaries on a selection of his own poems.[45] To anyone familiar with Romeo's penchant for oxymorons, the following example of Bruno's amatory style will be immediately recognisable even in translation:

Ah, what a condition, what a nature, or what a destiny is mine! I endure a living death, and a dead life! Ah me! Love has killed me by such a death, so that I am deprived of both life and death.[46]

Like Petrarch's *Rime sparse*, the poems in the *Eroici furori* have a philosophic meaning. Both collections are in effect allegories of the soul's progress. But they move in opposite directions. With Petrarch's recognition of the folly of his youthful passion, comes a growing sense of his own unworthiness; Bruno, inspired by a neo-Platonic belief in the soul's perfectibility, sees the lover's passions as a mark of his noble nature. And where Petrarch refers to the consummately beautiful *canzoniere* simply as *Rime sparse*, or scattered verses, Bruno gives his second-rate sonnets the grandiose title of *Heroic Frenzies*.

The idea that poets and lovers are the victims of an inspired frenzy derives from Plato's *Phaedrus* (245B) and *Ion* (534B–E). Its appeal in Elizabethan England was limited. George Chapman was one of the few poets who seems to have taken it seriously. But though it wasn't widely adopted, the idea of *furor poeticus* was sufficiently commonplace in

Renaissance poetics for poets to be able to joke about it (see chapter 8, p. 168). Sidney mocks it in *Astrophil and Stella* (74) while Shakespeare has fun with the same ideas in *A Midsummer Night's Dream* (v.i.2–27).

When Plato described the symptoms of love-sickness in the *Phaedrus*, he used the word ερως. This became the standard term for describing the malady of love in early Greek medical texts. Associating the word ερως with *herus* (master) and *heros* (hero), Latin translators of these treatises conflated them, and produced the word *hereos* to refer to love-sickness. The etymological confusion continued into the Middle Ages, with the result that the standard term for love-sickness in late medieval medical treatises is *amor heroycus*, or heroic love.[47] This is the malady that Chaucer's Arcite suffers from. With his hollow eyes, pallid complexion, solitary habits and incessant weeping, he's obviously a textbook case of heroic love:

> in his geere for al the world he ferde,
> Nat oonly lik the loveris maladye
> Of Hereos, but rather lyk manye,
> Engendred of humour malencolik[48]

It's equally obvious from Montague's account of Romeo's behaviour that he suffers from the same 'maladye of Hereos':

> Away from light steals home my heavy son,
> And private in his chamber pens himself,
> Shuts up his windows, locks fair daylight out,
> And makes himself an artificial night.
>   (1.i.135–8)

For Montague the prognosis is not good: 'Black and portentous must this humour prove', he says, 'Unless good counsel may the cause remove' (39–40). But for Bruno the torments of the lover as he wrestles with his malady are a sign of nobility: not all men are equally susceptible to beauty. Those who are endowed with such aesthetic sense 'fall in love more easily and more intensely and they also fall of out love more easily and are more intensely provoked'.[49] Not that there is anything wrong, in Bruno's view, with such 'mobility', as Dollimore would call it. All that matters is that you do it in the right aristocratic spirit. 'The heroic frenzy', writes Bruno, 'differs from other more ignoble frenzies not as virtue differs from vice, but as vice practised in a divine way by a more divine subject differs from vice practised in a bestial way by a more bestial subject'[50] – or as the old refrain goes, 'It's the rich what gets the pleasure, and the poor what gets the blame.' But the lover who can rise above the conflict between spirit and flesh and fix his attention on the Platonic good until he himself becomes a god is truly heroic:

Here his love is completely heroic and divine. And I would understand it as heroic and divine, even though because of it he speaks to himself as afflicted by such cruel tortures; for every lover who is separated from the beloved . . . finds himself in anguish and pain, crucifies himself and torments himself.[51]

Bruno dedicated the *Eroici furori* to Sidney in the belief that he was sympathetic to his neo-Platonic ideas. In fact, Sidney was sceptical of such theories, recognising that they were at best merely self-deceiving vanities (see for example, *Astrophil and Stella*, 5, 71, 72). And at worst? Debating the question of the fate of those heroic souls who fall short of the neo-Platonist's ideal, Bruno argues that 'a worthy and heroic death is preferable to an unworthy and vile triumph'. He then versifies these sentiments: 'fear not noble destruction, burst boldly through the clouds, and die content, if heaven destines us to so illustrious a death'.[52] It's one of the ironies of Petrarchism that a convention so commonplace as to be taken for granted by the mass of fifteenth and sixteenth-century love poets, was dismissed by Petrarch himself as an idle fiction. Writing shortly after Laura's death he said, 'I had never experienced such sorrow, nor do I now believe that one can die of grief' (271).[53] If a jilted Petrarchist like Donne dies of grief and then returns to play a deliciously tacky Halloween trick on his lover, no harm is done, since we know that the whole thing is just a literary joke. But what if the Petrarchan lover were to take Bruno's advice literally? That's exactly what happens in *Romeo and Juliet*. In *As You Like It*, Orlando is quickly brought down to earth when he tells 'Ganymede' that he will die of love if Rosalind refuses him: 'men have have died from time to time, and worms have eaten them', says Rosalind, 'but not for love' (IV.i.93–4). But Romeo has no one to tell him that tales of heroic love are, as Rosalind says, 'all lies'.

ERCLES' VEIN

When his servant brings news of Juliet's supposed death, Romeo resolves to 'defy [the] stars' (v.i.24), and immediately starts to plan his own death. Worried that his wild looks 'import / Some misadventure', Balthasar urges him to have patience (27–9). But Romeo dismisses him, remarking to himself: 'O mischief, thou art swift / To enter in the thoughts of desperate men' (35–6). In the final scene we see him in the same frenzied mood, muttering to himself, 'The time and my intents are savage-wild' (v.iii.37). When Paris confronts him at the Capulet tomb Romeo warns him not to tempt a desperate man (59). Recognising Tybalt's murderer, Paris tries to arrest him. Romeo is in no mood for argument and quickly dispatches him. With Paris out of the way he can now complete his heroic mission. As if in a melodramatic parody of Orpheus descending into Hades to win back his new bride from the gods of the underworld, Romeo goes down into the Capulet vault carrying the instrument, not of renewed life, but of a second death. His valedictory speech is rightly noted for its metaphoric invention. One critic, describing it as Romeo's best speech, writes: 'with it he gives dignity, meaning and finality to the one act he plans, and executes, however unwisely, without the help of friends, Friar, or Juliet. His language, like the deed, is his own.'[54] The truth is that the language of this speech is no more his own than the Petrarchan conceits that Mercutio had mocked in II.i; this time it's the inflated rhetoric of the Brunoesque heroic lover:

> O, here
> Will I set up my everlasting rest,
> And shake the yoke of inauspicious stars
> From this world-wearied flesh. Eyes, look your last.
> Arms, take your last embrace. And, lips, O you
> The doors of breath, seal with a righteous kiss
> A dateless bargain to engrossing death!
> Come, bitter conduct, come, unsavoury guide,
> Thou desperate pilot, now at once run on
> The dashing rocks thy sea-sick weary bark.
>   (109–18)

It's a widely accepted view shared by traditionalists and postmodernists alike that at the end of the play Romeo and Juliet are joined in some kind of mystical union. Coppélia Kahn argues that their death is at once a perverse 'birth' into death and a form of quasi-sexual fulfilment: 'Imagery and action combine to assert that death is a transcendent form of sexual consummation, and further, that it is a rebirth into a higher stage of existence – the counterpart of an adulthood never fully achieved in life'.[55] In *A Midsummer Night's Dream* Shakespeare burlesques the demise of the heroic lover in the wonderfully protracted nonsense of Pyramus' Herculean death-throes: 'Approach ye Furies fell. / O Fates, come, come', etc. (v.i.276–7). So close is Romeo's death speech to the kind of thing that Bottom is unintentionally parodying, that it's difficult to believe that Shakespeare meant us to understand the play's final scene in this sentimental way. The difference between the two scenes is that one satirises heroic pretensions by turning them into farce, the other by turning them into kitsch. When Shakespeare uses kitsch to expose senti-mental self deception he usually provides an alternative perspective.[56] In *Romeo and Juliet* we get that alternative view in the briefest moment of black comedy as Juliet wakes up and accuses her dead husband of churlishly thinking only of himself when he drained the cup of poison (v.iii.163–4). Grief is also turned into farce in iv.v as Paris, the Capulets and Juliet's Nurse all vie with each other to produce the most extravagant lament for Juliet. The Nurse easily takes the prize:

> O woe! O woeful, woeful, woeful day!
> Most lamentable day, most woeful day
> that ever, ever, I did yet behold!
> O day! O day! O day! O hateful day!
> Never was seen so black a day as this.
> O woeful day, O woeful day!
>
> (49–54)

It's the Friar who puts a stop to their hysterics: 'Peace ho, for shame! Confusion's cure lives not/In these confusions' (65–6).

A more serious contrast of attitudes is the pointed difference between Romeo's histrionic performance in the Capulet tomb and Mercutio's stoically understated death in the street in iii.i. This is not to say that Shakespeare is cynically denying the possibility of great passion. But you've only got to compare Romeo's sentiments with those of another Petrarchist to appreciate the difference between kitsch and a truly heroic grief. Milton's *Methought I saw my late espoused saint* is very close in spirit to the *canzoniere* that Petrarch wrote after Laura's death when she visits him in spirit, offering him a consolation that only intensifies his suffering; indeed Milton's is arguably the most genuinely Petrarchan sonnet that England produced. Like all Petrarchan poetry, its focus is on the male speaker and his torments, and takes no account of the feelings of the person who is the cause of his grief. But for all its generic limitations, there's no hint of self deception in Milton's poem. Like Petrarch, Milton doesn't consider suicide, but resigns himself to a life of mourning. Kitsch, however, is unable to confront unromantic reality, turning suffering instead into saccharine fantasy. It's not a question of whether or not you believe in an after-life. Petrarch's knowledge that he will one day meet Laura in a Christian heaven is fantasy as far as the atheist is concerned; but it's not kitsch, since there is no mitigation of present suffering, no attempt to escape from intolerable reality. But when Dryden's Cleopatra

gracefully expires on Antony's noble breast with the impression of a smile
left on her face to show 'she dy'd pleased with him for whom she liv'd, /
And went to charm him in another World',[57] that *is* kitsch: Shakespeare's
deeply ambivalent character has been reduced by Dryden to a terminally
simpering queen of hearts.

From the beginning of his career Shakespeare was a relentless critic of
sentimentality. Unlike *All for Love, Romeo and Juliet* has no hint of
reunion after death; the emphasis of the final scene is on the tragic waste
of two needless deaths, and how those who are left behind to mourn will
pick up the pieces. Talk of some kind of transcendent consummation in
death has no basis in the play; it's either a sentimental response to
Shakespeare's ironic kitsch, or else a misguided attempt to read him
against the grain. If you are looking for a lesson that's politically acceptable to modern feminist readers, you're more likely to find it by going
back to Shakespeare's sources than by invoking de Rougemont or Lacan,
or by attempting to demonstrate, as Catherine Belsey does in a recent
essay on *Romeo and Juliet*, that Shakespeare is 'a Saussurean *avant la
lettre*'.[58]

It's well known that there are close parallels between *Romeo and Juliet*
and Chaucer's *Troilus and Criseyde*.[59] Shakespeare took from Chaucer's
poem, not just a story of blighted youth, but also a view of masculinity
that subverts the *moralitas* traditionally associated with a story that was
one of the great showpieces of medieval antifeminism. As with *Romeo and
Juliet*, critics have spent much time debating the roles of fate and human
action in Chaucer's tragedy. It's a question that's never finally resolved in
Chaucer any more than it is in Shakespeare: fate does play a major role in
human affairs, but at the same time, human beings are capable of making
either the best or the worst of a bad situation. But Chaucer's poem
demands that we distinguish between the heroine's view of fate and the
hero's. Troilus' response to the news that he and Criseyde are to be cruelly
parted is dramatic: at first he is numbed with misery; then he becomes
hysterical, rushing about the room, beating his breast and dashing his
forehead against the wall in a paroxysm of despair; finally, when he has
calmed down enough to collect his thoughts, he launches into a vast
rhetorical complaint at the cruelty of fortune, concluding that the only
solution to his problem is suicide. Never once in this enormous *planctus*
does he mention Criseyde, or consider what effect his suicide might have
on her.

Her reaction to their mutual misfortune is quite different. Though
Criseyde, too, is devastated by the news of their impending separation,

she thinks, not of herself, but of Troilus and how he will cope with the sorrow of their parting:

> 'Gret is my wo,' quod she, and sighte soore,
> As she that feleth dedly sharp distresse;
> 'But yit to me his sorwe is muchel more,
> That love hym bet than he hymself, I gesse.
> Allas! for me hath he swich hevynesse?
> Kan he for me so pitously compleyne?
> Iwis, this sorwe doubleth al my peyne.
> 'Grevous to me, God woot, is for to twynne,'
> Quod she, 'but yet it harder is to me
> To sen that sorwe which that he is inne . . .'
> (IV.897–906)

Criseyde is not only less self-centred than Troilus; she's also more circumspect. Rejecting Troilus' plans for an elopement on practical grounds, she urges him not to do anything they might later regret (IV.1531). 'Thus maketh vertu of necessite / By pacience,' she concludes, 'and thynk that lord is he / Of Fortune ay, that naught wole of hire recche' (1586–8). One of the poem's many ironies is that so much Boethian wisdom is put into the mouth of a woman whose name was synonymous with infidelity. But it's not a simple case of saying one thing and doing another, as for example, when Lysander, under the influence of Love-in-idleness tells Helena 'The will of man is by his reason sway'd, / And reason says you are the worthier maid' (*A Midsummer Night's Dream*, II.ii.115–16). As we watch Troilus and Criseyde kissing, and arguing and quarreling it's clear that it's she who not only has a far more mature conception of love and sexuality, but who is the wiser and more philosophic of the two. He regards their crisis as a tragedy, something so devastating and irremediable that the only way out is suicide; she treats it as a misfortune, something to be born stoically and resolved by faith and endurance. Eventually she does of course betray Troilus, just as her own trust had originally been betrayed by him (ironically what first attracted her to him was the appearance of 'moral vertu, grounded upon trouthe' (IV.1672)). But instead of concluding his poem with the expected conventional misogynist warning against women, Chaucer cautions his women readers to beware of the blandishments of *men* (V.1784–5).

If much of this sounds familiar, it's because Shakespeare took from Chaucer, not just the story of two lovers separated by a combination of fate and human folly, but also the characters of the generous, loving woman and the poetical, egotistical, heroical male. Criticism has made surprisingly little of this difference.[60] Yet it forms the basis for one of the play's major patterns of symbolic imagery: Juliet is consistently associated with images of growing and blighted plants, Romeo with fire and gunpowder. The classic medieval belief in the dual nature of love – its harmonising power and also its destructive potential – is here expressed in fully realised characters who seem to have inner lives, but who at the same time have a symbolic dimension.[61] It's true that Romeo, almost as much as Juliet, is the unfortunate victim both of a series of unlucky accidents and of a culture that glorified masculine violence as a natural way of defending family honour. But although Romeo believes he is 'fortune's fool', it's not, finally, either the gods or human aggression that's responsible for his death, but his own hand. Like Chaucer's Troilus, Romeo behaves in a consistently egotistical way, dramatising himself as the heroic victim of a malicious destiny, and attempting suicide in iii.iii without any thought of how Juliet will cope with his death. If pressed, most critics will acknowledge the less attractive side of Romeo's character. However, it's commonly argued that, although he may begin the play as a thoroughly self-indulgent adolescent, by the final scene he has matured to the point where he can be said to show the true colours of his 'valiant and gentle manhood'.[62] I find little evidence of this new maturity in the play's final scene. Instead I see the same heroic attitude that had alarmed Juliet in the Balcony scene and worried Friar Lawrence when Romeo had tried to commit suicide for the first time.

Romeo and Juliet is Shakespeare's first domestic tragedy. Like the political tragedies that follow, the play suggests that there's something inherently dangerous in the heroic ideal that was enjoying such an extraordinary resurgence in the 1590s. From its brilliant flowering in the first two decades of the sixteenth century, English humanism had set itself in opposition to the old chivalric ideals. For men like Colet, Erasmus and More and their Elizabethan successors, a medieval culture of violence had no place in the new world of civic humanism. In his criticism of Malory's *Morte D'Arthur*, Queen Elizabeth's tutor Roger Ascham complained that medieval chivalry was nothing but 'open man's slaughter and bold bawdry'.[63] Now, in the final decade of the century, chivalric heroism was once more acquiring a fashionable appeal. With his obsession with honour, and his commitment to what Mervyn James has called 'the politics of violence',[64] the Earl of Essex seemed to his admirers like a symbol 'Of ancient honour near worn out of date'.[65] Like Tybalt, Essex believed that to defend 'the stock and honour of [one's] kin' (i.v.56) was no sin but an assertion of natural rights. In a tribute to the values that Essex stood for, his former military captain Gervase Markham described honour as 'the food of every great spirit, and the very god which creates in high minds heroical actions'.[66] Though Romeo is a reluctant fighter, he too has been infected by a dream of 'heroical actions'. In the form of *amor heroycus* the heroic ideal might seem like nothing more than an insignificant literary affectation. But as Chaucer showed so brilliantly in that great satire on heroic masculinity, *The Knight's Tale, amor heroycus* usually leads to other kinds of heroic action. When the heroic ideal takes the form of an idealisation of martial glory its capacity for destruction is limitless, as Shakespeare went on to show in plays like *Troilus and Cressida* and *Coriolanus.*

CHAPTER 7

History

Why did Shakespeare dramatise stories from the ancient world? If you asked a late Elizabethan historiographer that question he would probably say that Shakespeare went to Roman history for much the same reason that contemporary historians retold the story of the past, namely, that history is a storehouse of political lessons that can be applied to the modern world. Since human nature was thought to be much the same in all ages, an understanding of the reasons why people behaved as they did in the past could help you to understand the political problems of the modern world. In his *Discourses* on Livy Machiavelli wrote: 'If the present be compared with the remote past, it is easily seen that in all cities and in all peoples there are the same desires and the same passions as there always were. So that, if one examines with diligence the past, it is easy to foresee the future of any commonwealth, and to apply those remedies that were used of old.'[1] Machiavelli's 'politic' historiography was fashionable in England in the final decades of the sixteenth century and had begun to replace the older providentialist school of history that looked for the meaning of events in God's will. 'You cannot step into a scholar's study but (ten to one) you shall likely find open either Bodin's *de Republica* or Le Roye's *Exposition upon Aristotle's Politics* or some other like French or Italian Politic Discourses', wrote Gabriel Harvey in about 1580.[2]

However, a postmodern historiographer would give a very different answer to the question of why Shakespeare wrote historical dramas. Postmodernists also believe that human nature is the key to history. Where they differ from Renaissance historiographers is in their understanding of what it means to be human. 'Politic' historiographers like Machiavelli took it for granted that wherever you looked either in the ancient or the recent past you would find 'the same desires and the same passions'. But postmodernists see no constant elements in human nature. They argue that human beings are, in Jean Howard's words, '*created* by history': far from being what Marx called a *Gattungswesen*, or distinct species, with certain essential characteristics that recur in all cultures and all ages, human beings are 'the products of specific discourses and social processes';[3] there is no such thing as a 'defining human essence'.[4] These contrasting views of humanity have resulted in radically opposed views of history: for the Renaissance historiographer it's the universality of human nature that gives meaning to history; for the postmodernist it's the absence of any human universals that makes history 'politically valueless'.[5] Did Shakespeare share the humanist assumptions of his contemporaries, or was he, as postmodern Shakespeareans claim, a radical anti-essentialist? Did he believe that the past had something to tell us about the human condition, or was history for him no more than a tale told by an idiot, full of sound and fury, signifying nothing? I'll keep these questions in mind as we discuss *Julius Caesar*. It's an interesting play to consider in any discussion of Renaissance theories of history because, of all Shakespeare's historical dramas, it's probably the one that deals most directly with the kind of problems that concerned contemporary historiographers: the nature of historical evidence; the difference between fact and interpretation; the role (if any) of providence in human affairs; the significance of omens and portents; whether the past has anything to tell us about the present, and so on. Just as some of Shakespeare's plays – especially the late tragicomedies – offer a kind of running metadramatic commentary on the dramatist's own art, so *Julius Caesar* seems to concern itself, not merely with the events of republican Rome in its dying years, but with the very nature of historical drama. You might describe it as a metahistorical play.

HISTORIOGRAPHY, POSTMODERN AND EARLY MODERN

Postmodern theories of history owe much to Foucault.[6] In a tribute essay Hayden White suggested that, insofar as Foucault rejected all the conventional categories of historical description and explanation, he could best be described as an 'anti-historian'. 'Foucault', he explained, 'writes "history" in order to destroy it.'[7] Unlike the traditional historian, who sought to understand the past and to make it intelligible to his readers, partly by revealing the sequence of cause and effect in the unfolding of events, and partly by appealing to those constant elements in human nature that survive from one age to another, Foucault wanted to disrupt our false sense of coherence and defamiliarise the past. People imagine that there are certain human constants that transcend time and that link us with the past, explained Foucault in an essay on Nietzsche; but in reality '*nothing in man . . . is sufficiently stable to serve as a basis for . . . understanding other men*'. For Foucault the purpose of history is to expose that radical discontinuity: 'History becomes "effective" to the degree that it introduces discontinuity into our very being'.[8] Because there is in reality no universal *humanitas* and therefore no continuity in history, the past can have no more meaning for us than a theatre of the absurd. Foucault, wrote White, 'sought to show how we are isolated within our peculiar modalities of experience, so much so that *we could not hope to find analogues and models for the solution of the problems facing us, and thereby to enlighten us to the peculiar elements in our present situation*'. White argued that, insofar as Foucault tried to show how all systems of thought are 'little more than terminological formalisations of poetic closures with the world of words, rather than with the "things" they purport to represent and explain', he had more in common with the poet than the traditional historian.[9]

White's own sceptical historiography was heavily indebted to Foucault. In challenging what he believed were the false claims that traditional historians made to objectivity and neutrality, he developed Foucault's theme of the meaninglessness of any distinction between history and fiction. 'In general,' he wrote, 'there has been a manifest reluctance to consider historical narratives as what they most manifestly are: verbal fictions, the contents of which have more in common with their counterparts in literature than they have with those in the sciences.'[10] White's books – especially the seminal *Metahistory* (1973) – have in turn been influential in bringing about a radical shift of attitude among academic historians towards the nature of their discipline. White himself claimed in 1986 that 'the dominant opinion among professional historians themselves nowadays . . . [is that] narrative representations are to be accorded the status of literary, by which is meant "novelistic" or "fictional" accounts of the matters of which they treat'.[11] Though it's probably an exaggeration to say that White's textualist theory of history is now the dominant approach in modern history departments, it's certainly true that his ideas have been instrumental in creating a whole new school of postmodern historiography. Claims to objectivity had been subjected to critical scrutiny as long ago as the early decades of the last century (see chapter 9, pp. 188–9). But now the very possibility of knowing the past was questioned. Because history, like literature, is no more than representation, any truth claims that historians may make for their narratives are no more than wishful thinking. So too is the belief that you can learn from history. Since there's no such thing as a transhistorical *humanitas*, and no possibility of true contact, intellectual or emotional, between one age and another, the past can have little meaning for the present.

Popularising the new ideas, Keith Jenkins insists that 'we can never really know the past'. Historians, he argues, have traditionally sought the truth; but as Foucault has taught us, in reality truth itself is no more than a 'useful fiction' promulgated by the 'systems of power' that rule our lives. If we can rid ourselves of our obsession with truth, we can see that history is no more than 'a language game', and that the 'facts' on which we base our narratives are themselves merely 'a discursive construct'. Because facts have no intrinsic meaning until they have been selected, assembled and ordered by the historian, we are ineluctably brought to the conclusion that 'everything is ultimately interpretation'. And since there's no such thing as a universal human nature, any suggestion that the study of history can lead to 'empathy' – that is, 'an informed appreciation of the predicaments and viewpoints of people in the past' – is merely self-delusion.[12]

Postmodern historiographers make it clear exactly what's entailed when you claim that someone is an anti-essentialist. If you say that Shakespeare rejected the humanist idea of a universal *humanitas*, it's not just a matter of implying that he may perhaps have put rather more emphasis on education than nature, or of suggesting that he probably didn't attach much importance to the idea of an inner self. Anti-essentialism, as postmodernists themselves insist, involves a shift of perspective so radical that any engagement with a humanist mindset is impossible. For the historiographer it means that, once you accept that there's no such thing as a common humanity, you resign yourself to acknowledging that the past is a closed book, and that we are all, in White's words, 'isolated within our peculiar modalities of experience'.

In contrast to postmodern textualist theories of history with their insistence on the purely fictional nature of all historical writing, and their frank rejection of any notion of utility, is the emphasis that Renaissance 'politic' historiographers placed on the practical value of history. Whereas the medieval chronicler looked to history for examples of virtuous conduct within an all-encompassing providential framework, the politic historian was interested less in morality or divine will than the problem of survival. Politic history is about what works in political life and what doesn't: 'instead of discussing what princes ought to do in moral terms, the advocates of the new history sought to understand what they did in fact, how and why they did it, how effective their measures were'.[13] Though politic historians would often make a conciliatory reference to providence – possibly to placate the censor – they were primarily concerned with the analysis of human actions.[14]

Politic history is usually associated with the names of Machiavelli and his younger contemporary Francesco Guicciardini, both of whom were writing during the period of French occupation that followed the disastrous inter-city wars of the fifteenth century. It's been suggested that Machiavelli was an anti-essentialist who rejected the idea of a universal human nature.[15] This could hardly be further from the truth. 'God had not saved the Italians from their own folly, and the purpose of *The Prince*, and of Guicciardini's *History of Italy* was to turn the dominant role back to Man', wrote F. J. Levy in his classic study of Tudor historiography.[16] As we've seen, Machiavelli looked to history for practical lessons that could be applied to the present. If the past had a message for the modern world, that was because human nature is fundamentally the same in all ages. That's not to say that human beings are automata blindly following their maker's instructions. Like Cicero (see chapter 1, p. 10), Machiavelli distinguished between individual character and the universals that define humanity as a species. Individuals differ from one another – some politicians, for example, are innately cautious, others are impetuous – but those temperamental differences are not entirely random; they exist within a range of possibilities circumscribed by the nature of our humanity. It's those predictable elements in human nature that enable the political analyst to learn from the past.[17] Both in *The Prince* and in the *Discourses* you repeatedly find such phrases as these: 'men almost always follow in the footsteps of others, imitation being a leading principle of human nature'; 'men generally . . . are ungrateful, fickle, feigners and dissemblers'; 'men never do good unless necessity drives them to it'; 'nature has so constituted men that . . .'; 'the human mind is perpetually . . .', and so forth.[18] Guicciardini also insisted on the universality of human nature. In the *Ricordi* – a collection of aphorisms on life, politics and human nature – he wrote: 'One finds almost the same or similar proverbs, though in different words, in every country, and the reason is that proverbs are born of experience or observation of things which are everywhere alike';[19] because human nature is essentially unchanging, only the dull-witted are unable to learn from the past.[20] You find the same emphasis on the universality of human nature among English politic historians. 'Ambition, faction and affections, speak ever one language, wear like colours,' wrote Samuel Daniel in the dedicatory epistle to his *Civil Wars*, the reason being that 'man is a creature of the same dimension he [always] was: and how great and eminent soever he be, his measure and height is easy to be taken.'[21] The politic historian believed that, by observing the way people behaved in the past and noting the consequences of their actions, you could predict what outcome similar actions might have in the present. 'In a word we may gather out of history a policy no less wise than eternal', wrote Ralegh in the Preface to his *History of the World*.[22] The old civic-humanist emphasis on what Sir Thomas Elyot called 'good counsel'[23] as a way of encouraging princes to act virtuously had now shifted towards the politic art of analysing affairs of state. As one of Webster's characters puts it,

> Though some o'the court hold it presumption
> To instruct princes what they ought to do,
> It is a noble duty to inform them
> What they ought to foresee.[24]

Machiavelli and Guicciardini were both widely read in Elizabethan England. Guicciardini's *History of Italy* was translated into English in 1579 (with a new edition in 1599), and Machiavelli's *Florentine History* in 1595. Although there were no printed English translations of the *Discourses* on Livy and *The Prince* until 1636 and 1640 respectively, several manuscript translations of both texts were available in Elizabethan England, while printed Italian editions of both were also in circulation from the 1580s.[25] But it wasn't until the final decade of the century that politic historiography became truly fashionable in England. Its popularity owed much to the sponsorship of Robert Devereux, second Earl of Essex.

As interest in politic historiography spread to Northern Europe, Tacitus replaced Livy as the humanists' preferred Roman historian. In the disillusioned world of Elizabeth's final decade when, in Daniel's words, 'great men cloth[ed] their private hate / In those fair colours of the public good',[26] Tacitus' analysis of political corruption in imperial Rome seemed to have a direct message for those disaffected courtiers who believed that the queen was becoming erratic and tyrannical in old age.[27] 'In these four books of the story thou shalt see all the miseries of a torn and declining state', wrote the author of an anonymous epistle introducing the first English translation of Tacitus in 1591.[28] Rumour had it that it was the discontented Essex who wrote the book's anonymous foreword. And when John Hayward published England's first politic history in 1599 – *The Life and Reign of King Henry IIII* – he dedicated it to Essex. As a politic historian, Hayward was less interested in holding up examples of virtuous conduct for emulation than in providing what the author of his anonymous prefatory epistle called 'precepts for affairs of state'; the shrewdest politicians, the writer explained, have always taken advice from 'men skilful in histories' because their memories are a 'storehouse of the experiences not of one age or country, but of all times and all nations'.[29] In keeping with this advice, Hayward filled his own narrative with political maxims and *sententiae* from Essex's favourite historian, Tacitus.[30]

As it turned out, Hayward's dedication to Essex was disastrous for both men (though the *Life and Reign* was seized by the authorities in May 1599 when Essex was still in Ireland, Hayward wasn't actually prosecuted until after the earl's disgrace). While the failed *coup d'état* of 1601 appeared to confirm suspicions that Hayward's book was intended as 'a seditious prelude to put into people's heads boldness and faction',[31] the association of Essex's name with a supposedly dangerous writer counted against him at his own trial. The lesson of Hayward's unfortunate experience was clear: in such uncertain times it paid to exercise extreme caution in dealing with politically sensitive historical parallels, and above all to avoid declaring political allegiances. When he wrote *Julius Caesar* Shakespeare couldn't have known what was about to become of Hayward, or how spectacularly Essex's fortunes were to change. But Essex had a reputation for impulsiveness. You didn't have to be a fortune teller to know that if he *was* planning some kind of reckless action it could easily backfire: history provided all too many examples of bloody instructions returning to plague the inventor. In building into his play a number of pointed allusions to contemporary events, Shakespeare took good care not to betray sympathy for one party or another.

AFFAIRS OF STATE

The parallels between Shakespeare's Rome and Elizabethan England have been much discussed.[32] With its ailing, autocratic ruler toppled by a Machiavellian rebel who looks back to an heroic age when men were more warlike (1.iii.80–4), and its talk of a group of 'noblest-minded' aristocrats (121) 'factious for redress of [personal] griefs' (117), *Julius Caesar* would be bound to have put contemporary audiences in mind of the beliefs and ideals of the Essex circle. Essex's querulous *Apologie* – written at a time when rivalry between the two main factions in the Privy Council was at crisis point[33] – was published only just before Shakespeare wrote *Julius Caesar*. Like Cassius, Essex was a man with a grievance.[34] He surrounded himself with discontented nobles who shared his desire to remove what seemed to him a tyrannical ruler and reform government. His watchword was honour. And that meant a willingness to use violence if necessary in defence of personal or national reputation. In a pamphlet in praise of the aristocratic leaders of the Essex faction Gervase Markham described honour as 'the food of every great spirit, and the very god which creates in high minds heroical actions'.[35] For Cassius too honour is a word that has talismanic significance. 'Honour is the subject of my story,' he tells Brutus (1.ii.94).

These parallels are familiar to modern scholars. If Shakespeare took care to avoid committing himself to one side or the other, that's understandable. Essex was a figure of whom, in Markham's words, 'it behove[d] every man to be careful how to write'.[36] But the parallels go further than hints of a possible resemblance between the political situation of Rome before Caesar's assassination and London in 1598/9. Shakespeare makes pointed verbal allusion to the militant-Protestant faction and its values. For Essex's supporters, words like 'heroic', 'virtuous' and 'honourable', were a code that signalled commitment to an aggressively militarist political agenda.[37] The counterpart of these heroic epithets was a cluster of words to do with sleep, dreams, enchantment and idleness. As Blair Worden has shown, 'sleep' was widely used by members of the militant-Protestant faction as a metaphor for the false sense of security that they believed was blinding the government to political dangers at home and abroad.[38] In *Julius Caesar* there is much talk of heroic action. Cassius is an admirer of 'any bold or noble enterprise' (1.ii.298) and incites his supporters to 'undergo with me an enterprise / Of honourable-dangerous consequence' (1.iii.122–3), while Ligarius welcomes an 'exploit worthy the name of honour' (11.i.316). But the anonymous letter that Lucius finds in the window speaks of the need for Brutus to rouse himself from the 'sleep' of inaction: 'Brutus, thou sleep'st. Awake, and see thyself. / Shall Rome, et cetera? Speak, strike, redress.' Brutus then rereads the letter's key phrase: 'thou sleep'st. Awake' (11.i.46–8).[39] It's the combination of imagery of 'bloody, fiery, and most terrible' deeds (1.iii.129) on the one hand, and the exhortation to awake from the 'sleep' of 'security' (11.iii.7) on the other, that makes these allusions so pointed.

Such topical allusions would be meaningless if we weren't expected to see analogies between the final years of republic Roman and *fin-de-siècle* England. But what are we meant to deduce from them? Alan Sinfield sees *Julius Caesar* as politically straightforward; as a Cultural Materialist he believes that, like most tragedies and historical plays in this period, it's 'about gaining legitimacy for the exercise of state violence'.[40] But before the advent of Foucauldian Theory, critics saw *Julius Caesar's* politics as ambivalent. In the last century a long line of critics going back to A. P. Rossiter in the 1950s emphasised the dialectical nature of Shakespeare's plays. For critics like Rabkin, Elton, McElroy, Jones and Grudin, they were best seen as, in W. R. Elton's words, 'a dialect of ironies and ambivalences, avoiding in its complex movement and dialogue the simplification of direct statement and reductive resolution'.[41] *Julius Caesar* would seem to be typical of the tragedies and histories in its ambivalent treatment of political problems. 'After all the clear balancing of this against that, and for all the power of the figures on stage to move us,' writes David Daniell in his recent Arden edition of the play, 'there comes into view no alternative basis of authority at all, either divine or popular. There is only possession of power, the politics of the school playground'. But if, as Daniell rightly says, Shakespeare 'does not endorse anyone',[42] what are we expected to learn from this dramatisation of the most momentous event in Roman history? That republican politics is simply a power game from which we can deduce nothing of value? That history has no more to offer than a poet's fiction? This would be a truly Foucauldian view of history and literature.

The fact that Shakespeare is careful to avoid taking sides doesn't mean that the play has no view to offer on the historical events it dramatises. One of the central ironies of *Julius Caesar* is the fact that an action designed to deflect a feared event hastens that very outcome.[43] There is a similar structural irony in *Macbeth*. By attempting to avert destiny, Macbeth himself is instrumental in ensuring that the ancient prophecy of a re-united kingdom would be realised.[44] In *Julius Caesar*, too, fulfilment of prophecy is accelerated by an action that is intended to forestall it. Despite his republican sympathies, Plutarch considered Caesar to be a providential figure 'whom God had ordained of special grace to be governor of the empire of Rome, and to set all things again at quiet stay, the which required the counsel and authority of an absolute prince'.[45] Shakespeare doesn't refer in *Julius Caesar* to the 'time of universal peace' (*Antony and Cleopatra*, IV.vi.4) that was to follow the third stage of Rome's civil wars. Nor is there any proof that the many supernatural signs in the play apparently betokening divine displeasure are anything more than coincidence. However, contemporary audiences would have known perfectly well that Octavius' supremacy and the transformation of Rome into a dictatorship was brought forward by Caesar's murder. Instead of averting these events, the assassination hastened them.

On the question of whether or not there is a 'providence of some high powers / That govern us below' (V.i.106–7) the play is noncommittal. But looked at from a purely pragmatic point of view there's an inescapable irony in the fact that the immediate consequence of an action carried out in the name of 'Liberty, freedom, and enfranchisement!' (III.i.80) is

'Domestic fury and fierce civil strife' (III.i.266), followed by the deaths of all the conspirators. Cassius imagines the celebratory re-enactment of their 'lofty scene' (III.i.113) in future times. Has he read no history? Doesn't he know that conspiracies almost always end in disaster? 'There have been many conspiracies, but history has shown that few have succeeded', wrote Machiavelli in *The Prince*.[46] Machiavelli was not a monarchist defending the divine right of hereditary rulers. He was merely pointing out the facts of *realpolitik*. *The Prince* considers the consequences of conspiracies in principalities; the *Discourses* looks at them from a republican point of view. But the message is the same: 'there is . . . no enterprise . . . more dangerous or more rash than is this . . . those [who involve themselves in conspiracies] usually bring disaster both upon themselves and upon their country'.[47] Plutarch dwells on the brutality of the way in which Caesar was 'hacked and mangled among them, as a wild beast taken of hunters'.[48] But Machiavelli, also writing from a republican point of view, makes no appeal to the emotions, and no reference to heaven's will. His interest in the subject is pragmatic: conspiracies seldom achieve their intended effect. Describing how Caesar's death was avenged, he simply says: 'of the conspirators, after they had been driven out of Rome, one and all were killed at various times and in various places'.[49]

Machiavelli also considered the consequences of private acts of vengeance in his discussion of the Coriolanus story. As we know from Plutarch, Coriolanus was not noted for his diplomacy. So incensed were the plebeians by his contempt for them that, had it not been for the intervention of the tribunes, and their insistence that he appear before the senate, Coriolanus would probably have been murdered by the mob. But crisis was avoided because there was a legal outlet for public anger. Summing up the significance of these events, Machiavelli wrote:

all should reflect on the evils that might have ensued in the Roman republic had he been tumultuously put to death, for this would have been an act of private vengeance, which would have aroused fear; and fear would have led to defensive action; this to the procuring of partisans; partisans would have meant the formation of factions in the city; and factions would have brought about its downfall.

Thus far Machiavelli might almost have been describing Caesar's murder. But he continues:

As, however, the matter was settled by persons vested with the requisite authority, no opening was provided for the evils that might have resulted had the matter been settled by private authority.[50]

Machiavelli's observations on unauthorised action had a particular significance for English readers in 1599. *Julius Caesar* was written and performed while Essex was out of the country. Until news began to filter back to London of the truce that he had been forced to conclude with Tyrone in September 1599, no one could have predicted with certainty the outcome of the earl's mission to suppress the Irish rebellion. Success might lead to a reconciliation with the Queen and the rehabilitation of his own reputation as crusading national hero; failure would in all probability mean the end of his political career, at least while Elizabeth was alive. Given these uncertainties, it's difficult to imagine any intelligent Elizabethan watching a performance of *Julius Caesar* and not pondering the possible outcomes of a political *coup*. In his treatise on kingship St Thomas Aquinas wrote: 'to proceed against the cruelty of tyrants is an action to be undertaken, not through the private presumption of a few, but rather by public authority'.[51] Was this also Shakespeare's view? In *Macbeth* he presents us with the paradox of men resorting to extreme violence to depose a tyrant and restore civilised values. But *Julius Caesar* appears to confirm one of the central themes of the English history plays. Without giving away the writer's political sympathies, it suggests that rebellion is all too likely to be followed by 'Domestic fury and fierce civil strife'.

SHAKESPEARE'S POLITIC HISTORY

In his New Cambridge edition of *Julius Caesar* Marvin Spevack refers to changing fashions in Elizabethan historiography, arguing that 'it is self-evident that Shakespeare was very much in the tradition of the older providential view of history'.[52] This is a puzzling claim. Though Shakespeare's characters speculate about the significance of the omens that figure so prominently in the play, there's no evidence that Cassius is right when he claims that these are 'instruments of fear and warning' sent by the gods (1.iii.70), or indeed that there are any higher powers at all governing men's lives, as Brutus believes (v.i.106–7). Shakespeare's political vision would seem to have more in common with Machiavelli than it does either with Hall, Holinshed or *The Mirror for Magistrates*. Machiavelli's politic historiography was so well known in sixteenth-century England that traces of his ideas in literary works and political treatises aren't necessarily a sign of direct debt. In *The Jew of Malta* Marlowe capitalised unashamedly on the popular stereotype of the cunning schemer who takes a malicious delight in the spectacle of his own cruelty. *Julius Caesar* is Machiavellian in a different sense. Though Cassius has elements of the Machiavel of popular myth and uses systematic deception to realise his personal ambitions, he has little in common with Marlowe's buffoonish villain. Shakespeare's play is Machiavellian in the sense that it dramatises a pragmatic and sceptical view of politics which recognises that virtue and utility are not always compatible.[53]

Shakespeare's Brutus is a man who prides himself on his own integrity. 'Believe me for / mine honour, and have respect to mine honour, that/ you may believe', he tells the plebeians at Caesar's funeral (III.ii.14–16). During one of the childish arguments that break out on both sides after the assassination, Cassius complains that Brutus has done him wrong. Brutus replies that he would never wrong an enemy, much less a friend: 'Judge me, you gods: wrong I mine enemies? / And if not so, how should I wrong a brother?' (IV.ii.38–9). In response to Cassius' angry words later in the same scene he tells him that such threats mean nothing to him: 'I am armed so strong in honesty / That they pass by me as the idle wind' (122–3). Brutus believes that integrity is the only true guide to conduct: if you display honesty in all your actions you will be repaid in kind. In the moving final scene of the play he tells his audience: 'Countrymen, / My heart doth joy that yet in all my life / I found no man but he was true to me' (V.v.33–5). These are generous words and they help to explain why Brutus is regarded by friends and enemies alike as 'the noblest Roman of them all' (67). But noble as his intention may be, what Brutus is saying simply isn't true. Throughout the play he has been surrounded by deceivers. Indeed, though Cassius admires his honesty, he knows that not even Brutus himself is incorruptible:

> Well, Brutus, thou art noble; yet I see
> Thy honourable mettle may be wrought
> From that it is disposed. Therefore it is meet
> That noble minds keep ever with their likes;
> For who so firm that cannot be seduced?
>
> (I.ii.308–12)

Cassius is not a likeable character. But he is a much shrewder judge of human nature than Brutus is. In the space of two short scenes we see the truth of that judgement as Brutus allows himself to be persuaded that he must betray the man who loves him (I.ii.313). But though Brutus speaks of the 'even virtue' of the rebel cause (II.i.132) as justification for the deception he has always claimed he is above, the imagery he uses tells another story:

> O conspiracy,
> Sham'st thou to show thy dang'rous brow by night,
> When evils are most free? O then by day
> Where wilt thou find a cavern dark enough
> To mask thy monstrous visage? Seek none, conspiracy.
> Hide it in smiles and affability;
> For if thou put thy native semblance on,
> Not Erebus itself were dim enough
> To hide thee from prevention.
>
> (II.i.77–85)

It's a measure of the confusion in Brutus' mind that he should tell Cassius that those engaged in what he himself describes as a 'monstrous' act of political treachery need no 'other oath / Than honesty to honesty engaged' (II.i.125–6). Later he tells his fellow conspirators they must disguise their true intention and act their parts with 'untired spirits and formal constancy' (223–6). That Cassius should urge his friends to act like 'true Romans' (222) is not out of character: as a Machiavel he has no scruples about using trickery to achieve his political ends. But Brutus has always proclaimed his belief in honesty as the paramount value in public life. For such a man to represent unswerving commitment to treachery as 'formal constancy' is either hypocrisy or self-deception. What Brutus says in soliloquy suggests the latter. In a kind of Freudian slip he uses the traditional simile of political rebellion (compare Sidney's *Astrophil and Stella*, no. 5) to describe to himself his own mental confusion:

> Since Cassius first did whet me against Caesar
> I have not slept.
> Between the acting of a dreadful thing
> And the first motion, all the interim is
> Like a phantasma or a hideous dream.
> The genius and the mortal instruments
> Are then in counsel, and the state of man,
> Like to a little kingdom, suffers then
> The nature of an insurrection.
>
> (II.i.61–9)

But it's not just self-deception that Brutus is guilty of. A politic historian would probably say that his greatest crime is his political *naïveté*. Whether or not Brutus should have listened to Cassius' warning about Caesar's ambitions is a matter of opinion: a contemporary monarchist would probably say he was wrong; a republican might feel that he was right. What is indefensible, from whichever position you view his actions, is the credulity he shows in the decisions he makes after the assassination. His first mistake is to take Antony's offers of friendship at face value and allow him to speak at Caesar's funeral. His second is to suppose that the plebeians can be trusted to make responsible judgements based on reason. Knowing how easily swayed the plebeians are, Cassius is horrified at the prospect of so consummate a politician as Antony being allowed to address them (III.i.234–7). But Brutus is determined to be fair and honest with the enemy he has just created. The result is summed up in the short symbolic scene that follows Antony's oration. The murder of Cinna is a powerful piece of stage symbolism. Rome is now controlled by the mob. It has become a tyranny.

Tom McAlindon has recently argued that in the English history plays Machiavellian deception never works to the benefit of the state; Shakespeare, he claims, endorses the belief of an older generation of political moralists in truth as the only basis of justice and social order.[54] In an ideal world where 'noble minds keep ever with their likes' (I.ii.311), politicians would no doubt be able to dispense with any 'other oath / Than honesty to honesty engaged' and rely on mutual trust. But the world of *Julius Caesar* is far removed from that ideal. It's a world in which patricians employ systematic treachery, and plebeians are incapable of rational judgement. In such a world trust in the integrity of one's fellow politicians is the height of *naïveté*.

INSTRUMENTS OF FEAR

If *Julius Caesar* is thoroughly Machiavellian in its pragmatic view of politics, so too is it in its view of history. As many critics have noted, the play seems to be preoccupied with questions of meaning, interpretation and judgement.[55] An important question for the older school of providential historians was how to interpret portents, omens and other supernatural phenomena. If all things were ultimately subject to divine will, then it was important that you should be able to read correctly the signs by which God's anger or approval manifested itself. As Bishop Ponet explained in his *Short Treatise of Politic Power,*

There was never great misery, destruction, plague or visitation of God, that came on any nation, city or country, which as they be in deed, so may they justly be called wounds, but be sent of God for sin, and be not suddenly laid on the people, but are before prophesied and declared by the prophets and ministers of God's word, or by some revelations, wonders, monsters in the earth or tokens and signs in the element.[56]

The meaning of 'tokens and signs in the element' is something that occupies the minds of most of the major characters in *Julius Caesar*. But it's never clear whether their interpretation of the play's unnatural portents is correct, or indeed whether these phenomena are actually signs of divine interest, or merely chance events. Though Cassius and Caesar both change their minds on this question (I.iii.61–71; II.i.195–7; V.i.76–8), we are no nearer to a definitive answer at the end of the play than we were at the beginning. The disasters that befall Rome after the assassination certainly make the unnatural events reported in the play look like 'instruments of fear and warning'. But since the gods themselves make no appearance, we cannot know whether they were warning men against Caesar's ambition or Cassius' planned *coup*, or indeed whether they exist at all. Similarly with Calpurnia's dream: though her own interpretation seems to be borne out by events, and that of Decius exposed as intentionally misleading, there's no proven connection between the dream and the events it appears to prophesy. Cicero (Shakespeare's character) claims that, when it comes to interpreting omens, 'men construe things after their fashion / Clean from the purpose of the things themselves' (I.iii.34–5). This is to suppose that, given the right information, it should be possible to arrive at a correct answer. But the play doesn't give us this information; it offers us no way of determining which interpretation is correct. In the absence of any certainties, the 'true cause' (I.iii.62) of these portents can never be more than speculation and opinion. Is Shakespeare saying that the same is true of history, and that in the absence of determinate facts one interpretation has as much value as another? Is history, like poetry, merely representation? Richard Wilson believes that *Julius Caesar* 'appears to anticipate so much of postmodernism', particularly in the way it speaks 'directly to poststructuralist anxiety that there is nothing outside of texts and simulation'.[57] However, the play itself does not support this view.

In II.i there is a short episode that is striking in its seeming pointlessness. At the beginning of the scene Shakespeare gives us a marvellously convincing picture of an honest man wrestling with his conscience as he ponders the problem of whether or not to take action against a politician he thinks may become a tyrant. Then the conspirators arrive. The atmosphere is tense. Cassius draws Brutus aside. As they whisper together, Casca, Cinna and Decius talk amongst themselves. Since they are about to embark on an action that will transform Rome, you might expect them to reassure each other of the justice of their cause, or perhaps to reaffirm their resolve, or at least to run through their plans. But they talk of none of these things. Instead they argue about something completely inconsequential. Peering out at the night sky Decius says 'Here lies the east. Doth not the day break here?' Casca says bluntly, 'No'. Cinna joins in: 'O pardon, sir, it doth; and yon grey lines / That fret the clouds are messengers of day.' Casca replies:

> You shall confess that you are both deceived.
> (*He points his sword*)
> Here, as I point my sword, the sun arises.
> (II.i.100–5)

You could explain the scene in psychological terms – three men showing the pressure they are under by quarreling about trivia. But it's more than just a piece of psychological realism. The episode forms part of a pattern of opinion and counter-opinion that we've already glimpsed in Act I. However, this dispute is quite different from the discussion about the significance of omens. The latter is a question of belief; the former is about facts. One is fluid and open ended; the other is determinate. It's true that Decius and Casca interpret the signs in the night sky in different ways. But that doesn't mean that the points of the compass are a matter of opinion. Either Casca is right or he is not, and no amount of debate can alter the fact. Sunrise will soon show who interpreted the signs correctly. Insignificant in itself, the dispute anticipates the motif of conflicting evidence and misinterpretation in the last two acts.

After their second quarrel (during which Cassius discovers that he has misjudged Brutus), the two men receive conflicting reports of the actions of the Antony-Octavius alliance (IV.ii.225–30). They then discuss tactics (248–77). Brutus proposes that they march on the enemy immediately. Cassius disagrees. Brutus tells him they must cooperate with fortune when she is clearly working to their advantage ('There is a tide in the affairs of men') or suffer the consequences. Cassius reluctantly accepts Brutus' plan. But his misgivings are well founded. Once more Brutus has misjudged the situation. An immediate infantry attack is exactly what Octavius had hoped for: by initiating the engagement the enemy has sacrificed the advantage of higher ground (V.i.1–3).

Antony and Octavius too squabble about tactics: 'You said the enemy would not come down, / But keep the hills and upper regions. / It proves not so,' (V.i.2–3) Octavius tells Antony. 'Tut, I am in their bosoms, and I know / Wherefore they do it' replies Antony irritably (7–8). When Brutus and Cassius join them for a military conference, the two sides quarrel with each other. Only Octavius remains calm, coolly warning his enemies that he will never rest until every one of Caesar's wounds has been avenged. Once the battle of Philippi is under way, it is, contrary to Brutus' belief, misjudgement rather than fortune that determines the course of events. Believing that Titinius has been captured and that their situation is hopeless, Cassius falls on his sword. No sooner is he dead than Titinius enters wearing a wreath of victory. When he and Messala find Cassius' body, Messala comments on the irony of their predicament:

> Mistrust of good success hath done this deed.
> O hateful Error, Melancholy's child,
> Why dost thou show to the apt thoughts of men
> The things that are not?
>
> (v.iii.65–8)

With its formal personifications, Messala's speech is like a choric commentary on human credulity. It suggests, not that one interpretation is worth as much as another, but rather how easy it is to misinterpret the facts. Titinius shares Messala's sense of the irony of the situation: 'Why didst thou send me forth, brave Cassius?' he says when Messala has gone, 'Alas, thou hast misconstrued everything' (v.iii.79; 83).

As with the earlier debates over dreams and omens, and the arguments about political action, there is in Act v a mixture of conjecture, misjudgement and factual error. Was Cassius right to argue against taking the initiative at Philippi? There's no way of telling. Allowing the enemy to seek them out might have proved equally disastrous. But when Cassius commits suicide in the belief that their cause was lost, he was misinformed. This was not a matter of opinion. It was simple error. Pindarus was wrong; Titinius had not been captured. By returning repeatedly to the question of evidence and interpretation, *Julius Caesar* invites us to consider the problem that any historian must deal with in reconstructing the past. How reliable is our knowledge of the facts, and is our interpretation of them justified?

As we've seen, postmodern historiographers argue that there's no essential difference between fact and interpretation. According to Ellen Somekawa and Elizabeth Smith, 'within whatever rules historians can articulate, all interpretations are equally valid'.[58] Shakespeare doesn't appear to share this view. If, as Messala and Titinius observe, people often misinterpret the evidence, this presupposes that there are discoverable facts and that people are capable of getting them either right or wrong. There's no *a priori* reason for assuming that any character, major or minor, is voicing Shakespeare's own views. But in this case Messala and

Titinius happen to be right. The (symbolically) short-sighted Cassius (v.iii.21) was wrongly advised that Titinius had been captured by the enemy. No sooner had he killed himself than the truth was revealed. Titinius had been surrounded by friends, not enemies. This is no more a matter of opinion than the argument in Brutus' house about sunrise. In both cases Error was showing men's thoughts 'the things that are not'.

Julius Caesar is an imaginative retelling of one of the most important events in Roman history. With its metadramatic concern with truth, interpretation and judgement it's also an invitation to reflect on the value of history. It may be true that, unlike the historian, the poet, in Sidney's words, 'nothing affirms, and therefore never lieth'.[59] Nevertheless, without a clear understanding of the difference between fact and interpretation, history, as Foucauldians rightly argue, can have little meaning for the present. In *Julius Caesar* Shakespeare goes out of his way to emphasise that difference. While carefully avoiding commitment to either a monarchist or a republican point of view, he makes it clear that the story of Cassius' *coup* offers an instructive analogue for the present. But that analogue would only be meaningful if it told us something about the human condition. The Earl of Essex's followers admired their leader for his virility: so strong was his sense of masculine pride that he was even prepared to quarrel with his sovereign when honour was at the stake. In a passage from the *Discourses* that could not have helped but strike a chord with contemporary readers of Essex's *Apologie*, Machiavelli warned that, when faced with the potential threat of tyranny, it's usually better to temporise than risk violent action. If you do act precipitately you are likely to hasten the very evil you are seeking to avoid; the problem (as Essex watchers could see all too well) is that 'men are,' as Machiavelli wrote, 'by nature inclined to look with favour . . . on enterprises which seem to have in them a certain virility'.[60] He could almost have been writing about Essex.

Without an understanding of those human universals that Machiavelli comes back to time and again in his political writings, we would indeed be, as White puts it, 'isolated within our peculiar modalities of experience'. Though it's been fashionable for some two decades to claim that most leading intellectuals of the time were radical anti-essentialists, the historical evidence points overwhelmingly in the opposite direction. Major and minor writers in this period were united in their belief in a transhistorical core of human nature. If history had a lesson for the modern world that's because, as Samuel Daniel put it, 'man is a creature of the same dimension he [always] was'.

CODA: THE USES OF HISTORY

Julius Caesar makes a point of distinguishing between fact and interpretation. Was Shakespeare's historical vision fatally flawed by what postmodernists believe is a false distinction? Or is it the postmodern view of history itself that is logically flawed? In *Truth, Fiction, and Literature* Peter Lamarque and Stein Olsen argue that the postmodern reduction of all historical narrative to the status of fiction is based on a confusion between events in the sense of things that actually take place in the real world, and narrative *descriptions* of things:

As long as one talks about fiction, this confusion between the object sense and the description sense of the word does not matter: the events are invented, imagined, constructed, and they come into existence (or such existence as they have) through the construction of the verbal expressions that make up the story in which they occur . . . When one uses the word 'history', on the other hand, a confusion between the two senses of this word is fatal; such a confusion would mean that one talked about history in the object sense as if that could be constructed too. In other words, the confusion would legitimize a conclusion that in constructing an account of the past one was also constructing the past. But this is exactly where the analogy between the concept of fiction and the concept of history breaks down. . . . If past events were constructed, they would no longer be the past but simply fictional events.[61]

When debate about the nature of historical writing is conducted at the high level of abstraction that characterises much postmodern historiography, it's all too easy to overlook the kind of category errors that philosophers like Lamarque and Olsen object to. Before we leave this discussion of Shakespeare's use of history let's drop the Theory and consider an actual historical event that was dramatised for the stage at the end of the last century. It's a story that illustrates the similarities and, more important, the differences between a factual record and a fictional account of the same event.

In the winter of 1998/9 the London Tricycle Theatre company staged a play based on the public inquiry into the death of Stephen Lawrence, a young black man who was stabbed to death at a south-London bus stop by a group of white youths in April 1993. Apart from the sheer incompetence and apparent indifference that characterised the police investigation into the murder, what emerged with most shaming clarity in *The Colour of Justice* was the kind of racist attitudes that appeared to be endemic in some sections of British society at that time. After one of the suspects has stonewalled every question from the magistrates, the inquiry hears an extract from a secret recording of a conversation with his brother. 'Every nigger', says the suspect's brother, 'should be chopped up and they should be left with nothing but fucking stumps.'[62] In his review of the play in *The Guardian*, Michael Billington wrote: 'the supreme virtue of this staging . . . is that it allows the facts that emerged in the inquiry to speak for themselves'.[63]

A theatre reviewer writing to a tight deadline can be excused for coming out with the sort of cliché that most of us have used at some time or other. In reality we know that no theatrical performance, however faithful to the original events, can claim to let facts speak for themselves. In reducing over 10,000 pages of transcripts to a playscript John Norton-Taylor had to make decisions at every stage about objectivity, balance and emphasis, knowing full well that he might not have got it right.[64] Quite apart from the text, other matters – casting, staging, lighting, sound effects and so forth – all have a powerful effect on an audience's response to a play. Manifestly, there can be no such thing as an objective stage presentation of an historical event, a truism from which it would be difficult to imagine many literary critics dissenting.

It's equally true that, however much it might strive for impartiality, a purely factual report of a criminal inquiry would probably not succeed in eliminating bias altogether: the very act of selection and condensation involves judgement and choice. Does this mean that all accounts are equally contaminated? Of course not. A patient magistrate listening to all sides of the case and conscientiously seeking the truth may still be guilty of some unintentional bias; but his report is likely to be more reliable than any version offered by a policeman claiming to have lost his contemporaneous notes. However, a postmodernist would deny this distinction, claiming, not just that all narrative is rhetorical, but that there is no essential or meaningful difference between an historical record of an event and a fictional representation of that same event. As Keith Jenkins puts it, 'everything is ultimately interpretation'.

Following Foucault, postmodern historiographers like White and Jenkins claim that historical narratives are no more than verbal fictions, and have more in common with literature than they do with any kind of scientific document. If we apply this axiomatic postmodernist principle to the Lawrence affair, it means that the version of events offered by the five murder suspects is worth as much as anyone else's; it means also that police denial, in the face of overwhelming evidence to the contrary, of the existence of institutionalised racism in the force has as much validity as the opinion of those who claimed to have experienced police abuse. That being the case, what lesson can we draw from the Lawrence affair? The answer is simple: there is none. As Hindess and Hirst affirm, history for the postmodernist is 'politically valueless'.[65] If we can never determine the true facts; if we can never know who this man was murdered by and for what reason; if we can never know why the police were so slow to follow up informants' leads; if we can never know whether or not racial intolerance exists in our society, then we have no grounds for demanding the kind of official inquiries that were in fact subsequently conducted into prejudice in the British police and armed forces. In short, if we can never learn from the past, we have no rational grounds for seeking change. Before embracing postmodern theories of history we might do well to recall two other chilling stories of injustice and inhumanity. Having survived the Holocaust, Primo Levi wrote movingly and with the greatest clarity, in books like *If This is a Man* and *The Drowned and the Saved*, of his experiences in Auschwitz. What tormented him and contributed to the depression that finally drove him to suicide was the claim, fashionable in the 1970s and now once more gaining currency, that the truth can never be told. More recently, Sola Sierra, president of the Chilean Association of Relatives of the Disappeared, said: 'Remembering helps the people of a country avoid committing the same crime'.[66]

History has traditionally been valued for the perspective it provides on the present. If, as Plutarch's translator Jacques Amyot argued, history is 'the school of wisdom, to fashion men's understanding, by considering advisedly the state of the world that is past', that's because it 'teacheth us to judge of things present, and to foresee things to come: so as we may know what to like of, and what to follow, what to mislike, and what to eschew'.[67] But you can only learn from history if you are able to deduce certain principles of human behaviour from past examples. That's why Renaissance politic historiographers were so insistent on human universals: without them history really is no more than a tale told by an idiot, signifying nothing.

CHAPTER 8

Genius

Some years ago the neurologist Oliver Sacks met an autistic child called
Stephen Wiltshire. Like most autistic people, Stephen seemed to lack any
real sense of an inner self. That meant that he had no idea that other
people might have inner selves; he had, as cognitive psychologists would
say, no theory of mind.[1] This lack of mind theory makes it difficult for
autistic people to communicate with others. The physical signals that
most of us respond to intuitively, and that act as clues to what's going on
in someone else's mind, mean nothing to them. They seem to be indifferent to other people's feelings. But Stephen had an extraordinary talent.
Just as some musical *idiots savants* can play a piece of music note-for-note
after a single hearing,[2] Stephen was able to draw architecturally complex
buildings from memory with total recall. These delicate and beautiful
drawings were a best-seller when they were published as a book called
Floating Cities in 1991. Talking to Stephen, Sacks was struck by the
paradox of a person who had such prodigious gifts and such an apparent
void within. So strange was this paradox that he asked himself if it was
possible for a classically autistic person to be an artist in the conventional
sense of the term. That set him thinking about the whole question of
creativity. 'Creativity', he wrote,

as usually understood, entails not only a 'what', a talent, but a 'who' – strong
personal characteristics, a strong identity, personal sensibility, a personal style,
which flow into the talent, interfuse it, give it personal body and form. Creativity
in this sense involves the power to originate, to break away from existing ways of
looking at things, to move freely in the realm of the imagination, to create and
re-create worlds fully in one's mind – while supervising all this with a critical
inner eye. Creativity has to do with inner life – with the flow of new ideas and
strong feelings.[3]

Sacks' definition of artistic creativity would do nicely as an account of
literary genius. The greatest writers have traditionally been recognised as

men or women of an original cast of mind who tend to challenge the
orthodoxies of their time. They prompt us to rethink our most basic
assumptions about those perennial topics to which literature repeatedly
returns and about which we can be sure to have mixed feelings: war,
heroism, violence, religion, political manoeuvring, social injustice, growing up, courtship, sexual infidelity, and, of course, art itself. Distrusting
conventional solutions, writers of genius characteristically leave us with
questions rather than answers. Literary genius also expresses itself in
highly imaginative use of language and a fascination with complex artistic
structures. It transforms the genres within which it works. And though
environment – social, political, intellectual – plays a vital role in shaping
the imagination, genius leaves us with a sense of the inexplicable, a sense
that so much creative originality seems to come, not from a privileged
education, or from exceptional social circumstances, but from some
undiscovered region of the mind. Those who possess '*ingenium*', or
genius, wrote Ben Jonson paraphrasing the Spanish humanist Juan Luis
Vives, seem 'able by nature, and instinct, to pour out the treasure of
[their] mind'; literary language, it seems, 'springs out of the most retired,
and inmost parts of us, and is the image of . . . the mind'.[4]

This view of literary genius has not been fashionable in recent decades.
Genius, we are told, is undemocratic: 'asking who the geniuses are
presumes a particular type of hierarchical organization', writes one
scholar.[5] Postmodernists believe that the notion of genius as something
that springs from an invisible natural source inside us is mistaken. 'Great
art is not a matter of inspiration, or of being in tune with one's unconscious', writes Christine Battersby in a feminist study of genius; it's
socially constructed.[6] And because it's men on the whole who do the
constructing, conventional ideas of genius naturally privilege men and
devalue women.[7] Postmodernists object to the traditional view of genius, not just because they believe that it gives a misleading picture of
the way the mind works, but because it obscures the ideological nature
of artistic creation. The phenomenon we call genius is in reality no
more than a particular set of skills and accomplishments that serve to
endorse the interests of those in power, with the artist serving merely
as the voice through which ideology speaks. This is thought to be no less
true of Shakespeare than it is of any other author. Shakespeare's plays
weren't the expression of an exceptional mind responding in unpredictable ways to 'the very age and body of the time his form and pressure';
they were the product of the entertainment industry.[8] And because in
Elizabethan England that industry consisted almost entirely of men, it

follows that any play that such an industry assembled must reflect male prejudices.

In our post-Romantic world we are so familiar with the traditional idea that great works of art are produced by exceptional minds that people tend to assume that earlier centuries had similar views of artistic genius. But postmodernists tell us that Shakespeare's contemporaries were unfamiliar with the very idea of individual genius: 'in the Renaissance our modern concept of the genius simply did not exist', writes Battersby.[9] Because the notion of an inner self was alien to Renaissance writers, it didn't occur to them that a writer could be original. As Terence Hawkes explains, the idea of a literary text expressing its author's mind 'would have been unfamiliar to Shakespeare, involved as he was in the collaborative enterprise of dramatic production'.[10] Graham Holderness makes the same point: 'when we deconstruct the Shakespeare myth what we discover is not a universal individual genius . . . but a collaborative cultural process'.[11] Writers might have talent, but not genius in the modern sense of the term. The notion of a writer producing a work of great imaginative power as a result of exceptional inborn gifts wasn't invented until the eighteenth century, when writers like Addison, Akenside, Hurd and Young began for the first time to celebrate the principle of creative individuality as the true mark of literary greatness.[12] To apply these Romantic ideas to Shakespeare would be anachronistic. A play like *King Lear*, hailed by later generations as a work of consummate genius, was not 'the authentic statement of a coherent author'.[13] As the product of a team of script writers, technicians, craftsmen and entrepreneurs, it could do no more than echo the misogynist prejudices of its age. Genius, in short, is not some kind of universal human phenomenon that mysteriously springs up in certain exceptional individuals in all ages and in all human societies. It's the invention of a particular historical period and serves a specific ideological function. Hazlitt said that original genius is nothing but nature and feeling working in the artist's mind;[14] postmodernism says that it's nothing but ideology working in *our* minds.

These arguments are now widely accepted by the literary-critical establishment. They may not command universal assent, but they certainly represent mainstream academic opinion in the world of Shakespeare studies.[15] An unguarded remark about human nature or Shakespeare's genius at an international conference is sure to be met with incredulity. But what are the intellectual credentials of these ideas? In this chapter I will consider their origins in postmodern anti-humanism, the historical evidence for Shakespeare's supposed anti-essentialism, and classical and

Renaissance ideas of genius. Finally I will come back to the claim that *King Lear* does no more than endorse ideological commonplaces. Widely regarded as Shakespeare's most powerful, even if not his most dramatically successful tragedy, it's a good case for testing conventional ideas of genius.

ABOLISHING THE AUTHOR

Constructionist theories of genius are a product of the anti-humanism of the 1960s. In his seminal essay 'The Death of the Author' (1968) Roland Barthes famously declared that 'it is language which speaks, not the author'. Claiming that 'the author is a modern figure', the 'epitome and culmination of capitalist ideology', Barthes announced that 'a text is not a line of words releasing a single "theological" meaning (the "message of the Author-God") but a multi-dimensional space in which a variety of writings, none of them original, blend and clash'. Barthes thought that the modern notion of literary creativity was illusory. In reality the writer has no passions, humours, feelings, impressions; he is merely a repository of words and phrases culled from other writers; his 'only power is to mix [pre-existing] writings'.[16] In the following year Michel Foucault responded with an essay entitled 'What is an Author?' endorsing Barthes' radical ideas about writers and why they can never be original. Where Barthes had suggested vaguely that the author was a modern invention, Foucault was more specific: only since the eighteenth century, when, as he claimed, writers first 'became subject to punishment',[17] have we tried to give the false notion of the 'author' a semblance of reality by attributing to it such notions as 'profundity' or '"creative" power'.[18] Foucault claimed that these ideas are no more than projections of our own peculiarly modern ideas of authorship.

It's difficult to understand where Foucault can have got the idea that the concept of the author didn't exist before the eighteenth century. Even more puzzling is why literary critics accepted it so unquestioningly.[19] After all, the idea of authorship was as much a commonplace in the Middle Ages and the Renaissance as it was in the classical world.[20] For Jonson a poem was, quite simply, 'the work of the poet'.[21] It was the result of his 'labour and study', and his to alter as he saw fit. So too was it for Samuel Daniel. When Daniel issued a corrected version of some of his poems in 1607 he defended the right of an author to amend his work on the grounds that poetry is a personal testament:

> What I have done, it is mine own, I may
> Do whatsoever therewithal I will.
> I may pull down, raise, and re-edify:
> It is the building of my life, the fee
> Of nature, all the'inheritance that I
> Shall leave to those which must come after me;
> And all the care I have is but to see
> Those lodgings of m'affections neatly dressed.[22]

Medieval and Renaissance writers had just as clear a sense of stylistic individuality as we do. 'I know no work from man yet ever came / But had his mark, and by some error showed / That it was his', wrote Daniel.[23] Without a concept of authorial individuality the sophisticated games that Chaucer plays with his reader as he pretends to disclaim any responsibility for his own supremely inventive poetry on the grounds that he's simply following his 'auctour' would have been quite meaningless.[24] But Jonson wasn't joking when he spelt out in the title of his elegy on Shakespeare – 'To the Memory of My Beloved, The Author, Mr William Shakespeare' – the most important thing about his subject, namely, that he was a writer.[25]

Even disregarding Foucault's novel theory of the origins of authorship, neither his nor Barthes' essay was quite as original as its portentous tone suggested. The notion that any literary text could have a single meaning, 'theological' or humanistic, would have struck literary theorists of the 1940s and 1950s as distinctly old-fashioned. When W. K. Wimsatt and Monroe Beardsley declared in their celebrated essay, 'The Intentional Fallacy' (1946), that a poem doesn't belong to the writer, but goes its own way in the world regardless of its author's intentions,[26] they weren't so much laying down a radical new principle in critical thought as summarising ideas that had been current for some two decades. By the late 1960s anti-intentionalism had long been a new orthodoxy. In the same year that Barthes announced post-structuralism's startling discovery that literary texts don't have a single, authorised meaning, E. D. Hirsch wrote: 'there has been in the past *four decades* a heavy and largely victorious assault on the . . . belief that a text means what its author meant'. Protesting at the new orthodoxy, he wrote sardonically: 'it was not simply desirable that literature should detach itself from the subjective realm of the author's personal thoughts and feelings; it was, rather, an indubitable fact that all written language remains independent of the subjective realm'.[27] By the middle of the twentieth century it was a generally accepted view in British and American criticism that, far from

having a single, unalterable meaning, great works of literature are characterised by a plurality of meanings. Reflecting what he described as 'our
typical mid-century feeling for . . . unresolved dialectic', the medievalist
Charles Muscatine wrote: 'the perennial significance of great poems
depends on the multiplicity of meanings they interrelate'.[28] Like much
of the best post-war Anglo-American criticism, Muscatine's work combined an historicist approach to literature with a New Critical belief that
radical ambivalence was an essential criterion of literary excellence. As we
saw in chapter 1, W. R. Elton shared that 'mid-century feeling for
unresolved dialectic': for the new post-war generation of Shakespeare
scholars,[29] the structure of the typical Shakespeare play was 'a dialectic of
ironies and ambivalences, avoiding in its complex movement and multi-
voiced dialogue the simplifications of direct statement and reductive
resolution'.[30]

At first sight it seems puzzling that Barthes and Foucault should have
ignored the Anglo-American debate on authorial intention. However,
when you put these essays in their historical context the hyperbole is
understandable. 'The Death of the Author' was a political *jeu d'esprit*, a
protest against a literary establishment that was far more authoritarian
than anything that Britain and America had ever known.[31] The contrast
with the British and American literary establishment could hardly have
been greater. The truly surprising thing about Barthes' essay was not the
fact that it ignored the entire history of modern debate on intention, nor
that it was tilting at long-since demolished windmills, but rather that
American and British critics took its revolutionary call for a rejection of
authoritarian ideas about literary meaning seriously, and imported that
demand into what was an essentially pluralist critical environment.
Writing as if the new post-war critical movement that Muscatine was
part of had never existed, postmodern Shakespeareans defined their own
practice in opposition to ideas that had been abandoned in America and
Britain long before Barthes rose up in defiance of the French literary
establishment. Jonathan Dollimore, for example, asserted that traditional
Shakespeare criticism was 'concerned with discovering a single political
vision'.[32] Kathleen McLuskie claimed that traditional criticism posited a
fixed 'moral meaning [which is] the authentic statement of a coherent
author'.[33] Terence Hawkes said that traditionalists believed that each of
the plays 'offers once-for-all revelations about what Shakespeare
"thought" and "felt"'.[34]

It was in the 1980s that French theory rapidly took hold in Anglo-
American Shakespeare studies. It might be thought that after the excitement

had died down and people had had time to reflect on the ahistorical nature of Barthes' and Foucault's claims about the origins of authorship, scholars would have treated these essays with the same scepticism that they would any other body of unsupported assertions. But this didn't happen. Despite Foucault's own declared contempt for the bourgeois practice of naming celebrated writers as 'an index of truthfulness',[35] postmodern Shakespeareans continue to cite Barthes and Foucault as authorities on authorship, claiming that before the eighteenth century people neither placed value on originality nor considered the possibility that literary invention might come from within.[36] They also continue to echo Barthes' complaints about traditional criticism with its supposed insistence on the principle of authorised, univocal meaning. What was consistently emphasised in the radical criticism of the final decades of the twentieth century was postmodernism's role in liberating criticism from the strictures of a naïve intentionalism that in reality already belonged to the past. Asserting that traditional criticism was committed to such notions as 'the transcendent author . . . and transparent, single-levelled meaning', Hugh Grady explained that now, thanks to the 'clarity of focus provided by the new critical paradigms of our own day',[37] we have left all this behind. Catherine Belsey similarly claimed that it was 'current theory [that] permits us to see meaning as heterogeneous'.[38] The theme continues into the present century. In a collection of essays edited by Grady, John Joughin writes: 'poststructuralism . . . allows for the possibility that texts are open to a number of interpretations'.[39] It's as if the possibility that works of literature might have more than one definitive meaning had never crossed people's minds until postmodernism dared to suggest the idea. It's difficult to disagree with Terry Eagleton, formerly one of modern Theory's most widely read proselytisers, when he describes postmodernism as 'a game in which one solemnly sets up a grotesque travesty of one's opponent's view, and then proceeds self-righteously to bowl it over.'[40]

In their essays on the author Barthes and Foucault combined an extreme form of anti-intentionalism with a constructionist view of the self. But again, the constructionism was not so much a new position as an exaggerated version of an idea that had been current in anthropology and sociology since the early decades of the century. According to the constructionist theory of human nature that had dominated the social sciences since the 1920s, the individual is an effect of culture with minimal input from biological factors. In 1963 the American sociologist Peter Berger wrote: 'society not only controls our movements, but shapes our identity, our thought and our emotions. The structures of society become the structures of our consciousness.'[41] Barthes and Foucault took the familiar idea that the self is a social construct and inflated it to the point where it exploded, leaving nothing but tattered fragments that were incapable of thinking original thoughts or of making any kind of meaningful contact with other minds. They argued that the common-sense view of the self was merely an illusion conjured up by ideology's seductive powers of 'interpellation'.[42] Its function was to keep us in subjection while giving the illusion of intellectual independence. In reality our selves are fragmented and discontinuous; we are 'frail, precarious, dispersed across a range of discourses'[43] we are, in the postmodernist phrase, 'de-centred' beings.

If the self does not exist, it would obviously make little sense to talk of creative originality or genius. An *idiot savant* may have total musical recall, or extraordinary powers of draftsmanship, but no autistic person has ever written a great work of literature. For that you need an intuitive understanding of what makes other people tick – something that will always remain a mystery for autists. But postmodernism is sceptical of the notion of great literature produced by exceptional minds. Foucault argued that, since the notion of an 'originating subject' is an illusion, critics must ask the historian's question, 'under what conditions and through what forms can an entity like a subject appear in the order of discourse?' The task of criticism, he believed, was to strip away any false notions of creativity and analyse the subject 'as a complex and variable function of discourse'.[44] Popularising these ideas, Hawkes explained that

one of the major effects of latter-day post-structuralist thinking has been the subversion of a central ideological commitment to the idea of the individual, sovereign self, the human subject, as the fundamental unit of existence and the main negotiable instrument of meaning. In consequence, the notion of the text as the direct expression of that subject's innermost thoughts and feelings has also been abandoned.[45]

LOOK IN THY HEART AND WRITE

Let's turn now to the question of Renaissance anti-humanism and the claim that writers in this period had, at best, only a rudimentary notion of the self. According to Barthes and Foucault, the idea that books are written by 'originating subjects' with an inner life and '"deep" motives' is a modern invention. The fact that neither of them provided any evidence in support of these claims didn't prevent their assertions from quickly becoming accepted as statements of historical fact. Within a decade or so it had become an axiomatic principle in postmodern Shakespeare criticism that in Elizabethan England it hadn't yet occurred to people that they might have an inner self or that a literary text might be an expression of some form of inner being. Echoing Foucault, Jonathan Dollimore claimed that it wasn't until the Enlightenment that the individual became 'the origin and focus of meaning'.[46] Catherine Belsey confirmed the point, claiming that 'the unified subject of liberal humanism' didn't exist in early modern England: before the middle of the seventeenth century 'the representative human being has no unifying essence . . . Disunited, discontinuous . . . he has no single subjectivity . . . he is not a subject'.[47] Foucault had spoken: 'man' had not yet been 'invented'.[48]

Faced with an overwhelming body of evidence that Renaissance writers *did* believe in something called 'human-kindness' (that is, the nature of humankind), and that they *did* distinguish as a matter of course between inner and outer self, some critics shifted Foucault's epistemic revolution back a century or so and argued that it was the Elizabethans who invented the idea of the self. In 1998 Harold Bloom's *Shakespeare and the Invention of the Human* argued that the very notion of personality is something we owe to Shakespeare.[49] More recently Christopher Pye has argued, if I understand him correctly, that the flowering of the Elizabethan theatre coincided with the birth of 'the subject':

Here, in the era of spectacle and of a subjectivity bound less by established resources of narrativity and inwardness than by an as yet fragilely managed circuitry of exchange, the emergence of the subject is conditioned from the outset by history's proximity to the crypt, representation's proximity to demonic return, and all the possibilities of aggressive reversal and captivation implicit in theater's solicitous appeal.[50]

But there's nothing new in the Elizabethan commonplace that we have an outward self that takes many different forms, and a constant inner self that is largely hidden from the world. As the medievalist David Aers reminds us, 'the whole medieval penitential tradition involves a fundamental and perfectly explicit distinction between *inner* and *outer*, between that which is within and passes show and that which is without, the external act'.[51] Nor does the inner/outer distinction begin with medieval Christianity. St Augustine may have been responsible for introducing the idea of a spiritual journey into the self as the way to find God,[52] but he didn't invent the idea of the inner self any more than Freud invented the subconscious.[53] Indeed, it seems inherently unlikely that anyone actually 'invented' it: it's part of what it means to be human,[54] as Foucault himself seems to have realised in his final years.[55] Classical writers certainly believed that it was important to distinguish between the inner and outer man. Seneca, one of the Elizabethans' favourite Latin writers, knew only too well what it was like to live, like his own Thyestes, in daily fear of assassination,[56] and meditated on the problem of self-preservation both in the tragedies and in his essays. In 'On Tranquillity of Mind' he cautioned against the risks of candour in public life. But at the same time he warned that even under the most extreme pressure you should never lose contact with the inner man.[57] Seneca's evocation of the dangers of life under a tyranny had an obvious appeal for Renaissance writers, living as they did at a time when heresy was treason punishable by public torture and execution. Hamlet's confession that he has 'that within which passeth show' (i.ii.85) is a generic complaint of the Senecan hero. One of the most powerful expressions of this theme is the Duchess of Malfi's Senecan *planctus* on 'the misery of us that are born great'.[58] Though she recognises that those who have to live their lives in public are 'forced to express [their] violent passions / In riddles, and in dreams' (445–6), she retains a heroic sense of who and what she is despite all Bosola's attempts to destroy her identity: 'I am Duchess of Malfi still' (iv.ii.142).

A sense of difference between inner and outer selves is something you find everywhere in Elizabethan and Jacobean literature. 'Vertues seat is deepe within the mynd / And not in outward shows, but inward thoughts defynd', wrote Edmund Spenser.[59] 'I have unclasped / To thee the book even of my secret soul,' Orsino tells Viola (*Twelfth Night*, i.iv.13–14). 'I have that within that passes show', says Hamlet (i.ii.85). 'What is in thy mind / That makes thee stare thus?' wonders Imogen when she questions Posthumus' servant Pisanio about his odd behaviour: 'Wherefore breaks that sigh / From th' inward of thee?' (*Cymbeline*, iii.iv.4–6). 'Be careful', James I told Prince Henry, 'so to frame all your indifferent actions and outward behaviour, as they may serve for the furtherance and forth-setting of your inward virtuous disposition.'[60] 'A secret self I had enclosed within / That was not bounded with my clothes or skin', wrote Thomas Traherne.[61] That it would be unwise to judge the 'inward man' by his 'exterior' behaviour (*Hamlet*, ii.ii.6) was no more than common sense for Shakespeare's contemporaries.

What people also took for granted in Elizabethan and Jacobean England was that poetry 'springs out of the most retired, and inmost parts of us'. Jonson's words sound like a contradiction of one of the most fundamental principles of Renaissance poetic theory. As every graduate student knows, poetics in this period was dominated by mimetic theories of composition: a poet was someone who produced a copy either of the sensible or the intelligible world, his principal concern being how best to move and persuade his readers or listeners. 'Poesy', wrote Philip Sidney in the classic Elizabethan formulation of this axiomatic principle, 'is an art of imitation . . . that is to say, a representing, counterfeiting, or figuring forth – to speak metaphorically, a speaking picture – with this end, to teach and delight.'[62] Hamlet tells us that 'the purpose of playing . . . is to / hold as 'twere the mirror up to nature' (III.ii.20–2). Touchstone says that 'the truest poetry is the most feigning' (*As You Like It*, III.iii.16–17). Not for another century and a half did expressive theories of composition begin to dominate poetics. Only when the Romantic revolution had transformed thinking about the imagination did the poet come to be seen, not as a copier of nature, but as someone who gave expression to inner feelings and emotions. Metaphors of imitation and reflection gave way to images of overflowing springs and fountains. Or at least, that's what the standard books on poetic theory tell us. First published more than half a century ago, M. H. Abrams' *The Mirror and the Lamp* is still the definitive account of the rise of Romantic theories of poetry.[63] Abrams wrote:

Ancient rhetoric had bequeathed to criticism . . . its stress on affecting the audience . . . Gradually, however, the stress was shifted more and more to the poet's natural genius, creative imagination, and emotional spontaneity, at the expense of the opposing attributes of judgment, learning, and artful restraints. As a result the audience gradually receded into the background, giving place to the poet himself, and his own mental powers and emotional needs, as the predominant cause and even the end and test of art.[64]

Abrams' subject was Romantic theory and he couldn't be expected to treat Renaissance poetics in the same depth that he did eighteenth- and nineteenth-century poetic theory. But if he gave a rather schematic view of Renaissance thought, he did make it clear that the shift in critical orientation from affective to expressive theories of poetry was a gradual process. Foucault's theory of epistemic revolutions marking an unbridgeable chasm between mutually incompatible mindsets has been influential in recent decades. The central premise of Dollimore's *Radical Tragedy* was the claim that, sandwiched between two periods of essentialist thinking, was an anti-essentialist episteme when leading thinkers disavowed the idea of a universal human nature. But cultural change doesn't work in this neat, compartmentalising way. Abrams took care to point out that generalisations about any complex intellectual movement are bound to involve simplifications.[65] Although it's true that Renaissance and neoclassical theorists habitually employed a combination of Aristotelian and Horatian formulae when writing about poetry, and indeed continued to use metaphors of reflection and counterfeiting to describe the nature of the poetic process for at least another 150 years,[66] Jonson wasn't saying anything out of the ordinary when he declared that the most gifted writers 'pour out' the riches of the mind.

In medieval and Renaissance literature it's a commonplace that language is an expression of the inner self. The song that Chaucer's Troilus sings after his first meeting with Criseyde is 'a mirour of his mind' (1.365), while according to Chanticleer in *The Nun's Priest's Tale*, all the songs that his father sang came straight from the heart:'Certes, it was of herte, all that he song' (3303). For John Gower too 'the word is tokne [token] of that withinne'.[67] Spenser summed up the obvious when he said that words are 'ment / T'express the meaning of the inward mind' (*The Faerie Queene*, IV.viii.26). James I advised his son that 'the tongue's office [is] to be the messenger of the mind'.[68] Francis Bacon distinguished between oratory based on mere imitation of some excellent pattern of eloquence and the kind of speech that flows 'as from a fountain'.[69]

What was true of language in general applied *a fortiori* to poetry. George Puttenham claimed that true poets don't need to depend on literary models or empirical observation since they are able to generate poetic materials from their own brain.[70] Adapting the same Continental sources,[71] Sidney too argued that true poets are not tied to imitation of the sensible world, but range freely within the zodiac of their wit, creating in effect another nature.[72] Shakespeare's Duke Theseus (probably echoing Sidney) rehearses the same commonplace: the poetic imagination isn't restricted to the known world, but 'bodies forth / The forms of things unknown' (*A Midsummer Night's Dream*, v.i.14–15). Bacon repeated the point, arguing that, unlike historians and philosophers, poets create their own imaginative worlds.[73] John Harington said that you could never hope to emulate a poet like 'the great Sidney' by imitation; only through the imagination is it possible to ascend to the heights of poesy.[74]

If imagination is the key to true poetry, then it obviously makes sense to look within if you are in search of inspiration. Sidney's Astrophil hardly needs his muse to tell him to 'look in thy heart and write' since he confesses: 'I cannot choose but write my mind.'[75] Shakespeare compared the best poets with second-rate artists who 'draw but what they see, know not the heart' (sonnet 24). In the opening sonnet of *Idea* Michael Drayton wrote: 'My Verse is the true image of my Mind'.[76] What Drayton was saying may not actually be true: like Sidney's Astrophil, his speaker is probably just a fictional persona. But that's not the point. Behind his and Astrophil's claims to emotional authenticity is the commonplace assumption that poetry comes from within and is, as Daniel put it, 'the speaking picture of the mind' and 'extract of the soul'.[77] It's true that lyric poetry is a special case. Ostensibly it's the one genre in which poets are supposed by convention to give voice to their inner feelings, though we know that in practice Renaissance poets more often than not conceal their real thoughts under the cloak of a fictional persona. But does the fact that *Astrophil and Stella* is more like a tragicomedy[78] than a poetic autobiography make it any less authentic? Not according to Sidney's contemporary admirers. Thomas Nashe thought that every page of *Astrophil and Stella* was 'strewed with pearl'.[79] Samuel Daniel believed that Astrophil's name must have been 'registered in the annals of eternity'.[80]

And what of drama proper? A long tradition of scholarship going back to the early nineteenth century has made it clear that authorial collaboration was standard practice in the Elizabethan and Jacobean theatre.[81] Just as some of the most successful modern television sitcoms are put together by script-writing teams, so Elizabethan and Jacobean playwrights collaborated to satisfy the demands of the public theatre. Philip Henslowe paid his writing teams about £5 for every play they produced.[82] But that doesn't mean that all plays were team efforts. Nor does it mean that individual writers were incapable of originality when they were collaborating. Is it mere coincidence that the Chamberlain's Men (later the King's Men) were the most successful of the Elizabethan and Jacobean acting companies?

We have been taught that imitation was the paradigm for thinking about poetry in this period. In her groundbreaking *Elizabethan and Metaphysical Imagery* Rosemond Tuve claimed that the mimetic model was so powerful that alternatives were quite literally unthinkable. Poets might object to the stultifying force of convention, but those protests could never take the form of 'the heart, rebelliously bursting through the trammels of form': if Astrophil's muse tells him to look in his heart and write she must be talking about finding appropriate materials for invention; for Tuve it was inconceivable that his muse could mean what she plainly seems to be saying.[83] Yet everywhere we find writers insisting that poetry is 'a gift and not an art',[84] and that true poetry comes from the heart. For Elizabethan and Jacobean theorists, 'very' poets, as opposed to 'common rhymers',[85] are both imitators *and* creators. They certainly copy nature, but they are also 'able to devise and make . . . things of themselves, without any subject of verity';[86] they may be artificers, but they are also like 'creating gods';[87] they may spend years perfecting their skill, but writing also seems to come to them 'by nature, and instinct'.[88] Puttenham sums up the poet's dual nature on the first page of *The Arte of English Poesie* when he tells us that true poets are both 'counterfeiters' *and* 'makers':

A poet is as much to say as a maker . . . Such as (by way of resemblance and reverently) we may say of God: who without any travail to his divine imagination, made all the world of nought . . . Even so the very poet makes and contrives out of his own brain, both the verse and matter of his poem, and not by any foreign copy or example, as doth the translator, who therefore may well be said a versifier, but not a poet. The premises considered, it giveth to the name and profession no small dignity and pre-eminence, above all other artificers, scientific or mechanical. And nevertheless without any repugnancy at all, a poet may in some sort be said a follower or imitator, because he can express the true and lively of every thing is set before him, and which he taketh in hand to describe: and so in that respect is both a maker and a counterfeitor: and poesy an art not only of making, but also of imitation.[89]

To poets like Sidney or Shakespeare the suggestion that the greatest writers were incapable of expressing original thoughts whether in drama or in lyric poetry, or that literary texts could do no more than uncritically echo other texts would have been a baffling one.

LIKE CREATING GODS

Renaissance poets had a sophisticated and self-conscious interest in their own art. While polishing their technique through imitation of their predecessors, they also parodied second-rate versifiers. Much of their work is about poetry itself. Sidney's Astrophil ponders the nature of poetic originality (*Astrophil and Stella*, 1, 3, 6) and wrestles with the thoughts that 'swell and struggle' within as they try to form themselves in words (50). Shakespeare torments himself with the fact that his thoughts seem to be 'inhearsed' in his brain 'making their tomb the womb wherein they grew' (sonnet 86); but at the same time he knows that his 'gentle verse' will be read by 'eyes not yet created' (81). Spenser and Drayton also devised variations on the theme of poetry's immortalising power. Though poets affect to confer immortality on their patrons, they want us to know that in reality it's their own names that they are preserving for posterity. 'I know that I shall be read . . . so long as men speak English', wrote Daniel in the introductory epistle to one of his collections.[90] As for the idea, so long an unquestioned principle in modern scholarship, that Shakespeare wasn't interested in seeing his plays published and certainly wouldn't have regarded them as literature – that has recently been convincingly rejected by Lukas Erne, who argues that Shakespeare wrote for the stage *and* the page, producing different versions of his plays for the different media.[91]

But what of the claim that the *idea* of creative genius didn't exist in Renaissance England? It's true that people didn't begin to develop complex theories of genius until the eighteenth century; true also that this happened to coincide with Shakespeare's sentimental beatification as the tutelary spirit of Merrie England. But to say that the idea of creative individuality didn't enter people's heads for a hundred or so years after Shakespeare's death is like saying that homosexuality didn't exist in early-modern England because the word didn't happen to be in use,[92] or that romantic love was invented by the troubadours. De Quincey put it well when he said that the best writers are those 'that awaken into illuminated consciousness ancient lineaments of truth long slumbering in the mind'; the secret of Wordsworth's poetic genius, he believed, was that it gave expression to 'what is really permanent in human feelings'.[93] It's been unfashionable for some years to talk of universals in literature. But as Ian McEwan reminds us, the truth is that you can hardly read literature without encountering universals: 'that which binds us, our common nature, is what literature has always, knowingly and helplessly, given voice to'.[94] Far from being a construction of modern bourgeois society, the appearance in every generation of certain rare individuals with truly exceptional artistic ability seems to have been a constant feature of our humanity ever since people started decorating cave surfaces in the Upper Palaeolithic. Commentary on literary genius naturally has a shorter history. But people have speculated about the phenomenon of exceptional literary creativity for nearly 3,000 years.[95] In the classical world the usual explanation was that poets of genius must be inspired by the gods. Nor was it just Platonists who favoured the idea of divine inspiration. Even that soberest of statesmen, Cicero, declared that the greatest poets have some kind of 'inborn faculty' and seem to be 'infused with a strange supernal inspiration'.[96] These ideas were common knowledge in the Renaissance: Sidney was probably thinking of Cicero when he spoke of poetry holding children from play and old men from the chimney corner.[97] What occupied the minds of Renaissance theorists was not whether genius existed – that was a given – but two principal questions: what was the nature of genius? was it some kind of divine madness, or was it more a question of rational individuals who possessed innate gifts of an exceptional kind? and second, does great poetry owe more to art or to native genius?[98] Plato's cruelly witty satire on the professional rhapsode, Ion, is probably the origin of both debates.

As we know from the tenth book of *The Republic*, Plato had little time for the higher claims of poetry. In the satirical *Ion*, Socrates pretends to believe that the most exalted poetry has nothing to do with literary artistry in the conventional sense of rational control of verbal materials for an aesthetic purpose. Poets are such refined, ethereal creatures that they can only begin to compose when their minds have been taken over by some spiritual force: 'it is not by art that they compose and utter so many fine things . . . but by divine dispensation'.[99] (Not realising that Socrates is mocking him, Ion enthusiastically agrees.) In another dialogue, *Phaedrus*, Plato is somewhat franker about the nature of this 'divine dispensation': it's simply madness. In a passage that obviously appealed to Erasmus' sense of the absurd[100] (and probably Shakespeare's as well, though he could have got it from Erasmus),[101] Socrates claims that lovers and poets are both inspired with a kind of divine madness: 'the greatest of blessings come to us through madness, when it is sent as a gift of the gods'. So indispensable to the would-be poet is this lunacy that 'he who without the divine madness comes to the doors of the Muses . . . meets with no success, and the poetry of the sane man vanishes into nothingness before that of the inspired madmen'.[102] Translated by his commentators as '*furor poeticus*', Plato's divine madness became one of the essential elements in Renaissance discussions of genius.

Furor poeticus wasn't some esoteric idea that only neo-Platonist *cognoscenti* knew about. Among Elizabethan writers it was common knowledge.[103] Puttenham referred to it on the first page of his treatise on poetry.[104] Giordano Bruno published a whole book on the subject when he was in England in 1585.[105] Contemporaries thought that Spenser had clearly been touched by 'some sacred fury'.[106] Sidney's Astrophil says he's heard about 'poet's fury', but affects not to know what it means (no. 74), though his creator understood it perfectly well and repeated Landino's claim that some poets are 'so beloved of the gods that whatsoever they write proceeds of a divine fury'.[107] Shakespeare's Duke Theseus mocks the hackneyed figure of the inspired poet with his eye 'in a fine frenzy rolling' (*A Midsummer Night's Dream*, v.i.12). *Furor poeticus* was one of the standard ways of talking about the role of inspired genius in poetic composition in this period.

Some poets, like Chapman, took the notion of *furor poeticus* seriously and celebrated the role of inspired frenzy in poetic composition;[108] others, like Sidney and Shakespeare, satirised it. The self-confident critic of professionalism in *Astrophil and Stella,* 74 who prides himself on his own facility with words is in reality a linguistic buffoon. The bluff defender of common sense in the final scene of *A Midsummer Night's Dream* (v.i.4–8) who dismisses poetic imagination as little better than the fantasy of lunatics and lovers is a military ruler who is blind to the power of 'fancy's images'. The frenzied lover who has been reading too much Bruno and thinks he's suffering from the malady that the Middle Ages called *amor heroycus* (*Romeo and Juliet*, 1.i.135–8) is the object of his friends' scorn.[109] Only someone who has a sure sense of the value of his own art can afford to expose his work to ridicule in the way that both Sidney and Shakespeare did when they parodied the language of heroic frenzy. What they were mocking was not the idea of poetic genius itself, but the glib pretensions of second-rate poets like Bruno. The important point is that these ideas were commonplace: satire only works if everyone knows what you are talking about.

The other great Renaissance debate that derived from Plato's *Ion* has to do with the relative importance of art and native genius in poetic composition. As is usual with academic debates, a great deal of time was spent demolishing the opposition. But popularisers had no difficulty resolving conflicting positions in an easy synthesis. Horace simply said that *ingenium* and *studium* are equally important: 'of what avail is either study not enriched by Nature's vein, or native wit, if untrained'.[110] Boccaccio repeated the formula in the fourteenth century, though he was more interested in Platonic frenzy than Horace was. In his *Genealogy of the Pagan Gods* he claimed that, while few may be divinely inspired, when someone has been singled out in this way, the marks of genius are unmistakeable. 'This fervor of poesy is sublime in its effects: it impels the soul to a longing for utterance; it brings forth strange and unheard-of creations of the mind.' Yet as Horace said, what use is native talent without the discipline of art? 'Since nothing proceeds from this poetic fervor ... except what is wrought out by art,' wrote Boccaccio, 'poetry is generally called an art.'[111] Jonson said much the same thing: '*First,* we require in our *poet,* or maker ... a goodness of natural wit. For, whereas all other arts consist of doctrine, and precepts: the *poet* must bee able by nature, and instinct, to pour out the treasure of his mind'. But these natural gifts must be subjected to discipline: 'To this perfection of nature in our *poet,* we require exercise of those parts, and frequent.'[112]

Renaissance poets had a clear idea of what genius was; they knew perfectly well what it meant to drink from Aganippe well or to discover

the hidden secrets of Tempe (*Astrophil and Stella*, 74). As Jonson explained, it was divine instinct that 'the *Poets* understood by their *Helicon*,
Pegasus, or *Parnassus*'.[113] What's also obvious from the way they praised
their contemporaries is that, although writers may not have actually
used the word genius in its English form, they saw striking examples of
genius in the greatest poets of their own time. Nashe claimed that the
meanest line that Sidney wrote was a 'dowry of immortality'.[114] Harington
said that 'the *apex* of the *coelum empyrium* is not more inaccessable then is
the height of *Sidney's* poesy'.[115] Everard Guilpin described *The Faerie
Queene* as a 'master-piece of cunning'.[116] Lines on Shakespeare's memorial
bust praised him as possessing the genius of Socrates and the art of
Virgil,[117] while in his own memorial on Shakespeare Jonson said that
he was not of an age but for all time.[118] Heminge and Condell advised
buyers of their folio edition of the plays to 'Read him, therefore; and
again, and again.'[119]

When admirers wanted to evoke a sense of the seemingly miraculous
powers of their greatest contemporaries, they compared them, not just to
the classics – Sidney was usually compared with Petrarch (a modern
classic), and Spenser with Homer – but to the gods and heroes of
mythology. Nashe compared Sidney with Apollo;[120] someone signing
himself 'R. S.' described Spenser as 'this Britain Orpheus'.[121] To compare
a contemporary writer to Apollo or Orpheus was to suggest, not merely
the idea of remarkable talent, but innate powers of such a magical kind
as to defy comprehension. These comparisons are another way of expressing the familiar Renaissance claim that poets are like 'creating
gods'. The well-worn simile is more than just an abstract principle of
Renaissance poetic theory: the greatest poets have always known that
what they created would acquire a kind of immortality.[122] When someone mocked Euripides for producing only three lines in three days, he
is said to have retorted: 'thy verses will not last those three days; mine will
to all time'.[123] Horace compared his own poetry to an enduring monument built, not of corrodible brass or stone but imperishable words
(Odes, III.xxx). Shakespeare imitated him in sonnet 55, saying that his
own work would continue to be read by future generations. For all the
self-deprecation of sonnets like 85 and 86, he knew that it was his
eloquence, not the Friend's beauty, that would cause his poetry to be
read for as long as men could breathe or eyes could see. He was in effect
creating a future canon. That canon is the result, not of poets being
spoken by language, but of gifted individuals transforming the conventions of their age and writing with such imaginative power that, while

dealing with matters of personal or local interest, they give us insight into 'what is really permanent in human feelings', as De Quincey put it. Like a wedding-guest list, any canon will have doubtful cases that cause arguments. But at the heart of a literary canon is a stable list of exceptional writers who are not just linguistically gifted shapers of future taste, but individuals who see problems where others see only certainties. And though the list will continue to grow as new writers emerge, only time will tell who stays on it and who drops off.

CHALLENGING CONVENTION

Renaissance theorists tell us that true poets are like creating gods: they can make and contrive things out of their own brain; they range freely within the zodiac of their wit; it's as if they are inspired 'by a divine instinct'.[124] Yet when poets wrote for the theatre they seem to have relied entirely on earlier narrative sources. There isn't a single Shakespeare play that doesn't make use of someone else's stories. So was Barthes right when it comes to drama? Did Renaissance writers do no more than rearrange pre-existing materials? Let's consider *King Lear* as a test case and ask whether in this play Shakespeare is simply echoing the ideological prejudices of his *aucteurs*. According to Foucault, the task of criticism is to dispose of the notion of the author as originating subject and consider him instead as merely an effect of the structures of knowledge that characterise the particular episteme he happens to inhabit. Is that what's happening in *King Lear*? Or does Shakespeare rework his source materials in such a way as to challenge conventional thinking? Is *King Lear* a work of genius?

A charge frequently made in postmodern criticism is that the Western literary canon offers us politically motivated cant masquerading as eternal verities.[125] A play that certainly does aim to give us universal truths is *Gorboduc*, one of Shakespeare's imaginative sources for *King Lear*.[126] Barthes characterised the literary text as a space in which a variety of writings blend and clash. This describes *King Lear* rather well. *Gorboduc* is one of a group of writings that merge in Shakespeare's play. Others include Samuel Harsnett's *Declaration of Egregious Popish Impostures*, Raphael Holinshed's *Chronicles*, Sidney's *Arcadia*, and the anonymous *True Chronicle History of King Leir*. For the central story of the ancient British king and his three daughters Shakespeare went to Holinshed and the *True Chronicle History*,[127] adding the Gloucester story from Sidney, and elements of the mad scenes from Harsnett. Though *The True*

Chronicle History is closest to Shakespeare's play in its narrative outline – a
foolish old ruler imposes a love test on his three daughters only to find
that the child he disinherits is the one who loves him best – it did little to
stimulate Shakespeare's dramatic imagination. The play is a sentimental
tragicomedy with stereotyped characters, an implausibly happy ending,
and a simple moral summed up in Leir's *sententia*: 'O, let me warn all ages
that ensueth, / How they trust flattery, and reject the truth.'[128] Though
the play involves a disputed succession and a kingdom weakened by
internal divisions, its political interest is minimal. The author was clearly
less interested in developing constitutional or philosophic themes than in
milking the story for its emotional and sententious possibilities. *Gorboduc*,
by contrast, has a powerful political message that seems to have set
Shakespeare thinking, not just about fathers and daughters, but about
the largest philosophical questions.

Sackville and Norton wrote the play shortly after Elizabeth's accession.
They were both members of her government and devised their play partly
as a piece of cautionary advice (a prince's mirror) for their young queen,
and partly as a warning to parliament against allowing internal divisions
to compromise the common good. Like *The True Chronicle History*,
Gorboduc is set in ancient Britain; it too involves a ruler who unwisely
divides the kingdom between his children (in this case two sons).
Reminding us of how the legendary Brutus had divided the kingdom of
Albion between his three sons (1.ii.269–74), it develops the theme of an
uncertain succession and the resulting curse of civil war. Though the play
is essentially a political morality with good and evil counsellors appealing to the prince's conscience, its mode is Senecan tragedy. To emphasise
the horrors of civil war it paints a vivid picture of an ancestral penalty
going all the way back to Troy and blighting successive generations with
its unquenchable thirst for vengeance: 'Thus fatal plagues pursue the
guilty race, / Whose murderous hand, imbrued with guiltless blood, /
Asks vengeance still before the heaven's face / With endless mischiefs on
the cursed brood'.[129] The play advises the young Elizabeth to heed the
advice of wise counsellors.

Though *Gorboduc* is uncompromising in its condemnation of the
'giddy' rabble who 'headlong run with raging thoughts . . . To ruin
of the realm' (v.i.59–64), it makes it clear that ultimate responsibility
for the civil chaos of the final act lies with the prince himself. In the
familiar analogical argument, a prince is implicitly compared to a father:
'When fathers cease to know that they should rule, / The children cease to
know they should obey' (207–8). The consequences of irresponsible

behaviour are the same in families and states: abandon the principle of 'well ruling' (227) and you can be sure that the gods will punish human folly (1.i.59–67). Underpinning this analogical argument is the principle of natural law. Monarchy is not just pragmatically the best form of rule (1.ii.259–60); it's part of the natural order of things. As one of Gorboduc's counsellors explains, there are

> certain rules,
> Which kind [ie, nature] hath graft within the mind of man,
> That nature hath her order and her course,
> Which (being broken) doth corrupt the state
>
> (1.ii.218–21)

It's this system of universal ethical imperatives that Renaissance legal theorists called natural law.[130] As a postmodernist would say, *Gorboduc* presents its political message as an eternal truth that stands above controversy.

King Lear too gives us a portrait of a tyrannical ruler who brings chaos to the kingdom through his own folly and cruelty. (It's difficult to understand how McLuskie could see a play that owes so much to the tradition of the negative prince's mirror as an endorsement of patriarchal misogyny.) As in *Gorboduc*, the prince's wise counsellor foresees problems, not with the institution of monarchy itself, but with the abuse of royal authority.[131] Finally, like *Gorboduc* too, *King Lear* announces the theme of natural law in the first act. Cordelia's appeal to the reciprocal bond of love between parent and child (1.i.92–8), with its echo in Lear's invocation of 'The offices of nature, bond of childhood, / Effects of courtesy, dues of gratitude' (11.ii.351–2), establishes one of the play's central thematic concerns. But there the similarities end. *Gorboduc* offers its royal audience a series of unquestioned truths: 'one single rule is best. / Divided reigns do make divided hearts' (1.ii.259–60); 'timely knowledge may bring timely help' (111.i.44); 'nothing more may shake the common state, / Than sufferance of uproars without redress' (v.i.34–5); 'Though kings forget to govern as they ought, / Yet subjects must obey as they are bound' (v.i.42–3); and so on. Underwriting all these truths is the knowledge that nature has implanted certain immutable rules of conduct in our minds (1.ii.218–19). Shakespeare's play turns all these eternal verities into problems. *Gorboduc* gives us *sententiae*; *King Lear* gives us paradoxes.

The first 150 or so lines of the play show Lear rejecting Cordelia's appeal to the bonds of natural law and evoking as he does so an image of cannibal tribes that devour their own children. As so often in the tragedies, Shakespeare seems to be setting up a symbolic opposition between two opposing views of humanity and asking us to ponder the question that occupied the minds of all the great Renaissance humanists: the difference between civilised and barbarous behaviour. As the play unfolds, we are given an apocalyptic vision of cruelty and injustice so bleak that human beings seem no better than 'monsters of the deep' preying on one another (Quarto.xvi.49). In words that recall, not just the New Testament,[132] but also Senecan tragedy, Kent asks if such calamities are a sign of the promised end, to which Edgar replies, 'Or image of that horror'(v.iii.238–9).[133] But where *Gorboduc* does nothing to disprove Queen Videna's assurance that 'Jove's just judgement and deserved wrath' will inevitably fall on those who seek to 'transpose the course of governance' (1.i.59–67), *King Lear* undermines any sense that this is a just world in which heaven rewards virtue, punishes error, or indeed takes any interest at all in human affairs. On hearing that Edmund has given orders for Cordelia to be hanged, Albany cries 'the gods defend her!' (v.iii.231). His plea is followed by a symbolic action more eloquent than Lear's own howl of anguish. No sooner has Albany finished his prayer than we get the stage direction: 'Enter King Lear with Queen Cordelia in his arms'.

In a world where the gods, if they exist at all, are either cruel or indifferent, it would seem that Montaigne was right: what we take to be natural law is no more than the vanity of our own imagination.[134] Yet *King Lear's* vision isn't entirely bleak. Extremes of wickedness are matched by equally remarkable acts of selflessness, love and patient devotion. Echoing *The True Chronicle History's* pun on Cordella's name[135] in repeated iteration of the play's keyword, 'heart', Shakespeare inverts the conventional Renaissance hierarchy of intellect and emotion, suggesting that compassion rather than reason is the paramount human value.[136] It's easy enough to ask what good it does Cordelia to be 'most rich, being poor; / Most choice, forsaken; and most loved, despised' (1.i.250–1). The point, however, is not that the virtues enshrined in the Beatitudes are helpless in the Senecan world of the play – they clearly are – but that without them, society is no more than a 'stage of fools' (1v.v.179). Like the Sermon on the Mount, natural law may be simply myth; for all we know there may be no gods, kind or otherwise, sanctioning 'the offices of nature'. But that doesn't nullify those values. Since the consequences of abandoning the principles that we imagine to be 'rules of kind' is a world in which 'madmen lead the blind' (1v.i.47), the best we can do is to order our lives as if there were kindly gods responsible for implanting natural law in our hearts. At least that's what Edgar does, in effect, when he colludes with Gloucester's despair in a grotesque charade of suicide. Edgar doesn't know whether there are any gods or not. The important thing, he tells his father, is to live your life as if they did exist: 'Think that the clearest gods, who make them honours / Of men's impossibilities, have preserved thee' (IV.v.73–4).

Such metadramatic make-believe is a familiar device in Shakespeare, especially in *As You Like It* ('much virtue in "if"'), *The Winter's Tale* and *The Tempest*. What does it tell us about the kind of intellectual and imaginative activity involved in the composition of a play like *King Lear*? It suggests, not so much a de-centred, de-humanised scribe whose only power was to mix pre-existing writings, as an exceptionally self-conscious writer challenging the most fundamental religious and philosophical assumptions of his age, and asking us, as he does so, to think about the difference between art and life and to reflect on the way theatrical make-believe is capable of working on our imagination. The ability to question conventional thinking is not in itself a guarantee of genius; indeed it's no more than any self-respecting postmodernist would claim to be able to do (while denying the same power to creative writers from the past). For a time it was fashionable in postmodern criticism to 'refuse' any distinction between literature and other kinds of writing on the grounds that everything was simply 'text'.[137] But it's obvious to all but materialist critics that there's a difference in kind between a postmodernist critical essay and a Renaissance playtext. There's even a difference in kind between *The True Chronicle History* and *King Lear*. Both are historical dramas dealing with a fictional ancient Britain, yet one of them is never performed on the modern stage while the other is on most people's list of great works of literature. Is that simply because *King Lear* has the advantage of being associated with a powerful brand name? No doubt that helps. But it seems unlikely that it hasn't got something to do also with the fact that whoever wrote *The True Chronicle History* wasn't very good at creating interesting characters, wrote rather flat verse, and lacked artistic imagination, while Shakespeare excelled in all these things. Transforming an old fable about flattery into an apocalyptic critique of a society brought to chaos by tyrannical authority, he devised as the vehicle for his tragedy a complex artistic structure that involved psychologically plausible characters who also have a symbolic dimension, self-conscious references to the play's own style,[138] and language of extraordinary inventiveness. We know that in real life people don't talk in the way that Shakespeare's characters do. Yet paradoxically their linguistic virtuosity seems to hold the mirror up

to our nature and show us what we truly are. This is not to imply that
Shakespeare's interest in Christian quietism, his millenarian concerns, or
his qualified monarchism offer a message to the modern world.[139] Rather
it's to suggest that, if *King Lear* has moved so many playgoers in so many
different cultures, it's because his portrayal of the *problems* that confront
human beings – conflict between parents and children, the consequences
of sexual infidelity, rivalry between siblings, social injustice, irresponsible
rulers, the need to believe in some kind of metaphysical principle – is
rooted in a profound understanding of the human heart (or brain, as
modern neuroscientists would say).[140]

Does all this add up to genius? That will always be a matter of critical
opinion: we are, after all, only talking about degrees of originality and
artistic merit. But on the question of the validity of traditional ideas of
genius, the answer is fairly straightforward. Judging by postmodernism's
own negative criteria – the myth of human creativity (Foucault), the
impossibility of transforming earlier writings and making them into
something original (Barthes), our inability to challenge conventional
thinking (McLuskie), the illusion that we can exercise imaginative control
of verbal materials for an affective purpose (Hawkes) – Shakespeare would
seem to exemplify all the things that are deemed unthinkable in the
postmodernist episteme.

I began this chapter with a quotation from a neuroscientist who writes
about creativity far better than most literary critics manage to do. I'll
conclude with one from an entomologist on the same subject:

Behind Shakespeare, Leonardo, Mozart, and others in the foremost rank are a
vast legion whose realized powers form a descending continuum to those who are
merely competent. What the masters of the Western canon, and those of other
high cultures, possessed in common was a combination of exceptional
knowledge, technical skill, originality, sensitivity to detail, ambition, boldness,
and drive.

They were obsessed; they burned within. But they also had an intuitive grasp of
inborn human nature accurate enough to select commanding images from the
mostly inferior thoughts that stream through the minds of all of us. The talent
they wielded may have been only incrementally greater, but their creations
appeared to others to be qualitatively new. They acquired enough influence and
longevity to translate into lasting fame, not by magic, not by divine benefaction,
but by a quantitative edge in powers shared in smaller degree with those less
gifted. They gathered enough lifting speed to soar above the rest.[141]

CHAPTER 9

Anti-humanism

Let me begin by summarising the argument I set out in my Introduction. Anti-humanism, or anti-essentialism as it's usually termed, is the core theoretical principle of postmodern Shakespeare criticism. It's true that Cultural Materialism makes a particular point of studying literary texts in their historical context.[1] But so too did pre-theoretical historical scholarship. And contrary to what is uniformly claimed in postmodern Shakespeare criticism, twentieth-century historicists had a thoroughly sophisticated understanding of the problems involved in reconstructing the past (see below, pp. 188–9).[2] It's anti-essentialism, rather than an interest in historical context, that chiefly distinguishes Cultural Materialism from older forms of historical scholarship. It's also, despite the claim that it signalled 'the return of history in literary criticism',[3] what principally marks New Historicism off from earlier twentieth-century forms of literary historicism. Jean Howard is right when she says that the key to what's new about New Historicism is 'the basic issue of what one assumes to be the nature of man'; central to postmodern historicism on both sides of the Atlantic is 'the attack on the notion that man possesses a transhistorical core of being. Rather, everything from "maternal instinct" to conceptions of the self are now seen to be the products of specific discourses and social processes.' We know that this is true (as Howard says, it's something we can 'assume'), not because of what we might deduce from research into the mental capabilities of neonatal infants before they've had a chance to absorb culture, clinical experiments designed to test mind theory, cross-cultural studies of gender differences in a wide variety of urban and rural communities, or the epidemiology of culture (how ideas spread), but because, as Howard explains, we have it on Foucault's authority. For the postmodernist, 'nothing exists before the human subject is *created* by history'.[4]

Although anti-essentialism is what defines postmodern historicism as new, Cultural Materialists, New Historicists and materialist feminists believe that Renaissance thinkers and writers anticipated twentieth-century anti-essentialism by some 400 years. Because these writers were, in effect, postmodernists *avant la lettre*, it's 'incorrect', we are told, to read this period 'through the grid of an essentialist humanism'.[5] But as we've seen, these claims are without foundation. Not only did Renaissance humanists take it for granted that there was a universal essence of human nature underlying the cultural differences that distinguish one society from another; they insisted that an understanding of our human-kindness was 'the chief part of wisdom'. One of the justifications for reading literature was the belief that, by holding the mirror up to human nature, and showing us our generic human vices and virtues, poetry could have a civilising influence on the mind. Though radical Protestantism was fiercely opposed to humanist meliorism, it too held that there was an irreducible essence of human nature: the Thirty-nine Articles spelt out with great precision what the Church of England's Convocation agreed was 'the condition of man after the Fall of Adam'. And though the old microcosm/macrocosm analogy eventually became, in Sir Thomas Browne's words, no more than 'a pleasant trope of rhetoric', abandonment of the Pythagorean principles that buttressed the medieval view of humankind certainly didn't mean that human nature itself had been abandoned; all that had gone were the old metaphysical principles that had once supported it. In this concluding chapter I'll try to explain how such an unlikely notion as Renaissance anti-essentialism came about. I'll also suggest that, by listening to what other disciplines have to say about human nature, we can move on from an outdated anti-humanism that has its roots in the early decades of the last century to a more informed modern understanding of human universals. Finally, I'll argue that an acceptance of universals is essential if we want to avoid the kind of nihilistic postmodern world where, in the words of E.M. Forster's Mrs Moore, 'everything exists [and] nothing has value'.[6]

HUMAN NATURE AS IDEOLOGY

Postmodernists agree that the notion of a universal human nature is a bourgeois myth. 'The work of ideology is to present the position of the subject as fixed and unchangeable, an element in a given system of differences which is human nature', writes Catherine Belsey.[7] If capitalism emphasises the value of individual freedom, the argument goes, that's because it requires complicit, obedient subjects who willingly accept their subjection. In constructing us as its subjects, and persuading us that we are autonomous individuals blessed with free will and capable of making rational choices, ideology works in such a way as to obscure the oppression that is said to be the real driving force in all human relations. According to Louis Althusser it was Marx who first saw that human nature was a bourgeois myth. Althusser claimed that, in rejecting the bourgeois philosophy of 'man', Marx established the basis of a truly materialistic theory of history. It was this 'theoretical anti-humanism' that Althusser believed was Marx's true 'scientific discovery'.[8]

As Althusser's critics (and that includes Althusser himself) have shown, this anti-essentialist interpretation of Marx has no basis in Marx's own writing. The Marxist philosopher Scott Meikle has argued that in reality the essentialist categories of law, form, and necessity were 'the powerhouse of [Marx's] explanatory theories'.[9] The very notion of alienation, key to so much of Marx's thought, depends on the principle of an essential humanity from which man has been estranged under capitalism. Indeed without a sense of an integrated, uncorrupted humanity, the concept of alienation is meaningless. If you believe with Howard that 'nothing exists before the human subject is created by history', there's nothing to be alienated *from*; 'man' is merely a cipher. And you cannot be alienated from nothingness. Unlike Althusser and his followers, Marx saw humanity as a species ('*Gattungswesen*') whose essence was self-consciousness and sociability, and whose true potential would only be fully realised with the advent of a communist society. Only under communism, Marx believed, is 'the richness of human subjective sensibility (a musical ear, an eye for beauty of form – in short, senses capable of human gratification, senses confirming themselves as essential powers of man) either cultivated or brought into being'.[10] Communism, for Marx, meant a return to the human; his whole philosophy of history depended on the notion of a human *telos* that could be fully realised only when social conditions had been transformed. History for Marx was, in Meikle's phrase, 'the process of coming-to-be of human society'.[11] In what sounds oddly like an echo of Cicero (see chapter 1, p. 9), Marx wrote in *Capital*: 'He that would criticize all human acts, movements, relations, etc., by the principle of utility, *must first deal with human nature in general*.'[12]

Meikle's exposure of the flaws in anti-essentialist interpretations of Marx was, in effect, confirmed by Althusser himself. In his posthumously published autobiography he candidly admitted that his interpretation of Marx was no more than an imaginary construct which he had arrived at by suppressing everything in Marx that seemed incompatible with his own ideas:

I began to think about Marxism in my own way, though I realise that it was not exactly the way Marx himself thought . . . Naturally it meant that . . . specialists had the feeling I had invented my own view of Marx and an imaginary version of Marxism, which was far removed from the real Marx. I willingly accept this.[13]

In his Introduction to the autobiography, Althusser's editor, who had known him since the 1940s, wrote: 'he did not see history as a story of human effort or emancipation; he was not interested in humanism . . . He set out to show that Marxism was a scientific theory and he sought to complete it.'[14] With hindsight Althusser acknowledged that there was indeed something 'ridiculous' (his word) about his attempt to rewrite Marx's ideas in this way.[15] The Marxist historian E. P. Thompson put it in stronger terms. 'Althusserian "Marxism" is an intellectual freak', he wrote in *The Poverty of Theory*, 'what possible meaning is attached to "the Left" when it teaches lessons of anti-moralism, anti-humanism, and the closure of all the apertures of reason?'[16]

Althusser was taken up by British Cultural Materialists at a time when in France he was already a spent force. Even before the terrible events of the winter of 1980 Althusser was beginning to be seen as an irrelevancy;[17] after his arrest and hospitalisation, he ceased to take an active part in Parisian intellectual life. Discredited though it was, his anti-essentialist Marxism has nevertheless been extremely influential, especially in Cultural Materialist and materialist feminist criticism, and in a less specific way in postmodern criticism in general. Postmodern literary critics continue to reject the notion of a universal human nature with its characteristic, but supposedly illusory, sense of interior selfhood, and claim that human beings are the prisoners of an ideology into which they are born, and from which they can never completely escape; they have no existential 'centre' and no inner self; their sense of self-determination is an illusion. Even their gender is a social artefact. Because the human mind is exclusively the product of competing ideologies and owes nothing to biological nature,[18] it means that there are as many forms of human nature as there are human societies.

Catherine Belsey has recently claimed that 'A generation ago, cultural critics overthrew the tyranny of human nature, and put culture in its place'.[19] In reality the belief that culture is the sole determinant of human behaviour goes back at least as far as the early decades of the last century. In the 1920s and 1930s anthropologists and psychologists argued that human behaviour was determined entirely by environment. In 1925 the American behaviourist John Watson made his famous remark about taking any group of children and turning them into whatever kind of

adults he chose with the appropriate social conditioning.[20] Ten years later
the anthropologist Margaret Mead claimed that 'human nature is almost
unbelievably malleable, responding accurately and contrastingly to contrasting social conditions'.[21] But when other anthropologists later re-
studied the same tribes on which Mead had based her claim, they came
to the conclusion that she had misinterpreted the evidence: it turned out
that Samoan teenagers didn't have anything like the sexually carefree
existence that she had imagined; in reality male and female temperament
among the Tchambuli in New Guinea wasn't the inverse of what the
West regards as normal.[22] One of behaviourism's central clinching arguments had been demolished. With the spectacular failure of Stalinist,
Maoist and other twentieth-century experiments in changing human
nature, behaviourism lost much of the prestige it once enjoyed in the
social sciences. Rather than attempting to explain human behaviour
exclusively in terms of environmental influences, psychologists began to
recognise that it's the product of a complex interaction between genetic
and environmental factors (see pp. 193–5 below). However, postmodernism remains opposed in principle to any essentialist notion of innate
predispositions. Neil Badmington explains why in a recent book called
Posthumanism, arguing that if we are '*naturally* inclined to think, organise
and act in certain ways, it is difficult to believe that human society and
behaviour could ever be other than they are now'. That, he says, is why
'humanism' (in an Althusserian sense) must be opposed. Only if we reject
once and for all the notion of 'man' will radical social change become a
possibility.[23] The fact that throughout history the world has seen any
number of social and cultural revolutions that have not involved abandonment of the idea of a universal human nature is something that
Badmington doesn't discuss.

For much of the twentieth century behaviourism was universally
accepted in the social sciences; it was, so to speak, the official theory of
human behaviour. Nevertheless, there persisted in the popular mind the
notion that there was some kind of universal core of human nature
underlying the infinite variety of local beliefs and practices that characterise different cultures. Before they are introduced to Theory, university
students of English still tend to remark that a particular play has universal
themes, or that the dilemmas experienced by such-and-such a character
are timeless. Irrespective of whether they get these ideas from their school
teachers or from their own intuitions, the fact is that students often seem
to feel, not just sympathy for, but an empathetic affinity with, the figures
they encounter in literature from earlier centuries, experiencing the joys

and sorrows of those characters and responding intuitively to their moods.[24] That's what first drew them to literature. It's as if they imagine there's some kind of human bond linking them with the past, or with characters from cultures quite different from their own. Where did this supposedly illusory idea of a universal human nature originate? Althusser believed that Marx was the first to see that human nature was nothing more than a figment of ideology's imagination. But if the idea was well established in people's minds by the middle of the nineteenth century, where did it come from?

THE HISTORY OF 'MAN'

In the twentieth century a number of thinkers, including Althusser, Barthes, Benjamin, Derrida and Lévi-Strauss, either announced or called for the death of 'man'. But it was Foucault who first undertook to write a post-Nietzschean history of the birth and death of 'man'. His work is one of the formative influences on postmodern Shakespeare criticism. In *The Order of Things* Foucault declared that 'Before the end of the eighteenth century, *man* did not exist . . . man is an invention of recent date.'[25] It's generally assumed by postmodern Shakespeareans that he was claiming that the idea of a universal human nature didn't exist before the end of the eighteenth century.[26] But this is to misread *The Order of Things*. Foucault knew perfectly well that essentialist theories of 'man' go back to the ancient Greeks. He knew too that in the eighteenth century philosophers devoted much intellectual energy to the question of how to define human nature; indeed no other period had 'given it [human nature] a more stable, more definitive status'.[27] And unlike Althusser and his followers in American and British literary criticism, Foucault acknowledged that, far from lacking powers of agency or self-determination, human beings have 'almost unique autonomy'.[28] What interested Foucault at this stage in his career was not the study of human nature in a conventional sense – '*it is not a matter here of man's essence in general*'[29] – but the 'epistemological consciousness of man as such'.[30] What did he mean by this? It's not an easy question to answer.

In later volumes – especially *Discipline and Punish* and *The History of Sexuality* – Foucault charted the origins of our modern sense of selfhood as it's shaped and moulded by ideology until social norms have been completely internalised. *The Order of Things* deals with a more abstract philosophical question. The book is an examination of the conditions that govern the production of knowledge at any given period of history. The similarities and differences between Foucault's epistemes and Thomas Kuhn's scientific paradigms have been much discussed.[31] Though Foucault took over Kuhn's principle of incommensurability between different scientific models, his epistemes are not so much a set of operating principles shared by the scientific community in any period of history, as a series of largely *unconscious* and mutually incompatible mindsets that determine the way we conceptualise the world.[32] They probably owe as much to the French philosopher of science Gaston Bachelard (1884–1962) as they do to Kuhn. According to Bachelard, science isn't about the discovery of pre-existing, immutable facts; rather it's to do with the construction of a reality that itself changes as new questions are asked about it. In place of the traditional view of the history of science as a linear progression, with each generation either modifying or overturning the work of its predecessors, Bachelard proposed the idea of a series of dramatic intellectual ruptures or abrupt breaks with the past. Each age set its own intellectual agenda and established entirely new structures within which knowledge was produced.[33] In *The Order of Things* Foucault developed these ideas and made them the basis of a history of the frameworks that govern our knowledge systems in the post-medieval world. Where Bachelard and Kuhn concerned themselves with the history of science, Foucault took as his province the world of knowledge *tout court* and applied the notion of abrupt shifts between mutually incompatible mindsets to the history of what he called the human sciences.

Like Derrida, Foucault sensed in the mid-1960s that the world was on the brink of some kind of momentous intellectual crisis.[34] In language that seems to echo the portentous *fin-de-siècle* rhetoric of Max Nordau's *Degeneration*, he hinted at 'some event of which we can at the moment do no more than sense the possibility', an event of such cataclysmic proportions that it would bring about the total collapse of our present intellectual world order. As this apocalyptic disintegration took place the figure of 'man' would inevitably 'be erased, like a face drawn in sand at the edge of the sea'.[35] Though it was impossible to say what would follow the modern episteme, the causes of the present crisis were clear: a seismic rift had taken place in 'the order of things' as a result of the 'new position that [man] has so recently taken up in the field of knowledge'.[36] Like a reversal of the earth's magnetic polarity, the entire field of Western thought was once again about to be inverted.

This much is clear (though vigorously disputed):[37] just as the Renaissance and classical epistemes had abruptly given way to entirely new ways of producing and structuring knowledge, so all the familiar presuppositions and habits of thought that characterise the 'man'-centred modern episteme were destined to pass away and be replaced by a new framework of knowledge. What's not clear is how the modern conception of 'man' differs from that of the classical episteme.

Foucault acknowledges that in earlier periods of history scientists and philosophers had made a systematic study of human nature;[38] indeed for centuries humanity had been allotted 'a privileged position in the order of the world'.[39] What was distinctive about the new modern conception of 'man' was the fact that now for the first time you had the paradox of 'a figure in which the empirical contents of knowledge necessarily release, of themselves, the conditions that have made them possible'.[40] The essence of modernity, Foucault explains, consists, 'not [in] the attempt to apply objective methods to the study of man, but rather [in] the constitution of an empirico-transcendental doublet which was called *man*'.[41] Foucault has several goes at elucidating what he calls this 'strange' notion of an 'empirico-transcendental doublet'. But nowhere does he descend from metaphysical abstraction to the level of plain statement. Assuring his reader that all will shortly become clear, he promises that 'the motive of this new presence, the modality proper to it, the particular arrangement of the episteme that justifies it, the new relation that is established by means of it between words, things, and their order – all this can now be clarified'.[42] Foucault is fond of such proleptic reassurance. He tells us that the archaeologist of knowledge must proceed with the utmost intellectual rigour, examining 'each event in terms of its own evident arrangement', recounting how 'the configurations proper to each positivity were modified', analysing 'the alteration of the empirical entities which inhabit the positivities', and studying 'the displacement of the positivities in relation to the others'.[43] The outcome of such a systematic inquiry, he assures us, is 'a precise and extremely well-determined epistemological arrangement in history',[44] an arrangement whose outlines are 'very tight-knit, very coherent'.[45] In this way Foucault conveys the impression, to his followers at least, of a methodology that is at once rigorous, transparent, and scrupulously logical. 'Foucault's is a procedure of vigilance,' writes Jean Howard.[46] But the promised clarification is never delivered. Having assured us that all will now be revealed, he retreats once more into abstractions so impenetrable and so completely devoid of concrete example that we can only speculate about his real meaning. Summing up his theory of the 'empirico-transcendental doublet' that is modern 'man', Foucault writes:

If man is indeed . . . that paradoxical figure in which the empirical contents of knowledge necessarily release, of themselves, the conditions that have made them possible, then man cannot posit himself in the immediate and sovereign transparency of a *cogito*; nor, on the other hand, can he inhabit the objective inertia of something that, by rights, does not and never can lead to self-consciousness. Man is a mode of being which accommodates that dimension – always open, never finally delimited, yet constantly traversed – which extends from a part of himself not reflected in a *cogito* to the act of thought by which he apprehends that part; and which, in the inverse direction, extends from that pure apprehension to the empirical clutter, the chaotic accumulation of contents, the weight of experiences constantly eluding themselves, the whole silent horizon of what is posited in the sandy stretches of non-thought.[47]

Foucault's history of 'man' is irretrievably opaque. *The Order of Things* is concerned with the epistemological problem that arises when, for the first time, it comes to be recognised that 'man' is both an object that we represent to ourselves and at the same time the experiencing subject that does the representing. What's not clear is how and why this new consciousness suddenly supervened at the end of the classical episteme, how it transformed people's understanding of humanity in the conventional sense of 'man's essence in general', and what the impending demise of this 'empirico-transcendental doublet' might entail. Foucault's interminable 'sandy stretches of non-thought' are so resistant to lucid paraphrase that we have to resign ourselves to guessing at what he really had in mind. However, things become much clearer in Cultural Materialist versions of the invention of 'man'. Foucault's epistemes are still there, though now less watertight and with their boundaries shifted. But the invention and anticipated demise of 'man' has become much more straightforward. Indeed it's been completely transformed into something that Foucault would certainly have disowned.

When Foucault claimed that 'man' didn't exist before the end of the eighteenth century he made it clear that he was talking, not about 'man's essence in general' (to have claimed that universalist theories of human nature didn't exist before 1800 would have been demonstrably false), but 'man' in the sense of an object of knowledge which is at the same time a subject that creates that knowledge. Cultural Materialism interprets Foucault's statement about the invention of 'man' in an altogether simpler way, and in doing so turns an epistemological riddle into an uncompromising statement of historical fact. According to Catherine Belsey, the notion of 'man', in the sense of what Foucault calls a 'species or genus', simply didn't exist in the pre-modern world: before 1660 humanity was seen as fragmented and lacking in any kind of unifying essence. Only with the bourgeois revolution did there emerge the novel idea of a universal human nature, one of whose defining characteristics was a sense of interiority and selfhood. Belsey describes her book – *The Subject of Tragedy* – as 'a contribution to a history of man'. But it's a very different kind of history from Foucault's. *The Order of Things* deals with the intellectual frameworks that govern the production of knowledge in the post-medieval world; 'man' was a shorthand term, which Foucault usually put in italics as a way of distinguishing it from its more conventional meanings, for an epistemological problematic peculiar to the nineteenth and twentieth centuries. But for Belsey 'man' still has that conventional meaning from which Foucault took care to distance his own use of the term, namely, an essentialist view of humanity. Before 1660 'man' was a fragmented, de-centred being with no universal characteristics; after the revolution 'man' suddenly emerges, like some alien creature bursting from its chrysalis, as unified, autonomous, 'the unconstrained author of meaning and action'.[48] Quoting the final page of *The Order of Things*, she tells us that the present 'humanist' intellectual epoch is bound to pass away, and expresses the hope that her own work will help to bring about 'the end of the reign of man'.[49] Though she cites Foucault as an authority for her history of 'man', her book is really about the rise and anticipated fall of what she calls a 'liberal humanist' notion of human nature.

The Subject of Tragedy was published in 1985. In the previous year two other books advanced strikingly similar histories of 'man'. Using the Bachelard / Foucault notion of abrupt epistemic shifts in intellectual history, but interpreting 'man' in a very different sense from the way Foucault used the term, Francis Barker and Jonathan Dollimore also announced the sudden appearance, at a particular historical juncture, of a distinctively modern notion of human nature. 'The defining feature of the bourgeois discursive regime is the *in situ* control . . . of the newly interiorated subject', wrote Barker in *The Tremulous Private Body*.[50] 'It is the Enlightenment . . . which marks the emergence of essentialist humanism,' wrote Dollimore; it is at this moment that 'the individual becomes the origin and focus of meaning'.[51] Their claims were immediately accepted by postmodern Shakespeareans of most theoretical complexions. So high was Foucault's reputation in the 1980s, and so insuperable was the task of making sense of *The Order of Things*, that people failed to challenge assertions that apparently came with the backing of such a prestigious authority. It became an axiomatic principle in postmodern criticism that Shakespeare and his contemporaries were anti-essentialists.

Though Foucault is cited by postmodernists as the authority for this speculative history of man, the idea of a dramatic and sudden shift in sensibility resulting in a radically new conception of human nature was not a new one. Indeed in the second half of the nineteenth century it formed the basis of the standard view of the Renaissance. In 1855 Jules Michelet adopted the Hegelian notion of an antithesis between the medieval and Renaissance spirit and proposed in his great *History of France* the idea of the Renaissance as a reawakening of the human spirit. Five years later Jacob Burckhardt took up Michelet's view of 'man' in his influential *Civilization of the Renaissance* (1860), claiming that in the Middle Ages the notion of personality scarcely existed. There might have been rare cases of individuality in earlier centuries, but generally speaking, people were conscious of themselves only as members of a race or an institution. It was with the dawning of the Renaissance that 'the ban laid upon human personality was dissolved'. Now, for the first time, 'man became a spiritual individual'. This, for Burckhardt, was the spirit of the Renaissance.[52] It's a theory that modern scholarship revised many years ago. Following Petrarch's lead, Renaissance scholars like Leonardo Bruni and Bartolomeo della Fonte had emphasised the revolutionary nature of the humanist achievement. Taking these propagandist claims at face value, Burckhardt portrayed the Renaissance as an abrupt break with the past that allowed the spirit of self-assertive individualism to flourish for the first time. But modern scholarship has shown that much of what we think of as most characteristic of Renaissance humanism and its revival of classical culture had been anticipated in France at least a century earlier.[53] It has also shown that the idea that the medieval mind was incapable of conceiving of an inner self is without foundation (see above, chapter 8, p. 161). As one scholar puts it, 'the only clearly recognisable dividing line between the middle ages and the renaissance was the fact that the humanists had declared that there was a dividing line'.[54] The fact that Foucault seemed to be unaware of this body of modern scholarship when he wrote *The Order of Things* didn't concern Cultural Materialists. Mistakenly taking Foucault's claim that 'man is an invention of recent date' to mean that the notion of a universal human nature didn't exist in the early modern world, they revived the idea of an apocalyptic birth of modern 'man', but this time moving that nativity forward a couple of centuries and giving it an Althusserian inflection.

READING AGAINST THE GRAIN

In an interview he gave in 1967 Foucault described *The Order of Things* as 'a pure and simple "fiction"'.[55] The same might be said of Renaissance anti-essentialism. The idea seems to have originated in a misreading of *The Order of Things*, and was corroborated, in some cases by straightforward misunderstanding of the discourses operating in a particular Renaissance text,[56] in others by silent omission of textual counter-evidence,[57] in others again by what is sometimes called 'creative misreading' or 'reading against the grain'. In reality, you would be hard pressed to find a Renaissance writer, whether major or minor, conservative or radical, Calvinist or humanist, fideist or sceptic, who would have disagreed with Pierre Charron that 'the first lesson and instruction unto wisdom . . . is the knowledge of our selves and our human condition'.

But is there anything wrong with reading against the grain? After all, no work of literature has a definitive, authentic meaning; literary texts change their significance over time. Not only that, but our attempts to reconstruct an intellectual context for literature from earlier periods of history can never escape bias, intentional or otherwise. Try as we may to be objective, our view of the past is inevitably coloured by our own prejudices and preconceptions. In her widely cited essay on New Historicism Jean Howard explains that it's postmodern Theory that has taught us that the historian is 'a product of history and never able to recognize the otherness of the past in its pure form, but always in part through the framework of the present'.[58] Catherine Belsey has recently endorsed these arguments: 'we interpret, inevitably, from the present, and the present necessarily informs our account of the past . . . there is no "objective" account of the past'.[59] Postmodernists claim that pre-Theoretical historicists had an 'unproblematic concept of history' (see above, note 2). But this is not true. Historicists have been expressing much the same reservations about positivist theories of history since the early decades of the last century. 'Historians recognise formally the obvious, long known informally, namely, that any written history inevitably reflects the thought of the author in his time and cultural setting', wrote the American 'New Historian' Charles Beard in 1934.[60] Another American historian repeated the point two years later:

The historian is necessarily a selector of events. His interpretation, moreover, is not separable from the selection, rather does the former determine the latter, at least in part. When the historians tell us that they merely record, that 'the facts speak for themselves', they simply delude themselves. The facts, of course, do not speak: the historian speaks for them or makes them speak, and what they say depends upon the magic of his wand.[61]

The New Historians' reservations about naïve empiricism were part of a vigorous and sophisticated debate on historicism in the 1930s and were echoed by literary scholars on both sides of the Atlantic in the following decades.[62] In their *Theory of Literature* (1942) René Wellek and Austin Warren argued that, although the past must be judged in terms of its own values and principles, it's impossible in practice to exclude the critic's own attitudes and assumptions.[63] Helen Gardner shared their reservations about naïve empiricism. In a lecture she gave in 1953 entitled 'The Historical Approach' she argued that any attempt to define the past is bound to reflect the historian's own cultural assumptions: 'the historical imagination . . . is itself historically conditioned'.[64] She was particularly scornful of E. M. W. Tillyard's 'Elizabethan World Picture': 'We are rightly sceptical when we read statements about modern man and the modern mind and dismiss both as figments of journalism. We ought to be at least as sceptical about statements about "the Elizabethan mind"'.[65]

Given that complete objectivity is a chimera that will always elude us, isn't it best to acknowledge that there can be no such thing as a neutral reading of a work of literature, be frank about the political uses to which you want to put the text, and simply read it in such a way that it fits your own political agenda? That, at any rate, is what Alan Sinfield argues in a collection of essays called *Faultlines*. He suggests that, just as theatre directors often adapt classic playtexts in such a way as to produce something that may be flagrantly at odds with the spirit of the original, so the 'dissident' critic should be free to 'rework the authoritative text so that it is forced to yield, against the grain, explicitly oppositional kinds of understanding'.[66] Sinfield invites us to imagine how such an act of 'creative vandalism' might work with *Julius Caesar*. Having decided that, like so much Shakespeare, the play is all about 'gaining legitimation for the exercise of state violence',[67] he proposes that we turn it into a working-class play by moving the plebeians to the centre of the action and making it clear that they are the victims of a power struggle among the ruling elite.[68] In this way *Julius Caesar* becomes a sort of republican variation on the 'monarch-versus-the-rest' (sic) theme that Sinfield believes is typical of Shakespeare.[69]

So instead of a 'politic' analysis of the follies of unauthorised action in which blame for civil chaos is spread fairly evenly between the major power groups (see above, chapter 7), you now have something more clear-cut: on the one hand a pro-establishment play defending 'the exercise of state violence'; on the other a 'dissident' play about heroic workers exploited by their 'upper-class' rulers. This treatment of the play is in line with the Cultural Materialist principle that criticism should aim 'to judge the degree to which the drama was or was not complicit with the powers of the state'.[70] If it looks as if the play in question is supporting 'the state', you rewrite it so that it supports the people; if the play is difficult to pin down you get rid of the ambiguities.

Sinfield says he wants to scandalise the literary-critical establishment in order to shake it out of its political complacency (he believes that those who are not 'dissidents' like himself tend to be of 'the old Oxford-gentlemanly, dogged/dilettante schools').[71] However, there's such a long tradition of improving Shakespeare that it's difficult to understand why Sinfield thinks his kind of frank adaptation might shock the academic world. It's true that as a *critical* approach – he suggests that it might be called 'The New Reductionism'[72] – it does tend to encourage the weaker student to believe that all the great classics of Renaissance drama can be reduced to a simple state-versus-the-people formula.[73] But as a mode of theatrical adaptation, there doesn't seem to be anything particularly outrageous in Sinfield's reworking of *Julius Caesar*. After all, Shakespeare transformed his sources (though he tended to complicate his originals rather than simplifying them), while dramatists like D'Avenant and Dryden soon started rewriting *his* plays. Under the right kind of 'dissident' director, there's no reason why Sinfield's play about working-class heroes in ancient Rome – in his version the lynch mob that murders the innocent Cinna has been reduced to a handful of politically exploited 'louts' – shouldn't make uplifting political theatre for those who prefer not to be encumbered with awkward ambiguities.

Reading against the grain is certainly preferable to the more extreme form of reader-response approach that goes from one unlikely pole to another, arguing that, because Shakespeare's plays have no definitive or 'essential' meaning (critics like Wellek and Warren rejected this idea in the 1940s),[74] therefore they have no meanings at all beyond those that playgoers and readers attribute to them.[75] Against-the-grain readers do at least recognise that plays have some kind of historical meanings, even if they tend to simplify those meanings in order to justify their own protest. Reading against the grain only becomes a problem when its results are used as evidence to support claims about the intellectual culture of the past that have no basis in historical reality. If you read texts creatively, as Dollimore does in *Radical Tragedy*,[76] and then claim that their authors are *bona fide* postmodernists before their time, you risk losing all sense of historical perspective. Inspired by Foucault's masterplan of writing 'the history of the present',[77] postmodern critics sometimes refer to this rewriting of the past as 'presentism',[78] though with his interest in the bizarre otherness of the past, it's not an approach that Foucault himself would have recognised as his own.

Postmodern historiographers deny the possibility of factual accuracy, arguing with Foucault that historical narratives are no more than verbal fictions, with one interpretation counting for as much as another (see above, chapter 7, pp. 133–5). This being the case, they claim, quite logically, that 'the study of history is not only scientifically but also politically valueless'.[79] But historicists believe that it's still worth striving for historical truth (try telling an educated resident of Northern Ireland or postwar Iraq that the past has nothing to say to us about the problems of the modern world), even though they know that complete objectivity is an unattainable ideal. When pre-Theoretical literary theorists like Gardner, Warren and Wellek rejected nineteenth-century positivism in the 1940s and 1950s, they didn't abandon the pursuit of historical truth. They believed that, if the past contains a political lesson for our own time, that lesson is best elicited, not by obliterating intellectual differences and recruiting past thinkers as precursors of our own ideas, but by establishing a sense of historical perspective through the recovery of alien theories, beliefs and practices.[80] Indeed, it was only when Renaissance historiographers began to understand the gulf that stood between themselves and the ancient world that modern history was born. As G. K. Hunter put it,

the facts of the past only acquire shape and order when the mould of particular questions forces out specific meanings. It is the historian's act of asking questions that determines the hierarchy of facts in the answers; and the historian, of course, asks the questions that the age . . . thinks relevant, largely because these allow the past to contribute to the present and be understood by it.[81]

Samuel Johnson argued that 'To judge rightly of the present we must oppose it to the past.'[82] But when the whole of history is seen as a Manichaean struggle between authority and the subject – 'the monarch-versus-the-rest', in Sinfield's phrase – any sense of cultural perspective is lost and comparative judgement becomes impossible. Ironically, a critical project that began by rejecting the idea of a universal human nature has ended up with what Johnson called 'general and transcendental truths, which will always be the same'.[83]

History has traditionally been valued for the perspective it provides on the present. But you can only learn from history if you are able to deduce certain principles of human behaviour from past examples. That's why in the *Discourses* on Livy Machiavelli repeatedly insisted on human universals. The fact that the decisions we make as individuals are constrained by the nature of our humanity no more means that history can be reduced to a single formula than the fact that football is played according to internationally agreed rules means that every game is the same: it's the vagaries of individual character and temperament that make history endlessly varied. But if there were no unifying principles linking people in disparate cultures as members of the same species, we would be bound to begin each day afresh with no means of knowing how individuals or governments would be likely to behave in given circumstances. If you compound the postmodern historiographer's rejection of the notion of historical fact with anti-essentialism's denial of human universals, life really does become a tale told by an idiot, full of sound and fury, signifying nothing. Lisa Jardine puts it well when she writes: 'we are too deeply mired in the relativity of all things to risk truth claims. And on the whole we believe that in all of this, our age is one of loss – that we have lost something which the age of Erasmus possessed.'[84]

REDISCOVERING UNIVERSALS

So powerful is postmodernism's anti-humanist rhetoric that many left-wing intellectuals now find it embarrassing to talk of universals: to admit to a belief in something called human nature is to confess to the crassest kind of intellectual *naïveté*. Dryden defined a play as 'a just and lively image of human nature, representing its passions and humours, and the changes of fortune to which it is subject'.[85] But first-year university students are now taught that human nature is one of the bourgeois myths that Theory has exploded,[86] and it's left to other disciplines to remind us that great writers have always been 'the voice of the species'.[87] 'Works of art that prove enduring are intensely humanistic,' writes Edward O. Wilson, 'Born in the imagination of individuals, they nevertheless touch upon what was universally endowed by human evolution'.[88] If there were no universal passions and humours, we would have no means of evaluating literature from another age or another culture: a text would have value only for the community in which it was produced. 'There is no such thing as a literary work or tradition which is valuable in itself, regardless of what anyone might have said or come to say about it', writes Terry Eagleton, '"Value" is a transitive term: it means whatever is valued by certain people in specific situations, according to particular criteria and in the light of given purposes.'[89] That's why, as Peter Lamarque and Stein Olsen point out in *Truth, Fiction and Literature*, reception theory is increasingly taking the place of literary criticism.[90] In a world where 'everything exists and nothing has value', all criticism can do is record the history of a text's reception.

But there's no philosophic or scientific justification for our embarrassment about universals. Wilson claims that 'the greatest enterprise of the mind has always been and always will be the attempted linkage of the sciences and humanities'.[91] One of the most puzzling aspects of postmodern criticism is the fact that, despite its proclaimed interdisciplinarity, it has chosen to isolate itself from so many other disciplines. Concerned though it is with the history of 'man', postmodernism has ignored the rapidly growing body of work in archaeoanthropology, evolutionary psychology and neurobiology that has transformed modern thinking on social behaviour, the mind, and the mystery of human creativity. Catherine Belsey speaks for many postmodernists when she says she finds sociobiology 'deeply distasteful'.[92] Just as fundamentalist creationists prefer to disregard the scientific evidence of the fossil record because it conflicts with their religious beliefs, so postmodernists would rather ignore the extensive scientific literature on selfhood, gender, and consciousness because they believe that it's incompatible with their own political ideals.

Literary postmodernism prides itself on being the *avant-garde* of the modern intellectual world. It's ironic, therefore, that its intellectual models are thinkers who have long been regarded as obsolete in their own fields. Joseph Carroll writes:

The conceptual shift that takes place when moving from the Darwinian social sciences to the humanities can be likened to the technological shift that takes place when traveling from the United States or Europe to a country in the Third World . . . It is as if one were to visit a country in which the hosts happily believed themselves on the cutting edge of technological innovation and, in support of this belief, proudly displayed a rotary dial-phone, a manual typewriter, and a mimeograph machine.[93]

While postmodernists in Britain and America were popularising outdated Continental theories of 'man' based largely on intuition rather than empirical investigation, a revolution was taking place in the biological and social sciences.[94] In the decades immediately following the Second World War the application of evolutionary theory to the study of human nature was unthinkable. Though groundbreaking advances were being made in molecular biology – Francis Crick and James Watson cracked the riddle of DNA in 1953 – memories of the Holocaust, and the eugenicist theories that were used to justify it, were too close to contemplate studying the biological basis of human nature. In her autobiography Margaret Mead recalled how the danger of misinterpretation meant that any study of innate human characteristics would have to wait for 'less troubled times'.[95] However, by the 1960s sociobiologists had begun to challenge behaviourism's blank-sheet theory of human nature and to argue that universal patterns of human behaviour must owe something to our biological nature. Though sociobiology was well established by the mid 1970s – Edward Wilson's controversial *Sociobiology* was published in 1975 – it continued to face hostility from those who believed that it gave support to racist theories of humanity. But as the pioneering evolutionary psychologists Leda Cosmides and John Tooby point out, it's difficult to see how an attempt to provide empirical evidence for the existence of a universal nature common to all humanity can be accused of being racist.[96]

In his influential *The Interpretation of Cultures* the American anthropologist Clifford Geertz wrote: 'our ideas, our values, our acts, even our emotions, are, like our nervous system itself, cultural products'.[97] In a simile popular in constructionist theory, he compared the infant human with a computer before any software has been loaded. What provides us with the programmes we need for survival is culture. Without those programmes our life would be 'virtually ungovernable; a mere chaos of pointless acts and exploding emotions'.[98] But sociobiologists and evolutionary psychologists argue that if diverse cultures result in endlessly varied forms of social behaviour, that's not because the infant mind is like a computer before any software has been loaded. Rather it's because we come into the world with a pre-installed operating system specifically 'designed' to enable us to assimilate and interact with the culture that surrounds us from birth.[99] Evolutionary psychology has been criticised for substituting one form of determinism for another and allegedly insisting that all human behaviour can be explained in terms of inherited drives.[100] But this is to misrepresent evolutionary psychology. Far from denying the influence of culture in shaping human behaviour, evolutionary psychologists try to show how we are innately and uniquely equipped to interact with the cultural world and operate as cultural beings. As Edward Wilson explains, our minds are indeed shaped by culture. But it's our genetic inheritance that determines which parts of the cultural world we absorb. Those inherited predilections in turn shape culture. Wilson calls this process 'gene-culture coevolution'.[101]

The term that some evolutionary psychologists use to describe the universal human ability to integrate with the social world and become flexible and interactive participants in its discourses is 'metaculture'. In *The Adapted Mind* Leda Cosmides and John Tooby explain how

The variable features of a culture can be learned solely because of the existence of an encompassing universal human metaculture. The ability to imitate the relevant parts of others' actions, the ability to reconstruct the representations in their minds, the ability to interpret the conduct of others correctly, and the ability to co-ordinate one's behavior with others all depend on the existence of a human metaculture.[102]

Informing and co-ordinating all these specialised skills is the sense that we have both of our own subjectivity and that of others. We are born with an inbuilt theory of mind, a sense that other people too have inner selves.[103] Without that innate sense of subjectivity, discourse couldn't exist; we couldn't operate as social beings. In exceptional cases this inbuilt subjectivity 'module' is impaired or apparently non-existent, with devastating consequences.

In chapter 8 I discussed Oliver Sacks' encounter with Stephen Wiltshire and the thoughts about creativity that their meetings gave rise to. Could a classically autistic person who seemed to lack a sense of inwardness really be an artist in the conventional sense of the term? Sacks' impression that autistic people appear to lack an inner self was confirmed by his meeting with another well-known autistic person, the American biologist Temple Grandin. Grandin is unusual in having written, with the help of a journalist, an autobiography.[104] She is interested in her own condition, recognising that in subtle ways she is different from other people. 'She surmises,' writes Sacks, 'that her mind is lacking some of the "subjectivity", the inwardness, that others seem to have'.[105] Looking for words to describe the unusual phenomenon of people who seem to lack that sense of self which most of us take for granted, Sacks uses the phrase '*no living centre*'.[106] Autistic people are in effect de-centred human beings.

Sacks uses the same metaphor of an absent centre in his description of hebephrenia, a condition characterised by incessant facetiousness, punning and wisecracks:

'funny' and often ingenious as they appear – the world is taken apart, undermined, reduced to anarchy and chaos. There ceases to be any 'centre' to the mind, though its formal intellectual powers may be perfectly preserved. The end point of such states is an unfathomable 'silliness', an abyss of superficiality, in which all is ungrounded and afloat and comes apart.[107]

Wits might be tempted to suggest that Sacks' description of hebephrenia sounds like an uncannily accurate description of classic deconstruction of the kind that used to be practised by critics like Paul de Man and Geoffrey Hartman. But in truth it's not a joking matter. If we really want to know what it means to be a de-centred person with no inner self, 'frail, precarious, dispersed across a range of discourses', we cannot do better than read Sacks' poignant accounts of autists, hebephrenics and patients suffering from other neurological disorders.

It's a strange irony that postmodernism should have adopted as the basis for its theory of mind a pathological condition (promulgated in particular by a psychotic who ended his days in an institution for the insane) so disabling that it would appear to prevent the possibility of any true creativity. Indeed it's on the question of selfhood and agency that postmodernist arguments are most puzzling. Postmodernism says that culture is everything. Yet as Cosmides and Tooby argue, the development of culture depends on our ability to communicate with other people, which in turn depends on our ability to recognise that other people are intentional agents with minds of their own.[108] If our ancestors had all been autists there would be no advanced civilisations. In denying the reality of the self, postmodernists deny the very thing that makes culture possible. However, modern neuroscience appears to confirm what common sense has always told us about the inner self. Though we may play many roles over a lifetime, it's the sense of a constant inner core of our being that gives meaning and coherence to our lives: we may change our minds and even our most fundamental beliefs; we may put on antic dispositions; we may express our passions in riddles and dreams (as Webster's Duchess of Malfi puts it).[109] But we don't usually forget who we are. When we do forget as a result of some neurological disorder such as Alzheimer's disease or Korsakov's syndrome, the result is a catastrophic destruction of personality. For the gerontologist Raymond Tallis, senile dementia is 'an indirect reminder that to be human is to be explicitly extended in and across time'.[110] Modern neuroscientists believe that it's the brain's synapses – the interfaces between its neurons – that allow us to store memories of who we are and who we used to be. Without those memories 'personality would be merely an empty, impoverished expression of our genetic constitution', writes the neuro-biologist Joseph Ledoux; 'we wouldn't know if the person we are today jibes with the one we were yesterday or the one we expect to be tomorrow'.[111] If we didn't have a sense of a coherent inner self we would be like autistic people, who seem to have, as Sacks puts it, 'no living centre'.

No body of work that claims to offer insights into the mystery of human subjectivity can expect to be taken seriously beyond its own limited coterie if it systematically ignores developments in other disciplines that concern themselves with the study of mind and of social behaviour, especially when that new research has produced such a remarkable consensus in a wide range of subject areas. Biologists, from Darwin and Wallace to Dawkins and Gould have always disagreed over details of the evolutionary process;[112] but with only fundamentalist creationists and postmodern anti-humanists rejecting modern Darwinism, natural selection is now accepted in the scientific community as the only known way of accounting for what looks like complex 'design' in living organisms. As John Barrow puts it, 'wherever we find interwoven complexities, we find the hand of time, slowly fashioning adaptations'.[113]

If our bodies are the product of millions of years of selection, so too are our brains; they bear 'the stamp of 400 million years of trial and error, traceable by fossils and molecular homology in nearly unbroken sequence from fish to amphibian to reptile to primitive mammal to our immediate primate forerunners'.[114] Postmodernism claims that there's no such thing as a universal core of essential humanity. Yet as Steven Pinker reminds us,

In all cultures, people tell stories and recite poetry. They joke, laugh, and tease. They sing and dance. They decorate surfaces. They perform rituals. They wonder about the causes of fortune and misfortune, and hold beliefs about the supernatural that contradict everything else they know about the world. They concoct theories of the universe and their place within it.

As if that weren't enough of a puzzle, the more biologically frivolous and vain the activity, the more people exalt it. Art, literature, music, wit, religion, and philosophy are thought to be not just pleasurable but noble. They are the mind's best work, what makes life worth living.[115]

To Pinker's list of human universals we can add the propensity to devise complex systems of moral values. Opinion on human nature has traditionally been divided: pessimists tend to agree with Machiavelli that people never do good unless necessity drives them to it; optimists share the belief of the eighteenth-century *philosophes* in humanity's natural benevolence. Many so-called materialists are also optimists, believing that, if only you can get the economic conditions right, class will disappear and people will live naturally in egalitarian harmony. Evolutionary psychologists argue that both the potential for brutality *and* the benevolence are intrinsic to our nature. History shows that we seem to have an innate capacity for collective cruelty,[116] but at the same time, a sense of right and wrong is a feature of all known human societies. Evolutionary psychologists may differ among themselves on the question of whether our sense of morality originally served a survival function or evolved through sexual selection.[117] But they agree that, insofar as human value systems have arisen out of the basic drives of human nature, they have a biological rather than a transcendental origin, and are therefore just as truly universal as if they had been god-given. That's not to say that the laws of every society throughout history are fundamentally the same; not even Renaissance proponents of natural law argued that. What *is* universal is the tendency for both civilised and pre-civilised societies to frame laws or codes of conduct that seek to regulate the ruthlessness, violence, cunning and powers of deception that we share with our closest and most Machiavellian simian relations.[118] Those laws or codes are an expression of our equally innate desire for truth, justice and fair play, and are unique to our species. Matt Ridley writes: 'The conspicuously virtuous things we all praise – cooperation, altruism, generosity, sympathy, kindness, selflessness – are all unambiguously concerned with the welfare of others. This is not some parochial Western tradition. It's a bias shared by the whole species.'[119] Moral and political values will inevitably vary from one writer to another and one culture to another, but the problems are always recognisably human.

There will always be conflict between different sides of our evolved nature, with some societies privileging one side and some another (*Hamlet* dramatises this conflict in its contrast between the archaic world of heroic values represented by Hamlet's father on the one hand, and Horatio's philosophic stoicism on the other). Any enlightened system of human justice is bound to involve compromise as it seeks to allow freedom to the individual while protecting others from the consequences of unlicensed behaviour. But the basic conflicts will always be there and can never be completely resolved. That may be one reason why great literature typically concerns itself with conundrums rather than the 'eternal verities' that postmodernists allege are the stock-in-trade of the Western canon.

Of course not all literature deals with those high moral and political conundrums. Despite the solemn tone of the typical humanist treatise on poetics, much of the best Renaissance poetry and drama was anything but serious. Ask a class of English literature students to name their favourite poem from this period and they are more likely to say 'The Flea' than 'An Anatomy of the World'. Geoffrey Miller has an interesting theory about our fascination with ingeniously frivolous poetic word games. It's all to do with sex. According to Miller our creative intelligence has evolved through sexual selection. While peacocks appeal to their mates' visual sense, we appeal to the mind: 'We load our courtship displays with meaning, to reach deeper into the minds of those receiving the signals'. Just as the peacock's tail serves no practical function, so evolution has added 'baroquely ornamental towers of creativity to our plainly utilitarian foundations of perception, memory, motor control and social intelligence'. But that doesn't mean that creativity continues to serve an exclusively sexual function. Once our brains have been wired up for creative thought, the same hardware can be used to run a seemingly endless variety of programmes. The result is 'a human creative intelligence that can flood the planet with fictions, but that judges such displays more often for their capacity to excite, intrigue, entertain, and distract, than for their capacity to remind us of the stark, mortal lonely truths of human life'.[120]

Neo-Darwinian theory is worth listening to, not just because it provides us with an amusingly plausible explanation for our human predilection for the fantastic and the useless (including postmodern literary theory), but because it can give us the confidence to return to those human universals without which the very notion of literature is, as postmodernism itself insists, meaningless.

IN DEFENCE OF LITERATURE

Postmodernism has always been suspicious of the idea of literature, with its suggestion of independent minds having original thoughts and writers using language in imaginative ways. One of the tasks it set itself was to question the difference between 'literature' and other kinds of writing, using inverted commas to indicate the doubtful nature of the category. 'Materialist criticism refuses to privilege "literature" in the way that literary criticism has done hitherto', writes Jonathan Dollimore.[121] 'The newer historical criticism is *new* in its refusal of unproblematised distinctions between "literature" and "history", between "text" and "context"', argues Louis Montrose.[122] Terence Hawkes thinks we should abandon the distinction altogether and just call everything 'text'.[123] Rejection of the idea of 'literature' in favour of undifferentiated 'text' originates in the work of Barthes, Derrida, Kristeva and other contributors to the Parisian journal *Tel quel* in the late 1960s and early 1970s.[124] Barthes' theory of the polysemous text with its free play of signifiers held out the possibility of an infinite number of readings while at the same time abolishing the notion of authorial agency. But as Lamarque and Olsen point out, there's something oddly perverse in the very notion of textual polysemy: 'With the free play of the meanings of the text we are back in the essentially unordered triviality of daily life . . . And we do not need a realm of art that simply duplicates the triviality of life.'[125]

Some years ago John Ellis proposed a more logical approach to the question of what literature is and how you define it. Before Theory we all knew that *Pride and Prejudice* was literature and the London telephone directory wasn't. The problem was how to *explain* the difference. To most people it's obvious that Jane Austen wrote works of literature and the compilers of the telephone directory don't. But what about the indeterminate cases? Many people write verses that we would hesitate to call literature, while conversely there are countless examples of books that were not conceived of by their authors as literature, but which commonly feature on university literature syllabuses. How do you decide which of these is literature and which isn't? Ellis argued that literary texts can be thought of as 'those that are used by . . . society in such a way that the text is not taken as specifically relevant to the immediate context of its origin'.[126] In other words, whether or not something counts as literature depends on how it's used rather than on who wrote it, or what it's like in itself. Both literary and non-literary texts can be either ornate or plain; both can be highly organised or relatively formless. But the fact that a literary text may have formal properties in common with other kinds of writing doesn't mean that the category 'literature' is worthless. Just as gardeners usually have no trouble telling what is a weed and what isn't, even though two plants may belong to the same botanical genus, so most people would agree that *King Lear* is literature and the 1606 *Acte to Restraine Abuses of Players* isn't. Literary historians read the Act of Abuses, not for its own sake, but to find out what James I's government thought about blasphemy and how that might have affected the sort of plays that people wrote at the time. But the reason why theatre directors in so many different cultures keep coming back to *King Lear* is because of the play's intrinsic human interest. It's true that academics ask what we can learn from Shakespeare about such matters as Renaissance theories of natural law, pre-modern cosmology, or humoural psychology. But theatre audiences aren't generally concerned with these things. They go to see a performance of *King Lear* because they know that it will speak to them of what Geoffrey Miller calls 'the stark, mortal lonely truths of human life'.

Ellis's functional theory of literature is useful in dispelling some postmodern misconceptions about literature.[127] But it's not entirely true to say that there are no qualities that are inherently and uniquely literary. One universal characteristic of great literature that isn't a feature of non-literary writing is complex imaginative treatment of human relationships and moral dilemmas. An interest in human relationships, states of mind and social networks seems to be universal; it could be described as one of the defining characteristics of our human nature. What literature does is to take that universal human interest in our own nature and give it a local habitation and a name.

But in defending the idea of literature as a special category we need to beware of making false claims about its power to change the world. Great literature may not be the obedient servant of ideology that postmodernism would like us to imagine it is (as Ellis reminds us, great writers have a way of discomfiting their masters rather than reassuring them, which is why dictators have usually tried to control or suppress them).[128] But nor, despite persuasive Renaissance humanist advocacy of the *humanae litterae*, does it do much to transform the structures of society. *King Lear* may have made some contemporary playgoers think a bit harder about social injustice; but a political historian would be hard pressed to show that it had much effect on Stuart governance. Wordsworth tells us that one impulse from a vernal wood can teach us more about good and evil than we can ever get from moral philosophy; but *The Prelude* didn't result in large numbers of people relocating to Patterdale and becoming more beneficent beings. Even the great Victorian social problem novels were written long after the reforming legislation they dealt with.[129] Shelley said that poets are the unacknowledged legislators of the world. But a more truthful image of the writer is Conrad's Marlow sitting in a boat in the pitch darkness, unable to see his audience, not knowing if they are awake or asleep, and certain only that these captains of industry and finance don't wish to hear his embarrassing message.

Literature's record of bringing about social change is not impressive. But with its unique ability to give us the illusion of getting inside another person's mind, one thing it *can* do is tell us about how people think in cultures that are remote, either geographically or chronologically, from our own. In his great book on Freud, Richard Webster writes: 'one of the satisfactions afforded by literature is to be found in the way it allows readers to recognise as a part of common humanity feelings which they had previously regarded as individual or private'.[130] This is one of the chief justifications for the study of literature: imaginative contact with other minds in periods or cultures remote from our own helps us to appreciate that our common humanity is more important than the ethnic and religious differences that continue to create so much havoc in the modern world. In short, literature can help to teach us the value of tolerance. But deny that there is such a thing as a common humanity, and one of the most powerful arguments for tolerance immediately vanishes. Combine that with postmodernism's extreme relativism – which logically means that in the absence of human universals there can be no rational grounds for preferring one set of values to another – and tolerance acquires a quite different meaning: it means that we are obliged to tolerate regimes that are themselves brutal and *in*tolerant.[131] It's time we got over our misplaced embarrassment about human nature and recognised anti-humanism for what it really is.

CONCLUSION

Confrontational in style, and contemptuously dismissive of all that preceded it, anti-humanist Theory has made many enemies.[132] E. P. Thompson, one of Theory's first opponents, made it clear that Althusserian Marxism was, in his view, one of the great intellectual frauds of the twentieth century. Thompson never had any time for Theory. But when even its former champions acknowledge their disillusionment with literary postmodernism, it's obvious that in its more radical form Theory has reached an impasse. In *The Illusions of Postmodernism* Terry Eagleton asks: 'What if the left were suddenly to find itself . . . simply washed up, speaking a discourse so quaintly out of tune with the modern era that, as with the language of Gnosticism or courtly love, nobody bothered any longer to enquire into its truth value? What if the vanguard were to become the remnant, its arguments still dimly intelligible but spinning rapidly off into some metaphysical outer space'. He answers his own question: 'There is, of course, no need to imagine such a period at all. It is the one we are living in, and its name is postmodernism'.[133]

  Anti-essentialism, and the cultural relativism that is its corollary, are the core of postmodernist thought, and inevitably lead us into a world where, to quote Forster once more, 'everything exists and nothing has value'. But we don't have to take this route. An alternative lies in a neo-Darwinian view of human nature. Darwinism has been described as 'amongst the most comprehensively successful achievements of the human intellect'.[134] The evolutionary psychology that Darwin himself hinted at,[135] but which has only flourished in such a remarkable way over the last twenty years, offers a way out of our present theoretical impasse. Neo-Darwinism may not provide the basis for a new critical practice, and there's no reason for insisting that we import evolutionary psychology into literary criticism (though it certainly provides a sounder basis for thinking about human behaviour than Lacanian psychology does). What neo-Darwinism does offer is a body of evidence powerful enough and sufficiently well established to give us the confidence to challenge the orthodoxies that are seldom questioned in modern primers on Theory, and to re-endorse the human universals without which criticism cannot exist, and history becomes impossible. It may even help us to recognise Shakespeare's humanism for what it is.

Notes

INTRODUCTION

1 Noam Chomsky, 'Language and Freedom', *TriQuarterly*, 23–4 (1972), pp. 29–30.
2 Bruce Smith, *Shakespeare and Masculinity* (Oxford University Press, 2000), pp. 131–2.
3 John Locke, *An Essay Concerning Human Understanding*, ed. Peter H. Nidditch (Oxford: Clarendon Press, 1975), p. 105.
4 'God . . . hath furnished man with those faculties, which will serve for the sufficient discovery of all things requisite to the end of [his] being' (*An Essay*, p. 91). In the previous chapter (1.iii) Locke wrote: 'Nature . . . has put into man [certain] innate practical principles, which do continue constantly to operate and influence all our actions, without ceasing: these may be observed in all persons and all ages, steady and universal . . . I deny not, that there are natural tendencies imprinted on the minds of men' (p. 67).
5 Virginia Woolf, *Mr Bennett and Mrs Brown* (London: Hogarth Press, 1924), p. 4.
6 Bernard Shaw, Preface to *On the Rocks* (London: Constable, 1934), p. 166.
7 See chapter 9, p. 194.
8 See Leda Cosmides and John Tooby, 'The Psychological Foundations of Culture', *The Adapted Mind: Evolutionary Psychology and the Generation of Culture*, ed. Jerome H. Barkow, Leda Cosmides and John Tooby (New York and Oxford: Oxford University Press, 1992), pp. 19–136.
9 Edward O. Wilson, *Consilience: the Unity of Knowledge* (London: Little, Brown, 1998), p. 139.
10 In her seminal *Critical Practice* (London and New York: Methuen, 1980) Catherine Belsey rejected any notion of 'an essential human nature' based on 'a quasi-biological theory of instincts' (p. 131). Yet in a more recent essay she describes the interaction between biology and culture in a way that is virtually indistinguishable from that of an evolutionary biologist like Edward O. Wilson: 'the biology that constitutes human beings always interacts with the relatively autonomous culture their evolved brains make possible, and culture too exercises determinations' ('Biology and Imagination: The Role of Culture', conference paper, The Institute of Contemporary Arts, London,

8 May 2004). To acknowledge that human beings are the product of 'gene-culture coevolution', to use Wilson's phrase (*Consilience*, p. 139) is to challenge one of the defining principles of postmodern theory.

11 'The New Historicism in Renaissance Studies', *English Literary Renaissance*, 16 (1986), pp. 20–1.

12 In *An Essay Concerning Civil Government* (1698) Locke wrote: 'Man [is] born with a title to perfect freedom, and an uncontrolled enjoyment of all the rights and privileges of the law of nature' (*Two Treatises of Government*, ed. Peter Laslett (Cambridge University Press, 1960), p. 348).

13 'The New Historicism in Renaissance Studies', p. 21 (my italics).

14 'Resonance and Wonder', *Learning to Curse: Essays in Early Modern Culture* (New York and London: Routledge, 1990), p. 165. Though Greenblatt has now moved sufficiently far from his former anti-humanism to be able to write a biography of Shakespeare (*Will in the World: How Shakespeare Became Shakespeare* (London: Jonathan Cape, 2004)), the majority of his followers have been less quick to abandon the constructionism he helped bequeath to English studies.

15 *Faultlines: Cultural Materialism and the Politics of Dissident Reading* (Oxford: Clarendon Press, 1992), p. 10.

16 *Radical Tragedy: Religion, Ideology and Power in the Drama of Shakespeare and his Contemporaries*, 3rd edn (Basingstoke: Palgrave Macmillan, 2004), p. xxv.

17 Michel Foucault, *The Order of Things: An Archaeology of the Human Sciences*, trans. anon (1970; repr. London: Tavistock, 1977), p. 308.

18 *Radical Tragedy*, p. 250.

19 Foreword to 3rd edn of *Radical Tragedy*, p. xiii.

20 Frank Kermode has recently claimed that in the world of Shakespeare studies the discourse of postmodernism is now 'virtually omnipotent' (Introduction to *The Shakespearean International Yearbook*, 3 (2003), ed. Graham Bradshaw, John M. Mucciolo, Angus Fletcher and Tom Bishop, p. 5). Although this is maybe a slight exaggeration, it's certainly true that postmodernism continues to dominate the Shakespeare sections of academic publishers' catalogues, the major Shakespeare journals and most international Shakespeare conferences. Academics find that it's not easy to get a paper hostile to postmodern orthodoxy published in *PMLA* or the top Shakespeare journals.

21 *Radical Tragedy*, p. 155.

22 Catherine Belsey, 'The Name of the Rose in *Romeo and Juliet*', *Yearbook of Shakespeare Studies*, 23 (1993), pp. 141, 133.

23 Terence Hawkes, ed., *Alternative Shakespeares Volume 2* (London and New York: Routledge, 1996), pp. 9–10. What was true of Shakespeare was of course true of literature in general. In *Critical Practice* Belsey set out to dispel the myth that 'literary texts . . . tell us truths . . . about the world in general or about human nature' (p. 2).

24 Philippa Berry and Margaret Tudeau-Clayton, eds., Introduction to *Textures of Renaissance Knowledge* (Manchester University Press, 2003), p. 4.

25 Catherine Belsey, *The Subject of Tragedy* (London and New York: Methuen, 1985), p. 18. In the present century, student primers continue to inform their readers that the notion of a conscious inner self was alien to Shakespeare's contemporaries. In *Shakespeare and Masculinity* Bruce Smith explains that self-knowledge for the Elizabethans meant knowing, not your inner being, but merely your body (p. 8). As we shall see (chapters 1 and 8), this is quite untrue.

26 Terence Hawkes, *That Shakespeherian Rag: Essays on a Critical Process* (London: Methuen, 1986), p. 75.

27 Christine Battersby, *Gender and Genius: Towards a Feminist Aesthetics* (London: Women's Press, 1989), p. 28.

28 Laura Levine, *Men in Women's Clothing: Anti-Theatricality and Effeminization, 1579–1642* (Cambridge University Press, 1994), p. 4.

29 Bruce Smith writes: 'there was no such thing in early modern England as a "homosexual"' (*Homosexual Desire in Shakespeare's England: A Cultural Poetics* (University of Chicago Press, 1991), p. 12). Following Foucault (*The History of Sexuality: An Introduction*, trans. Robert Hurley (London: Penguin, 1979), p. 43), Smith sees homosexuality, like any other kind of sexuality, as a cultural artefact: 'No one in England during the sixteenth or seventeenth centuries would have thought of himself as "gay" or "homosexual" for the simple reason that those categories of self-definition did not exist' (pp. 11–12).

30 'Machiavelli's *Via Moderna*: Medieval and Renaissance Attitudes to History', *Niccolò Machiavelli's The Prince: New Interdisciplinary Essays*, ed. Martin Coyle (Manchester University Press, 1995), p. 50.

31 In his recent *Shakespeare and Renaissance Politics* (London: Arden Shakespeare, 2004) Andrew Hadfield implies that belief in a universal human nature is incompatible with an interest in politics (p. vii). Renaissance historians and political theorists would have found this a puzzling idea. As I shall show in the chapters that follow (especially 4 and 7), knowledge of human nature was generally regarded in this period as the key to an informed understanding of history and politics.

32 Pierre Charron, *Of Wisdome* (1601); trans. Samson Lennard (London, 1606), p. 223.

33 I discuss Cicero in chapter 1. In *What is Good?* Grayling writes: 'Before one can get far with thinking about the good for humankind, one has to have a view about human nature, for the very simple and obvious reason that a theory about the human good that drew only on considerations about what, say, dogs and horses are like (and what dogs and horses like) would be of exceedingly little use' (*What is Good? The Search for the Best Way to Live* (London: Weidenfeld and Nicolson, 2003), p. 210).

34 *The Rambler*, ed. W. J. Bate and Albrecht B. Strauss, *The Yale Edition of the Works of Samuel Johnson*, 16 vols., general eds. Allen T. Hazen and John H. Middendorf, (New Haven, Conn. and London: Yale University Press, 1958–90), vol. 4 (1969), p. 120.

35 'The Great Odyssey', *Guardian Saturday Review*, 9 June 2001, p. 3.

1 SHAKESPEARE AND ENGLISH HUMANISM

1 Jane Austen, *Northanger Abbey*, ed. K. M. Lobb (London: University of London Press, 1956), p. 65.

2 Catherine Belsey, *The Subject of Tragedy* (London and New York: Methuen, 1985) p. 14.

3 Desiderius Erasmus, *Enchiridion militis christiani: An English Version*, ed. Anne M. O'Donnell, SND (Oxford: Early English Text Society, 1981), p. 59.

4 Hamlet was echoing a commonplace. Stephen Gosson wrote: 'every man in a play may see his own faults, and learn by this glass, to amend his manners' (*The Schoole of Abuse* (1579), ed. Edward Arber (London: English Reprints, 1869), p. 31).

5 In a more specialised sense humanism involved the application of classical political theory to the problems of the modern world. It used to be thought that, after flourishing in the early years of the sixteenth century, humanist political thought declined in England until republican ideas were revived during the Civil War. But as Markku Peltonen has shown, humanist ideas and values were being 'strenuously restated' at precisely the time Shakespeare began his writing career (*Classical Humanism and Republicanism in English Political Thought 1570–1640* (Cambridge University Press, 1995), p. 19).

6 One of the best discussions of humanist elements in Shakespeare is Emrys Jones, *The Origins of Shakespeare* (Oxford: Clarendon Press, 1977). An excellent modern introduction to English humanism is Mike Pincombe, *Elizabethan Humanism: Literature and Learning in the later Sixteenth Century* (London: Longman, 2001). See also Jonathan Bate, 'The Humanist *Tempest*', *Shakespeare: La Tempête: Etudes Critiques*, ed. Claude Peltrault (University of Besançon Press, 1993), pp. 5–20; Wolfgang G. Müller, 'Shakespeare and Renaissance Humanism', *Literaturwissenschaftliches Jahrbuch*, 44 (2003), pp. 47–63; Jennifer Richards, *Rhetoric and Courtliness in Early Modern Literature* (Cambridge University Press, 2003).

7 Abraham Fleming used the word 'humanist' in the sense of a classical scholar in the introduction to his translation of Virgil's *Georgics* ('To the Reader', *The Bucoliks of Publius Virgilius Maro* (London, 1589)).

8 Vito R. Giustiniani, 'Homo, Humanus, and the Meanings of "Humanism"', *Journal of the History of Ideas*, 46 (1985), pp. 167–95. See also Paul Oskar Kristeller, *Renaissance Thought*, 2 vols. (New York: Harper and Row, 1961), vol. I, pp. 8–10; 110–11; Kristeller, 'Humanism', *The Cambridge History of Renaissance Philosophy*, ed. Charles B. Schmitt, Quentin Skinner, Eckhard Kessler, et al. (Cambridge University Press, 1988), pp. 113–37; Charles Trinkaus, *The Scope of Renaissance Humanism* (Ann Arbor: University of Michigan Press, 1983), pp. 368–9.

9 Cicero wrote: 'it is [speech] that has united us in the bonds of justice, law and civil order, this has separated us from savagery and barbarism' (*De*

natura deorum, ii.lix.148, trans. H. Rackham, Loeb Classical Library (London: Heinemann, 1951), p. 267).

10 In his heroic poem *Africa* Petrarch celebrated Rome's victories and had his hero's father prophesy that one day Rome would 'conquer every land from the Red Sea/to the far regions of the frozen North' (*Petrarch's Africa*, trans. and annotated Thomas G. Bergin and Alice S. Wilson (New Haven and London: Yale University Press, 1977), p. 29). In the second of a pair of letters to the Doge and Council of Genoa during the war between Genoa and Venice in 1352 Petrarch urged the Council to 'pursue your enemies and overtake them, and . . . in the words of the Psalmist, smite them until they are unable to resist' (*Letters on Familiar Matters*, trans. Aldo S. Bernado (Baltimore and London: Johns Hopkins University Press, 1982), p. 243). Erasmus, by contrast, was strongly opposed to nationalist wars of expansion (see 'Dulce bellum inexpertis', *The 'Adages' of Erasmus,* ed. and trans. Margaret Mann Phillips (Cambridge University Press, 1964), p. 348).

11 Pierre Charron, *Of Wisdome* (1601); trans. Samson Lennard (London, 1606), p. 223.

12 *Peace with her Four Guarders* (1622), quoted by Pincombe, *Elizabethan Humanism*, p. 6.

13 Ibid., p. 6.

14 On the republican element in Elizabethan humanist political theory see Peltonen, *Classical Humanism*, pp. 1–118.

15 The question of definitions is complicated by postmodernism's use of the word 'humanism' to mean 'the ideology of the West since the seventeenth century, which presupposes a human being to be a sovereign and spontaneous individual subject, who is the origin and author of her/his own meaning' (definition of 'Humanism' in glossary of *New Historicism and Renaissance Drama*, ed. Richard Wilson and Richard Dutton (London and New York: Longman, 1992), p. 229). I will discuss postmodernism's theory of the humanist 'subject' in chapter 9.

16 Sir Thomas Elyot, *The Boke Named the Governour*, ed. Foster Watson (London: Dent, 1907), p. 293.

17 *Discoveries, Ben Jonson*, 11 vols., ed. C. H. Herford and Percy and Evelyn Simpson (Oxford: Clarendon Press, 1925–52), vol. 8 (1947), p. 636.

18 *De legibus*, trans. Clinton Walker Keyes, Loeb Classical Library (London: Heinemann, 1948), pp. 315–17.

19 Kristeller expressed a widely held view when he wrote: 'Renaissance humanists were . . . interested in human values, but this was incidental to their major concern, which was the study and imitation of classical, Greek and Latin literature' (*Renaissance Thought*, vol. 1, p. 120).

20 *Petrarch's Letters to Classical Authors*, trans. M. E. Cosenza (University of Chicago Press, 1910), p. 18.

21 *De officiis*, trans. Walter Miller, Loeb Classical Library (London: Heinemann, 1913), pp. 73–5.

22 Ibid., p. 109.

23 Ibid., p. 113.

24 *On Education: a Translation of the De tradendis disciplinis,* trans. Foster Watson (Cambridge University Press, 1913), p. 232.

25 See, for example, Rolf Soellner, *Shakespeare's Patterns of Self-Knowledge* (Columbus: Ohio State University Press, 1972).

26 Quoted by Jonathan Dollimore, *Radical Tragedy: Religion, Ideology and Power in the Drama of Shakespeare and his Contemporaries,* 3rd edn (Basingstoke: Palgrave Macmillan, 2004), p. 11.

27 See Tom McAlindon, 'Cultural Materialism and the Ethics of Reading: or the Radicalizing of Jacobean Tragedy', *Modern Language Review,* 90 (1995), p. 833.

28 *The Essayes or Counsels Civill or Morall* (London: Dent, 1906), p. 117.

29 *The Passions of the Mind in General* (1601), ed. William Webster Newbold (New York and London: Garland, 1986), pp. 92–3 (my italics).

30 John Donne, *Devotions upon Emergent Occasions,* ed. Anthony Raspa (Montreal and London: McGill-Queen's University Press, 1975), p. 86.

31 For an excellent discussion of Machiavelli's distinction between individual character and humanity's universal nature see Janet Coleman, 'Machiavelli's *Via Moderna*: Medieval and Renaissance Attitudes to History', *Niccolò Machiavelli's The Prince: New Interdisciplinary Essays,* ed. Martin Coyle (Manchester University Press, 1995), pp. 40–64; see also Coleman, *Ancient and Medieval Memories: Studies in the Reconstruction of the Past* (Cambridge University Press, 1992), pp. 584–6.

32 Francesco Petrarca, 'On his Own Ignorance and that of Many Others', trans. Hans Nachod, in *The Renaissance Philosophy of Man,* ed. Ernst Cassirer, Paul Oskar Kristeller and John Hermann Randall, Jr (University of Chicago Press, 1948), p. 59.

33 *Praise of Folly,* trans. Betty Radice, *Collected Works of Erasmus,* 32 vols., ed. Peter D. Bietenholz, Alexander Dalzell, Anthony T. Grafton and others (University of Toronto Press, 1974–89), vol. 27 (1986), pp. 126–8.

34 *Enchiridion Militis Christiani,* p. 55.

35 St.Thomas More, *Selected Letters,* ed. Elizabeth Frances Rogers (New Haven and London: Yale University Press, 1961), p. 99.

36 Henry Peacham the Elder, *The Garden of Eloquence* (1593), with an introduction by William G. Crane (Gainesville, Fla.: Scholars' Facsimiles and Reprints, 1954), sig. Abiii^v.

37 *De oratore,* i.viii.33, trans. E. W. Sutton, Loeb Classical Library, 2 vols (London: Heinemann, 1948), vol. i, p. 25.

38 *Pro Archia Poeta,* ed. and trans. N. H. Watts, Loeb Classical Library (London: Heinemann, 1923).

39 *Ars poetica,* ed. and trans. H. Rushton Fairclough, Loeb Classical Library (London: Heinemann, 1970), p. 483.

40 See for example George Puttenham, *The Arte of English Poesie,* ed. Gladys Doidge Willcock and Alice Walker (Cambridge University Press, 1936), p. 6; Henry Peacham the Elder, *The Garden of Eloquence* (1593), with an

introduction by William G. Crane (Gainesville, Fla., Scholars' Facsimiles and Reprints, 1954), sig. ABiii^v.

41 The best-known version of the story in Elizabethan England was Arthur Golding's translation of Ovid's *Metamorphoses*, 1.113–312 (*Shakespeare's Ovid*, ed. W. H. D. Rouse (London: Centaur Press, 1961), pp. 22–4). Spenser paraphrases Ovid's version of the four ages of the world in *The Faerie Queene*, II.vii.16–17.

42 Giovanni Pico della Mirandola, 'Oration on the Dignity of Man', *The Renaissance Philosophy of Man*, ed. Ernst Cassirer, Paul Oskar Kristeller and John Herman Randall, trans. Elizabeth Livermore Forbes (University of Chicago Press, 1948), p. 225.

43 Dollimore, *Radical Tragedy*, p. 169.

44 St Augustine of Hippo, *Confessions*, trans. William Watts (1631), Loeb Classical Library, 2 vols. (London: Heinemann, 1922–5), vol. 1 (1922), pp. 449–51.

45 *The Heroic Frenzies*, trans. Paul Eugene Memmo, Jr (Chapel Hill: University of North Carolina Press, 1964), p. 137.

46 'Oration', ed. Cassirer, Kristeller and Randall, p. 225.

47 *The Faerie Queene*, II.ix.1, *The Poetical Works*, ed. J. C. Smith and E. de Selincourt (London, New York and Toronto: Oxford University Press, 1912), p. 112.

48 Sir Philip Sidney, *An Apology for Poetry*, ed. Geoffrey Shepherd (London: Nelson, 1965), p. 104.

49 See Robin Headlam Wells, *Elizabethan Mythologies: Studies in Poetry, Drama and Music* (Cambridge University Press, 1994), p. 140.

50 *Peace with her Four Guarders*, quoted by Pincombe, *Elizabethan Humanism*, p. 6.

51 *The Grounds of Criticism in Poetry* (1704), facsimile edn (Menston, Scolar Press, 1971), p. 6.

52 Quoted by Stanley Wells, *Times Literary Supplement*, 26 September 2003, p. 14. Scott's manuscript is in an identified private collection.

53 St Thomas More, *Utopia*, ed. Edward Surtz, S. J. and J. H. Hexter, *The Complete Works of St Thomas More*, 15 vols. (New Haven and London: Yale University Press, 1963–85), vol. 4 (1965), pp. 105–7.

54 See, for example, Quentin Skinner, *The Foundations of Modern Political Thought*, 2 vols: (Cambridge University Press, 1978), vol. 1, pp. 255–62; Dollimore, *Radical Tragedy*, pp. 169–70.

55 See *Utopia*, ed. Surtz and Hexter, p. 384, n. 112/1–2.

56 Ibid., pp. 243–5.

57 The *Dialogue* was never published in Starkey's lifetime. For the likely date of composition see *A Dialogue Between Pole and Lupset*, ed. T. F. Mayer (London: The Royal Historical Society, 1989), pp. x–ii.

58 Thomas F. Mayer, *Thomas Starkey and the Commonweal: Humanist Politics and Religion in the Reign of Henry VIII* (Cambridge University Press, 1989), p. 3.

59 *A Dialogue*, pp. 6–7.

60 Peter Martyr, *De novo Orbe, or The Historie of the west Indies*, trans. Richard Eden and Michael Lok (London, 1612), quoted by Harry Levin, *The Myth of the Golden Age in the Renaissance* (London: Faber and Faber, 1970), p. 60.

61 *De novo Orbe*, quoted by Levin, p. 62.

62 Levin notes that a survey of more than 500 travel books published in France before 1610 (Geoffroy Atkinson, *Les Nouveaux Horizons de la Renaissance Française* (Paris: Droz, 1935)) shows that reporters 'fall repeatedly into the vocabulary of the golden age' (*The Myth of the Golden Age*, p. 65).

63 See Fritz Caspari, *Humanism and the Social Order in Tudor England* (Chicago University Press, 1954), pp. 1–27.

64 R. Weiss, *Humanism in England during the Fifteenth Century*, 2nd edn (Oxford: Blackwell, 1957), pp. 13–21.

65 *Utopia*, ed. Surtz and Hexter, p. 27.

66 Letter to Robert Fisher, trans. R. A. B. Mynors and D. F. S. Thomson, *Collected Works of Erasmus*, vol. 1 (1974), pp. 235–6.

67 Charles H. George and Katherine George, *The Protestant Mind of the English Reformation 1570–1640* (Princeton University Press, 1961), p. 55.

68 Article X states that 'The condition of man after the Fall of Adam is such that he cannot turn and prepare himself by his own natural strength and good works, to faith and calling upon God: Wherefore we have no power to do good works, pleasant and acceptable to God, without the grace of God by Christ preventing us' (E. J. Bicknell, *A Theological Introduction to the Thirty-Nine Articles of the Church of England*, 2nd edn (London, New York and Toronto: Longmans, Green, 1925), p. 172).

69 What Montaigne was challenging in an essay such as 'Of Custome' was natural law, not the notion of a transhistorical human nature. When he claimed, for example, that 'every man hold[s] in special regard, and inward veneration the opinions approved and customes received about him', Montaigne was asking us to consider a universal tendency of humankind as a species (*The Essays of Montaigne*, trans. John Florio, 3 vols. (London: David Nutt, 1892–3), vol. 1 (1892), p. 112). Like Machiavelli's *Discourses*, the *Essays* are full of such generalisations about human nature.

70 *The Humanism of Leonardo Bruni: Selected Texts*, ed. and trans. Gordon Griffeths, James Hankins and David Thompson (Binghamton: Renaissance Society of America, 1987), pp. 96–7.

71 Eugenio Garin, *Italian Humanism: Philosophy and Civic Life in the Renaissance* (1947), trans. Peter Munz (Oxford: Basil Blackwell, 1965), p. 12.

72 Kristeller, *Renaissance Thought*, vol. 2, p.14.

73 Quoting John 1:9 in 'On his Own Ignorance', Petrarch wrote of the classical world, 'The true light had not yet begun to shine, which lights every man who comes into this world' (trans. Hans Nachod, p. 75).

74 T. E. Mommsen, 'Petrarch's Conception of the "Dark Ages"', *Speculum*, 17 (1942), pp. 226–42.

75 *Petrarch's Africa*, ii.362–4, p. 32.

76 Quoted by Charles Trinkaus, *The Scope of Renaissance Humanism* (Ann Arbor: University of Michigan Press, 1983), p. 55.

77 Wallace K. Ferguson writes: 'It was of course grossly unfair to confuse the contemporary exponents of a decadent scholasticism with the great medieval doctors. But Erasmus was too deeply involved in conflict with the former to make troublesome distinctions. For him all were barbarians, and the culture of the medieval centuries which the schoolmen had dominated was therefore barbarous' (*The Renaissance in Historical Thought: Five Centuries of Interpretation* (Cambridge, Mass.: Houghton Mifflin, 1948), p. 41).

78 Letter to Cornelis Gerard, *Collected Works of Erasmus*, vol. 1 (1974), p. 40.

79 *Antibarbari*, trans. Margaret Mann Phillips, *Collected Works*, vol. 23 (1978), pp. 42–3.

80 *De linguae Anglicae scriptione*, trans. and quoted by Pincombe, *Elizabethan Humanism*, p. 63.

81 *The 'Historia Regum Britanniae' of Geoffrey of Monmouth*, ed. Acton Griscom (London: Longmans, 1929), p. 239.

82 See Robin Headlam Wells, *Spenser's 'Faerie Queene' and the Cult of Elizabeth* (London and Totowa, NJ: Croom Helm and Barnes & Noble, 1983), pp. 10–14.

83 In *Pierce's Supererogation* Harvey wrote: 'It is not long, since the goodliest graces of the most noble commonwealths upon earth, eloquence in speech, and civility in manners, arrived in these remote parts of the world: it was a happy revolution of the heavens . . . when Tiberis flowed into the Thames; Athens removed to London; pure Italy, and fine Greece planted themselves in rich England' (quoted by Pincombe, *Elizabethan Humanism*, p. 59).

84 *Orchestra*, stanzas 120–6, *The Poems of Sir John Davies*, ed. Robert Krueger (Oxford: Clarendon Press, 1975), pp. 122–3.

85 Nabil Matar, *Islam in Britain 1558–1685* (Cambridge University Press, 1998), pp. 158–62.

86 *Enchiridion Militis Christiani*, p. 152. In *Othello* Shakespeare's hero seems to turn the second part of Erasmus' maxim into symbolic action while forgetting the first.

87 *The Generall Historie of the Turkes* (London, 1603), sig. Aiv^v.

88 'The Lepanto', *The Poems of James VI of Scotland*, ed. James Craigie (Edinburgh and London: Blackwood, 1955), p. 254. 'The Lepanto' was written in 1585 and republished in James' *Poeticall Exercises* of 1591 (see editor's introduction, p. xlviii).

89 *Toxophilus* (1545), ed. Edward Arber (London: Constable, 1895), p. 81.

90 *Report and Discourse of the Affairs and State of Germany* (1570), quoted by Pincombe, *Elizabethan Humanism*, p. 71.

91 Spenser used it in his description of the rebel forces besieging the Castle of Alma (*The Faerie Queene*, II.xi.5–16); Donne used it in Holy Sonnet x ('Batter my heart'). Both are based on the familiar analogy in which a 'public weal' is compared with 'a body living, compact or made of sundry estates and degrees of men . . . governed by the rule and moderation of reason' (Elyot, *The Governour*, p. 1).

92 In *Troilus and Criseyde* Chaucer makes a sustained analogy between the siege of Troy and Troilus' siege of Criseyde's heart.

93 For example, when Thomas More praised Colet for implanting the new learning in England he compared him to the Greeks: 'just as the Greeks who destroyed the barbarian Troy came out of the Trojan horse, so from your school come those who reprove and overthrow *their* ignorance' (*Selected Letters*, ed. Rogers, p. 6).

94 According to some versions of the Troy story, it was Antenor who sealed the city's fate by secretly advising the Greeks to build the Wooden Horse. In his own version of the story Chaucer comments wryly on the fact that the Trojans were so eager to exchange Criseyde for Antenor, the very man who 'was after traitor to the town/Of Troye' (*Troilus and Criseyde*, IV.204–5, *The Works of Geoffrey Chaucer*, 2nd edn, ed. F. N. Robinson (London: Oxford University Press, 1957), p. 443). For further discussion of the Trojan theme in *Hamlet* see Robin Headlam Wells, *Shakespeare on Masculinity* (Cambridge University Press, 2000), pp. 75–9.

95 Kenneth Charlton, *Education in Renaissance England* (London and Toronto: Routledge and Kegan Paul, 1965), p. 130.

96 On the Elizabethan grammar-school curriculum see T. W. Baldwin, *William Shakespere's Small Latine and Lesse Greeke*, 2 vols. (Urbana: University of Illinois Press, 1944); Peter Mack, *Elizabethan Rhetoric: Theory and Practice* (Cambridge University Press, 2002).

97 Philemon Holland's translation of Livy's *The Roman Historie* (1600) included Florus' abridgement of Livy.

98 *The Arte of English Poesie*, p. 60.

99 Thomas Wilson, *The Arte of Rhetorique*, ed. G. H. Mair (Oxford: Clarendon Press, 1909), dedicatory epistle, sig. Avii.

100 See Baldwin, *William Shakespere's Small Latine and Lesse Greeke*. See also Robert S. Miola, *Shakespeare and Classical Tragedy: The Influence of Seneca* (Oxford: Clarendon Press, 1992); Jonathan Bate, *Shakespeare and Ovid* (Oxford: Clarendon Press, 1993).

101 For a recent discussion of humanist drama in this period see Kent Cartwright, *Theatre and Humanism: English Drama in the Sixteenth Century* (Cambridge University Press, 1999).

102 Jonathan Dollimore, Introduction to *Political Shakespeare: New Essays in Cultural Materialism*, ed. Dollimore and Alan Sinfield (Manchester University Press, 1985), pp. 10–13.

103 See Rosalie Colie, *Paradoxia Epidemica: the Renaissance Tradition of Paradox* (Princeton University Press, 1966); Emrys Jones, *The Origins of Shakespeare*,

pp. 13–15; Joel B. Altman, *The Tudor Play of Mind: Rhetorical Inquiry and the Development of Elizabethan Drama* (Berkeley, Los Angeles and London: University of California Press: 1978); M. T. Jones-Davies, 'Shakespeare in the Humanist Tradition: The Skeptical Doubts and their Expression in Paradoxes', *Shakespeare and Cultural Traditions*, ed. Tetsuo Kishi, Roger Pringle and Stanley Wells (London and Toronto: Associated University Presses, 1994), pp. 99–109.

104 Colie, *Paradoxia Epidemica*, p. 10.

105 *Shakespeare and the Common Understanding* (1967; repr. University of Chicago Press, 1984), p.12.

106 W. R. Elton, 'Shakespeare and the Thought of his Age', *A New Companion to Shakespeare Studies*, ed. Kenneth Muir and S. Schoenbaum (Cambridge University Press, 1971), p. 197.

107 For some recent discussion of political issues in the middle and later Shakespeare see Alvin Kernan, *Shakespeare, the King's Playwright: Theater in the Stuart Court 1603–1613* (New Haven, Conn. and London: Yale University Press, 1995); Robin Headlam Wells, *Shakespeare on Masculinity*; Debora Kuller Shuger, *Political Theologies in Shakespeare's England: The Sacred and the State in 'Measure for Measure'* (Basingstoke: Palgrave, 2001); Andrew Hadfield, *Shakespeare and Renaissance Politics* (London: Arden Shakespeare, 2004).

108 See Lukas Erne, *Shakespeare as Literary Dramatist* (Cambridge University Press, 2003) who argues that Shakespeare wrote for the stage *and* the page, producing different versions of his plays for the different media.

109 See for example Sidney, *An Apology for Poetry*, p. 108.

110 *Microcosmographia: A Description of the body of Man* (London, 1618), sig. b^{v}.

111 The French humanist Pierre de La Primaudaye gave a classic account of the doctrine of analogy in the popular *The French Academie*: 'As we see that . . . the whole world being compounded of unlike elements, of earth, water, air and fire, is notwithstanding preserved by analogy and proportion . . . and as we see in a man's body, head, hands, feet, eyes, nose, ears; in a house the husband, wife, children, master, servants; in a politic body, magistrates, nobles, common people, artificers; and that every body mingled with heat, cold, dry and moist, is preserved by the same reason of analogy and proportion which they have together, so it is in every commonwealth . . .' (London, 1586, p. 744). For modern discussions of the microcosm/macrocosm analogy see J. B. Bamborough, *The Little World of Man* (London, New York and Toronto: Longmans, Green & Co, 1952); S. K. Heninger Jr, *Touches of Sweet Harmony: Pythagorean Cosmology and Renaissance Poetics* (San Marino: Huntington Library, 1974); James Daly, 'Cosmic Harmony and Political Thinking in Early Stuart England', *Transactions of the American Philosophical Society*, 69 (1979), pp. 3–40.

112 See chapter 2, p. 37.

113 On the idea of sudden change as a characteristic feature of the pre-modern universe see T. McAlindon, *Shakespeare's Tragic Cosmos* (Cambridge University Press, 1991); McAlindon, 'What is a Shakespearean Tragedy?',

The Cambridge Companion to Shakespearean Tragedy, ed. Claire McEachern (Cambridge University Press, 2002), pp. 1–22.
114 *Microcosmographia*, sig. B^v.
115 *The Advancement of Learning and the New Atlantis*, ed. Arthur Johnston (Oxford: Clarendon Press, 1974), p. 105.
116 Sir Walter Ralegh, *The History of the World* (London, 1614), p. 25.
117 Sir Thomas Browne, *The Religio Medici* (London: Dent, 1962), p. 39.
118 *A Dialogue Between Pole and Lupset*, p. 10.
119 'Apology for Raimond Sebond', *The Essays*, vol. 2, p. 144.
120 Ibid., p. 144.
121 'An Anatomy of the World', p. 213, *The Epithalamions, Anniversaries and Epicedes*, ed. W. Milgate (Oxford: Clarendon Press, 1978), p. 28.
122 Rejection of the supposedly false notion of a universal human nature was a popular theme among intellectuals in post-war Europe (see chapter 9). If, as Althusser claimed, human nature was a bourgeois myth, there must obviously have been a time when people's minds hadn't yet been contaminated by this false ideology. But while there was a general sense that the modern concept of human nature was coeval with the rise of capitalism, no one had ventured to put a date on its first appearance. It was Foucault who seemed for the first time to provide authority for the idea of a definitive history of 'man', even going so far as to identify a particular decade when the concept was invented. But as I'll explain in chapter 9, Foucault didn't mean quite what he seemed to be saying when he made the notorious claim: 'before the end of the eighteenth century, *man* did not exist'.

2 GENDER

1 Ronald Hutton, *The Rise and Fall of Merry England: The Ritual Year 1400–1700* (Oxford and London: Oxford University Press, 1994), p. 211. This and the following paragraph are based on Hutton. On seventeenth-century attitudes towards traditional seasonal revelry see also Leah S. Marcus, *The Politics of Mirth: Jonson, Herrick, Milton, Marvell and the Defense of Old Holiday Pastimes* (University of Chicago Press, 1986).
2 C. L. Barber, *Shakespeare's Festive Comedy: A Study of Dramatic Form and its Relation to Social Custom* (Princeton University Press, 1959), p. 7.
3 Philip Stubbes, *The Anatomie of Abuses*, ed. Frederick J. Furnivall (London: New Shakespeare Society, 1877–9), pp. 146–7.
4 William Warner, *Albions England*, revised and enlarged edn (London, 1601–2), p. 121.
5 *Albions England*, p. 121.
6 Robert Devereux, *An Apologie of the Earl of Essex* (London, 1598), sig. E^v.
7 Stephen Gosson, *The Schoole of Abuse* (1579), ed. Edward Arber (London: English Reprints, 1869), p. 34.
8 For discussion of Shakespeare's satirical treatment of *amor heroycus* see chapter 6, pp. 124; 130.

9 On this aspect of the play see Robin Headlam Wells, *Elizabethan Mythologies: Studies in Poetry, Drama and Music* (Cambridge University Press, 1994), pp. 208–24.

10 The most likely date of *Twelfth Night*'s composition was 1601 (see Elizabeth Story Donno, ed., *Twelfth Night* (Cambridge University Press, 1985), pp. 1–4). The Earl of Essex's rebellion took place in February 1601.

11 Laura Levine, *Men in Women's Clothing: Anti-theatricality and Effeminization, 1579–1642* (Cambridge University Press, 1994), p. 3. See also Catherine Belsey, 'Disrupting Sexual Difference: Meaning and Gender in the Comedies', *Alternative Shakespeares*, ed. John Drakakis (London and New York: Methuen, 1985) pp. 166–90; Stephen Greenblatt, 'Fiction and Friction', *Shakespearean Negotiations: The Circulation of Social Energy in Renaissance England* (Oxford: Clarendon Press, 1988), pp. 66–93; Jean E. Howard, 'Crossdressing, The Theatre, and Gender Struggle in Early Modern England', *Shakespeare Quarterly*, 39 (1988), pp. 419–20; Marjorie Garber, *Vested Interests: Cross-Dressing and Cultural Anxiety* (New York and London: Routledge, 1992), pp. 32–7; Peter Stallybrass, 'Transvestism and the "body beneath": Speculating on the Boy Actor', in *Erotic Politics: Desire on the Renaissance Stage*, ed. Susan Zimmerman (London: Routledge, 1992), pp. 64–83; Valerie Traub, *Desire and Anxiety: Circulations of Sexuality in Shakespearean Drama* (London and New York: Routledge, 1992); Jonathan Crewe, 'In the Field of Dreams: Transvestism in *Twelfth Night* and *The Crying Game*', *Representations*, 50 (1995), 101–21; Stephen Orgel, *Impersonations: The Performance of Gender in Shakespeare's England* (Cambridge University Press, 1996); Dympna Callaghan, *Shakespeare Without Women: Representing Gender and Race on the Renaissance Stage* (London: Routledge, 1999), pp. 26–48.

12 'Fiction and Friction', *Shakespearean Negotiations*, p. 76.

13 Ibid., p. 77.

14 Ibid., p. 86.

15 Ibid., p. 87.

16 Helkiah Crooke, *Microcosmographia: A Description of the Body of Man* (London, 1618), Preface.

17 Annibale Romei, *The Courtier's Academy*, trans. J. K[eper] (London, 1598), p. 17.

18 See for example the illustration reproduced in Robin Headlam Wells, *Elizabethan Mythologies*, p. 124 of a human figure representing the Boethian categories of *musica mundana*, *musica humana* and *musica instrumentalis*.

19 Pierre de La Primaudaye, *The French Academie*, revised edn, trans. Thomas Bowes (London, 1618), p. 523.

20 See J. B. Bamborough, *The Little World of Man* (London, New York and Toronto: Longmans, Green and Co, 1952), p. 60.

21 *Cynthia's Revels*, II.iii.124–5, *Ben Jonson*, 11 vols., ed. C. H. Herford and Percy and Evelyn Simpson (Oxford: Clarendon Press, 1925–52), vol. 4 (1932), p. 74.

22 'I am a little world', *The Divine Poems*, ed. Helen Gardner (Oxford: Clarendon Press, 1952), p. 13.

23 In his introduction Crooke explained, 'because . . . the body carrieth in it a representation of all the most glorious and perfect workes of God, as being an Epitome or compend of the whole creation . . . hence it is that man is called a *Microcosme*, or little world' (*Microcosmographia*, sig. B^v).
24 See Bamborough, *The Little World of Man*, passim.
25 Levinus Lemnius, *The Secret Miracles of Nature* (1571), trans. anon. (London, 1658), p. 310.
26 See Sir Philip Sidney, *An Apology for Poetry*, ed. Geoffrey Shepherd (London: Nelson, 1965), p. 104.
27 *An Apology for Poetry*, p. 86.
28 'Transvestism and the "body beneath"', pp. 64–83.
29 Jonas Barish, *The Antitheatrical Prejudice* (Berkeley, Los Angeles and London: University of California Press, 1981), pp. 80–131. See also Michael Shapiro, *Gender in Play on the Shakespearean Stage: Boy Heroines and Female Pages* (Ann Arbor: University of Michigan Press, 1994), pp. 15–28.
30 Anon., *A Word to Mr Wil Pryn* (London, 1649), p. 8.
31 William Prynne, *Histriomastix* (1633), facsimile edn with a preface by Arthur Freeman (New York and London: Garland, 1974), p. 171, quoted by Stallybrass, 'Transvestism and the "body beneath"', p. 76.
32 Ibid., p. 77.
33 William M. Lamont, *Marginal Prynne 1600–1669* (London: Routledge and Kegan Paul, 1963), p. 2.
34 *Histriomastix*, p. 171.
35 Ibid., p. 207, quoted by Stallybrass, 'Transvestism and the "body beneath"', p. 76 (Prynne's italics).
36 Ibid., p. 76.
37 *Histriomastix*, p. 208.
38 *Hic Mulier: Or, the Man-Woman* (London, 1620), sig. B2^v.
39 'Transvestism and the "body beneath"', p. 79.
40 Compare Traub: 'However much we might discredit the anti-theatricalists as "fanatics" or crude mimeticists, their intuitions about erotic arousal should not be presumed to be incidental to theatrical production' (*Desire and Anxiety*, p. 119).
41 Levine, *Men in Women's Clothing*, p. 4.
42 Ibid., p. 3.
43 Ibid., p. 10.
44 Ibid., p. 4.
45 Ibid., p. 10.
46 Ibid., pp. 3; 10.
47 *The Schoole of Abuse*, pp. 26; 29 (I have italicised the phrase that Levine quotes). Thomas Lodge makes a riposte to Gosson's 'disprayses of Musik' in *A Reply to 'Gosson's Schoole of Abuse'* (facsimile edn with a preface by Arthur Freeman (New York and London: Garland, 1973), pp. 24–5). In *An Apologie of the Schoole of Abuse* Gosson responds to the complaint (probably Lodge's) that 'I condemne Musique' by saying that it's not music

itself that he is attacking, but its abuse (printed in *The Schoole of Abuse*, p. 65).

48 *The Anatomie of Abuses*, p. 73.

49 *Men in Women's Clothing*, p. 4.

50 *The Anatomie of Abuses*, p. 73.

51 Ibid., p. 144.

52 Robert Browne, *An Answere to Master Cartwright* (London, n.d. [1585?]), sig. Aii; p. 6.

53 See Andrew Gurr, 'Metatheatre and the Fear of Playing', in *Neo-Historicism: Studies in English Renaissance Literature, History and Politics*, ed. Robin Headlam Wells, Glenn Burgess and Rowland Wymer (Cambridge: D. S. Brewer, 2000), pp. 91–110.

54 Robert Browne, *The Life and Manners of all True Christians* (Middleburg, 1582), sig. D2ᵛ.

55 William Perkins, *A Discourse of the Damned Art of Witchcraft* (Cambridge, 1608), quoted by Gurr, 'Metatheatre and the Fear of Playing', p. 92.

56 *Histriomastix*, p. 159.

57 Levine's *Men in Women's Clothing* has received high praise from postmodern Shakespeareans. Patricia Parker describes Levine as 'a critic of the first rank' (quotation on cover of paperback edition).

58 *Impersonations*, p. 26.

59 *Shakespeare Without Women*, p. 33.

60 Stephen Cohen, '(Post)modern Elizabeth: Gender, Politics, and the Emergence of Modern Subjectivity', in *Shakespeare and Modernity: Early Modern to Millenium* ed. Hugh Grady (London and New York: Routledge, 2000), p. 32.

61 Valerie Traub, 'Gender and Sexuality in Shakespeare', *The Cambridge Companion to Shakespeare*, ed. Margreta De Grazia and Stanley Wells (Cambridge University Press, 2001), pp. 141–2.

62 David Scott Kastan, *Shakespeare After Theory* (New York and London: Routledge, 1999), p. 152.

63 'Disrupting Sexual Difference', p. 188.

64 Linda Charnes, *Notorious Identity: Materializing the Subject in Shakespeare* (Cambridge, Mass.: Harvard University Press, 1993), 10. See also Ivo Kamps ed., *Materialist Shakespeare: A History* (London and New York: Verso, 1995); Margreta de Grazia, Maureen Quilligan and Peter Stallybrass, eds., *Subject and Object in Renaissance Culture* (Cambridge University Press, 1996); Elizabeth Hanson, *Discovering the Subject in Renaissance England* (Cambridge University Press, 1998); Christopher Pye, *The Vanishing: Shakespeare, the Subject, and Early Modern Culture* (Durham, NC and London: Duke University Press, 2000).

65 'Crossdressing, The Theatre, and Gender Struggle', p. 419 n 4.

66 Karen Newman, *Fashioning Femininity and English Renaissance Drama* (Chicago and London: University of Chicago Press, 1991), p. xviii.

67 *Impersonations*, p. xiv.

68 See for example Belsey, 'Disrupting Sexual Difference', p. 188; Garber, *Vested Interests*, p. 12; Levine, *Men in Women's Clothing*, p. 11.

69 Judith Butler, *Gender Trouble: Feminism and the Subversion of Identity* (New York: Routledge, 1990), p. 136.

70 See Leda Cosmides and John Tooby, 'The Psychological Foundations of Culture', in *The Adapted Mind: Evolutionary Psychology and the Generation of Culture,* ed. Jerome H. Barkow, Leda Cosmides and John Tooby (New York and Oxford: Oxford University Press, 1992), pp. 19–136.

71 Orgel writes: 'Elizabethan children of both sexes were dressed in skirts until the age of seven or so; the "breeching" of boys was the formal move out of the common gender of childhood' (*Impersonations*, pp. 15; 18).

72 Richard D. Gross, *Psychology: The Science of Mind and Behaviour* (London, Sydney and Auckland: Hodder and Stoughton, 1992), p. 686.

73 See John Colapinto, *As Nature Made Him: The Boy Who was Raised as a Girl* (New York: HarperCollins, 2000).

74 John Money and Anke A. Ehrhardt, *Man and Woman Boy and Girl: The Differentiation and Dimorphism of Gender Identity from Conception to Maturity* (Baltimore and London: Johns Hopkins University Press, 1972), pp. 117–45.

75 According to Colapinto, it's not just children whose gender has been re-assigned in infancy who feel that there is something wrong with their sexual identity; other children sense it too, and unerringly single out the victim for bullying (*As Nature Made Him*, pp. 216–17).

76 David Reimer speaking in 'The Boy Who Was Turned into a Girl', BBC, Horizon, 2000. Reimer committed suicide in May 2004.

77 *Vested Interests*, p. 15.

78 D. F. Swaab has shown that, as is the case with many mammalian species, the prenatal human brain is differentially modified by sex hormones, with the result that the 'sexually dimorphic nucleus . . . of the human hypothalamus contains twice as many cells in young adult men as in women' ('Sex and Gender Differences in the Human Brain: Behavioural Consequences', *European Journal of Neuroscience*, 10 (1998), Supplement, 330). See also Dick F. Swaab, Jiang-Ning Zhou, Mariann Fodor, et al., 'Sexual Differentiation of the Human Hypothalamus: Differences According to Sex, Sexual Orientation, and Transsexuality', *ART in the Year 2000*, ed. K. Diedrich and R. Felberbaum (Oxford University Press, 1999), pp. 129–50; Simon Baron-Cohen, *The Essential Difference: Men, Women and the Extreme Male Brain* (London: Allen Lane, 2003).

79 Jan Morris, *Conundrum* (London: Faber and Faber, 1974), p. 14.

80 Sarah Brewer, *A Child's World* (London: Headline, 2001), pp. 93–129.

81 *Impersonations*, p. 57.

82 *Vested Interests*, p. 10.

83 Postmodernists give the impression that the quarrel in modern studies of gender is between social constructionists and biological determinists. This is misleading. As Joseph Carroll explains, the real antithesis is between

constructionists, who believe that social conditioning is everything, and evolutionary psychologists, who argue that gender identity is the product of a combination of genetic and environmental factors (*Evolution and Literary Theory* (Columbia and London: University of Missouri Press, 1995), pp. 271–2). Edward O. Wilson writes well on what he calls 'gene-culture coevolution': 'Culture is created by the communal mind, and each mind in turn is the product of the genetically structured human brain. Genes and culture are therefore inseverably linked. But the linkage is flexible, to a degree still mostly unmeasured' (*Consilience: the Unity of Knowledge* (London: Little, Brown, 1998), p. 139).

84 Diane N. Ruble, 'Sex-Role Development', *Social, Emotional, and Personality Development*, ed. Marc H. Bornstein and Michael E. Lamb, 2nd edn (London and Hillsdale: Lawrence Erlbaum Associates, 1988), p. 430.

85 See for example Lodge, *A Reply to 'Gosson's Schoole of Abuse'*, pp. 36–7; Sidney, *An Apology for Poetry*, pp. 117–18; Thomas Heywood, *An Apology for Actors* (1612) (London: Shakespeare Society, 1841), p. 28.

86 Linda Woodbridge, *Women and the English Renaissance: Literature and the Nature of Womankind, 1540–1620* (Brighton: Harvester, 1984), p. 154.

87 Peter Ackroyd, *Dressing Up: Transvestism and Drag, The History of an Obsession* (London: Thames and Hudson, 1979), p. 21.

88 Richard F. Doctor, *Transvestites and Transsexuals: Toward a Theory of Cross-Gender Behaviour* (New York and London: Plenum Press, 1988), p. 70.

89 *Erotic Politics*, p. 8.

90 Jeanette Winterson, 'What Planet is Doris on?', *Guardian Review*, 15 August 2001, p. 7.

91 In a survey of cross-dressing plays in this period David Cressy concludes that 'Theatrical cross-dressing is not portrayed as threatening, effeminizing, and certainly not an abomination unto the lord. But how should it be otherwise, since the plays were not the voices but the targets of reformist propaganda' ('Gender Trouble and Cross-Dressing in Early Modern England', *Journal of British Studies*, 35 (1996), p. 458).

92 Quoted by Magnus Hirschfeld, *Transvestites: The Erotic Drive to Cross Dress*, trans. Michael A. Lombardi-Nash (Buffalo: Prometheus Books, 1991), p. 351.

93 Despite the play's satire on male vanity, foolishness and self-deception, there seems to be an assumption in much recent criticism that in its sexual politics *Twelfth Night* is anti-women. Jean Howard sees it as 'a fairly oppressive fable about the containment of gender' that 'disciplines independent women like Olivia' ('Crossdressing, The Theatre, and Gender Struggle', pp. 431; 433). Dympna Callaghan describes it as a 'social enactment of women's oppression' (*Shakespeare Without Women*, p. 40).

94 Enid Welsford, *The Court Masque: A Study of the Relationship Between Poetry and the Revels* (Cambridge University Press, 1927), pp. 38–9.

95 *The Court Masque*, p. 38.

96 *Vested Interests*, p. 9.

97 Waldemar Januszczak writes: 'when the Taliban blew up the giant outdoor Buddha of Bamiyan [in 2001] any sane observer would have shuddered at the misguided bellicosity of the deed and recognised it immediately as an act of barbarism. Yet what we did to our artistic heritage five centuries ago was of an altogether more barbaric order . . . A thousand years of artistic evolution, the sum total of Britain's cultural history so far, was attacked by rioting mobs of religious maniacs, while the rest of the country cheered them on' (*The Sunday Times*, 'Culture' section, 30 September 2001, p. 10).

3 VALUE PLURALISM

1 See Richard Halpern, *Shakespeare Among the Moderns* (Ithaca and London: Cornell University Press, 1997), pp. 163–6.

2 David S. Katz, *The Jews in the History of England 1485–1850* (Oxford: Clarendon Press, 1994), pp. 49–101. See also Hermann Sinsheimer, *Shylock: the History of a Character* (1947; repr. New York: Benjamin Blom, 1968), p. 37; James Shapiro, *Shakespeare and the Jews* (New York: Columbia University Press, 1996), p. 43.

3 *Discoveries, Ben Jonson*, 11 vols., ed. C. H. Herford and Percy and Evelyn Simpson (Oxford: Clarendon Press, 1925–52), vol. 8 (1947), p. 565.

4 For a brilliant discussion of the ironic parallels between Christians and Jews in Shakespeare's play see René Girard, '"To Entrap the Wisest": A Reading of *The Merchant of Venice*', *Literature and Society: Selected Papers of the English Institute*, ns 3, ed. Edward W. Said (Baltimore and London: Johns Hopkins University Press, 1980), pp. 100–19.

5 *Geneva Bible*, facsimile of 1560 edn with an introduction by Lloyd E. Berry (Madison, Milwaukee and London: University of Wisconsin Press, 1969), sig. ⲦⲦii.

6 Shapiro, *Shakespeare and the Jews*, p. 144.

7 Leslie Fiedler writes: 'the play in some sense celebrates, certainly releases ritually the full horror of anti-Semitism . . .no racist's Jew is more terrible, more absolute in his obduracy than Shylock' (*The Stranger in Shakespeare* (London: Croom Helm, 1973), pp. 98; 121).

8 On the puritan campaign against the theatre see Jonas Barish, *The Antitheatrical Prejudice* (Berkeley, Los Angeles and London: University of California Press, 1981), pp. 80–131. On the factional battles to control government policy in the late 1590s, including Essex's systematic patronage of puritan clergy, see Mervyn James, *Society, Politics and Culture: Studies in Early Modern England* (1978; repr. Cambridge University Press, 1986), pp. 308–415; R. B. Wernham, *The Making of Elizabethan Foreign Policy, 1558–1603* (Berkeley, Los Angeles and London: University of California Press, 1980), pp. 82–7; John Guy, *Tudor England* (Oxford and New York: Oxford University Press, 1988), p. 449. On the puritan campaign to criminalise adultery see Debora Kuller Shuger, *Political Theologies in Shakespeare's England: The*

Sacred and the State in 'Measure for Measure' (Basingstoke: Palgrave, 2001), p. 30. On the so-called 'puritan' articles devised by parliament to extend the law of treason against Catholics see Penry Williams, *The Later Tudors: England 1547–1603*, The New Oxford History of England (Oxford: Clarendon Press, 1995), p. 290.

 9 Quoted by Shapiro, *Shakespeare and the Jews*, p. 143.

10 Werner Sombart, *The Jews and Modern Capitalism*, trans. M. Epstein (Glencoe, Ill.: Free Press, 1951), p. 250.

11 *Der Calvinische Judenspiegel*, quoted by Sombart, *The Jews and Modern Capitalism*, p. 251.

12 Eldred D. Jones, *The Elizabethan Image of Africa* (Washington: Folger Shakespeare Library, 1971), p. 20.

13 See R. S. White, *Natural Law in English Renaissance Literature* (Cambridge University Press, 1996), pp. 160–4; B. J. Sokol and Mary Sokol, 'Shakespeare and the English Equity Jurisdiction: *The Merchant of Venice* and the two texts of *King Lear*', *Review of English Studies*, ns 50 (1999), pp. 417–39.

14 White, *Natural Law in English Renaissance Literature*, p. 164; Sokol and Sokol, 'Shakespeare and the English Equity Jurisdiction', p. 419.

15 'It is the province of a prince to surpass all in stainless character and wisdom . . . [the characteristics of a good prince are] clemency, affability, fairness, courtesy, and kindliness' (Desiderius Erasmus, *The Education of a Christian Prince*, trans. with an introduction by Lester K. Born (New York: Columbia University Press, 1936), pp. 153; 209).

16 Niccolò Machiavelli, *The Prince*, ed. Quentin Skinner and Russell Price (Cambridge University Press, 1988), p. 55.

17 Ben Jonson, *Discoveries*, ed. Herford and Simpson, vol. 7, p. 599.

18 Gentillet described Machiavelli as 'a most pernicious writer, which . . . utterly destroyed, not this or that virtue, but even all virtues at once' (Innocent Gentillet, *A Discourse upon the Meanes of Wel Governing . . . Against Nicholas Machiavell*, trans. S. Patericke (London, 1602), sig. ¶iii^v). The *Discours contre Machiavel* went through nine editions between 1577 and 1609 and was translated into Dutch, English, German, and Latin. On Machiavelli's influence in England see Felix Raab, *The English Face of Machiavelli: A Changing Interpretation 1500–1700* (London: Routledge and Kegan Paul, 1964); F. J. Levy, *Tudor Historical Thought* (San Marino: The Huntington Library, 1967), pp. 238–42; Anne Barton, 'Livy, Machiavelli, and Shakespeare's *Coriolanus*', *Shakespeare Survey*, 38 (1985), pp. 115–29; Victoria Kahn, *Machiavellian Rhetoric: From the Counter-Reformation to Milton* (Princeton: Princeton University Press, 1994).

19 John Rainoldes, *Th' overthrow of Stage-Playes*, facsimile edn with a preface by Arthur Freeman (New York and London: Garland, 1974), pp. 9–10.

20 For discussion of the modern critical debate on Shakespeare and the anti-theatricalists see chapter 2.

21 Justus Lipsius, *Six Bookes of Politickes or Civil Doctrine*, trans. William Jones (London, 1594), p. 114.

22 'To the memory of my beloved, The Author, Mr. William Shakespeare', line 56, ed. Herford and Simpson, vol. 7 (1947), pp. 390–2.

23 *Discoveries*, ed. Herford and Simpson, vol. 7, p. 584.

24 A passage in the anonymous *Greene's Groats-worth of witte* (1592) describes Shakespeare as 'an upstart Crow, beautified with our feathers, that with his *Tiger's heart wrapped in a Player's hide*, supposes he is as well able to bombast out a blank verse as the best of you: and being an absolute *Johannes factotum*, is in his own conceit the only Shake-scene in a country' (sig. A3ᵛ). Katherine Duncan-Jones, who quotes this remark (p. 27) in her provocatively titled biography, challenges the notion of a liberal, unselfish, unprejudiced Shakespeare: 'I don't believe that any Elizabethans, even Shakespeare, were what might now be called "nice" ' (*Ungentle Shakespeare: Scenes from His Life* (London: Arden Shakespeare, 2001), p. x).

25 On Shakespeare's punning on 'gentle' (rank and conduct) and 'gentile' in *The Merchant of Venice* see Frank Kermode, 'The Mature Comedies', *Early Shakespeare*, ed. John Russell Brown and Bernard Harris, Stratford-upon-Avon Studies, 3 (London: Edward Arnold, 1961), pp. 221–2.

26 Compare Graham Bradshaw: '[*The Merchant of Venice* is] a comedy concerned with diverse acts of valuing' (*Shakespeare's Scepticism* (Brighton: Harvester Press, 1987), p. 31).

27 See in particular A. P. Rossiter, 'Ambivalence: The Dialectic of the Histories' (1951), *Angel with Horns: Fifteen Lectures on Shakespeare*, ed. Graham Storey, 1961; repr. with an introduction by Peter Holland (London and New York: Longman, 1989), pp. 40–64; Bernard McElroy, *Shakespeare's Mature Tragedies* (Princeton University Press, 1973); Emrys Jones, *The Origins of Shakespeare* (Oxford: Clarendon Press, 1977); Robert Grudin, *Mighty Opposites: Shakespeare and Renaissance Contrariety* (Berkeley, Los Angeles and London: University of California Press, 1979); W. R. Elton, 'Shakespeare and the Thought of his Age', *The Cambridge Companion to Shakespeare Studies*, ed. Stanley Wells (Cambridge University Press, 1986), pp. 17–34; Graham Bradshaw, *Shakespeare's Scepticism*; Bradshaw, *Misrepresentations: Shakespeare and the Materialists* (Ithaca and London: Cornell University Press, 1993).

28 See Rosalie Colie, *Paradoxia Epidemica: the Renaissance Tradition of Paradox* (Princeton University Press, 1966), p. 10; Jones, *The Origins of Shakespeare*, pp. 13–15; Joel B. Altman, *The Tudor Play of Mind: Rhetorical Inquiry and the Development of Elizabethan Drama* (Berkeley, Los Angeles and London: University of California Press, 1978).

29 The translation has been lost. See M. T. Jones-Davies, 'Shakespeare in the Humanist Tradition: The Skeptical Doubts and their Expression in Paradoxes', *Shakespeare and Cultural Traditions*, ed. Tetsuo Kishi, Roger Pringle and Stanley Wells (London and Toronto: Associated University Presses, 1994), pp. 99–109.

30 Prefatory epistle to *Syr P. S. His Astrophel and Stella*, quoted by Jones-Davies, pp. 99–100.

31 Sextus Empiricus, *Outlines of Pyrrhonism*, I.12, trans. R. G. Bury, Loeb Classical Library (London: Heinemann, 1933), p. 9.

32 For Berlin's central statement of value pluralism see 'Two Concepts of Liberty', first given as an inaugural lecture at Oxford University, 1958, reprinted in *Four Essays on Liberty* (Oxford and New York: Oxford University Press, 1969), pp. 118–72. For discussion of Berlin's value pluralism see John Gray, *Isaiah Berlin* (London: HarperCollins, 1995), pp. 38–75; see also papers by Aileen Kelly, Ronald Dworkin, Steven Lukes, Charles Taylor and Bernard Williams in *The Legacy of Isaiah Berlin*, ed. Mark Lilla, Ronald Dworkin and Robert Silver, (New York: New York Review of Books, 2001).

33 John Donne, *The Divine Poems*, ed. Helen Gardner (Oxford: Clarendon Press, 1952), p. 13.

34 White, *Natural Law in English Renaissance Literature*. See also Robert Hoopes, *Right Reason in the English Renaissance* (Cambridge, Mass.: Harvard University Press, 1962), pp. 1–32; George C. Herndl, *The High Design: English Renaissance Tragedy and the Natural Law* (Lexington, Ky: University of Kentucky Press, 1970), pp. 13–40; John S. Wilks, *The Idea of Conscience in Renaissance Tragedy* (London and New York: Routledge, 1990), pp. 9–23; Richard A. McCabe, *Incest, Drama and Nature's Law 1550–1700* (Cambridge University Press, 1993), pp. 55–61.

35 *Of the Laws of Ecclesiastical Polity*, I.viii.9, 2 vols. (London: Dent, 1907), vol. I, p. 182.

36 Thomas Starkey, *A Dialogue Between Pole and Lupset*, ed. T. F. Mayer, Camden Fourth Series, 37 (London: The Royal Historical Society, 1989), p. 12

37 *A Dialogue*, p. 11.

38 'Two Concepts of Liberty', pp. 168–9.

39 *Shakespeare and the Common Understanding* (1967; repr. Chicago and London: University of Chicago Press, 1984), p. 27. Jonathan Bate also refers to Bohr (though not to Rabkin), and draws similar conclusions, in *The Genius of Shakespeare* (London and Basingstoke: Picador, 1997), pp. 312–15. In another book Rabkin argued that *The Merchant of Venice* illustrates this principle in the way it refuses to allow an unequivocal resolution of its conflicts in favour of one side or the other (*Shakespeare and the Problem of Meaning* (Chicago and London: University of Chicago Press, 1981), pp. 28–9).

40 See Ernest Gellner, *Relativism and the Social Sciences* (Cambridge University Press, 1985), pp. 84–5.

4 SOCIAL JUSTICE

1 Theodor W. Adorno and Max Horkheimer, *Dialectic of Enlightenment* (1944), trans. John Cumming (London: Allen Lane, 1973), p. 37.

2 *Dialectic of Enlightenment*, p. 35.

3 Herbert Marcuse, *One Dimensional Man: Studies in the Ideology of Advanced Industrial Society* (London: Routledge and Kegan Paul, 1964), pp. 18; 15–16.

4 *One Dimensional Man*, p. x.
5 Quoted in *One Dimensional Man*, p. 84.
6 Adorno and Horkheimer, *Dialectic of Enlightenment*, p. 3.
7 Raymond Tallis writes: 'Real crimes tend . . . to be relatively neglected by Cultural Critics, or simply regarded as logical extensions of the symbolic crimes; they are of lesser interest because they require no hermeneutic skills to uncover them' (*Enemies of Hope: A Critique of Contemporary Pessimism* (Basingstoke and London: Macmillan, 1997), p. 209).
8 Michel Foucault, *Discipline and Punish: The Birth of the Prison*, trans. Alan Sheridan (London: Allen Lane, 1977), p. 31.
9 Ibid., p. 78.
10 Ibid., p. 24.
11 Ibid., p. 11.
12 Ibid., p. 194.
13 Ibid., p. 301.
14 Ibid., pp. 302; 308.
15 Ibid., p. 24.
16 Ibid., p. 304.
17 Joseph Carroll, *Evolution and Literary Theory* (Columbia and London: University of Missouri Press, 1995), p. 435.
18 *Discipline and Punish*, p. 304.
19 'The Discourse of History', trans. John Johnston, *Foucault Live: Interviews 1961–1984*, ed. Sylvère Lotringer (New York: Semiotext(e), 1989), p. 24.
20 J. G. Merquior, *Foucault*, 2nd edn (London: Fontana, 1991), p. 102.
21 Jonathan Dollimore, 'Transgression and Surveillance in "Measure for Measure"', *Political Shakespeare: New Essays in Cultural Materialism*, ed. Jonathan Dollimore and Alan Sinfield (Manchester University Press, 1985), pp. 72–87.
22 Ibid., p. 72.
23 Michel Foucault, *The History of Sexuality: An Introduction*, trans. Robert Hurley (London: Penguin, 1979), p. 148 (Foucault's italics).
24 'Transgression and Surveillance', p. 85.
25 Ibid., p. 73.
26 Ibid., p. 81.
27 For discussion of the controversies that form the background of the opposition between the duke's penitential model of justice and Angelo's puritan disciplinary ideal see Debora Kuller Shuger, *Political Theologies in Shakespeare's England: The Sacred and the State in 'Measure for Measure'* (Basingstoke: Palgrave, 2001), pp. 102–37.
28 I will discuss some of the theoretical issues involved in the quarrel between presentism and historicism in chapter 9, pp. 188–92.
29 'Now for the poet, he nothing affirms, and therefore never lieth' (Sir Philip Sidney, *An Apology for Poetry*, ed. Geoffrey Shepherd (London: Nelson, 1965), p. 123.).

30 What Quentin Skinner says of the history of ideas is true also of literary scholarship: 'The understanding of texts . . . presupposes the grasp of what they were intended to mean and of how that meaning was intended to be taken' (*Visions of Politics*, 3 vols. (Cambridge University Press, 2002), vol. 1, p. 86.).

31 Roland Barthes, 'The Death of the Author', *Image Music Text*, trans. Stephen Heath (London: Fontana, 1977), p. 143.

32 See Shuger, *Political Theologies*, pp. 102–3.

33 James VI and I, *Basilicon Doron*, *The Political Works of James VI and I*, ed. Johann P. Sommerville (Cambridge University Press, 1994), pp. 20–2; 26–7.

34 *Faultlines: Cultural Materialism and the Politics of Dissident Reading* (Oxford: Clarendon Press, 1992), p. 37.

35 Richard Waswo, 'How To Be (or Not Be) a Cultural Materialist', *The European English Messenger*, 6 (1997), p. 65.

36 'Transgression and Surveillance', p. 83.

37 Innocent Gentillet, *A Discourse upon the Meanes of Wel Governing . . . Against Nicholas Machiavell*, trans. S. Patericke (London:, 1602), sig. ¶iii^v.

38 Justus Lipsius, *Sixe Bookes of Politickes or Civil Doctrine*, trans. William Jones (London, 1594), p. 114.

39 Jean Bodin, *The Six Bookes of a Commonweale* (1576), trans. Richard Knolles (London, 1606), pp. 216–17.

40 *The Six Bookes of a Commonweale*, p. 216.

41 *The Prince*, ed. Quentin Skinner and Russell Price (Cambridge University Press, 1988), p. 23.

42 'Transgression and Surveillance', p. 84.

43 He concludes his list with the example of the Athenian statesman Solon: 'Especially crafty and shrewd was the device of Solon, who, to make his own life safer and at the same time to do considerably larger service for his country, feigned insanity' (*De officiis*, trans. Walter Miller, Loeb Classical Library (London: Heinemann, 1947), p. 111).

44 *De officiis*, p. 113. I am indebted to Tom McAlindon for this point.

45 'On Tranquility of Mind', *Moral Essays*, trans. John W. Basore, Loeb Classical Library, 3 vols. (London: Heinemann, 1932), vol. 2, pp. 112–13; 235.

46 Sidney, *An Apology for Poetry*, p. 120.

47 *On Education: a Translation of the De tradendis disciplinis*, trans. Foster Watson (Cambridge University Press, 1913), p. 232.

48 *The Passions of the Mind in General* (1601), ed. William Webster Newbold (New York and London: Garland, 1986), pp. 92–3.

49 *De officiis*, pp. 339–41.

50 The classic Elizabethan statement of natural law is Hooker's *Laws of Ecclesiastical Polity*. Hooker wrote: 'Law rational, which men commonly use to call the law of nature, meaning thereby the law which human nature knoweth itself in reason universally bound unto . . . comprehendeth all those things which men by the light of their natural understanding evidently

know . . . to be beseeming or unbeseeming, virtuous or vicious, good or evil for them to do' (*Of the Laws of Eccelesiastical Polity*, Folger Library edn, general ed. W. Speed Hill, 4 vols. (Cambridge, Mass. and London: Harvard University Press, 1977), vol. 1, p. 90).

51 *De legibus*, trans. Clinton Walker Keyes (London: Heinemann, 1948), pp. 315–17.

52 'Transgression and Surveillance', p. 84.

53 *Will Power: Essays on Shakespearean Authority* (New York and London: Harvester Wheatsheaf, 1993), p. 126.

54 See Robin Headlam Wells, *Shakespeare on Masculinity* (Cambridge University Press, 2000), pp. 53–8.

5 MEN, WOMEN AND CIVILISATION

1 For further discussion of this point see Robin Headlam Wells, *Shakespeare on Masculinity* (Cambridge University Press, 2000), pp. 108–9.

2 F. D. Hoeniger, ed., *Pericles* (London and New York: Methuen, 1979), pp. lxxxviii–xci; Mimi Still Dixon, 'Tragicomic Recognitions: Medieval Miracles and Shakespearean Romance', *Renaissance Tragicomedy: Explorations in Genre and Politics*, ed. Nancy Klein McGuire (New York: AMS Press, 1987), pp. 56–79; Peter Milward, *The Catholicism of Shakespeare's Plays* (Tokyo: Renaissance Institute, 1997); Thomas Rist, *Shakespeare's Romances and the Politics of Counter-Reformation* (Lewiston, Queenston, Lampeter: Edwin Mellen Press, 1999).

3 Rist, *Shakespeare's Romances*, p. 48.

4 Ibid., p. 48.

5 On Ovid as a source for the Perdita story see E. A. J. Honigmann, 'Secondary Sources of *The Winter's Tale*', *Philological Quarterly*, 34 (1955), pp. 27–38. For critical discussion of Shakespeare's use of the Proserpina myth see Jonathan Bate, *Shakespeare and Ovid* (Oxford: Clarendon Press, 1993), pp. 233–9; T. G. Bishop, *Shakespeare and the Theatre of Wonder* (Cambridge University Press, 1996), pp. 150–60.

6 *Shakespeare's Romances*, p. 54.

7 Sir Philip Sidney, *An Apology for Poetry*, ed. Geoffrey Shepherd (London: Nelson, 1965), p. 104.

8 Quoted by Stanley Wells, *Times Literary Supplement*, 26 September 2003, p. 14.

9 See Bernard Weinberg, *A History of Literary Criticism in the Italian Renaissance*, 2 vols. (Chicago University Press, 1961), vol. 1, pp. 191, 254, 275, 283, 311, 497.

10 'Of Education', *Complete Prose Works of John Milton*, 8 vols., ed. Douglas Bush and others (New Haven and London: Yale University Press and Oxford University Press, 1953–82), vol. 2 (1959), pp. 366–7.

11 *The Grounds of Criticism in Poetry* (1704), facsimile edn (Menston: Scolar Press, 1971), p. 6.

12 See George Puttenham, *The Arte of English Poesie*, ed. Gladys Doidge Willcock and Alice Walker (Cambridge University Press, 1936), p. 303–4.

13 See Baxter Hathaway, *The Age of Criticism: The Late Renaissance in Italy* (Ithaca: Cornell University Press, 1962), pp. 437–59; E. W. Tayler, *Nature and Art in Renaissance Literature* (New York and London: Columbia University Press, 1964).

14 For discussion of the modern debate on art and nature in *The Faerie Queene* see Robin Headlam Wells, *Elizabethan Mythologies: Studies in Poetry, Drama and Music* (Cambridge University Press, 1994), pp. 25–43.

15 Arthur O. Lovejoy and George Boas, *Primitivism and Related Ideas in Antiquity* (Baltimore: Johns Hopkins University Press, 1935), p. 207.

16 Ekbert Faas, *Shakespeare's Poetics* (Cambridge University Press, 1986), p. 191.

17 Frank Kermode, ed., *The Winter's Tale* (New York: New American Library, 1963), p. xxxv.

18 *Shakespeare's Poetics*, p. 193 (my italics).

19 Pauline Kiernan, *Shakespeare's Theory of Drama* (Cambridge University Press, 1996), p. 81.

20 *Shakespeare's Theory of Drama*, p. 81.

21 See Hathaway, *The Age of Criticism*, pp. 437–59.

22 Catherine Belsey, *Shakespeare and the Loss of Eden: The Construction of Family Values in Early Modern Culture* (Basingstoke and London: Macmillan, 1999), p. 103. Stephen Orgel also discusses the 'dangerous condition' of marriage in his edition of *The Winter's Tale* (Oxford and New York: Oxford University Press, 1996), pp. 26–8.

23 Raymond Tallis, 'The Shrink from Hell', review of Elizabeth Roudinesco, *Jacques Lacan and Co: A History of Psychoanalysis in France, 1925–1985*, *Times Higher Education Supplement*, 31 October 1997, p. 20.

24 *Apology for Poetry*, ed. Shepherd, p. 108. Cf Horace, *Epistles*, 1.ii.62; Seneca, *De ira*, 1.i.

25 John Gower, *Confessio Amantis*, Prol, 121; 731, *The Complete Works of John Gower*, ed. G. C. Macaulay, 4 vols. (Oxford: Clarendon Press, 1899–1902), vol. 3 (1901), pp. 6; 25.

26 *Confessio Amantis*, Prol., 169.

27 William M. Hamlin notes that Montaigne was by no means consistent in his primitivism (*The Image of America in Montaigne, Spenser and Shakespeare: Renaissance Ethnography and Literary Reflection* (New York: St Martin's Press, 1995), pp. 50–5). See also David Lewis Schaefer, *The Political Philosophy of Montaigne* (Ithaca and London: Cornell University Press, 1990), pp. 177–88.

28 'The Name of the Rose in *Romeo and Juliet*', *Yearbook of Shakespeare Studies*, 23 (1993), pp. 141; 133.

29 'Transgression and Surveillance in "Measure for Measure"', *Political Shakespeare: New Essays in Cultural Materialism*, ed. Jonathan Dollimore and Alan Sinfield, (Manchester University Press, 1985), pp. 72–87.

30 Richard Wilson, ed., *Julius Caesar*, New Casebook (Basingstoke: Palgrave, 2002), p. 1.

31 See Robin Headlam Wells, *Elizabethan Mythologies*, pp. 12–16; Tom McAlindon, 'Cultural Materialism and the Ethics of Reading: or the Radicalizing of Jacobean Tragedy', *Modern Language Review*, 90 (1995), pp. 830–46.

32 *Radical Tragedy: Religion, Ideology and Power in the Drama of Shakespeare and his Contemporaries*, 3rd edn (Basingstoke: Palgrave Macmillan, 2004), p. 225.

33 Giovanni Pico della Mirandola, 'Oration on the Dignity of Man', *The Renaissance Philosophy of Man*, ed. Ernst Cassirer, Paul Oskar Kristeller and John Herman Randall, trans. Elizabeth Livermore Forbes (University of Chicago Press, 1948), p. 225.

34 In the words of Alan of Lille: 'just as concord in discord, unity in plurality, harmony in disharmony, agreement in disagreement of the four elements unite the structure of the royal palace of the universe, so too, similarity in dissimilarity, equality in inequality, like in unlike, identity in diversity of four combinations bind together the house of the human body' (*The Plaint of Nature*, ed. and trans. James J. Sheridan (Toronto: Pontifical Institute of Medieval Studies, 1980), pp. 118–19). For modern discussion of Pythagorean ideas in Renaissance thought see S. K. Heninger Jr *Touches of Sweet Harmony: Pythagorean Cosmology and Renaissance Poetics* (San Marino: Huntington Library, 1974).

35 See 'Oration', ed. Cassirer, Kristeller and Randall, p. 235.

36 Plato, *Timaeus*, 47D, trans. R. G. Bury, Loeb Classical Library (London: Heinemann, 1929), p. 109.

37 Marsilio Ficino, *De vita coelitus comparanda, Opera Omnia* (Basel, 1576), quoted and trans. D. P. Walker, *Spiritual and Demonic Magic from Ficino to Campanella* (London: Warburg Institute, 1958), p. 16.

38 See Sears Jayne, introduction to Marsilio Ficino, *Commentary on Plato's Symposium on Love*, ed. and trans. Jayne (Dallas: Spring Publications, 1985), p. 21.

39 Wayne Shumaker, 'Literary Hermeticism: Some Test Cases', *Hermeticism and the Renaissance: Intellectual History and the Occult in Early Modern Europe*, ed. Ingrid Merkel and Allen G. Debus (Washington: Folger Shakespeare Library, 1988), p. 296.

40 *Hermeticism and the Renaissance*, p. 297.

41 Baldassare Castiglione, *The Book of the Courtier*, trans. Sir Thomas Hoby, ed. W. H. D. Rouse (London: Dent, 1928), p. 75.

42 On the Pythagorean tradition that lies behind Lorenzo's speech see James Hutton, 'Some English Poems in Praise of Music', *Essays on Renaissance Poetry*, ed. Rita Guerlac (Ithaca and London: Cornell University Press, 1980), pp. 17–173.

43 *The Arte of English Poesie*, p. 6.

44 Henry Peacham the Elder, *The Garden of Eloquence* (1593), with an introduction by William G. Crane (Gainesville, Fla.: Scholars' Facsimiles and Reprints, 1954), sig. ABiii^v.

45 Francis Bacon, 'The Wisdom of the Ancients', *The Philosophical Works*, ed. John M. Robertson (London: Routledge, 1905), p. 835.

46 One of the best discussions of Shakespeare's use of Ovid in *The Winter's Tale* is Leonard Barkan, 'Living Sculptures: Ovid, Michelangelo, and *The Winter's Tale*', *Journal of English Literary History*, 48 (1981), pp. 639–7. See also Bate, *Shakespeare and Ovid*, pp. 233–9.

47 Jean H. Hagstrum, *The Sister Arts: The Tradition of Literary Pictorialism and English Poetry from Dryden to Gray* (1958; repr. University of Chicago Press, 1965), p. 87, quoted by Faas, *Shakespeare's Poetics*, p. 193.

48 *Shakespeare's Theory of Drama*, p. 81 (when Leontes discovers that the statue is warm he says, 'If this be magic, let it be an art / Lawful as eating' – v. iii.110–11).

49 *Shakespeare's Poetics*, p. 193.

50 The phrases quoted are from the first two sections of 'The Tower' (*The Collected Poems of W. B. Yeats*, 2nd edn (London: Macmillan, 1950), pp. 218, 220).

51 Letter to John Hamilton Reynolds, 21 September 1819, *The Letters of John Keats*, ed. Hyder Edward Rollins, 2 vols. (Cambridge University Press, 1958), vol. 2, p. 167.

52 *The Arte of English Poesie*, p. 154.

53 See above note 15.

54 *A Dialogue Between Pole and Lupset*, ed. T. F. Mayer (London: The Royal Historical Society, 1989), pp. 6–7.

55 *A Dialogue*, p. 7.

56 Thomas Wilson, *The Arte of Rhetorique*, ed. G. H. Mair (Oxford: Clarendon Press, 1909), Preface, Sig. Avii.

57 Michel de Montaigne, 'Of the Caniballes', *The Essays of Montaigne*, trans. John Florio, 3 vols. (London: David Nutt, 1892–3), vol. 1 (1892), p. 221.

58 'The Humanist *Tempest*', *Shakespeare: La Tempête: Etudes Critiques*, ed. Claude Peltrault (University of Besançon Press, 1993), p. 13.

59 Though Erasmus took a more optimistic view of human nature than many humanists did, he was critical of sentimental primitivism. In the *Praise of Folly* he satirised primitivist ideas by having Folly appeal, like Gonzalo, to the golden age when people needed no other guiding principle than instinct (*Praise of Folly*, trans. Betty Radice, *Collected Works of Erasmus*, 32 vols., ed. Peter D. Bietenholz, Alexander Dalzell, Anthony T. Grafton and others (University of Toronto Press, 1974–89), vol. 27 (1986), p. 107).

60 Stephen Greenblatt, 'Learning to Curse: Aspects of Linguistic Colonialism in the Sixteenth Century', *First Images of America: the Impact of the New World on the Old*, ed. Fred Chiappelli, 2 vols. (Berkeley, Los Angeles and London: University of California Press, 1976), vol. 2, pp. 561–80; Francis Barker and Peter Hulme, '"Nymphs and reapers heavily vanish": the Discursive Contexts of *The Tempest*', *Alternative Shakespeares*, ed. John Drakakis (London: Methuen, 1985), pp. 191–205; Paul Brown, '"This thing of darkness I acknowledge mine": *The Tempest* and the Discourse of Colonialism',

Political Shakespeare: New Essays in Cultural Materialism, ed. Jonathan Dollimore and Alan Sinfield (Manchester University Press, 1985), pp. 48–71; Malcolm Evans, *Signifying Nothing: Truth's True Contents in Shakespeare's Texts* (Brighton: Harvester, 1986), pp. 74–9.

61 Robin Headlam Wells, *Shakespeare on Masculinity*, pp. 177–206.
62 'Of the Caniballes', p. 221.
63 *Astrophil and Stella*, 6, *The Poems of Sir Philip Sidney*, ed. William A. Ringler, Jr (Oxford: Clarendon Press, 1962), p. 167.
64 John Lee, 'Reanimating Criticism: Towards a Materialist Shakespeare', *English*, 53 (2004), p. 3.

6 LOVE AND DEATH

1 *Tales of Love*, trans. Leon S. Roudiez (New York: Columbia University Press, 1987), pp. 216–20; 222; 221. See also Nicholas Brooke, *Shakespeare's Early Tragedies* (London: Methuen, 1968), who also believes that Juliet is in love with death (pp.101ff.).
2 *Astrophil and Stella*, no. 6, *The Poems of Sir Philip Sidney*, ed. William A. Ringler, Jr (Oxford: Clarendon Press, 1962), p. 167.
3 *Tales of Love*, p. 214.
4 Ibid., p. 221.
5 Denis de Rougemont, *Love in the Western World* (1939), trans. Montgomery Belgion (New York: Schocken Books, 1990), p.18.
6 Ibid., p. 45.
7 Ibid., p. 52.
8 Ibid., p. 46.
9 Ibid., p. 52.
10 Ibid., p. 190.
11 Ibid., p. 53.
12 'The ring was visible on her finger; / he pulled at it gently, without moving her finger. / Originally, it had been very tight, / but her fingers were now so thin / that it came off effortlessly. / The king was able to remove it without difficulty' (Béroul, *The Romance of Tristran*,(2043–8), ed. and trans. Norris J. Lacy (New York and London: Garland, 1989), p. 97).
13 *Love in the Western World*, p. 40.
14 Alberto Varvaro does not include de Rougemont in his extensive bibliography in *Beroul's 'Romance of Tristran'*, trans. John C. Barnes (Manchester University Press, 1972).
15 'Desire is Death', *Subject and Object in Renaissance Culture*, ed. Margreta de Grazia, Maureen Quilligan and Peter Stallybrass (Cambridge University Press, 1996), p. 379.
16 Ibid., p. 380.
17 See Jill L. Levenson, *Romeo and Juliet, Shakespeare in Performance* (Manchester University Press, 1987).
18 Levenson, *Romeo and Juliet*, p. 381.

19 *An Anthropologist on Mars* (London and Basingstoke: Picador, 1995), pp. 262–3.

20 Philippe Ariès, *Centuries of Childhood* (Harmondsworth: Penguin, 1962), pp. 39, 125.

21 Lawrence Stone, *The Family, Sex and Marriage in England 1500–1800* (London: Weidenfeld and Nicholson, 1977), pp. 2, 112, 117.

22 C.S. Lewis wrote: 'French poets, in the eleventh century, discovered or invented, or were the first to express, that romantic species of passion which English poets were still writing about in the nineteenth' (*The Allegory of Love: A Study in Medieval Tradition* (London: Oxford University Press, 1936), p. 4). See also Alexander J. Denomy: 'a glance at classical antiquity or the Dark Ages at once shows us that what we took for "nature" [romantic love] is really a special state of affairs, which will probably have an end, and which certainly had a beginning in eleventh-century Provence' (*The Heresy of Courtly Love* (Gloucester, Mass.: Peter Smith, 1947), p. 3).

23 Michel Foucault, *The History of Sexuality: An Introduction*, trans. Robert Hurley (London: Penguin, 1979), p. 43. Like his notorious statement about the invention of 'man' at the end of the eighteenth century (see chapter 9, p. 182), Foucault's dramatic claim that homosexuality is a relatively recent invention has been widely misinterpreted. What he meant was not that same-sex love and erotic practices didn't exist until the word homosexuality was coined, but that homosexuality as a 'psychological, psychiatric, medical category' (p. 43) was only constructed in 1870 when the German psychiatrist Carl Westphal published an article in which he defined 'contrary sexual feeling' as a neuropathic condition (see Graham Robb, *Strangers: Homosexual Love in the Nineteenth Century* (London: Picador, 2003), pp. 11 43; see also David M. Halperin, *How to Do the History of Homosexuality* (University of Chicago Press, 2002), p. 192, n 61).

24 Steven Ozment, *Ancestors: The Loving Family in Old Europe* (Cambridge, Mass. and London: Harvard University Press, 2001), p. 109. See also Shulamith Shahar, *Childhood in the Middle Ages*, trans. Chaya Galai (London and New York: Routledge, 1990); Nicholas Orme, *Medieval Children* (New Haven and London: Yale University Press, 2001). The fact that some women experience maternal love less strongly than others, and some not at all, doesn't alter the fact that strong emotional bonds with infants, and feelings of intense grief and despair when they die, seems to be a universal human trait.

25 David M. Buss, *The Evolution of Desire: Strategies of Human Mating* (New York: Basic Books, 1994), p. 2.

26 Joseph Cady, '"Masculine Love," Renaissance Writing, and the "New Invention" of Homosexuality', *Homosexuality in Renaissance England: Literary Representations in Historical Context*, ed. Claude J. Summers (New York, London and Norwood (Australia): Haworth Press, 1992), pp. 9–40. I haven't got space in a chapter on heterosexual love to do justice to Cady's subtle and complex argument. For a recent rebuttal of Foucault's

constructionist theory of homosexuality see Robb, *Strangers: Homosexual Love in the Nineteenth Century* pp. 11, 42–3.

27 Lacan believed that aggression plays a central role in 'the economy of the psyche' (Jacques Lacan, *Écrits: A Selection*, trans. Alan Sheridan (London: Tavistock, 1977), p. 8). Among the characteristic '*imagos*' that betray this aggression are 'the images of castration, mutilation, dismemberment, dislocation, evisceration, devouring, bursting open of the body . . . One only has to listen to children aged between two and five playing, alone or together, to know that the pulling off of the head and ripping open of the belly are themes that occur spontaneously to their imagination' (*Écrits*, p. 11).

28 On the revival of chivalric and heroic values in late Elizabethan England see Arthur B. Ferguson, *The Chivalric Tradition in Renaissance England* (Washington, London and Toronto: Folger Shakespeare Library, 1986). See also Sydney Anglo, ed., introduction to *Chivalry in the Renaissance* (Woodbridge: Boydell Press, 1990), pp. xi–vi; Ferguson, *The Indian Summer of English Chivalry: Studies in the Decline and Transformation of Chivalric Idealism* (Durham, NC: Duke University Press, 1960); Richard C. McCoy, *The Rites of Knighthood: The Literature and Politics of Elizabethan Chivalry* (Berkeley, Los Angeles and London: University of California Press, 1989); Roy Strong, *The Cult of Elizabeth* (London: Thames & Hudson, 1977); Frances Yates, *Astraea: The Imperial Theme in the Sixteenth Century* (London and Boston: Routledge & Kegan Paul, 1975), pp. 88–111.

29 Joan Bennett, *Five Metaphysical Poets*, 2nd edn (Cambridge University Press, 1966), p. 17.

30 Donald L. Guss, *John Donne, Petrarchist: Italianate Conceits and Love Theory in 'The Songs and Sonets'* (Detroit: Wayne State University Press, 1966), pp. 53–60.

31 See Guss, *John Donne, Petrarchist*; Thomas M. Greene, *The Light in Troy: Imitation and Discovery in Renaissance Poetry* (New Haven and London: Yale University Press, 1982); Roland Greene, *Post-Petrarchism: Origins and Innovations of the Western Lyric Sequence* (Princeton University Press, 1991).

32 A. J. Smith, *The Metaphysics of Love: Studies in Renaissance Love Poetry from Dante to Milton* (Cambridge University Press, 1985), p. 148.

33 'O tempo, O ciel volubil che fuggendo / inganni I ciechi et miseri mortali, / O dì veloci più che vento et strali! / ora *ab experto* vostre frodi intendo' (*Petrarch's Lyric Poems: the 'Rime sparse' and Other Lyrics*, trans. and ed. Robert M. Durling (Cambridge, Mass. and London: Harvard University Press, 1976), p. 552).

34 *Lord Morley's Tryumphes of Fraunces Petrarcke: the First English Translation of the Trionfi* (c. 1553–6) (Cambridge, Mass.: Harvard University Press, 1971), pp. 151–2.

35 *Lord Morley's Tryumphes*, p. 124.

36 See Guss, *John Donne, Petrarchist*, p. 18.

37 Dorothea Waley Singer, *Giordano Bruno: His Life and Thought* (New York: Henry Schuman, 1950), pp. 3–4.

38 *Giordano Bruno and the Embassy Affair* (New Haven and London: Yale University Press, 1991).
39 See Frances A. Yates, 'Giordano's Conflict with Oxford', *Journal of the Warburg Institute*, 2 (1938–39), pp. 227–42.
40 Quoted and trans. by Frances A. Yates, *Giordano Bruno and the Hermetic Tradition* (London: Routledge and Kegan Paul, 1964), p. 237.
41 Yates, *Giordano Bruno and the Hermetic Tradition*, pp. 208–9.
42 Hermetic neo-Platonists were of course also interested in the recovery of ancient texts. But where humanists placed the highest value on philological accuracy, the later phase of Italian neo-Platonism was typified by what Frances Yates has described as Ficino's 'unfailing gullibility' regarding the provenance of Greek texts (*Giordano Bruno*, p. 160). She wrote: 'if the Magi had devoted more time to . . . grammatical studies and made themselves into good philological scholars they might have seen through the prisci theologi, and so never become Magi' (*Giordano Bruno*, p. 162).
43 *Giordano Bruno*, p.168. In *Shakespeare and the Goddess of Complete Being* (London: Faber and Faber, 1992), Ted Hughes claims that Bruno was an avant-garde thinker who 'made an impact' on London intellectuals in the 1580s (p. 23). However there's little evidence that his influence extended beyond the limited circle of John Dee and his associates.
44 *The Heroic Frenzies*, trans. Paul Eugene Memmo, Jr (Chapel Hill: University of North Carolina Press, 1964), p. 82.
45 See John Charles Nelson, *Renaissance Theory of Love: the Context of Giordano Bruno's 'Eroici Furori'* (New York: Columbia University Press, 1958).
46 *The Heroic Frenzies*, pp. 101–2.
47 Ibid., translator's introduction, pp. 17–18. See also D. W. Robertson Jr., *A Preface to Chaucer: Studies in Medieval Perspectives* (Princeton University Press, 1962), pp. 49, 108–10, 457–60.
48 'The Knight's Tale', 1372–6, *The Works of Geoffrey Chaucer*, 2nd edn, ed. F. N. Robinson (London: Oxford University Press, 1957), p. 30.
49 *The Heroic Frenzies*, p. 112.
50 Ibid., p. 100.
51 Ibid., p. 114.
52 Ibid., p. 118.
53 'né giamai tal peso / provai, né credo ch'uom di dolor mora' (*Petrarch's Lyric Poems*, pp. 450–1).
54 J. A. Bryant ed., Introduction to *The Tragedy of 'Romeo and Juliet'* (New York: New American Library, 1964), p. xxxii.
55 'Coming of Age in Verona', *The Woman's Part: Feminist Criticism of Shakespeare*, ed. Carolyn Ruth Swift Lenz, Gayle Greene and Carol Thomas Neely (Urbana, Chicago and London: University of Illinois Press, 1980), p. 188.
56 On Shakespeare's use of kitsch for satiric purposes see the article on which this chapter is based: Robin Headlam Wells, 'Neo-Petrarchan Kitsch in *Romeo and Juliet*', *Modern Language Review*, 93 (1998), pp. 913–33.

57 *All for Love*, v.i.510–12, *The Works of John Dryden*, 20 vols, ed. Edward Niles Hooker, Alan Roper and H. T. Swedenborg, Jr (Berkeley, Los Angeles and London: University of California Press, 1956–89), vol. 13 (1984), p. 110.

58 'The Name of the Rose in *Romeo and Juliet*', *Yearbook of Shakespeare Studies*, 23 (1993), pp. 141, 133.

59 See Ann Thompson, *Shakespeare's Chaucer: A Study in Literary Origins* (Liverpool University Press, 1978; E. T. Donaldson, *The Swan at the Well: Shakespeare Reading Chaucer* (New Haven: Yale University Press, 1985).

60 Ann Thompson notes that both Criseyde and Juliet come off rather well in a comparison with their lovers (*Shakespeare's Chaucer*, p. 103), but in general both traditional and feminist criticism has tended to treat Shakespeare's lovers almost indistinguishably as the twin victims of tragic circumstances.

61 The dual nature of love was usually expressed symbolically in the two Venuses (see Plato, *Symposium*, 180E). The contrast between them informs the symbolic structure of Chaucer's *Knight's Tale*.

62 T. McAlindon, *Shakespeare's Tragic Cosmos* (Cambridge University Press, 1991), p. 73. In his Introduction to the Arden edition of the play Brian Gibbons argues that 'By the beginning of the last scene, Romeo's transformation of personality is expressed in a new note of resolution and command, compressed, resonant and personal' (*Romeo and Juliet* (London and New York: Routledge, 1980), p. 50). Evelyn Gajowski also believes that Romeo achieves maturity by the end of the play: 'Finally worthy of Juliet, he seems capable of a mutuality of devotion with her based upon confidence, generosity, and an intimacy of expression that honestly conveys his emotions' (*The Art of Loving: Female Subjectivity and Male Discursive Traditions in Shakespeare's Tragedies* (Newark: University of Delaware Press, 1992), p. 50).

63 Roger Ascham, *The Scholemaster, English Works*, ed. W. A. Wright (Cambridge University Press, 1904), p. 231.

64 Mervyn James, *Society, Politics and Culture: Studies in Early Modern England* (1978; repr. Cambridge University Press, 1986), p. 309.

65 *The Civil Wars*, Book II, stanza 130, *The Complete Works in Verse and Prose of Samuel Daniel*, 5 vols., ed. Alexander B. Grosart (London, 1885–96), vol. 2 (1885), p. 98. Daniel cancelled his compliment to Essex in the 1601 edition of his poem.

66 Gervase Markham, *Honour in his Perfection* (London, 1624), p. 4.

7 HISTORY

1 *The Discourses of Niccolò Machiavelli*, ed. and trans. Leslie J. Walker, 2 vols. (London: Routledge and Kegan Paul, 1950), vol. 1, p. 302.

2 *Letter-Book of Gabriel Harvey, 1573–1580*, ed. E. J. L. Scott (London: Camden Society, 1884), p. 79.

3 Jean Howard, 'The New Historicism in Renaissance Studies', *English Literary Renaissance*, 16 (1986), pp. 20–1 (author's italics).

4 Stephen Greenblatt, 'Resonance and Wonder', *Learning to Curse: Essays in Early Modern Culture* (New York and London: Routledge, 1990), p. 165.

5 Barry Hindess and Paul Q. Hirst, *Pre-Capitalist Modes of Production* (London and Boston: Routledge and Kegan Paul, 1975), p. 311.

6 The following two paragraphs are based on Robin Headlam Wells, Glenn Burgess and Rowland Wymer, eds., Introduction to *Neo-Historicism: Studies in English Renaissance Literature, History and Politics* (Cambridge: D. S. Brewer, 2000), pp. 1–27.

7 'Foucault Decoded: Notes from Underground', *Tropics of Discourse: Essays in Cultural Criticism* (Baltimore: Johns Hopkins University Press, 1985), p. 239.

8 Michel Foucault, 'Nietzsche, Genealogy, History', *Language, Counter-Memory, Practice*, ed. and trans. Donald F. Bouchard (Oxford: Blackwell, 1977), pp. 153–4 (my italics).

9 'Foucault Decoded', 234; 257; 259 (my italics).

10 *Tropics of Discourse*, p. 82.

11 'Historical Pluralism', *Critical Inquiry* 12 (1986), p. 486.

12 Keith Jenkins, *Re-thinking History* (London and New York: Routledge, 1991), pp. 19; 32; 33; 38; 39; 46; 48. Jenkins supports his remarks on the ideological nature of truth (pp. 28–32) with a quotation from Foucault's *Power/Knowledge* (New York: Pantheon, 1981), pp. 131–3. In his recent *On the Future of History: The Postmodernist Challenge and its Aftermath* (Chicago and London: Chicago University Press, 2003), Ernst Breisach confirms that in postmodern historiography truth 'has no privileged authority' (p. 24).

13 S. L. Goldberg, 'Sir John Hayward, "Politic" Historian', *Review of English Studies*, ns 6 (1955), p. 234. See also F. J. Levy, *Tudor Historical Thought* (San Marino: The Huntington Library, 1967), pp. 237–85; George K. Hunter, '"A Roman Thought": Renaissance Attitudes to History Exemplified in Shakespeare and Jonson', *An English Miscellany Presented to W. S. Mackie*, ed. Brian S. Lee (Cape Town, London and New York: Oxford University Press, 1977), pp. 93–115.

14 In his *The Life and Raigne of King Henrie IIII* John Hayward wrote: 'Assuredly, howsoever in regard of inferior causes some things are imputed to wisdom, some to folly, and some to chance, yet in regard of the first and highest cause all things are most certainly, most orderly, most justly decreed' (ed. with an introduction by John J. Manning, Camden Fourth Series, vol. 42 (London: Royal Historical Society, 1991), p. 222). Richard Knolles similarly considered a combination of human action, fortune and divine will in his discussion of the success of the Ottoman Empire (*The Generall Historie of the Turkes* (London, 1603), sig. Aiv^v).

15 *Radical Tragedy: Religion, Ideology and Power in the Drama of Shakespeare and his Contemporaries*, 3rd edn (Basingstoke: Palgrave Macmillan, 2004), pp. 170–1.

16 *Tudor Historical Thought*, p. 238.

17 See Janet Coleman, 'Machiavelli's *Via Moderna*: Medieval and Renaissance Attitudes to History', *Niccolò Machiavelli's The Prince: New Interdisciplinary Essays*, ed. Martin Coyle (Manchester University Press, 1995), pp. 40–64.

18 *The Prince*, ed. Quentin Skinner; trans. Russell Price (Cambridge University Press, 1988), pp. 19, 59; *The Discourses*, ed. Walker, vol. I, pp. 217, 295, 356.

19 Francesco Guicciardini, *Selected Writings*, ed. Cecil Grayson, trans. Margaret Grayson (London: Oxford University Press, 1965), p. 8.

20 'Everything which was in the past and is now, will be in the future, but the names change, and the outward appearance of things, so that anyone who lacks perspicacity does not recognize them and cannot draw conclusions or form an opinion from what he observes' (*Selected Writings*, p. 23).

21 *The Civil Wars*, ed. Lawrence Michel (New Haven: Yale University Press, 1958), p. 68.

22 Sir Walter Ralegh, *The History of the World* (London, 1614), sig. A2.

23 Sir Thomas Elyot, *The Boke Named the Governour*, ed. Foster Watson (London: Dent, 1907), p. 293.

24 *The Duchess of Malfi*, I.i.19–22, Revels Plays edn, ed. John Russell Brown (London: Methuen, 1964), p. 9.

25 Felix Raab, *The English Face of Machiavelli: A Changing Interpretation 1500–1700* (London: Routledge and Kegan Paul, 1964), p. 53. Raab wrote: 'everything indicates that, at least from the middle 'eighties onwards, Machiavelli was being quite widely read in England and was no longer the sole preserve of "Italianate" Englishmen and their personal contacts' (p. 53). On Machiavelli's influence in Elizabethan England see also Levy, *Tudor Historical Thought*, pp. 238–42; Anne Barton, 'Livy, Machiavelli, and Shakespeare's *Coriolanus*', *Shakespeare Survey 38* (1985), pp. 115–29; Victoria Kahn, *Machiavellian Rhetoric: From the Counter-Reformation to Milton* (Princeton University Press, 1994); John Roe, *Shakespeare and Machiavelli* (Cambridge: D. S. Brewer, 2002).

26 *Philotas*, III.iii.1135–6, *The Complete Works in Verse and Prose of Samuel Daniel*, 5 vols., ed. Alexander B. Grosart (London, 1885–96), vol. 3 (1885), p. 144.

27 On the fashion for Tacitean history in late Elizabethan England see Levy, *Tudor Historical Thought*, pp. 249–51; P. Burke, 'Tacitism', *Tacitus*, ed. T. A. Dorey (London: Routledge and Kegan Paul, 1969), pp. 149–71; Mervyn James, *Society, Politics and Culture: Studies in Early Modern England* (1978; repr. Cambridge University Press, 1986), pp. 418–20; John J. Manning, Introduction to *Hayward's The Life and Raigne of King Henrie IIII*, pp. 34–42; Malcolm Smuts, 'Court-Centred Politics and the Uses of Roman Historians *c.* 1590–1630', *Culture and Politics in Early Stuart England*, ed. Kevin Sharpe and Peter Lake (Basingstoke and London: Macmillan, 1994), pp. 21–43; Blair Worden, 'Ben Jonson Among the Historians', *Culture and Politics in Early Stuart England*, ed Sharpe and Lake, pp. 67–89.

28 *Fower Books of the Histories of Tacitus*, trans. Sir Henry Savile (London, 1591), quoted by Smuts, 'Court-Centred Politics and the Uses of Roman Historians', p. 26.

29 'A. P.' to the Reader, *Hayward's The Life and Raigne of King Henrie IIII*, ed. Manning, pp. 62–3.

30 According to Francis Bacon, Hayward had 'taken most of the sentences of Cornelius Tacitus, and translated them into English, and put them into his text' (Sir *Francis Bacon his Apologie, in Certain Imputations Concerning the Late Earle of Essex*, quoted by John Manning, ed, *John Hayward's The Life and Raigne of King Henrie IIII*, p. 2).

31 *Francis Bacon his Apologie*, quoted by Manning, *John Hayward's The Life and Raigne of King Henrie IIII*, p. 2.

32 See for example Tom McAlindon, *Shakespeare's Tragic Cosmos* (Cambridge University Press, 1991), pp. 76–8; David Daniell, ed., *Julius Caesar*, The Arden Shakespeare (Walton-on-Thames: Nelson, 1998), pp. 23–4.

33 See Wallace T. MacCaffrey, *Elizabeth I: War and Politics 1588–1603* (Princeton University Press, 1992), pp. 453ff.; see also Wernham, *The Making of Elizabethan Foreign Policy*, passim; John Guy, *Tudor England* (Oxford and New York: Oxford University Press, 1988), pp. 439ff; Penry Williams, *The Later Tudors: England 1547–1603 The New Oxford History of England* (Oxford: Clarendon Press, 1995), p. 364.

34 Compounding Essex's policy differences with Elizabeth was a sense of personal grievance. While he feigned helpless susceptibility to Elizabeth's beauty, in reality he deeply resented being subject to a woman's authority (see James, *Society, Politics and Culture*, p. 444).

35 *Honour in his Perfection* (London, 1624), p. 4.

36 Ibid., p. 26.

37 See James, *Society, Politics and Culture*, pp. 308–415. For discussion of the politically nuanced use of these terms by Shakespeare and his contemporaries see Robin Headlam Wells, *Shakespeare on Masculinity* (Cambridge University Press, 2000), pp. 7–10.

38 *The Sound of Virtue: Philip Sidney's Arcadia and Elizabethan Politics* (New Haven and London: Yale University Press, 1996), p. 62.

39 Shakespeare takes the phrase 'Brutus, thou sleep'st' from Plutarch. It occurs, in slightly different forms, in the lives both of Brutus and Julius Caesar (*Plutarch's Lives of the Noble Grecians and Romans*, trans. Sir Thomas North, 6 vols. (London: David Nutt, 1895–6), vol. 5 (1896), p. 63; vol. 6 (1896), p. 190).

40 *Faultlines: Cultural Materialism and the Politics of Dissident Reading* (Oxford: Clarendon Press, 1992), p. 10.

41 'Shakespeare and the Thought of his Age' (1971), *The Cambridge Companion to Shakespeare Studies*, ed. Stanley Wells (Cambridge University Press, 1986), p. 32. See also Norman Rabkin, *Shakespeare and the Common Understanding* (1967; repr.Chicago and London: University of Chicago Press, 1984); Bernard McElroy, *Shakespeare's Mature Tragedies* (Princeton University Press, 1973),

Emrys Jones, *The Origins of Shakespeare* (Oxford: Clarendon Press, 1977); Robert Grudin, *Mighty Opposites: Shakespeare and Renaissance Contrariety* (Berkeley, Los Angeles and London: University of California Press, 1979).

42 *Julius Caesar*, ed. Daniell, pp. 38; 34. See also Robert S. Miola, '*Julius Caesar* and the Tyrannicide Debate', *Renaissance Quarterly*, 38 (1985), pp. 271–89.

43 Joseph S. M. J. Chang notes that, by joining the conspiracy Brutus 'incites the civil war which destroys the very Republic he seeks to preserve' ('*Julius Caesar* in the Light of Renaissance Historiography', *Journal of English and Germanic Philology*, 69 (1970), p. 70). However, in taking Brutus' protestations of honesty at face value, Chang does not allow for the fact that Shakespeare may be commenting ironically on Brutus' political *naïveté*. I discuss this question below.

44 In *Poly-Olbion* Drayton explains how, by murdering Banquo and causing Fleanch (Shakespeare's Fleance) to flee to Wales, Macbeth was indirectly responsible for bringing about a marriage that would unite the houses of Plantagenet and Tudor. Fleanch married the daughter of Llewellin, the Prince of Wales. His descendant, Henry VII, married Elizabeth of York, and it was their eldest daughter, Margaret, who married James IV. James VI and I could thus claim both to unite the houses of York and Lancaster, and also to restore the ancient British line (*The Works of Michael Drayton*, 5 vols., ed. J. William Hebel (Oxford: Blackwell, 1931–41), vol. 4 (1933), p. 167).

45 *Plutarch's Lives*, trans. North, vol. 6, p. 237.

46 *The Prince*, ed. Skinner, p. 65.

47 *The Discourses*, ed. Walker, vol. 1, pp. 470–1.

48 *Plutarch's Lives*, vol. 5, p. 68.

49 *The Discourses*, vol. 1, p. 487.

50 Ibid., p. 228.

51 Thomas Aquinas, *On Kingship: To the King of Cyprus*, trans. Gerald B. Phelan, revised by I. Th. Eschmann (Toronto: Pontifical Institute of Medieval Studies, 1949), p. 27.

52 *Julius Caesar*, ed. Spevack (Cambridge University Press, 1988), p. 19 n. 1.

53 Machiavelli wrote: 'how men live is so different from how they should live that a ruler who does not do what is generally done, but persists in doing what ought to be done, will undermine his power rather than maintain it' (*The Prince*, ed. Skinner, p. 54).

54 'Swearing and forswearing in Shakespeare's Histories: The Playwright as Contra-Machiavel', *Review of English Studies*, 51 (2000), pp. 208–29.

55 See for example, Chang, '*Julius Caesar* in the Light of Renaissance Historiography', 63–71; René E. Fortin, '*Julius Caesar*: An Experiment in Point of View', *Shakespeare Quarterly*, 19 (1976), pp. 341–7; Robert S. Miola, *Shakespeare's Rome* (Cambridge University Press, 1983), pp. 76–115.

56 John Ponet, *A Short Treatise of Politic Power* (1556), facsimile edn (Menston: Scolar Press, 1970), sig. Kii^v.

57 Richard Wilson, ed., *Julius Caesar*, New Casebook (Basingstoke: Palgrave, 2002), p. 1.

58 Ellen Somekawa and Elizabeth A. Smith, 'Theorizing the Writing of History', *Journal of Social History*, 22 (1988), p. 154.
59 Sir Philip Sidney, *An Apology for Poetry*, ed. Geoffrey Shepherd (London: Nelson, 1965), p. 123.
60 *The Discourses*, ed. Walker, vol. 1, p. 287.
61 Peter Lamarque and Stein Haugom Olsen, *Truth, Fiction, and Literature: a Philosophical Perspective* (Oxford: Clarendon Press, 1994), p. 309.
62 From a transcript of the Stephen Lawrence inquiry, quoted in *The Colour of Justice*, ed. Richard Norton-Taylor (London: Oberon Books, 1999), p. 126.
63 'Guilty as charged officer', review of *The Colour of Justice*, *The Guardian G2*, 14 January 1999, p. 9.
64 'Why I wrote it', *The Observer Review*, 17 January 1999, p. 7.
65 See above, note 5.
66 *The Observer*, 29 November 1998, p. 28.
67 *Plutarch's Lives*, vol. 1, pp. 12; 10.

8 GENIUS

1 See Simon Baron-Cohen, *Mindblindness: An Essay on Autism and Theory of Mind* (Cambridge, Mass. and London: MIT Press, 1997).
2 See Darold A. Treffert, *Extraordinary People* (London: Bantam Press, 1989).
3 Oliver Sacks, *An Anthropologist on Mars* (London and Basingstoke: Picador, 1995), pp. 230–1.
4 *Discoveries, Ben Jonson*, 11 vols., ed. C. H. Herford and Percy and Evelyn Simpson (Oxford: Clarendon Press, 1925–52), vol. 8 (1947) pp. 637; 625. '*Ingenium*' has a variety of meanings: disposition, aptitude, mental facility, or genius in our modern sense of the word. Jonson uses the word in different ways in different contexts. Here he is using it in the sense in which Horace uses in the *Ars poetica* (409–10) as exceptional native talent in contrast to mere *studium*.
5 Tia DeNora, *Beethoven and the Construction of Genius: Musical Politics in Vienna, 1792–1803* (Berkeley, Los Angeles and London: University of California Press, 1995), p. 190.
6 Christine Battersby, *Gender and Genius: Towards a Feminist Aesthetics* (London: Women's Press, 1989), p. 160.
7 Battersby writes: 'the Romantic conception of genius is peculiarly harmful to women' (*Gender and Genius*, p. 23).
8 Kathleen McLuskie, 'The Patriarchal Bard: Feminist Criticism and Shakespeare', *Political Shakespeare: New Essays in Cultural Materialism*, ed. Jonathan Dollimore and Alan Sinfield (Manchester University Press, 1985), p. 92.
9 Battersby, *Gender and Genius*, p. 28.
10 *That Shakespeherian Rag: Essays on a Critical Process* (London: Methuen, 1986), p. 75. In *Shakespeare in the Present* (London and New York:

Routledge, 2002) Hawkes mocks the misguided attempts by some (unnamed) critics to restore to Shakespeare 'the genuine monarchy of genius' (p. 2).

11 Graham Holderness, 'Bardolatry: or, The Cultural Materialist's Guide to Stratford-upon-Avon', *The Shakespeare Myth*, ed. Graham Holderness (Manchester University Press, 1988), p. 13.

12 Jonathan Bate, 'Shakespeare and Original Genius', *Genius: the History of an Idea*, ed. Penelope Murray (Oxford: Blackwell, 1989), pp. 76–97; see also Murray, 'Poetic Genius and its Classical Origins', *Genius: The History of an Idea*, ed. Murray, pp. 9–31. In *The Genius of Shakespeare* (London and Basingstoke: Picador, 1997) Bate argues that '"genius" was a category invented in order to account for what was peculiar about Shakespeare' (p. 163).

13 McLuskie, 'The Patriarchal Bard', p. 93.

14 'On Genius and Common Sense', *Table Talk* (London: Dent, 1908), p. 43.

15 In academia, as elsewhere, there is strong pressure not to appear unfashionable. Many scholars acknowledge a debt to postmodern theoretical principles even when those principles are in conflict with the evidence they adduce. For example, in an otherwise excellent recent book on Shakespeare's language Russ McDonald claims that the Foucauldian notion of collaborative literary agency 'properly rebuts the fiction of imaginative autonomy' (*Shakespeare and the Arts of Language* (Oxford University Press, 2001), p. 4). Yet in the next paragraph he talks about 'Shakespeare's unparalleled poetic imagination' (p. 5). Another example is Elizabeth Heale, who in *Autobiography and Authorship in Renaissance Verse: Chronicles of the Self* (Basingstoke: Palgrave Macmillan, 2003) writes: 'Foucault is surely right in rejecting the idea of an author as the extra-textual source of a work'. In her next paragraph she explains that 'autobiographical writing and a sophisticated sense of the self as subject of discourse existed, of course, long before the sixteenth century' (p. 5).

16 Roland Barthes, 'The Death of the Author', *Image Music Text*, trans. Stephen Heath (London: Fontana, 1977), pp. 142–3; 146.

17 Foucault wrote: 'Speeches and books were assigned real authors . . . only when the author became subject to punishment and to the extent that discourse was considered transgressive' ('What is an Author?', *Language, Counter-Memory, Practice: Selected Essays and Interviews*, ed. and trans. Donald F. Bouchard (Oxford: Blackwell, 1977), p. 124).

18 'What is an Author?', p. 127.

19 Introducing a collection of essays on authorship Peter Jaszi and Martha Woodmansee take it as generally acknowledged truth that 'the modern regime of authorship, far from being timeless and universal, is a relatively recent formation' (*The Construction of Authorship: Textual Appropriation in Law and Literature*, ed. Jaszi and Woodmansee (Durham, NC and London: Duke University Press, 1994), pp. 2–3).

20 In *Shakespeare, Co-Author: A Historical Study of Five Collaborative Plays,* (Oxford University Press, 2002), pp. 509–27 Brian Vickers provides a survey of classical and Renaissance ideas of authorship showing that Foucault's claim has no basis whatever in history.

21 *Discoveries,* p. 636.

22 'To the Reader', 17–24, *Certaine Small Workes, The Complete Works in Verse and Prose of Samuel Daniel,* 5 vols., ed. Alexander B. Grosart (London: Hazell, Watson, and Viney, 1885–96), vol I (1885), pp. 12–13. Writers were also concerned to protect their reputations against false attribution. In *The Duchess of Malfi* John Webster added against the song in III: 'The author disclaims this ditty to be his' (ed. John Russell Brown (London: Methuen, 1964), p. 96).

23 'To the Reader', 43–5, *Certaine Small Workes,* ed. Grosart, p. 13.

24 See for example, *Troilus and Criseyde,* II.15–21, *The Works of Geoffrey Chaucer,* 2nd edn, ed. F. N. Robinson (London: Oxford University Press, 1957), p. 401.

25 *Poems,* ed. Ian Donaldson (London, Oxford and New York: Oxford University Press, 1975), p. 307.

26 W. K. Wimsatt and Monroe C. Beardsley, 'The Intentional Fallacy', reprinted in *The Verbal Icon* (Lexington: University of Kentucky Press, 1954), p. 5.

27 E. D. Hirsch, Jr, *Validity in Interpretation* (New Haven, Conn.: Yale University Press, 1967), p. 1 (my italics).

28 *Chaucer and the French Tradition: A Study in Style and Meaning* (Berkeley, Los Angeles and London: University of California Press, 1957), p. 9.

29 The key figures of the post-war critical movement in Shakespeare studies are A. P. Rossiter, 'Ambivalence: The Dialectic of the Histories' (1951), *Angel with Horns: Fifteen Lectures on Shakespeare,* ed. Graham Storey, 1961; repr. with an introduction by Peter Holland (London and New York: Longman, 1989), pp. 40–64; Norman Rabkin, *Shakespeare and the Common Understanding* (University of Chicago Press, 1967); Bernard McElroy, *Shakespeare's Mature Tragedies* (Princeton University Press, 1973); Emrys Jones, *The Origins of Shakespeare* (Oxford: Clarendon Press, 1977); Robert Grudin, *Mighty Opposites: Shakespeare and Renaissance Contrariety* (Berkeley, Los Angeles and London: University of California Press, 1979).

30 W. R. Elton, 'Shakespeare and the Thought of his Age', *A New Companion to Shakespeare Studies,* ed. Kenneth Muir and S. Schoenbaum (Cambridge University Press, 1971), p. 197.

31 See John M. Ellis, *Against Deconstruction* (Princeton University Press, 1989), p. 84. See also Seán Burke, *The Death and Return of the Author: Criticism and Subjectivity in Barthes, Foucault and Derrida,* 2nd edn (Edinburgh University Press, 1998), pp. 20–61; Brian Vickers, *Appropriating Shakespeare: Contemporary Critical Quarrels* (New Haven and London: Yale University Press, 1993), pp. 101–5.

32 Introduction to *Political Shakespeare*, pp. 5–6.
33 'The Patriarchal Bard', p. 93.
34 *Meaning by Shakespeare* (London: Routledge, 1992), p. 6.
35 'What is an Author?', p. 126.
36 Catherine Belsey speaking on BBC Radio 4, 'In Our Time', 21 March 2003. See also Jeffrey Masten, *Textual Intercourse: Collaboration, Authorship, and Sexualities in Renaissance Drama* (Cambridge University Press, 1997), p. 10; Gordon McMullan ed., *King Henry VIII*, Arden Shakespeare, 3rd series (London: Thomson, 2000), pp. 196–7.
37 *Shakespeare's Universal Wolf: Studies in Early Modern Reification* (Oxford: Clarendon Press, 1996), pp. 7–8.
38 *Shakespeare and the Loss of Eden* (Basingstoke and London: Macmillan, 1999), p. 15.
39 'Shakespeare, Modernity and the Aesthetic: Art, Truth and Judgement in *The Winter's Tale*', *Shakespeare and Modernity: Early Modern to Millenium*, ed. Hugh Grady (London and New York: Routledge, 2000), p. 66.
40 Review of M. J. Devaney, *'Since at least Plato . . .' and Other Postmodernist Myths*, *Times Literary Supplement*, 2 January 1998, p. 12.
41 *Invitation to Sociology* (1963; repr. Harmondsworth: Penguin, 1975), p. 140. On the social construction of the self see also Hans H. Gerth and C.Wright Mills, *Character and Social Structure* (New York: Harcourt Brace, 1953); Erving Goffman, *The Presentation of Self in Everyday Life* (Garden City, NY: Doubleday Anchor, 1959); George H. Mead, *Mind, Self, and Society* (1934; repr. University of Chicago Press, 1970).
42 The term 'interpellation' was coined by Louis Althusser to refer to the way ideology addresses the reader in such a way as to 'construct' him or her as a mythical subject (see 'Ideology and Ideological State Apparatuses', *Lenin and Philosophy and other Essays*, trans. Ben Brewster (London: NLB, 1971), pp. 162–3).
43 Catherine Belsey, *The Subject of Tragedy* (London and New York: Methuen, 1985) p. 14.
44 'What is an Author?', pp. 137–8.
45 *Meaning by Shakespeare*, p. 5.
46 *Radical Tragedy: Religion, Ideology and Power in the Drama of Shakespeare and his Contemporaries*, 3rd edn (Basingstoke: Palgrave Macmillan, 2004), p. 250.
47 *The Subject of Tragedy*, pp. 33; 18.
48 '*On peut être sûr que l'homme y est une invention récente*', *Les Mots et les Choses: Une Archéologie des Sciences Humaines* (Paris: Gallimard, 1966), p. 398. In chapter 9 I explain that Foucault didn't mean quite what he seemed to be saying in this much-quoted remark.
49 Bloom suggests that 'self-overhearing' is the key to Shakespeare's innovative characterisation: 'self-overhearing is their royal road to individuation, and no other writer, before or since Shakespeare, has accomplished so well the virtual miracle of creating utterly different yet self-consistent voices for his

more than one hundred major characters' (*Shakespeare: the Invention of the Human* (London: Fourth Estate, 1999), p. xvii).

50 *The Vanishing: Shakespeare, the Subject, and Early Modern Culture* (Durham, NC and London: Duke University Press, 2000), p. 37.

51 David Aers, 'A Whisper in the Ear of Early Modernists: or, Reflections on Literary Critics Writing the "History of the Subject"', *Culture and History 1350–1600: Essays on English Communities, Identities and Writing*, ed. Aers (London and New York: Harvester Wheatsheaf, 1992), p. 185. See also Anne Ferry, *The 'Inward' Language: Sonnets of Wyatt, Sidney, Shakespeare, Donne* (University of Chicago Press, 1983); Katharine Eisaman Maus, *Inwardness and Theater in the English Renaissance* (University of Chicago Press, 1995); John Lee, *Shakespeare's 'Hamlet' and the Controversies of the Self* (Oxford: Clarendon Press, 2000).

52 Charles Taylor, *Sources of the Self: The Making of the Modern Identity* (Cambridge University Press, 1989), p. 131.

53 As Richard Webster reminds us, 'the notion that some aspects of the self are sometimes hidden from ordinary consciousness is as old, almost, as human consciousness itself. Versions of the idea were put forward by Plotinus in the third century, by St Augustine in the fourth, and by countless other thinkers in practically every century since' (*Why Freud Was Wrong: Sin, Science and Psychoanalysis* (London: Harper Collins, 1996), p. 243).

54 Anthony Low writes 'Probably consciousness of an inner self has always been an aspect of human experience' (*Aspects of Subjectivity: Society and Individuality from the Middle Ages to Shakespeare and Milton* (Pittsburgh: Duquesne University Press, 2003), p. x).

55 In what amounted to a retraction of the position on which he had built his entire reputation as an historian of the self, Foucault acknowledged, in a lecture he gave two years before his death in 1984, that the self was not only alive and well in the classical world, but that knowledge of oneself was the 'most important moral principle in ancient philosophy', adding that 'perhaps our philosophical tradition has . . . forgotten [this fact]' (*Technologies of the Self: A Seminar with Michel Foucault*, ed. Luther H. Martin, Huck Gutman and Patrick H. Hutton (London: Tavistock, 1988), p. 19). For discussion of Foucault's *volte-face* see Lee, *Shakespeare's 'Hamlet' and the Controversies of the Self*, pp. 82–4.

56 *Thyestes*, 449, *Seneca's Tragedies*, trans. Frank Justus Miller, Loeb Classical Library, 2 vols. (London: Heinemann, 1927), vol. 2, p. 128.

57 *Moral Essays*, trans. John W. Basore, Loeb Classical Library, 3 vols. (London: Heinemann, 1932), vol. 2, pp. 112–13.

58 *The Duchess of Malfi*, 1.i.441, ed. Russell Brown, p. 34.

59 *The Faerie Queene*, vi.proem.5, *The Poetical Works*, ed. J. C. Smith and E. de Selincourt (London, New York and Toronto: Oxford University Press, 1912), p. 337.

60 *Basilicon Doron, Political Writings*, ed. Johann P. Sommerville (Cambridge University Press, 1994), p. 50.

61 'Nature', 19–20, *Centuries, Poems, and Thanksgivings*, 2 vols., ed. H. M. Margoliouth (Oxford: Clarendon Press, 1958), vol. 2, p. 60.

62 *An Apology for Poetry*, p. 101.

63 The eighteenth-century volume in the new *Cambridge History of Literary Criticism* lacks a chapter on poetics. By contrast, the Renaissance volume has twenty-two chapters on poetics (*The Renaissance*, ed. Glyn P. Norton, *The Cambridge History of Literary Criticism* (Cambridge University Press, 1999)).

64 M. H. Abrams, *The Mirror and the Lamp: Romantic Theory and the Critical Tradition* (New York: Oxford University Press, 1953), p. 21.

65 *The Mirror and the Lamp*, p. 70.

66 In 1751 Richard Hurd wrote: 'All *Poetry*, to speak with Aristotle and the Greek critics . . . is, properly, *imitation*' ('Discourse on Poetical Imitation', *The Works* (1811), 8 vols., facsimile edn (Hildesheim: Georg Olms Verlag, 1969), vol. 2, p. 111.

67 *Confessio Amantis*, VII.1737, *The Complete Works of John Gower*, 4 vols., ed. G. C. Macaulay (Oxford: Clarendon Press, 1899–1902), vol. 2 (1901), p. 280.

68 *Basilicon Doron*, ed. Sommerville, p. 54.

69 Francis Bacon, *The Advancement of Learning and the New Atlantis*, ed. Arthur Johnston (Oxford: Clarendon Press, 1974), p. 2.

70 *The Arte of English Poesie*, pp. 3–4.

71 Sidney's principal source for the idea of the poet as creator was Scaliger (see *An Apology for Poetry*, ed. Geoffrey Shepherd (London: Nelson, 1965), pp. 155–6).

72 *An Apology for Poetry*, ed. Shepherd, p. 100.

73 *The Advancement of Learning*, ed. Johnston, p. 80.

74 John Harington, *Epigrams*, facsimile edn (Menston: Scolar Press, 1970), sig. A3^v.

75 *Astrophil and Stella*, nos. 1; 50, *The Poems of Sir Philip Sidney*, ed. William A. Ringler, Jr (Oxford: Clarendon Press, 1962), pp. 165; 189.

76 'To the Reader', *Idea* (1619), *The Works of Michael Drayton*, 5 vols., ed. J. William Hebel (Oxford: Blackwell, 1931–41), vol. 2 (1932), p. 310.

77 *Musophilus*, 178–9, *The Complete Works*, ed. Grosart, vol. 1, p. 231.

78 Thomas Nashe described *Astrophil and Stella* as 'a tragicomedy of love . . . performed by starlight' (prefatory epistle to *Syr P. S. His Astrophel and Stella* (London, 1591), sig. A3).

79 Prefatory epistle to *Syr P. S. His Astrophel and Stella*, sig. A3.

80 Dedicatory epistle to *Delia*, *The Complete Works*, ed. Grosart, vol. 1, p. 33.

81 See Vickers, *Shakespeare, Co-Author*.

82 *Henslowe's Diary*, ed. R. A. Foakes and R. T. Rickert (Cambridge University Press, 1961), p. 86.

83 *Elizabethan and Metaphysical Imagery: Renaissance Poetics and Twentieth-Century Critics* (1947; repr. Chicago and London: Phoenix Books, 1961), p. 39.

84 Sir John Harington, Preface to translation of *Orlando Furioso*, *Elizabethan Critical Essays*, ed. G. Gregory Smith, 2 vols. (London: Oxford University Press, 1904), vol. 2, p. 197.

85 Jonson, *Discoveries*, p. 637.

86 Puttenham, *The Arte of English Poesie*, p. 4; cf. Sidney's *Apology*, p. 100.

87 Puttenham, *The Arte of English Poesie*, p. 4.

88 Jonson, *Discoveries*, p. 637.

89 *The Arte of English Poesie*, p. 3.

90 'To the Reader', 60–1, *Certaine Small Workes*, ed. Grosart, p. 14.

91 Lukas Erne, *Shakespeare as Literary Dramatist* (Cambridge University Press, 2003).

92 See chapter 6, note 26.

93 Thomas De Quincey, 'On Wordsworth's Poetry' (1845); repr. In *De Quincey's Literary Criticism*, ed. H. Darbishire (London: Henry Frowde, 1909), pp. 234; 241.

94 'The Great Odyssey', *Guardian Saturday Review*, 9 June 2001, p. 3.

95 See below n. 122.

96 *Pro Archia poeta*, viii.18, ed. and trans. N. H. Watts, Loeb Classical Library (London: Heinemann, 1923).

97 *An Apology for Poetry*, p. 113; cf. *Pro Archia poeta*, vii.6.

98 Platonists tended to debate the former question, Horatians the latter. See Bernard Weinberg, *A History of Literary Criticism in the Italian Renaissance*, 2 vols. (Chicago University Press, 1961), pp. 272–3, 599, 716, and pp. 102–3, 186, 229–30, 721, 742, 1007 respectively.

99 *Ion*, 534C, ed. and trans. W. R. M. Lamb, Loeb Classical Library (London: Heinemann, 1952), p. 423.

100 Erasmus refers to the *Phaedrus* in the final pages of the *Praise of Folly* (*Collected Works of Erasmus*, 32 vols., ed. Peter D. Bietenholz, Alexander Dalzell, Anthony T. Grafton and others (Toronto, Buffalo and London: University of Toronto Press, 1974–89), *Praise of Folly*, trans. Betty Radice, vol. 27 (1986), pp. 152–3).

101 On Shakespeare's debt to Erasmus see Walter Kaiser, *Praisers of Folly: Erasmus, More, Shakespeare* (London: Gollancz, 1964). See also Emrys Jones, *The Origins of Shakespeare*, pp. 10–18.

102 *Phaedrus*, 244A; 245B, ed. W. R. M. Lamb; trans. Harold N. Fowler, Loeb Classical Library (London: Heinemann, 1919), p. 469.

103 E. C. Pettet, 'Shakespeare's Conception of Language', *Essays and Studies*, 3 (1950), p. 31.

104 Puttenham wrote: 'this science [of poetry] in his perfection, can not grow, but by some divine instinct, the platonics call it furor' (*The Arte of English Poesie*, p. 3).

105 Giordano Bruno, *The Heroic Frenzies*, trans. Paul Eugene Memmo, Jr (Chapel Hill: University of North Carolina Press, 1964).

106 Anonymous commendatory verses on *The Faerie Queene* in Edmund Spenser, *The Poetical Works*, ed. J. C. Smith and E. de Selincourt (London, New York and Toronto: Oxford University Press, 1912), p. 409.

107 *An Apology for Poetry*, p. 142.

108 See, for example, the neo-Platonic *Shadow of Night*. In consecrating his life to 'blacke shades and desolation' ('Hymnus in Noctem', 270), Chapman tells us that he hopes that the spirit of Night will inspire in him that state of tortured frenzy which alone is capable of allowing man access to nature's hidden secrets (*The Poems of George Chapman*, ed. Phyllis Brooks Bartlett (New York: Russell & Russell, 1962), p. 26).

109 See chapter 6, pp. 114; 120–1; 124.

110 *Ars poetica*, 409–10, ed. and trans. H. Rushton Fairclough, Loeb Classical Library (London: Heinemann, 1970), p. 485.

111 *Boccaccio on Poetry: Being the Preface and the Fourteenth and Fifteenth Books of Boccaccio's Genealogia Deorum Gentilium*, ed. and trans. Charles G. Osgood (Indianapolis and New York: Bobbs-Merrill, 1956), pp. 39–40.

112 *Discoveries*, p. 637.

113 Ibid., p. 637.

114 Prefatory epistle to *Syr P. S. His Astrophel and Stella*, sig. A3.

115 *Epigrams*, sig. A3ᵛ.

116 Everard Guilpin, *Skialetheia: Or Shadow of Truth, in Certaine Epigrams and Satyres*, ed. D. Allen Carroll (Chapel Hill: University of North Carolina Press, 1974), Satire VI, 75, p. 90.

117 The first full line of the Shakespeare monument in Holy Trinity Church, Stratford-upon-Avon reads 'IUDICIO PYLUM, GENIO SOCRATEM, ARTE MARONEM'. See the photograph of the monument on plate 6 of *The Riverside Shakespeare*, ed. G. Blakemore Evans, et al., 2nd edn (Boston: Houghton Mifflin, 1997).

118 'To the Memory of . . . Shakespeare', 43, *Poems*, ed. Donaldson, p. 309.

119 'To the Great Variety of Readers', 1623 Folio edn of *Mr. William Shakespeare's Comedies, Histories, & Tragedies*, quoted by Erne, *Shakespeare as Literary Dramatist*, p. 25.

120 Prefatory epistle to *Syr P. S. His Astrophel and Stella*, sig. A3ᵛ.

121 Spenser, *The Poetical Works*, ed. Smith and de Selincourt, p. 409.

122 One of the earliest expressions of this theme is by Theognis (*c.* 570?–490? BC). See D. A. Russell and M. Winterbottom, eds., *Ancient Literary Criticism: The Principal Texts in New Translations* (Oxford: Clarendon Press, 1972), p. 3.

123 Jonson, *Discoveries*, p. 638.

124 *Discoveries*, p. 637.

125 Many postmodernists see the classics of the Western canon as, in effect, 'a form of complicity, another manifestation of the lies and hypocrisy through

which the ruling class has maintained its power' (Gerald Graff, *Literature Against Itself: Literary Ideas in Modern Society* (University of Chicago Press, 1979), p. 31). For a rebuttal of such claims see John M. Ellis, *Literature Lost: Social Agendas and the Corruption of the Humanities* (New Haven, Conn. and London: Yale University Press, 1997), pp. 47–8.

126 Barbara H. C. De Mendonça, 'The Influence of *Gorboduc* on *King Lear*', *Shakespeare Survey*, 13 (1960), pp. 41–8.

127 For parallels between the *True Chronicle History* and *King Lear* see Richard Knowles, 'How Shakespeare Knew *King Leir*', *Shakespeare Survey*, 55 (2002), pp. 12–35.

128 *The True Chronicle History of King Leir*, xxiv.2148–9, facsimile edn (London: Malone Society Reprints, 1907), sig. H2.

129 Thomas Sackville and Thomas Norton, *Gorboduc, or Ferrex and Porrex*, III. i.182–5, ed. Irby B. Cauthen, Jr. (University of Nebraska Press, 1970), p. 44.

130 In a classic statement of this principle Richard Hooker explained that natural law 'comprehendeth all those things which men by the light of their natural understanding evidently know . . . to be beseeming or unbeseeming, virtuous or vicious, good or evil, for them to do' (*Of the Laws of Ecclesiastical Polity*, I.viii.9, 2 vols. (London: Dent, 1907), vol. I, p. 182). On natural law in this period see White, *Natural Law in English Renaissance Literature*. See also Robert Hoopes, *Right Reason in the English Renaissance* (Cambridge, Mass.: Harvard University Press, 1962), pp. 1–32; George C. Herndl, *The High Design: English Renaissance Tragedy and the Natural Law* (Lexington, Ky: University of Kentucky Press, 1970), pp. 13–40; John S. Wilks, *The Idea of Conscience in Renaissance Tragedy* (London and New York: Routledge, 1990), pp. 9–23; Richard A. McCabe, *Incest, Drama and Nature's Law 1550–1700* (Cambridge University Press, 1993), pp. 55–61.

131 'Reserve thy state', Kent tells Lear, 'And in thy best consideration check / This hideous rashness' (I.i.149–151). In other words, 'behave as a true king should do and exercise your authority'.

132 Mary Lascelles, 'King Lear and Doomsday', *Shakespeare Survey 26* (1973), pp. 69–79; Joseph Wittreich, *'Image of that Horror': History, Prophecy and Apocalypse in King Lear* (San Marino: Huntington Library, 1984).

133 Cf *Thyestes*' Chorus: 'Have we of all mankind been deemed deserving that heaven, its poles uptorn, should overwhelm us? In our time has the last day come?', 876–8 (*Seneca's Tragedies*, trans. Miller, vol. 2, p. 163).

134 'This [natural] law thou allegest is but a municipal law, and thou knowest not what the universal is' ('An Apologie of Raymond Sebond', *The Essays of Montaigne*, trans. John Florio, 3 vols. (London: David Nutt, 1892–3), vol. 2 (1893), p. 233). In another essay Montaigne wrote: 'The laws of conscience, which we say to proceed from nature, rise and proceed of custom' ('Of Custome', *Essays*, vol. I (1892), p. 112).

135 Declaring his love the French King says 'Ah, dear *Cordella*, cordial to my heart' (vii.709).

136 T. McAlindon, *Shakespeare's Tragic Cosmos* (Cambridge University Press, 1991), pp. 174–83.

137 Louis Montrose writes: 'the newer historical criticism is *new* in its refusal of unproblematized distinctions between "literature" and "history", between "text" and "context"' ('Renaissance Literary Studies and the Subject of History', *English Literary Renaissance*, 16 (1986), p. 6). Cf. Jonathan Dollimore Introduction to *Political Shakespeare: New Essays in Cultural Materialism*, ed. Dollimore and Alan Sinfield (Manchester University Press, 1985), p. 4; Jean Howard, 'The New Historicism in Renaissance Studies', *English Literary Renaissance*, 16 (1986), p. 42; Leonard Tennenhouse, *Power on Display: the Politics of Shakespeare's Genres* (New York and London: Methuen, 1986), pp. 14–15.

138 See E. A. J. Honigmann, 'Shakespeare's "bombast"', *Shakespeare's Styles: Essays in Honour of Kenneth Muir Philip Edwards*, ed. Inga-Stina Ewbank and G. K. Hunter (Cambridge University Press, 1980), pp. 151–62.

139 On *King Lear*'s changing reception in response to political developments in the twentieth century see R. A. Foakes, *Hamlet versus Lear: Cultural Politics and Shakespeare's Art* (Cambridge University Press, 1993), pp. 45–77.

140 In *The Bard on the Brain: Understanding the Mind through the Art of Shakespeare and the Science of Brain Imaging* (New York: Dana Press, 2003) Paul M. Matthews and Jeffrey McQuain argue that modern neurology confirms what common sense has always known, namely, that Shakespeare had an exceptionally acute understanding of human psychology.

141 Edward O. Wilson, *Consilience: the Unity of Knowledge* (London: Little, Brown, 1998), pp. 236–7.

9 ANTI-HUMANISM

1 According to Terence Hawkes, Cultural Materialism's 'project' involves 're-inserting [texts] into the cultural history of their own time . . . and merging them back into the context of the circulating discourses from which "English" has prised them' ('Bardbiz', review article, *London Review of Books*, 22 February 1990, p. 13). Alan Sinfield similarly describes Cultural Materialism's 'strategy' as 'repudiat[ing] the supposed transcendence of literature' by 'placing a text in its context' (*Faultlines: Cultural Materialism and the Politics of Dissident Reading* (Oxford: Clarendon Press, 1992), p. 22). However, given such a long tradition of historical scholarship in twentieth-century English studies, it's not easy to see how 'English' can be said to have 'prised' literary texts from their historical context, or which school of modern criticism believes in 'the transcendence of literature'.

2 Terence Hawkes' suggestion that historicists concern themselves with 'the recovery of a lost purity, of a final arrival at truth-revealing origins' is a travesty of modern historical scholarship (*Shakespeare in the Present* (London and New York: Routledge, 2002), p. 2), as is Richard Wilson's claim that

'old historicists' had an 'unproblematic concept of history' (*New Historicism and Renaissance Drama*, ed. Wilson and Richard Dutton (London and New York: Longman, 1992), p. xi), or Jean Howard's assertion that they believed that 'history is knowable; and that historians and critics can see the facts of history objectively' ('The New Historicism in Renaissance Studies', *English Literary Renaissance*, 16 (1986), p. 18). For discussion of the debates on historicism that were taking place in the 1930s, '40s and '50s among historians and literary scholars see Introduction to *Neo-Historicism: Studies in English Renaissance Literature, History and Politics*, ed. Robin Headlam Wells, Glenn Burgess and Rowland Wymer (Cambridge: D. S. Brewer, 2000), pp. 1–27.

3 Richard Wilson, Introduction to *New Historicism and Renaissance Drama*, p. 1.

4 Howard, 'The New Historicism in Renaissance Studies', pp. 20–1.

5 Jonathan Dollimore, *Radical Tragedy: Religion, Ideology and Power in the Drama of Shakespeare and his Contemporaries*, 3rd edn (Basingstoke: Palgrave Macmillan, 2004), p. 155.

6 *A Passage to India* (1924; repr. Melbourne, London and Baltimore: Penguin, 1936), p.147.

7 *Critical Practice* (London and New York: Methuen, 1980), p. 90.

8 'Marxism and Humanism', *For Marx*, trans. Ben Brewster (London: Penguin, 1969), pp. 227–9.

9 Scott Meikle, *Essentialism in the Thought of Karl Marx* (London: Duckworth, 1985), p. viii.

10 *Economic and Philosophical Manuscripts of 1844*, quoted by Bertell Ollman, *Alienation: Marx's Conception of Man in Capitalist Society* (Cambridge University Press, 1971), p. 95.

11 Meikle, *Essentialism in the Thought of Karl Marx*, p. 57. See also Kate Soper, *Humanism and Anti-Humanism* (London: Hutchinson, 1986), p. 21.

12 Quoted by Ollman, *Alienation*, p. 75 (my italics).

13 Louis Althusser, *The Future Lasts a Long Time*, ed. Olivier Corpet and Yann Moulier Boutang, trans. Richard Veasey (London: Chatto and Windus, 1993), p. 221.

14 Douglas Johnson, Introduction to *The Future Lasts a Long Time*, p. xii.

15 *The Future Lasts a Long Time*, p. 222.

16 E. P. Thompson, *The Poverty of Theory* (London: Merlin Press, 1978), pp. 195, 381.

17 Johnson, Introduction to *The Future Lasts a Long Time*, p. xiv

18 In rejecting the idea that biology might have anything to do with human behaviour postmodernists appeal to French Theory. Catherine Belsey explains that 'Lacan consistently rejects a concept of humanity based on a quasi-biological theory of instincts' (*Critical Practice*, p. 131); Jean Howard cites Foucault in support of her similar claim that what we suppose to be instincts have nothing to do with biology (see above, note 4). Belsey has recently retreated from her earlier radical anti-humanism, but in doing so

she has rejected one of the founding principles of postmodern theory (see Introduction, note 10).

19 *Culture and the Real*, New Accents, (London: Routledge, 2005), p. xi.

20 'Give me a dozen healthy infants, well-formed, and my own specified world to bring them up in and I'll guarantee to take any one at random and train him to become any type of specialist I might select – doctor, lawyer, artist, merchant-chief, and yes, even beggar-man and thief, regardless of his talents, penchants, tendencies, abilities, vocations, and race of his ancestors' (John B. Watson, *Behaviorism* (London: Kegan Paul, Trench, Trubner and Co, 1925), p. 82). However, not even Watson went so far as to deny that there is a universal human nature (p. 238).

21 Margaret Mead, *Sex and Temperament in Three Primitive Societies* (London: Routledge and Kegan Paul, 1935), p. 280.

22 Donald E. Brown, *Human Universals* (Philadelphia: Temple University Press, 1991), pp. 9–10.

23 Neil Badmington, ed., *Posthumanism* (Basingstoke: Palgrave, 2000), p. 7.

24 On the psychology of empathy see Simon Baron-Cohen, *The Essential Difference: Men, Women and the Extreme Male Brain* (London: Allen Lane, 2003), chapter 3.

25 *The Order of Things: An Archaeology of the Human Sciences*, trans. anon (1970; repr. London: Tavistock, 1977), pp. 308, 387.

26 Jean Howard, for example, writes: 'For a striking investigation of the relatively late emergence of the concept of "man" as a self-sufficient autonomous being possessed of interiority and self-presence see Michel Foucault, *The Order of Things*' ('The New Historicism in Renaissance Studies', p. 20 n13).

27 *The Order of Things*, p. 309.

28 Ibid., p. 352.

29 Ibid., p. 344 (my italics).

30 Ibid., p. 309.

31 J. G. Merquior, *Foucault*, 2nd edn (London: Fontana, 1991), pp. 36–8.

32 Kuhn explained that his paradigm shifts involve conscious re-evaluation by the scientific community of traditional experimental procedures and theoretical presuppositions; such changes cause scientists to see the world differently (Thomas S. Kuhn, *The Structure of Scientific Revolutions* (Chicago University Press, 1962), pp. 7; 110).

33 Merquior, *Foucault*, pp. 39–40.

34 Compare the final sentence of Derrida's seminal Johns Hopkins lecture on 'Structure, Sign, and Play in the Discourses of the Human Sciences': '[we now face] the as yet unnamable which is proclaiming itself and which can do so, as is necessary whenever a birth is in the offing, only under the species of the nonspecies, in the formless, mute, infant, and terrifying form of monstrosity' (*Writing and Difference*, trans. Alan Bass (London: Routledge, 1978), p. 293).

35 *The Order of Things*, p. 387.

36 Ibid., p. xxiii.
37 For a critique of Foucault's theory of unitary epistemes see Merquior, *Foucault*, pp. 57–70. For an incisive analysis of *The Order of Things* and its 'pseudo-prophetic vacuity of meaning' see John Weightman, 'On Not Understanding Michel Foucault', *The American Scholar*, 58 (1989), pp. 383–406.
38 *The Order of Things*, p. 308.
39 Ibid., p. 318.
40 Ibid., p. 322.
41 Ibid., p. 319.
42 Ibid., p. 312.
43 Ibid., p. 218.
44 Ibid., p. 346.
45 Ibid., p. 384.
46 'The New Historicism in Renaissance Studies', p. 22.
47 *The Order of Things*, pp. 322–3.
48 *The Subject of Tragedy* (London and New York: Methuen, 1985), p. 8. Cf. Antony Easthope: 'The notion of the transcendent subject is a relatively recent innovation. It is well known that it did not exist in the ancient world, nor in any developed form in the feudal period' ('Poetry and the Politics of Reading', *Re-Reading English*, ed. Peter Widdowson (London and New York: Methuen, 1982), p. 142).
49 *The Subject of Tragedy*, pp. 13–14, 33.
50 Francis Barker, *The Tremulous Private Body: Essays in Subjection* (Methuen: London and New York, 1984), p. 52.
51 *Radical Tragedy*, p. 250.
52 Jacob Burckhardt, *The Civilization of the Renaissance*, trans. S. G. C. Middleton, 2nd edn (Oxford and London: Phaidon, 1945), p. 81.
53 See Charles Homer Haskins, *The Renaissance of the Twelfth Century* (Cleveland, Ohio and New York: Meridian, 1957); Christopher Brooke, *The Twelfth Century Renaissance* (London: Thames and Hudson, 1969); Winthrop Wetherbee, *Platonism and Poetry in the Twelfth Century: the Literary Influence of the School of Chartres* (Princeton University Press, 1972); Walter Ullman, Medieval Foundations of Renaissance Humanism (London: Paul Elek, 1977); Robert L. Benson and Giles Constable, eds., *Renaissance and Renewal in the Twelfth Century* (Oxford: Clarendon Press, 1982).
54 Peter Munz, Introduction to Eugenio Garin, *Italian Humanism: Philosophy and Civic Life in the Renaissance* (1947), trans. Munz (Oxford: Blackwell, 1965), p. xii. See also Wallace K. Ferguson, *The Renaissance in Historical Thought: Five Centuries of Interpretation* (Cambridge, Mass.: Houghton Mifflin, 1948), pp. 290–5.
55 'The Discourse of History', trans. John Johnston, *Foucault Live: Interviews 1961–1984*, ed. Sylvère Lotringer (New York: Semiotext(e), 1989), p. 24.

56 For a discussion of Catherine Belsey's misreading of Donne's 'Hymn to God my God, in my sickness' as an expression of an anti-essentialist view of the self see Robin Headlam Wells, *Elizabethan Mythologies: Studies in Poetry, Drama and Music* (Cambridge University Press, 1994), p. 141.

57 See for example chapter 1, pp. 10–11; chapter 2 pp. 39–40.

58 'The New Historicism in Renaissance Studies', p. 23.

59 *Shakespeare and the Loss of Eden: The Construction of Family Values in Early Modern Culture* (Basingstoke and London: Macmillan, 1999), p. 10.

60 'Written History as an Act of Faith', *American Historical Review* 39 (1934), p. 221.

61 A. A. Goldenweiser, 'The Nature and Tasks of the Social Sciences', *Journal of Social Philosophy* (1936), quoted by Harry Elmer Barnes, *A History of Historical Writing* (1937) revised edn (New York: Dover, 1962), pp. 268–9.

62 See Peter Novick, *That Noble Dream: The 'Objectivity Question' and the American Historical Profession* (Cambridge University Press, 1988). See also Introduction to *Neo-Historicism*, ed. Headlam Wells, Burgess and Wymer, pp. 1–27.

63 'It is simply not possible to stop being men of the twentieth century while we engage in a judgment of the past: we cannot forget the associations of our own language, the newly acquired attitudes, the impact and import of the last centuries' (René Wellek and Austin Warren, *Theory of Literature* (New York: Harcourt, Brace and Co, 1942), p. 32).

64 Helen Gardner, *The Business of Criticism* (Oxford: Clarendon Press, 1959), p. 32.

65 *The Business of Criticism*, p. 34.

66 *Faultlines*, p. 22.

67 Ibid., p. 10. For Cultural Materialists this is a familiar theme in Shakespeare. According to Sinfield *Othello* and *Macbeth* are also about the legitimation of state violence (pp. 34, 95).

68 *Faultlines*, p. 19.

69 Ibid., p. 98.

70 Hawkes, 'Bardbiz', p. 13. Paradoxically, the radical Left shares a view of politics associated with the extreme right: as George W. Bush, echoing Margaret Thatcher, so memorably put it after the bombing of the World Trade Centre, 'you are either for us or against us'.

71 *Faultlines*, p. 8.

72 Ibid., p. 20.

73 In recent years I've examined a number of PhD dissertations that have taken exactly this approach to a heterogeneous selection of Renaissance plays, citing Sinfield as their theoretical model.

74 'If we should really be able to reconstruct the meaning which *Hamlet* held for its contemporary audience, we would merely impoverish it. We should suppress the legitimate meanings which later generations found in *Hamlet*. We would bar the possibility of a new interpretation' (*Theory of Literature*, p. 32).

75 Terence Hawkes, *Meaning by Shakespeare* (London: Routledge, 1992), p. 3.
76 For discussion of Cultural Materialism's 'creative misreading' of Renaissance texts see Headlam Wells, *Elizabethan Mythologies*, pp. 13–15; Tom McAlindon, 'Cultural Materialism and the Ethics of Reading: or the Radicalizing of Jacobean Tragedy', *Modern Language Review*, 90 (1995), pp. 830–46.
77 Michel Foucault, *Discipline and Punish: The Birth of the Prison*, trans. Alan Sheridan (London: Allen Lane, 1977), p. 31.
78 See Hawkes, *Shakespeare in the Present*.
79 Barry Hindess and Paul Q. Hirst, *Pre-Capitalist Modes of Production* (London and Boston: Routledge and Kegan Paul, 1975), p. 311.
80 In a lecture on 'The Historical Sense' Gardner argued that if we simply impose our own critical paradigms on the past we are in danger of 'emptying it of its own historical reality' (*The Business of Criticism*, p. 135).
81 George K. Hunter, '"A Roman Thought": Renaissance Attitudes to History Exemplified in Shakespeare and Jonson', *An English Miscellany Presented to W.S. Mackie*, ed. Brian S. Lee (Cape Town, London and New York: Oxford University Press, 1977), p. 93.
82 *Rasselas, The Yale Edition of the Works of Samuel Johnson*, 16 vols., ed. Gwin J. Kolb (New Haven and London: Yale University Press, 1958–1990), vol. 16 (1990), p. 112.
83 *Rasselas*, p.44.
84 Erasmus, *Man of Letters: the Construction of Charisma in Print* (Princeton University Press, 1993), p. 5.
85 *Of Dramatic Poesy and Other Critical Essays*, 2 vols., ed. George Watson (London and New York: Dent, 1962), vol. 1, p. 25.
86 Peter Barry, *Beginning Theory: An Introduction to Literary and Cultural Theory* (Manchester University Press, 1995), p. 18.
87 Steven Pinker, *The Blank Slate: The Modern Denial of Human Nature* (London: Allen Lane, 2002), p. 421.
88 *Consilience: the Unity of Knowledge* (London: Little, Brown, 1998), p. 243.
89 Terry Eagleton, *Literary Theory: An Introduction* (Oxford: Blackwell, 1983), p. 11.
90 Peter Lamarque and Stein Haugom Olsen, *Truth, Fiction, and Literature: a Philosophical Perspective* (Oxford: Clarendon Press, 1994), p. 441.
91 *Consilience*, p. 6. For a recent attempt to bring modern psychological theory to bear on the study of literature see Joseph Carroll, *Evolution and Literary Theory* (Columbia and London: University of Missouri Press, 1995).
92 *Desire: Love Stories in Western Culture* (Oxford: Blackwell, 1994), p. 14. However, in recent years Belsey has adopted a more accommodating view of modern science (see Introduction, n. 10).
93 *Literary Darwinism: Evolution, Human Nature, and Literature* (New York and London: Routledge, 2004), p. x.

94 For a survey of the origins of sociobiology and evolutionary psychology see Kenan Malik, *Man, Beast and Zombie: What Science Can and Cannot tell us about Human Nature* (London: Weidenfeld and Nicolson, 2000), chapter 7.

95 Margaret Mead, *Blackberry Winter* (New York: Simon and Schuster, 1972), p. 222. A similar political sensitivity continues to surround the question of gender. In *The Essential Difference* Simon Baron-Cohen writes: 'I have spent more than five years writing this book. This is because the topic was just too politically sensitive to complete in the 1990s. I postponed finishing this book because I was unsure whether a discussion of psychological sex differences could proceed dispassionately' (p. 11).

96 'The Psychological Foundations of Culture', *The Adapted Mind: Evolutionary Psychology and the Generation of Culture*, ed. Jerome H. Barkow, Leda Cosmides and John Tooby (Oxford University Press, 1992), pp. 19–36.

97 Clifford Geertz, *The Interpretation of Cultures* (New York: Basic Books, 1973), p. 50.

98 *The Interpretation of Culture*, p. 46. It was Geertz's constructionism that inspired Stephen Greenblatt to make anti-humanism an integral part of the New Historicist credo.

99 See Cosmides and Tooby, 'The Psychological Foundations of Culture'.

100 Malik, *Man, Beast and Zombie*, chapter 10.

101 *Consilience*, p. 139.

102 'The Psychological Foundations of Culture', p. 92.

103 Simon Baron-Cohen, *Mindblindness: An Essay on Autism and Theory of Mind* (Cambridge, Mass. and London: MIT Press, 1997); Pinker, *The Blank Slate*, pp. 61–2; 223–4.

104 Temple Grandin and Margaret M. Scariano, *Emergence: Labeled Autistic* (Tunbridge Wells: Costello, 1986).

105 Oliver Sacks, *An Anthropologist on Mars* (London and Basingstoke: Picador, 1995), p. 275.

106 Oliver Sacks, *The Man Who Mistook His Wife for a Hat* (London: Duckworth, 1985), p. 188.

107 *The Man Who Mistook His Wife for a Hat*, p. 113.

108 As Cosmides and Tooby, point out, 'humans everywhere include as part of their conceptual equipment the idea that the behavior of others is guided by invisible internal entities, such as "beliefs" and "desires"' ('The Psychological Foundations of Culture', p. 89). See also Matt Ridley, *Nature Via Nurture: Genes, Experience and What Makes Us Human* (London: Harper Collins, 2003), pp. 210–11.

109 John Webster, *The Duchess of Malfi* (I.i.445–6), ed. John Russell Brown (London: Methuen, 1964), p. 34.

110 'A Dark Mirror: Reflections on Dementia', *News from the Republic of Letters*, 2 (1997), p. 15.

111 *Synaptic Self: How Our Brains Become Who We Are* (London: Macmillan, 2002), p. 9.

112 Helena Cronin, *The Ant and the Peacock: Sexual Selection from Darwin to Today* (Cambridge University Press, 1991).

113 John D. Barrow, *The Artful Universe* (Oxford: Clarendon Press, 1995), p. 82.

114 Wilson, *Consilience*, p. 116.

115 *How the Mind Works* (London and New York: Allen Lane, 1998), p. 521.

116 Evelyn Waugh didn't exaggerate when he said 'Barbarism is never finally conquered; given propitious circumstances, men and women who seem quite orderly will commit every conceivable atrocity' (quoted by Geoffrey Wheatcroft, 'A Prophet Without Honour', *Times Literary Supplement*, 24 October 2003, p. 14). Anyone who doubts the truth of this should read Jared Diamond, *The Rise and Fall of the Third Chimpanzee* (London: Vintage, 1988; repr. 1992).

117 See Matt Ridley, *The Origins of Virtue* (London: Viking, 1996); Geoffrey Miller, *The Mating Mind: How Sexual Choice Shaped the Evolution of Human Nature* (London: Heinemann, 2000).

118 See Frans de Waal, *Chimpanzee Politics: Power and Sex among Apes* (London: Jonathan Cape, 1982).

119 *The Origins of Virtue*, p. 38.

120 I've taken these phrases from Miller's *Times Literary Supplement* article 'Looking to be entertained: three strange things that evolution did to our minds' (16 October 1998, p. 14). However, the book on which the article is based, *The Mating Mind: How Sexual Selection Shaped the Evolution of Human Nature* (Oxford: Heinemann, 2000), is continuously stimulating.

121 Jonathan Dollimore and Alan Sinfield, eds., *Political Shakespeare: New Essays in Cultural Materialism* (Manchester University Press, 1985), p. 4.

122 Louis Montrose, 'Renaissance Literary Studies and the Subject of History', *English Literary Renaissance*, 16 (1986), p. 6.

123 'Bardbiz', p. 13.

124 See Patrick Ffrench, *The Time of Theory : A History of 'Tel Quel' (1960–1983)* (Oxford: Clarendon Press, 1995).

125 *Truth, Fiction, and Literature*, p. 455.

126 John M. Ellis, *The Theory of Literary Criticism: A Logical Analysis* (Berkeley, Los Angeles and London: University of California Press, 1974), p. 44.

127 In a later book Ellis corrected Terry Eagleton's misreading of *The Theory of Literary Criticism*: 'Eagleton seizes [in *Literary Theory: An Introduction*] on the idea that literature is not a category based strictly on physical similarity in order to dissolve literature as a real category, but that argument would dissolve most of the other categories that we live by' (*Literature Lost: Social Agendas and the Corruption of the Humanities* (New Haven, Conn. and London: Yale University Press, 1997), p. 45).

128 *Literature Lost*, pp. 47–8.

129 See Louis Cazamian, *The Social Novel in England 1830–1850*, trans. Martin Fido (London: Routledge and Kegan Paul, 1973); Josephine M. Guy, *The Victorian Social-Problem Novel: The Market, the Individual and Communal Life* (Basingstoke and London: Macmillan, 1996).

130 *Why Freud Was Wrong: Sin, Science and Psychoanalysis*, revised edn (London: HarperCollins, 1996), p. 480.

131 See Ernest Gellner, *Relativism and the Social Sciences* (Cambridge University Press, 1985), pp. 84–5.

132 The following is a selection of books, in addition to those that I have already cited in the notes for this chapter, that are critical of Theory: Graham Bradshaw, *Misrepresentations: Shakespeare and the Materialists* (Ithaca and London: Cornell University Press, 1993); Joseph Carroll, *Evolution and Literary Theory* (Columbia and London: University of Missouri Press, 1995); Frederick Crews, *Skeptical Engagements* (New York and Oxford: Oxford University Press, 1986); M. J. Devaney, '*Since at least Plato*' *and Other Postmodernist Myths* (New York: St Martin's Press, 1997); John M. Ellis, *Against Deconstruction* (Princeton, NJ: Princeton University Press, 1989); Richard A. Etlin, *In Defense of Humanism: Value in the Arts and Letters* (Cambridge University Press, 1996); Richard Freadman and Seumas Miller, *Re-thinking Theory: A Critique and an Alternative Account* (Cambridge University Press, 1992); Leonard Jackson, *The Poverty of Structuralism: Literature and Structuralist Theory* (London and New York: Longman, 1991) and *The Dematerialisation of Karl Marx* (London and New York: Longman, 1994); John Lee, *Shakespeare's 'Hamlet' and the Controversies of the Self* (Oxford: Clarendon Press, 2000); Alan Sokal and Jean Bricmont, *Intellectual Impostures* (London: Profile Books, 1998); Raymond Tallis, *Not Saussure: a Critique of Post-Saussurean Literary Theory* (Basingstoke and London: Macmillan, 1988) and *Enemies of Hope: A Critique of Contemporary Pessimism* (Basingstoke and London: Macmillan; 1997); Brian Vickers, *Appropriating Shakespeare: Contemporary Critical Quarrels* (New Haven and London: Yale University Press, 1993).

133 *The Illusions of Postmodernism* (Oxford: Blackwell, 1996), pp. 1; 20.

134 Cronin, *The Ant and the Peacock*, p. 431.

135 Charles Darwin, *The Descent of Man*, chapter 5 (Princeton University Press, 1981), pp, 158–84.

Select bibliography

PRIMARY SOURCES

Anon. *Haec-Vir. Or, the Womanish-Man* (London, 1620).
    Hic Mulier. Or, the Man-Woman (London, 1620).
    A Word to Mr. Wil Pryn (London, 1649).
    The True Chronicle History of King Leir, facsimile edn (London: Malone Society Reprints, 1907).
Ascham, Roger. *Toxophilus (1545)*, ed. Edward Arber (London: Constable, 1895).
Augustine, St. *Confessions*, trans. William Watts (1631), Loeb Classical Library, 2 vols. (London: Heinemann, 1922–5).
Bacon, Francis. *The Works of Francis Bacon*, ed. James Spedding, Robert Leslie Ellis and Douglas Denon Heath, 7 vols. (London: Longman, 1879–87).
    The Philosophical Works, ed. John M. Robertson (London: George Routledge, 1905).
    The Essayes or Counsels Civill or Morall (London: Dent, 1906).
    The Advancement of Learning and the New Atlantis, ed. Arthur Johnston (Oxford: Clarendon Press, 1974).
Boccaccio, Giovanni. *Boccaccio on Poetry: Being the Preface and the Fourteenth and Fifteenth Books of Boccaccio's Genealogia Deorum Gentilium*, ed. and trans. Charles G. Osgood, (Indianapolis and New York: Bobbs-Merrill, 1956).
Bodin, Jean. *The Six Bookes of a Commonweale* (1576), trans. Richard Knolles (London, 1606).
Browne, Sir Thomas. *The Religio Medici* (London: Dent, 1962).
Bruni, Leonardo. *The Humanism of Leonardo Bruni: Selected Texts*, ed. and trans. Gordon Griffeths, James Hankins and David Thompson (Binghamton: Renaissance Society of America, 1987).
Bruno, Giordano. *The Heroic Frenzies*, trans. Paul Eugene Memmo, Jr (Chapel Hill: University of North Carolina Press, 1964).
Castiglione, Baldassare. *The Book of the Courtier*, trans. Sir Thomas Hoby, ed. W. H. D. Rouse (London: Dent, 1928).
Chapman, George. *The Poems of George Chapman*, ed. Phyllis Brooks Bartlett (New York: Russell and Russell, 1962).
Charron, Pierre. *Of Wisdome*, trans. Samson Lennard (London, 1606).

Chaucer, Geoffrey. *The Works of Geoffrey Chaucer*, 2nd edn, ed. F. N. Robinson (London: Oxford University Press, 1957).

Cicero, Marcus Tullius. *Pro Archia poeta*, ed. and trans. N. H. Watts, Loeb Classical Library (London and New York: Heinemann, 1923).

De amicitia, trans. William Armistead Falconer; Loeb Classical Library (London and New York: Heinemann, 1927).

De legibus, trans. Clinton Walker Keyes, Loeb Classical Library (London and New York: Heinemann, 1948).

De re publica, trans. Clinton Walker Keyes, Loeb Classical Library (London and New York: Heinemann, 1948).

De natura deorum, trans. H. Rackham, Loeb Classical Library (London and New York: Heinemann, 1951).

De officiis, trans. Walter Miller, Loeb Classical Library (London and New York: Heinemann, 1913).

De oratore, trans. E. W. Sutton, Loeb Classical Library, 2 vols. (London and New York: Heinemann, 1948).

Tusculan Disputations, trans. J. E. King, Loeb Classical Library (London and New York: Heinemann, 1927).

Crooke, Helkiah. *Microcosmographia: A Description of the body of Man* (London, 1618).

Daniel, Samuel. *The Complete Works in Verse and Prose of Samuel Daniel*, ed. Alexander B. Grosart, 5 vols. (London: Hazell, Watson and Viney, 1885–96).

The Civil Wars, ed. Lawrence Michel (New Haven: Yale University Press, 1958).

Davies, John of Hereford. *Microcosmos* (London, 1603).

Davies, Sir John. *The Poems of Sir John Davies*, Robert Krueger (Oxford: Clarendon Press, 1975).

Dennis, John. *The Grounds of Criticism in Poetry* (1704), facsimile edn (Menston: Scolar Press, 1971).

Donne, John. *The Divine Poems*, ed. Helen Gardner (Oxford: Clarendon Press, 1952).

The Epithalamions, Anniversaries and Epicedes, W. Milgate (Oxford: Clarendon Press, 1978).

Devotions upon Emergent Occasions, ed. Anthony Raspa (Montreal and London: McGill-Queen's University Press, 1975).

Drayton, Michael. *The Works of Michael Drayton*, ed. J. William Hebel, 5 vols. (Oxford: Blackwell, 1931–41).

Dryden, John. *The Works of John Dryden*, ed. Edward Niles Hooker, Alan Roper and H. T. Swedenborg, Jr, 20 vols. (Berkeley, Los Angeles and London: University of California Press, 1956–89).

Of Dramatic Poesy and Other Critical Essays, ed. George Watson, 2 vols. (London and New York: Dent, 1962).

Elyot, Sir Thomas. *The Boke Named the Governour*, ed. Foster Watson (London: Dent, 1907).

Empiricus, Sextus. *Outlines of Pyrrhonism*, trans. R. G. Bury, Loeb Classical Library (London and New York: Heinemann, 1933).

Erasmus, Desiderius. *The Education of a Christian Prince*, trans. with an introduction by Lester K. Born (New York: Columbia University Press, 1936).

The 'Adages' of Erasmus, ed. and trans. Margaret Mann Phillips (Cambridge University Press, 1964).

Collected Works of Erasmus, ed. Peter D. Bietenholz, Alexander Dalzell, Anthony T. Grafton and others, 32 vols. (Toronto, Buffalo and London: University of Toronto Press, 1974–89).

Enchiridion militis christiani: An English Version, ed. Anne M. O'Donnell, SND (Oxford: Early English Text Society, 1981).

Gentillet, Innocent. *A Discourse upon the Meanes of Wel Governing . . . Against Nicholas Machiavell*, trans. S. Patericke (London, 1602).

Gorges, Sir Arthur. *The Poems of Sir Arthur Gorges* (Oxford: Clarendon Press, 1953).

Gosson, Stephen. *The Schoole of Abuse* (1579), ed. Edward Arber (London: English Reprints, 1869).

Playes Confuted in Five Actions (1582), facsimile edn (New York and London: Garland, 1972).

Gower, John. *The Complete Works of John Gower*, ed. G. C. Macaulay, 4 vols. (Oxford: Clarendon Press, 1899–1902).

Guicciardini, Francesco. *Selected Writings*, ed. Cecil Grayson, trans. Margaret Grayson (London: Oxford University Press, 1965).

Harvey, Gabriel. *Letter-Book of Gabriel Harvey, 1573–1580*, ed. E. J. L. Scott (London: Camden Society, 1884).

Gabriel Harvey's Marginalia, ed. G. C. Moore Smith (Stratford-upon-Avon: Shakespeare Head, 1913).

Hayward, John. *The First and Second Part of John Hayward's The Life and Raigne of King Henrie IIII*, Camden Fourth Series, vol. 42 (London: Royal Historical Society, 1991).

Heywood, Thomas. *An Apology for Actors* (1612) (London: Shakespeare Society, 1841).

Horace (Quintus Horatius Flaccus). *Ars poetica*, ed. and trans. H. Rushton Fairclough, Loeb Classical Library, (London and New York: Heinemann, 1970).

James VI. *The Poems of James VI of Scotland*, ed. James Craigie (Edinburgh and London: William Blackwood, 1955).

James VI and I. *Political Writings*, ed. Johann P. Sommerville (Cambridge University Press, 1994).

Jonson, Ben. *Ben Jonson*, ed. C. H. Herford and Percy and Evelyn Simpson, 11 vols. (Oxford: Clarendon Press, 1925–52).

La Primaudaye, Pierre de. *The French Academie* (London, 1586).

Lemnius, Levinus. *The Secret Miracles of Nature* (1571), trans. anon. (London, 1658).

Lipsius, Justus. *Six Bookes of Politickes or Civil Doctrine* (1589), trans. William Jones (London, 1594).

Locke, John. *An Essay Concerning Human Understanding*, ed. Peter H. Nidditch (Oxford: Clarendon Press, 1975).

Two Treatises of Government, ed. Peter Laslett (Cambridge University Press, 1960), p. 348.

Machiavelli, Niccolò. *The Discourses of Niccolò Machiavelli*, ed. and trans. Leslie J. Walker, 2 vols. (London: Routledge and Kegan Paul, 1950).

The Prince, ed. Quentin Skinner, trans. Russell Price (Cambridge University Press, 1988).

Montaigne, Michel de. *The Essays of Montaigne*, trans. John Florio, 3 vols. (London: David Nutt, 1892–3).

More, St.Thomas. *Selected Letters*, ed. Elizabeth Frances Rogers (New Haven and London: Yale University Press, 1961).

The Complete Works of St Thomas More, ed. Edward Surtz, S. J. and J. H. Hexter, 15 vols. (New Haven and London: Yale University Press, 1963–85).

Petrarca, Francesco. *Petrarch's Letters to Classical Authors*, trans. M. E. Cosenza (Chicago University Press, 1910).

'On his Own Ignorance and that of Many Others', *The Renaissance Philosophy of Man*, ed. Ernst Cassirer, Paul Oskar Kristeller and John Herman Randall, Jr., trans. Hans Nachod (Chicago University Press, 1948), pp. 47–133.

Petrarch's Africa, trans. and annotated Thomas G. Bergin and Alice S. Wilson (New Haven and London: Yale University Press, 1977).

Letters on Familiar Matters, trans. Aldo S. Bernado (Baltimore and London: Johns Hopkins University Press, 1982).

Pico della Mirandola, Giovanni. 'Oration on the Dignity of Man', *The Renaissance Philosophy of Man*, ed. Ernst Cassirer, Paul Oskar Kristeller and John Herman Randall, trans. Elizabeth Livermore Forbes (Chicago University Press, 1948), pp. 223–54.

Plato. *Phaedrus*, ed. W. R. M. Lamb, trans. Harold N. Fowler, Loeb Classical Library (London and New York: Heinemann, 1919).

Ion, ed. and trans. W. R. M. Lamb, Loeb Classical Library (London and New York: Heinemann, 1952).

Ponet, John. *A Short Treatise of Politic Power* (1556), facsimile edn (Menston: Scolar Press, 1970).

Prynne, William. *Histriomastix* (1633), facsimile edn with a preface by Arthur Freeman (New York and London: Garland, 1974).

Puttenham, George. *The Arte of English Poesie*, ed. Gladys Doidge Willcock and Alice Walker (Cambridge University Press, 1936).

Rainoldes, John. *Th' overthrow of Stage-Plays*, facsimile edn with a preface by Arthur Freeman (New York and London: Garland, 1974).

Ralegh, Sir Walter. *The History of the World* (London, 1614).

Sackville, Thomas and Norton, Thomas. *Gorboduc, or Ferrex and Porrex*, ed. Irby B. Cauthen, Jr (Lincoln, Nebr.: University of Nebraska Press, 1970).

Seneca, Lucius Annaeus. *Moral Essays*, ed. and trans. John W. Basore, 3 vols, Loeb Classical Library (London and New York: Heinemann, 1932), pp. 202–85.

Shakespeare, William. *The Complete Works*, ed. Stanley Wells and Gary Taylor (Oxford: Clarendon Press, 1986).

Sidney, Sir Philip. *The Poems of Sir Philip Sidney*, ed. William A. Ringler, Jr (Oxford: Clarendon Press, 1962).

An Apology for Poetry, ed. Geoffrey Shepherd (London: Nelson, 1965).

Spenser, Edmund. *The Poetical Works*, ed. J. C. Smith and E. de Selincourt (London, New York and Toronto: Oxford University Press, 1912).

Starkey, Thomas. *A Dialogue Between Pole and Lupset*, ed. T. F. Mayer (London: The Royal Historical Society, 1989).

Stubbes, Philip. *The Anatomie of Abuses* (1583), ed. Frederick J. Furnivall (London: New Shakespeare Society, 1877–9).

Warner, William. *Albions England* (London, 1602).

Wright, Thomas. *The Passions of the Mind in General* (1601), ed. William Webster Newbold (New York and London: Garland, 1986).

SELECTED SECONDARY SOURCES

Abrams, M. H. *The Mirror and the Lamp: Romantic Theory and the Critical Tradition* (New York: Oxford University Press, 1953).

Ackroyd, Peter. *Dressing Up: Transvestism and Drag, The History of an Obsession* (London: Thames and Hudson, 1979).

Adams, Robert P. *The Better Part of Valor: More, Erasmus, Colet, and Vives on Humanism, War, and Peace 1496–1535* (Seattle: University of Washington Press, 1962).

Adorno, Theodor W. and Horkheimer, Max. *Dialectic of Enlightenment* (1944), trans. John Cumming (London: Allen Lane, 1973).

Aers, David. 'A Whisper in the Ear of Early Modernists: or, Reflections on Literary Critics Writing the "History of the Subject"', *Culture and History 1350–1600: Essays on English Communities, Identities and Writing*, ed. David Aers (London and New York: Harvester Wheatsheaf, 1992), pp. 177–202.

Althusser, Louis. *For Marx*, trans. Ben Brewster (London: Allen Lane, 1969).

'Ideology and Ideological State Apparatuses', *Lenin and Philosophy and other Essays* (London: NLB, 1971), pp. 121–73.

The Future Lasts a Long Time, ed. Olivier Corpet and Yann Moulier Boutang; trans. Richard Veasey (London: Chatto and Windus, 1993).

Altman, Joel B. *The Tudor Play of Mind: Rhetorical Inquiry and the Development of Elizabethan Drama* (Berkeley, Los Angeles and London: University of California Press, 1978).

Badmington, Neil, ed. *Posthumanism* (Basingstoke: Palgrave, 2000).

Baldwin, T. W. *William Shakespere's Small Latine and Lesse Greeke*, 2 vols. (Urbana: University of Illinois Press, 1944).

Bamborough, J. B. *The Little World of Man* (London, New York and Toronto: Longmans, Green and Co, 1952).

Barish, Jonas. *The Antitheatrical Prejudice* (Berkeley, Los Angeles and London: University of California Press, 1981).

Barkan, Leonard. *Nature's Work of Art: The Human Body as Image of the World* (New Haven and London: Yale University Press, 1975).

Barker, Francis. *The Tremulous Private Body: Essays in Subjection* (London and New York: Methuen, 1984).

Barkow, Jerome H., Cosmides, Leda and Tooby, John, eds. *The Adapted Mind: Evolutionary Psychology and the Generation of Culture* (New York: Oxford University Press, 1992).

Barnes, Harry Elmer. *A History of Historical Writing*, (1937; revised edn. New York: Dover, 1962).

Baron-Cohen, Simon. *Mindblindness: An Essay on Autism and Theory of Mind* (Cambridge, Mass. and London: MIT Press, 1997).
  The Essential Difference: Men, Women and the Extreme Male Brain (London: Allen Lane, 2003).

Barrow, John D. *The Artful Universe* (Oxford: Clarendon Press, 1995).

Barthes, Roland. 'The Death of the Author', *Image Music Text* (London: Fontana, 1977), pp. 142–8.

Bate, Jonathan. 'Shakespeare and Original Genius', *Genius: the History of an Idea*, ed. Murray, Penelope (Oxford: Blackwell, 1989), pp. 76–97.
  'The Humanist Tempest', *Shakespeare: La Tempête: Etudes Critiques*, ed. Claude Peltrault (Besançon: University of Besançon, 1993), pp. 5–20.
  Shakespeare and Ovid (Oxford: Clarendon Press, 1993).
  The Genius of Shakespeare (London and Basingstoke: Picador, 1997).

Battersby, Christine. *Gender and Genius: Towards a Feminist Aesthetics* (London: The Women's Press, 1989).

Belsey, Catherine. *Critical Practice* (London and New York: Methuen, 1980).
  The Subject of Tragedy (London and New York: Methuen, 1985).
  'The Name of the Rose in *Romeo and Juliet*', *Yearbook of Shakespeare Studies*, 23 (1993), pp. 126–42.
  Desire: Love Stories in Western Culture (Oxford: Blackwell, 1994).
  Shakespeare and the Loss of Eden: The Construction of Family Values in Early Modern Culture (Basingstoke and London: Macmillan, 1999).

Benson, Robert L., Constable, Giles, eds. *Renaissance and Renewal in the Twelfth Century* (Oxford: Clarendon Press, 1982).

Berlin, Isaiah. 'Two Concepts of Liberty', *Four Essays on Liberty* (Oxford and New York: Oxford University Press, 1969), pp. 118–72.

Bevington, David. *Tudor Drama and Politics: a Critical Approach to Topical Meaning* (Cambridge, Mass.: Harvard University Press, 1968).

Bloom, Harold. *Shakespeare: the Invention of the Human* (London: Fourth Estate, 1999).

Bossy, John. *Giordano Bruno and the Embassy Affair* (New Haven and London: Yale University Press, 1991).

Bradshaw, Graham. *Shakespeare's Scepticism* (Brighton: Harvester Press, 1987).
  Misrepresentations: Shakespeare and the Materialists (Ithaca and London: Cornell University Press, 1993).
Brooke, Christopher. *The Twelfth Century Renaissance* (London: Thames and Hudson, 1969).
Brown, Donald E. *Human Universals* (Philadelphia: Temple University Press, 1991).
Burckhardt, Jacob. *The Civilization of the Renaissance*, 2nd edn, trans. S. G. C. Middleton (Oxford and London: Phaidon, 1945).
Burke, Peter. *The Renaissance* (Basingstoke: Macmillan, 1987).
Bush, Douglas. *The Renaissance and English Humanism* (1939; repr. Toronto: University of Toronto Press, 1958).
Buss, David M. *The Evolution of Desire: Strategies of Human Mating* (New York: Basic Books, 1994).
Cady, Joseph. '"Masculine Love," Renaissance Writing and the "New Invention" of Homosexuality', *Homosexuality in Renaissance England: Literary Representations in Historical Context*, ed. Claude, J. Summers (New York, London and Norwood (Australia): Haworth Press, 1992), pp. 9–40.
Carroll, Clare. 'Humanism and English Literature in the Fifteenth and Sixteenth Centuries', *The Cambridge Companion to Renaissance Humanism*, ed. Jill Kraye (Cambridge University Press, 1996), pp. 246–68.
Carroll, Joseph. *Evolution and Literary Theory* (Columbia and London: University of Missouri Press, 1995).
  Literary Darwinism: Evolution, Human Nature, and Literature (New York and London: Routledge, 2004).
Caspari, Fritz. *Humanism and the Social Order in Tudor England* (Chicago University Press, 1954).
Charlton, Kenneth. *Education in Renaissance England* (London and Toronto: Routledge and Kegan Paul, 1965).
Chomsky, Noam. 'Language and Freedom', *TriQuarterly*, 23–4 (1972), pp. 13–33.
Colapinto, John. *As Nature Made Him: The Boy Who was Raised as a Girl* (New York: HarperCollins, 2000).
Coleman, Janet. 'Machiavelli's *Via Moderna*: Medieval and Renaissance Attitudes to History', *Niccolò Machiavelli's The Prince: New Interdisciplinary Essays*, ed. Martin Coyle (Manchester University Press, 1995), pp. 40–64.
Colie, Rosalie. *Paradoxia Epidemica: the Renaissance Tradition of Paradox* (Princeton University Press, 1966).
Collins, Stephen L. *From Divine Cosmos to Sovereign State: An Intellectual History of Consciousness and the Idea of Order in Renaissance England* (New York and Oxford: Oxford University Press, 1989).
Cosmides, Leda and Tooby, John. 'The Psychological Foundations of Culture', *The Adapted Mind: Evolutionary Psychology and the Generation of Culture*, ed. Jerome H. Barkow, Leda Cosmides and John Tooby (New York and Oxford: Oxford University Press, 1992), pp. 19–136.

Cressy, David. 'Foucault, Stone, Shakespeare and Social History', *English Literary Renaissance*, 21 (1991), pp. 121–33.

'Gender Trouble and Cross-Dressing in Early Modern England', *Journal of British Studies*, 35 (1996), pp. 438–65.

Cronin, Helena. *The Ant and the Peacock: Sexual Selection from Darwin to Today* (Cambridge University Press, 1991).

Daly, James. 'Cosmic Harmony and Political Thinking in Early Stuart England', *Transactions of the American Philosophical Society*, 69 (1979), pp. 3–40.

Daniel, Norman. *Islam, Europe and Empire* (Edinburgh University Press, 1966).

The Arabs and Medieval Europe (London: Longman, 1975).

Dean, Paul. 'Tudor Humanism and the Roman Past: A Background to Shakespeare', *Renaissance Quarterly*, 41 (1988), pp. 84–111.

DeNora, Tia. *Beethoven and the Construction of Genius: Musical Politics in Vienna, 1792–1803* (Berkeley, Los Angeles and London: University of California Press, 1995).

Dollimore, Jonathan. 'Transgression and Surveillance in *Measure for Measure*', *Political Shakespeare: New Essays in Cultural Materialism*, ed. Jonathan Dollimore and Alan Sinfield (Manchester University Press, 1985), pp. 72–87.

'Desire is Death', *Subject and Object in Renaissance Culture*, ed. Margreta de Grazia, Maureen Quilligan and Peter Stallybrass (Cambridge University Press, 1996), pp. 369–86.

Radical Tragedy: Religion, Ideology and Power in the Drama of Shakespeare and his Contemporaries, 3rd edn. (Basingstoke: Palgrave Macmillan, 2004).

Duncan-Jones, Katherine. *Ungentle Shakespeare: Scenes from His Life* (London: Arden Shakespeare, 2001).

Dust, Philip C. *Three Renaissance Pacifists: Essays on the Theories of Erasmus, More, and Vives* (New York: Peter Lang, 1987).

Eagleton, Terry. *The Illusions of Postmodernism* (Oxford: Blackwell, 1996).

Ellis, John M. *The Theory of Literary Criticism: A Logical Analysis* (Berkeley, Los Angeles and London: University of California Press, 1974).

Erne, Lukas. *Shakespeare as Literary Dramatist* (Cambridge University Press, 2003).

Faas, Ekbert. *Shakespeare's Poetics* (Cambridge University Press, 1986).

Ferguson, Wallace K. *The Renaissance in Historical Thought: Five Centuries of Interpretation* (Cambridge, Mass.: Houghton Mifflin, 1948).

Ferry, Anne. *The 'Inward' Language: Sonnets of Wyatt, Sidney, Shakespeare, Donne* (Chicago and London: Chicago University Press, 1983).

Foucault, Michel. *The Order of Things: An Archaeology of the Human Sciences*, (1970; repr. London: Tavistock, 1977).

Discipline and Punish: The Birth of the Prison, trans. Alan Sheridan (London: Allen Lane, 1977).

Language, Counter-Memory, Practice: Selected Essays and Interviews, ed. and trans. Donald F. Bouchard (Oxford: Blackwell, 1977).

The History of Sexuality: An Introduction, trans. Robert Hurley (London: Penguin, 1979).

Power/Knowledge (New York: Pantheon, 1981).

Technologies of the Self: A Seminar with Michel Foucault, ed. Luther H. Martin, Huck Gutman and Patrick H. Hutton (London: Tavistock, 1988).

Foucault Live: Interviews 1961–1984, ed. Sylvère Lotringer, trans. John Johnston (New York: Semiotext(e), 1989).

Garber, Marjorie. *Vested Interests: Cross-Dressing and Cultural Anxiety* (New York and London: Routledge, 1992).

Gardner, Helen. *The Business of Criticism* (Oxford: Clarendon Press, 1959).

Garin, Eugenio. *Italian Humanism: Philosophy and Civic Life in the Renaissance* (1947), trans. Peter Munz (Oxford: Blackwell, 1965).

George, Charles H., George, Katherine. *The Protestant Mind of the English Reformation 1570–1640* (Princeton University Press, 1961).

Giustiniani, Vito R. 'Homo, Humanus, and the Meanings of "Humanism"', *Journal of the History of Ideas*, 46 (1985), pp. 167–95.

Goldberg, S. L. 'Sir John Hayward, "Politic" Historian', *Review of English Studies*, ns 6 (1955), pp. 233–44.

Greenblatt, Stephen. *Learning to Curse: Essays in Early Modern Culture* (New York and London: Routledge, 1990).

Shakespearean Negotiations: The Circulation of Social Energy in Renaissance England (Oxford: Clarendon Press, 1988).

Haskins, Charles Homer. *The Renaissance of the Twelfth Century* (Cleveland, Ohio and New York: Meridian, 1957).

Hawkes, Terence. *That Shakespeherian Rag: Essays on a Critical Process* (London: Methuen, 1986).

Meaning by Shakespeare (London: Routledge, 1992).

ed., *Alternative Shakespeares Volume 2* (London and New York: Routledge, 1996).

Shakespeare in the Present (London and New York: Routledge, 2002).

Hirsch, E. D. Jr. *Validity in Interpretation* (New Haven, Conn.: Yale University Press, 1967).

Howard, Jean. 'The New Historicism in Renaissance Studies', *English Literary Renaissance*, 16 (1986), pp. 13–43.

'Crossdressing, The Theatre, and Gender Struggle in Early Modern England', *Shakespeare Quarterly*, 39 (1988), pp. 419–20.

Hunter, George K. '"A Roman Thought": Renaissance Attitudes to History Exemplified in Shakespeare and Jonson', *An English Miscellany Presented to W. S. Mackie*, ed. Brian S. Lee (Cape Town, London and New York: Oxford University Press, 1977), pp. 93–115.

Hutton, Ronald. *The Rise and Fall of Merry England: The Ritual Year 1400–1700* (Oxford and London: Oxford University Press, 1994).

The Stations of the Sun: A History of the Ritual Year in Britain (Oxford and New York: Oxford University Press, 1996).

James, Mervyn. *Society, Politics and Culture: Studies in Early Modern England*, (1978; repr. Cambridge University Press, 1986).

Jones, Emrys. *The Origins of Shakespeare* (Oxford: Clarendon Press, 1977).

Jones-Davies, M. T. 'Shakespeare in the Humanist Tradition: The Skeptical Doubts and their Expression in Paradoxes', *Shakespeare and Cultural Traditions*, ed. Tetsuo Kishi, Roger Pringle and Stanley Wells (London and Toronto: Associated University Presses, 1994), pp. 99–109.

Kaiser, Walter. *Praisers of Folly: Erasmus, More, Shakespeare* (London: Gollancz, 1964).

Kelley, Donald R. *Renaissance Humanism* (Boston, Mass.: Twayne, 1991).

Kiernan, Pauline. *Shakespeare's Theory of Drama* (Cambridge University Press, 1996).

Knowles, Richard. 'How Shakespeare Knew *King Leir*', *Shakespeare Survey*, 55 (2002), pp. 12–35.

Kraye, Jill, ed. *The Cambridge Companion to Renaissance Humanism* (Cambridge University Press, 1996).

Kristeller, Paul Oskar. *Renaissance Thought*, 2 vols. (New York: Harper and Row, 1961).

'Humanism', *The Cambridge History of Renaissance Philosophy*, ed. Charles B. Schmitt, Quentin Skinner, Eckhard Kessler and others (Cambridge University Press, 1988), pp. 113–37.

Kristeva, Julia. *Tales of Love*, trans. Leon S Roudiez (New York: Columbia University Press, 1987).

Lamarque, Peter and Olsen, Stein Haugom. *Truth, Fiction, and Literature: a Philosophical Perspective* (Oxford: Clarendon Press, 1994).

Lee, John. *Shakespeare's 'Hamlet' and the Controversies of the Self* (Oxford: Clarendon Press, 2000).

Levin, Harry. *The Myth of the Golden Age in the Renaissance* (London: Faber and Faber, 1970).

Levine, Joseph. *Humanism and History: Origins of Modern English Historiography* (Ithaca and London: Cornell University Press, 1987).

Levine, Laura. *Men in Women's Clothing: Anti-theatricality and Effeminization, 1579–1642* (Cambridge University Press, 1994).

Levy, F. J. *Tudor Historical Thought* (San Marino: The Huntington Library, 1967).

Low, Anthony. *Aspects of Subjectivity: Society and Individuality from the Middle Ages to Shakespeare and Milton* (Pittsburgh: Duquesne University Press, 2003).

Malik, Kenan. *Man, Beast and Zombie: What Science Can and Cannot tell us about Human Nature* (London: Weidenfeld and Nicolson, 2000).

Marcuse, Herbert. *One Dimensional Man: Studies in the Ideology of Advanced Industrial Society* (London: Routledge and Kegan Paul, 1964).

Maus, Katharine Eisaman. *Inwardness and Theater in the English Renaissance* (Chicago University Press, 1995b).

Mayer, Thomas F. *Thomas Starkey and the Commonweal: Humanist Politics and Religion in the Reign of Henry VIII* (Cambridge University Press, 1989).

McAlindon, Tom. 'Cultural Materialism and the Ethics of Reading: or the Radicalizing of Jacobean Tragedy', *Modern Language Review*, 90 (1995), pp. 830–46.

'What is a Shakespearean Tragedy?', *The Cambridge Companion to Shakespearean Tragedy*, ed. Claire McEachern (Cambridge University Press, 2002), pp. 1–22.

McLuskie, Kathleen. 'The Patriarchal Bard: Feminist Criticism and Shakespeare', *Political Shakespeare: New Essays in Cultural Materialism*, ed. Jonathan Dollimore and Alan Sinfield (Manchester University Press, 1985), pp. 88–108.

Meikle, Scott. *Essentialism in the Thought of Karl Marx* (London: Duckworth, 1985).

Merquior, J. G. *Foucault*, 2nd edn (London: Fontana, 1991).

Miller, Geoffrey (1998). *The Mating Mind: How Sexual Selection Shaped the Evolution of Human Nature* (Oxford: Heinemann, 2000).

Mommsen, T. E. 'Petrarch's Conception of the "Dark Ages"', *Speculum*, 17 (1942), pp. 226–42.

Murray, Penelope. 'Poetic Genius and its Classical Origins', *Genius: The History of an Idea*, ed. Penelope Murray (Oxford: Blackwell, 1989), pp. 9–31.

Nauert, Charles G. Jr. *Humanism and the Culture of Renaissance Europe* (Cambridge University Press, 1995).

Norton, Glyn P., ed. *The Renaissance, The Cambridge History of Literary Criticism* (Cambridge University Press, 1999).

Ollman, Bertell. *Alienation: Marx's Conception of Man in Capitalist Society* (Cambridge University Press, 1971).

Orgel, Stephen. *Impersonations: The Performance of Gender in Shakespeare's England* (Cambridge University Press, 1996).

Ovid. *Shakespeare's Ovid*, trans. Arthur Golding; ed. W. H. D. Rouse, trans. Arthur Golding; ed. W. H. D. Rouse (London: Centaur Press, 1961).

Peltonen, Markku. *Classical Humanism and Republicanism in English Political Thought 1570–1640* (Cambridge University Press, 1995).

Pincombe, Mike. *Elizabethan Humanism: Literature and Learning in the later Sixteenth Century* (London: Longman, 2001).

Pinker, Steven. *How the Mind Works* (London and New York: Allen Lane, 1998). *The Blank Slate: The Modern Denial of Human Nature* (London: Allen Lane, 2002).

Raab, Felix. *The English Face of Machiavelli: A Changing Interpretation 1500–1700* (London: Routledge and Kegan Paul, 1964).

Rabkin, Norman. *Shakespeare and the Problem of Meaning* (Chicago and London: Chicago University Press, 1981). *Shakespeare and the Common Understanding* (1967; repr. Chicago and London: Chicago University Press, 1984).

Ridley, Matt. *The Origins of Virtue* (London: Viking, 1996). *Nature Via Nurture: Genes, Experience and What Makes Us Human* (London: HarperCollins, 2003).

Rist, Thomas. *Shakespeare's Romances and the Politics of Counter-Reformation* (Lewiston, Queenston, Lampeter: Edwin Mellen Press, 1999).

Roe, John. *Shakespeare and Machiavelli* (Cambridge: D. S. Brewer, 2002).

Rougemont, Denis de. *Love in the Western World* (1940) trans. Montgomery Belgion, (New York: Schocken Books, 1990).

Russell, D. A. and Winterbottom, M., eds. *Ancient Literary Criticism: The Principal Texts in New Translations* (Oxford: Clarendon Press, 1972).

Sacks, Oliver. *The Man Who Mistook His Wife for a Hat* (London: Duckworth, 1985).

An Anthropologist on Mars (London and Basingstoke: Picador, 1995).

Shapiro, James. *Shakespeare and the Jews* (New York: Columbia University Press, 1996).

Shuger, Debora Kuller. *Political Theologies in Shakespeare's England: The Sacred and the State in 'Measure for Measure'* (Basingstoke: Palgrave, 2001).

Sinfield, Alan. *Faultlines: Cultural Materialism and the Politics of Dissident Reading* (Oxford: Clarendon Press, 1992).

Skinner, Quentin. *The Foundations of Modern Political Thought*, 2 vols. (Cambridge University Press, 1978).

Visions of Politics, 3 vols. (Cambridge University Press, 2002).

Slater, Ann Pasternak. 'Petrarchism Comes True in Romeo and Juliet', *Images of Shakespeare: Proceedings of the Third Congress of the International Shakespeare Association, 1996*, ed. Werner Habicht, D. J. Palmer and Roger Pringle (Newark, Del.: University of Delaware Press, 1988), pp. 129–50.

Smith, Bruce R. *Shakespeare and Masculinity* (Oxford University Press, 2000).

Soellner, Rolf. *Shakespeare's Patterns of Self-Knowledge* (Columbus: Ohio State University Press, 1972).

Sokol, B. J. 'Prejudice and Law in *The Merchant of Venice*', *Shakespeare Survey 51* (1998), pp. 159–73.

Sokol, B. J. and Sokol, Mary. 'Shakespeare and the English Equity Jurisdiction: *The Merchant of Venice* and the two texts of *King Lear*', *Review of English Studies*, ns 50 (1999), pp. 417–39.

Soper, Kate. *Humanism and Anti-Humanism* (London: Hutchinson, 1986).

Stallybrass, Peter. 'Transvestism and the "Body Beneath": Speculating on the Boy Actor', *Erotic Politics: Desire on the Renaissance Stage*, ed. Susan Zimmerman (London: Routledge, 1992), pp. 64–83.

Thompson, E. P. *The Poverty of Theory* (London: Merlin Press, 1978).

Traub, Valerie. *Desire and Anxiety: Circulations of Sexuality in Shakespearean Drama* (London and New York: Routledge, 1992).

Trinkaus, Charles. *The Scope of Renaissance Humanism* (Ann Arbor: University of Michigan Press, 1983).

Tuve, Rosemond. *Elizabethan and Metaphysical Imagery: Renaissance Poetics and Twentieth-Century Critics* (1947; repr. Chicago and London: Phoenix Books, 1961).

Weightman, John. 'On Not Understanding Michel Foucault', *The American Scholar*, 58 (1989), pp. 383–406.

Weinberg, Bernard. *A History of Literary Criticism in the Italian Renaissance*, 2 vols. (Chicago University Press, 1961).

Weiss, R. *Humanism in England during the Fifteenth Century*, 2nd edn (Oxford: Blackwell, 1957).

Wells, Robin Headlam. *Spenser's 'Faerie Queene' and the Cult of Elizabeth* (London and Totowa, NJ: Croom Helm and Barnes and Noble, 1983).

Elizabethan Mythologies: Studies in Poetry, Drama and Music (Cambridge University Press, 1994).

Shakespeare on Masculinity (Cambridge University Press, 2000).

White, Hayden. *Metahistory: The Historical Imagination in Nineteenth-Century Europe* (Baltimore and London: Johns Hopkins University Press, 1973).

Tropics of Discourse: Essays in Cultural Criticism (Baltimore: Johns Hopkins University Press, 1985).

The Content of the Form: Narrative Discourse and Historical Representation (Baltimore and London: Johns Hopkins University Press, 1987).

White, R. S. *Natural Law in English Renaissance Literature* (Cambridge University Press, 1996).

Wilson, Edward O. *Consilience: the Unity of Knowledge* (London: Little, Brown, 1998).

Wilson, Richard. *Will Power: Essays on Shakespearean Authority* (New York and London: Harvester Wheatsheaf, 1993).

Wilson, Richard and Dutton, Richard, eds. *New Historicism and Renaissance Drama* (London and New York: Longman, 1992).

Worden, Blair. *The Sound of Virtue: Philip Sidney's Arcadia and Elizabethan Politics* (New Haven and London: Yale University Press, 1996).

Yates, Frances A. 'Giordano's Conflict with Oxford', *Journal of the Warburg Institute*, 2 (1938–39), pp. 227–42.

Giordano Bruno and the Hermetic Tradition (London: Routledge and Kegan Paul, 1964).

Index

intersex 35–36
Ion (Plato) 123, 168, 169

James I (VI of Scotland) 77, 79, 106, 164
James, Mervyn 130
Jardine, Lisa 192
Jenkins, Keith 135, 151
Jew of Malta (Marlowe) 53, 142
Johnson, Samuel 5, 191
Jonson, Ben
  on author as genius 154, 156, 157, 164, 169,
    170, 240
  Cynthia's Revels 37
  on poetry 8
  on self-knowledge 51
  on Shakespeare 61
Joughin, John 159
Julius Caesar **132–152**
  politics in 25, 34, 104
  Sinfield, Alan on 189–190
  and theories of history 133
  Wilson, Richard on 95

Kahn, Coppélia 126
Kastan, David Scott 43
Kermode, Frank 92, 205
Kiernan, Pauline 92, 99, 101
King Lear **171–176**
  barbarism in 24, 173–176
  human nature in 30
  humoural psychology in 37
  as literature 200
  microcosm and macrocosm in 29
  self-knowledge in 24
Knight's Tale (Chaucer) 124, 131, 235
Knolles, Richard 22, 236
Kristeller, Paul Oskar 208
Kristeva, Julia 43, 109–111, 114, 200
Kuhn, Thomas 183, 251
Kyd, Thomas 111

Lacan, Jacques 43, 94, 118, 203, 233, 250
Lamarque, Peter 150, 193, 200
La Primaudaye, Pierre de 37, 214
Lawrence, Stephen 150, 151
Laws of Ecclesiastical Polity (Hooker) 226
Ledoux, Joseph 197
Lee, John 106
Lemnius, Levinus 38
Leonardo da Vinci 37
Letters to Classical Authors (Petrarch) 9
Levi, Primo 152
Levin, Harry 211
Levine, Laura 40, 218
Levy, F. J. 391.20

Lewis, C.S. 232
liberal arts 12, 89, 91, 94, 96, 99, 103
Life of Petrarch (Bruni) 19
The Life and Reign of King Henry IIII (Hayward)
  137, 236
Linacre, Thomas 17
Lipsius, Justus 79
literature 199–202
Locke, John 1, 3, 204, 205
Lodge, Thomas 217
love and death *see Romeo and Juliet*
Love in the Western World (Rougemont) 111–114
Low, Anthony 244
Luhrmann, Baz 115
Lyly, John 27, 46

McAlindon, Tom 145
Macbeth 28, 140, 142, 253
McDonald, Russ 241
McEwan, Ian 5, 167
Machiavelli, Niccolò
  Discourses 132, 136, 137, 141, 149, 192
  Florentine History 137
  Gentillet, Innocent on 57, 79, 222
  on human nature 14, 19, 30
  politic history of 136, 142
  The Prince 56, 80, 83, 136, 137, 141–142, 239
McLuskie, Kathleen 158, 173, 176
Malory, Thomas 130
Man, Paul de 196
Marcuse, Herbert 68
Markham, Gervase 138
Marlowe, Christopher 26, 53, 87
Marx, Karl 68, 132, 179, 182
Marxism 202
materialism 197, 199
materialist feminism 177, 180
maternal love 116, 232
Mead, Margaret 2, 181, 194
Measure for Measure **67–88**
  art and nature in 92
  debate form of 75–81
  Dollimore, Jonathan on 72–74, 79, 80, 85, 95
  humanism in 8, 27
  presentist readings of 67
  puritanism in 53
  religious fundamentalism in 18
  Wilson, Richard on 86
Meikle, Scott 179
*Men in Women's Clothing: Anti-theatricality and
  Effeminization* (Levine) 40–42
The Merchant of Venice **50–66**
  art and nature in 54
  conundrums in 57–61
  Shylock as puritan 51–54

Lightning Source UK Ltd.
Milton Keynes UK
UKOW02f2224150515

251639UK00001B/66/P